Life-Span Developmental Psychology:

Perspectives on Stress and Coping

Life-Span Developmental Psychology:

Perspectives on Stress and Coping

Edited by

E. Mark Cummings
Anita L. Greene
Katherine H. Karraker
West Virginia University

LEA
1991

LAWRENCE ERLBAUM ASSOCIATES, PUBLISHERS
Hillsdale, New Jersey   Hove and London

Lawrence Erlbaum Associates, Inc., Publishers
365 Broadway
Hillsdale, New Jersey 07642

Library of Congress Cataloging-in-Publication Data

Life-span developmental psychology : perspectives on stress and coping
/ edited by E. Mark Cummings, Anita L. Greene, Katherine H.
Karraker.
    p. cm.
    Papers presented at the Eleventh Biennial West Virginia University
Conference on Life-Span Development, held in Morgantown on March
24-27, 1988.
    Includes bibliographical references and index.
    ISBN 0-8058-0371-8
    1. Stress (Psychology)—Congresses. 2. Adjustment (Psychology)—
Congresses. 3. Developmental psychology—Congresses.
I. Cummings, E. Mark. II. Greene, Anita L. III. Karraker,
Katherine H. IV. West Virginia University Conference on Life-Span
Developmental Psychology (11th : 1988) V. Title: Perspectives on
stress and coping.
BF575.S75L5 1991
155.2′4—dc20
                                          90-22087
                                            CIP

Printed in the United States of America
10 9 8 7 6 5 4 3 2 1

Contents

Part VII: *Epilogue*

     and Coping: Discussion of Papers From the West Virginia
     Conference   **297**
     Bertram J. Cohler

     Author Index   **327**

     Subject Index   **341**

List of Contributors

Toni C. Antonucci, PhD, Institute for Social Research, University of Michigan

Karen Caplovitz Barrett, PhD, Department of Psychology, Colorado State University

Emily Borman, BA, Department of Psychiatry, Harvard Medical School

Mary K. Bowlds, BA, formerly of Department of Psychiatry, Harvard Medical School

Joseph J. Campos, PhD, Institute of Human Development, University of California, Berkeley

Sheldon Cohen, PhD, Department of Psychology, Carnegie Mellon University

Bertram J. Cohler, PhD, Committee on Human Development, University of Chicago

Bruce Compas, PhD, Department of Psychology, University of Vermont

Paul T. Costa, Jr. PhD, Gerontology Research Center, National Institute of Aging

E. Mark Cummings, PhD, Department of Psychology, West Virginia University

Byron R. Egeland, PhD, Institute of Child Development, University of Minnesota

Mona El-Sheikh, PhD, Department of Psychology, West Virginia University

Tiffany Field, PhD, Mailman Center for Child Development, University of Miami Medical School

Susan Folkman, PhD, Department of Medicine, University of California, San Francisco

Norman Garmezy, PhD, Department of Psychology, University of Minnesota

Anita Greene, PhD, Department of Psychology, West Virginia University

Stuart Hauser, PhD, MD, Department of Psychiatry, Harvard Medical School and Joslin Diabetes Center

Alan Jacobson, MD, Department of Psychiatry, Harvard Medical School and Joslin Diabetes Center

Katherine H. Karraker, PhD, Department of Psychology, West Virginia University

Kristen Knoebber, BA, Department of Psychology, Virginia Commonwealth University

Terrie Kreutzer, PhD, Department of Educational Psychology, University of Minnesota

Margaret A. Lake, BA, Department of Psychology, West Virginia University

Reed Larson, PhD, Department of Human Development and Family Ecology, University of Illinois at Urbana–Champaign

Ann Masten, PhD, Institute of Child Development, University of Minnesota

Robert McCrae, PhD, Gerontology Research Center, National Institute of Aging

Gil Noam, EdD, Department of Psychiatry, Harvard Medical School

Vicky Phares, PhD, Department of Psychiatry, University of California, San Francisco

Sally Powers, EdD, Department of Psychology, University of Massachusetts, Amherst

Peggy Thoits, PhD, Department of Sociology, Indiana University

Alan B. Zonderman, PhD, Gerontology Research Center, National Institute of Aging

Preface

This volume contains the papers presented at the 11th Biennial West Virginia University Conference on Life-Span Development. The conference was held in Morgantown on March 24–27, 1988. The topic selected for the conference was "Stress and Coping Across the Life Span."

The choice of this topic was motivated by the significant increase in studies of stress and coping processes in recent years. Many clinically and developmentally relevant questions about individuals' responses to threatening or challenging events currently are being addressed. This research also promises to lead toward the development of increasingly sophisticated and integrative models of stress and coping. However, researchers often have approached stress and coping from rather narrow and constrained perspectives. Further, little communication across disciplines and research directions has taken place, leading to the emergence of several relatively isolated literatures. The goal of this conference, therefore, was to foster exchanges between researchers studying stress and coping in different age groups and from different theoretical perspectives. We hoped to facilitate communication and a broadening of perspectives by emphasizing two major themes through our selection of participants and paper topics for the conference.

The first theme of the conference was the importance and usefulness of taking a life-span approach to the study of stress and coping. We, therefore, brought together researchers working in each of the major periods of the life span: infancy, childhood, adolescence, adulthood, and older adulthood. Investigators concentrating on each of these age periods typically have paid little attention to comparable research in other age periods. For example, researchers who have focused on childhood stressors have seldom considered the implications of early stressful experiences for later development. Similarly, researchers who have focused on the coping strategies of adults have only infrequently considered the contributions of early experiences and learned coping mechanisms to development in later life. Increased understanding of individuals' responses to stress and abilities to cope with stressors clearly can be fostered by emphasizing a life-span perspective.

The second theme of the conference was an emphasis on the development of new and more complete conceptual models of stress and coping processes. We attempted to bring together researchers whose work reflected a variety of conceptual perspectives. Two general approaches to understanding stress and coping were identified: (a) a focus on cognitive mediators and processes in stress and coping reactions (e.g., Folkman and Lazarus, 1980); and (b) a focus on affective or emotional components of stress and coping reactions (e.g., Barrett & Campos, 1987). Both approaches were represented at the conference. Both cognitive and affective processes are likely to operate when an individual encounters and copes with a stressor; thus, an integration of these approaches will be needed for a complete understanding of stress and coping reactions.

These two themes of the conference are linked in that different processes tend to be emphasized in studies of different age periods. For example, research on children tends to focus on socioemotional responding to stress, whereas research on adults tends to emphasize cognitive mediators of stress and coping reactions. These differences in focus are further accentuated by differences in preferred methodology. Research on children often relies on observational methodologies and the study of specific stress events, whereas research on adults often relies on self-report methodologies and relatively global characterizations of multiple stress events.

We did not expect any major reformulations of stress and coping theory to immediately emerge from this conference. Our hope was that by facilitating communication among researchers with diverse views of the stress and coping process that a broadening and integration of perspectives would eventually ensue. Similarly this volume will not provide the reader with a broadly integrated conceptual model of stress and coping. Rather the volume includes chapters representing many of the major current directions in stress and coping research across the life span. We invite the reader to take the information presented here and use it to enhance his or her own efforts to understand and conceptualize the stress and coping process.

The chapters based on the 15 papers presented at the conference are organized into several sections. The first section highlights theoretical issues and includes chapters on the cognitive and socioemotional perspectives on stress and coping. The next sections present work concerned with stress and coping in infancy, childhood, adolescence, adulthood, and older adulthood. A final chapter provides an integrative overview of the volume.

E. M. Cummings
A. L. Greene
K. H. Karraker

REFERENCES

Barrett, K., & Campos, J. (1987). Perspectives on emotional development II: A functionalist approach to emotions. In J. Osofsky (Ed.), *Handbook of infant development* (2nd ed., pp. 555–578). New York: Wiley.

Folkman, S., & Lazarus, R. (1980). An analysis of coping in a middle-aged community sample. *Journal of Health and Social Behavior, 21,* 219–239.

Acknowledgments

The success of the eleventh West Virginia Conference on Life-Span Developmental Psychology is the result of the efforts of many persons. Gerald Lang, Dean of the College of Arts and Sciences, assisted in providing university funds and support. William Fremouw, Chair of the Department of Psychology, was instrumental in helping with obtaining funding and also provided departmental funds and resources. Special thanks are due to the graduate students in developmental psychology at West Virginia University, who worked with the cochairs throughout the planning stages of the conference and during the conference itself: Mary Ballard, David Daniel, Mona El-Sheikh, Suzanne Evans, Frank Jurden, Paul Klaczynski, Joseph Laipple, Margaret Lake, Leslee Pollina, Eileen Reamy, Ruth Tunick, Mary Valaik, and Dena Vogel.

THEORETICAL ISSUES

Coping Across the Life Span: Theoretical Issues

Susan Folkman
University of California, San Francisco

At first glance, the questions that are asked about coping, when it is viewed from a life-span perspective, appear to differ from those that are asked about coping when it is viewed only at specific ages such as infancy, adolescence, or middle age. Research about coping over the life span is motivated by interest in *changes* in coping and the factors that influence such change. Research about coping at various ages is motivated largely by an interest in the *influence* or *effect* coping has on the relationship between stress, both chronic and acute, and outcomes such as behavior, psychological well-being, and physical health.

Despite the seeming differences in the questions that are suggested by the two perspectives, the questions in fact overlap a great deal. Both perspectives share a fundamental interest in *coping efficacy*. Those who ask about coping from the life-span perspective are generally interested not just in changes in coping qua coping but in changes in coping effectiveness over the life span. Do people become better or worse, more mature or immature, in their coping as they grow older? Those who are interested in the effects of coping on the relationship between stress and adaptational outcomes are also interested in efficacy: Are the effects positive or negative, salubrious or harmful? Both perspectives, thus, depend on having a method for evaluating coping that can be used in research settings. This evaluation presents some of the most difficult problems for coping researchers.

Many theorists and researchers, including Baltes, Block, Caspi, Costa, Elder, Levinson, Neugarten, and Thomae, have extended our understanding of adaptation over the life span by investigating stable properties of the person and the environment such as status variables, personality dispositions, biological and

3

psychological vulnerabilities, motivational structures, history, and cohort effects. The influence such variables have on adaptation over the life span is significant.

If coping makes only a minor contribution to adaptational outcomes over and above the variables I just mentioned, this contribution is potentially highly significant, because coping, unlike most structural variables, can be modified. Analyses of coping provide us with information about thoughts and behaviors that people use in managing the acute and enduring demands of their lives. These thoughts and behaviors can be changed through educational and therapeutic interventions (cf. Meichenbaum & Jaremko, 1983). Thus, even if coping has only a minimal influence on long-range adaptational outcomes, it is potentially a critical point of entry for modifying an individual's trajectory over the life span.

Our understanding of coping over the life span is shaped by the model of coping that is used in research. In this chapter, I shall briefly describe the two models of coping that have been most widely used in life-span coping research. I shall then focus on one of these two models, namely the contextual model, and summarize the findings from empirical research on age differences in coping and highlight some of the issues that are involved in evaluating coping over the life span.

TWO MODELS OF COPING

Two major approaches have been used to consider coping from a life-span perspective, one that is organized around developmental themes, and a second that is organized around contextual themes. The developmental approach is usually based on ego psychology models in which coping is viewed essentially as an aspect of personality. The contextual approach is usually based on relational models of stress in which coping is viewed in the context of the person–environment relationship.

The ego psychology model of coping is based on the concept of defenses, which are unconscious adaptive mechanisms that are a major means of managing instinct and affect. Vaillant's (1977) well-known study of adaptation over the life span uses this model. Vaillant arranged defense mechanism hierarchically according to their maturity. The highest or most mature group of these mechanisms consists of adaptive processes such as sublimation, altruism, suppression, and humor. The next lower group consists of neurotic mechanisms, including intellectualization, repression, reaction formation, displacement, and dissociation. Next are the immature mechanisms, including fantasy, projection, hypochondriasis, passive–aggressive behavior, and acting out. Finally the least mature are the psychotic mechanisms, including denial of external reality, distortion, and delusional projection. Ego psychology models have also been proposed by Haan (1977) and Menninger (1963). The term "coping," when used in the context of these models, refers to the most advanced or mature of the ego processes.

Contextual models of coping are widely used in current coping research (e.g., Aldwin & Revenson, 1987; Billings & Moos, 1982; Forsythe & Compas, 1987; Felton & Revenson, 1984; Manne & Sandler, 1984; McCrae, 1982, 1984; Parkes, 1984, 1986; Pearlin & Schooler, 1978; Quayhagen & Quayhagen, 1982; Stone & Neale, 1984; Thoits, 1986, 1987; Vitaliano, Maiuro, Russo, & Becker, 1987). This model serves as the basis of the coping research that Richard Lazarus and I and our colleagues on the Berkeley Stress and Coping Project conducted over a ten-year program of research.

Within this model, we defined coping as the changing thoughts and acts the individual uses to manage the external and/or internal demands of a specific person–environment transaction that is appraised as stressful (Lazarus & Folkman, 1984). Three features distinguish this definition of coping from the one that is provided by the ego psychology model. First, coping is defined as what the person actually thinks and does to manage the demands of a particular encounter: no attempts are made to infer unconscious processes. Second, the definition points to coping as a changing process. The ego psychology model, in contrast, tends to emphasize defensive styles that are stable properties of the person. Third, coping is not equated with efficacy or maturity. The efficacy or maturity of a coping process is judged on the basis or its relationship to the demands, constraints, and resources of a particular context; in contrast, the ego psychology model judges the maturity of a defense mechanism on an a priori basis.

THE COPING PROCESS AS VIEWED
FROM THE CONTEXTUAL MODEL

As I noted earlier, contextual formulations of coping focus on specific thoughts and actions that a person uses to manage the demands of a specific stressful encounter. The behavioral flow begins with a person's cognitive appraisal of a person–environment relationship. The appraisal includes an evaluation of the personal significance of the encounter (primary appraisal) and an evaluation of the options for coping (secondary appraisal). In primary appraisal, the person asks, "What do I have at stake in this encounter?" and in secondary appraisal the question is "What can I do?" (Lazarus, 1966; Lazarus & Folkman 1984). Together, primary appraisal and secondary appraisal shape emotion quality and intensity and influence the coping response.

Appraisals are influenced by antecedent person and situation characteristics. Thus, the personal significance of an encounter is determined on the one hand by the pattern of motivation (e.g., values, commitments, and goals), beliefs about oneself and the world, and personal resources for coping such as financial means, social and problem-solving skills, and health and energy. Individual differences in these variables help explain why an encounter may be appraised as a threat by one person and as neutral or a challenge by another. As an example, being passed over for a promotion is likely to be appraised as a harm or loss for a person for whom career advancement is a major goal, whereas it may be only mildly stressful or even a relief for a person whose goal is to preserve as much time as possible for family life. Appraisal processes are also influenced by situation characteristics such as the nature of the danger, its imminence, ambiguity, and duration, and the existence and quality of social support resources to facilitate coping.

Coping as a Dynamic Process

Coping processes continuously change as a function of continuous appraisals and reappraisals of the shifting person–environment relationship. Shifts may be due to coping efforts directed at changing the environment or the meaning or understanding of the event. Shifts may also be the result of changes in the environment that are independent of the person. Any shift leads to a reappraisal of the situation, which in turn influences subsequent coping efforts. Thus, coping changes during an encounter as it unfolds, and it changes from encounter to encounter.

The Multidimensional Nature of Coping

Coping has two major functions: the management of the problem (problem-focused coping) and the regulation of emotion (emotion-focused coping). These two functions have been recognized by a number of coping researchers, including Kahn, Wolfe, Quinn, Snoek, & Rosenthal (1964), Mechanic (1962), and Billings and Moos (1981).

In addition to the problem-focused and emotion-focused distinction, several broad categories of coping have been suggested. Pearlin and Schooler (1978), for example, were concerned with the following: responses that change the situation out of which the stressful experience arises (which is similar to problem-focused coping), responses that control the meaning of the stressful experience after it occurs but before the emergence of distress emotion (emotion-focused coping), and responses that control distress emotion (emotion-focused coping). Folkman and Lazarus (1988a) referred to cognitive activity that influences the deployment of attention (this can be either problem-focused or emotion-focused), cognitive activity that alters the subjective meaning or significance of the encounter for well-being (emotion-focused), and actions that alter the actual terms of the person–environment relationship (problem-focused coping).

Additional distinctions have been made at the empirical level. Pearlin and Schooler (1978), for example, defined 17 types of coping processes, some of which are limited to specific role areas such as family, marriage, parenting, and work. McCrae (1982) defined 28 types of coping, and Stone and Neale (1984) defined eight types, including distraction, situation redefinition, direct action, catharsis, acceptance, seeking social support, relaxation, and religion. Folkman, Lazarus, Dunkel-Schettel, DeLongis, and Gruen (1986) also defined eight types, including intrapersonal processes that are directed at problem solving and regulation of emotion (distancing, self-control, positive reappraisal, and escape-avoidance) and interpersonal problem-focused processes (confrontation) and emotion-focused processes (the seeking of informational and emotional support). Regardless of the taxonomy of coping that is used, what is clear is that coping is a complex, multidimensional process that includes a variety of intrapersonal and interpersonal strategies for managing problems and regulating emotions.

A fascinating finding that has been reported by all the contextually oriented researchers cited previously is that people use a wide range of these strategies in any given encounter. For example, in a study of 150 community resident subjects of 45 to 64 years of age, we found that people used both problem-focused and emotion-focused coping in over 95% of the more than 1,300 stressful encounters they reported (Folkman & Lazarus, 1980). In subsequent studies with two other community samples in which 8 types of coping were assessed, we found that, on the average, people used between 6 and 7 different types of coping in each stressful encounter (Folkman, Lazarus, Dunkel-Schetter, DeLongis, & Gruen, 1986).

EMPIRICAL FINDINGS

The contextual model has been used to evaluate the relationship between coping and age in a relatively small number of cross-sectional studies, which I summarize here. My discussion is limited to studies of adults. To read about coping development in children and adolescents, see Compas (1987), Garmezy and Rutter (1983), and Murphy and Moriarty (1976).

Pearlin and Schooler (1978) investigated coping in a large sample of adults that was representative of the Chicago area. The ages of subjects ranged from 18 to 65 years. Pearlin and Schooler were interested in the persistent life strains that people encounter as they act as parents, job holders and breadwinners, husbands, and wives. As noted earlier, they assessed 17 types of coping. The questions about coping were designed to assess how the person usually coped with the strains associated with each of the role domains. Several age differences in coping were observed. For example, in coping with marital problems, older people were more disposed to self-reliance (less often seeking advice) and more likely to engage in a controlled reflection of the marital problems than were the young people. However, neither the young nor the older appeared to have any overall advantage in coping efficacy, which was defined as the reduction of emotional stress.

Billings and Moos (1981) assessed coping in a randomly selected community sample. They asked respondents to describe how they had coped with a specific stressful event. Coping strategies were classified according to method of coping (active-cognitive, active-behavioral, avoidance), and focus (problem-focused and emotion-focused). They found no relation between coping and age.

McCrae (1982) evaluated age differences in coping in two studies, one which examined coping with life events that were classified a priori as losses, threats, and challenges, and a second that examined coping with respondent-defined losses, threats, and challenges. The sample was drawn from the Augmented Baltimore Longitudinal Study of Aging. The age range was 24 to 91. Twenty-eight coping mechanisms were evaluated. McCrae found that in most respects older people coped in much the same way as younger people. Where they employed different mechanisms, it appeared largely to be a function of the different types of stress they faced. Only two of the 28 coping mechanisms showed consistent age effects: Middle-aged and older individuals relied less on the theoretically immature mechanisms of hostile reaction and escapist fantasy than did younger individuals.

Felton and Revenson (1987 examined age differences in coping in the context of chronic illness. Their sample ranged in age from 41 to 89. They assessed coping with six subscales derived from the Ways of Coping Checklist. They found age differences in two forms of coping: Younger people used more information seeking and more emotional expression than did older people.

LaBouvie-Vief, Hakim-Larson, and Hobart (1987) used the contextual approach to evaluate coping in a sample of males and females that ranged in age from 10 to 77 years. Their study is notable, because in addition to assessing coping (using the eight scales from the Ways of Coping Checklist that were used by Folkman, Lazarus, Dunkel Schetter, Delongis, Gruen, 1986), LaBouvie-Vief and her colleagues assessed ego development and defensive style. With respect to coping, they found that those who were older and developmentally more mature used less escape/avoidance and distancing than those who were younger and less developmentally mature.

My colleagues and I examined age differences in two studies. The first involved 45- to 64-year-old community residents who reported an average of 13 stressful encounters over a year (Foldman & Lazarus, 1980). Two forms of coping, problem-focused and emotion-focused, were assessed with the Ways of Coping. No relationship between age and coping was found.

The second study involved a comparison of two samples, one that included 35- to 44-year-old women and their husbands, who reported five stressful encounters over a six-month period, and another that included 65- to 74-year-old men and women, who reported four stressful encounters over a five-month period (Folkman, Lazarus, Pimley, & Novacek, 1987). Eight types of coping were assessed with scales derived from the Ways of Coping. A scoring technique that controlled for individual differences in response rates was used. Encounters were classified according to what the event was about, the primary appraisal of stakes, and the secondary appraisal of coping options. Age differences in coping were marked and for the most part consistent across contexts. The younger people used proportionately more confrontive coping, seeking of social support, and planful problem solving than did the older people, and the older people used more distancing, acceptance of responsibility, and positive reappraisal than did the younger people.

The latter study differed from the previous studies primarily in the way coping was scored. Most of the previous studies summed raw scores across items. The latter study used a proportional scoring technique whereby the coping scores were standardized, and each type of coping was evaluated as a proportion of the person's total coping score (see also Vitaliano, Katon, et al., 1987). This technique produced relative scores that controlled for individual differences in response rate. The findings from the studies in which coping was scored by the raw score method of summing ratings suggests that on the whole older people seem to do less coping than do younger people. The proportional scoring technique controlled for this group difference and enabled us to see age differences in the relative use of each type of coping that were not apparent using the raw score technique.

Despite differences in age range, definitions of stressful events, the assessment of coping, and designs, the previous studies suggest interesting common patterns of age differences in coping. Younger people appear to use more interactive coping, such as expression of emotion and information seeking, and older people appear to use more intrapersonal coping, such as reflection and positive reappraisal.

The extent to which such differences are a function of changes in the context of coping or developmental changes is not at all clear. On the one hand, the contextual explanation for these differences cannot be ruled out. Although several of the investigators tried to group stressful encounters according to common contextual themes in order to control for effects due to context, these efforts undoubtedly fell short of their mark. For example, Folkman et al. (1987) examined coping within family encounters. However, the family encounters of the younger group typically involved young children at home, whereas those of the older group did not. Similarly the category of health encounters included everything from problems with weight control to problems surrounding life-threatening illnesses. The older group's health encounters were probably more serious than those of the younger group. On the other hand, the developmental explanation also cannot be ruled out in that some age differences were apparent across diverse contexts. Probably both explanations apply.

THE ISSUE OF COPING EFFICACY

The extent to which age differences in coping are developmentally and contextually determined, although an interesting question in and of itself, is in many respects secondary to the question of coping effectiveness over the life span. From infancy to old age, people are faced with multiple adaptational demands.

The key question with respect to coping is whether people become more or less effective in the ways they cope with these adaptational demands as they grow older. Our ability to advance understanding of this question has been seriously constrained by difficult issues that are involved in the evaluation of coping effectiveness. I shall turn to two aspects of this issue. The first has to do with finding stability in a process that is inherently variable. The second has to do with the kinds of outcomes that are chosen to evaluate coping effects. I shall then describe an approach to evaluating coping that focuses more on the process than on the outcome.

The Search for Stability

There has to be some stability in coping processes for them to have an effect on outcomes of importance such as psychological well-being, physical health, and social functioning. However, we know that coping, at least as we have been assessing it with contextually oriented measures, is not a stable process. People vary their coping from context to context, depending, for example, on whether the event is a harm, loss, or threat (McCrae, 1984); the social role that is involved (Menaghan, 1982); environmental and social factors (Parkes, 1986); and what is at stake and what the options for coping are (Folkman & Lazarus, 1980, 1985; Folkman, Lazarus, Gruen, & DeLongis, 1986). The challenge, therefore, is how to determine stability in a process that is inherently variable.

First, to determine stability in coping, we must repeatedly assess an individual's coping across contexts. It is likely that this approach will reveal at least some stability in some types of coping. For example, Folkman, Lazarus, Gruen et al. (1986) found that average intraindividual autocorrelations on eight types of coping over five encounters ranged from .17 (for seeking social support) to .47 (for positive reappraisal). The latter indicates a relatively high degree of stability. (See also Epstein, 1979, for a full discussion of this issue in relation to emotion.) Unfortunately most research on the relationship between coping and various outcomes is based on one or two samples of a person's coping processes in specific contexts, which does not provide a reliable estimate of the individual's stable patterns of coping across contexts, let alone over time. To expect a small, unreliable sample of coping to predict an outcome such as depression or anxiety is asking a great deal of coping; in many ways, this expectation is analogous (although in the opposite direction) to expecting a broad personality disposition to predict how a person would behave in an isolated instance.

Second, coping is multidimensional, which means that combinations of coping strategies must be considered. To date, most coping research based on the contextual model has evaluated individual types of coping strategies. A few investigators have attempted to assess patterns of problem-focused and emotion-focused coping by looking at their relative amounts in specific stressful events

(Billings & Moos, 1981; Folkman & Lazarus, 1980). However, reducing coping to these two categories tends to mask the rich variety of coping strategies that they subsume. The challenge is to find the critical number of types of strategies to evaluate. Two are too few, but as Stone and his colleagues have noted (Stone, Helder, & Schneider, 1988), eight are too many; they create an overwhelming number of combinations of coping. We need to address this issue from both conceptual and empirical perspectives.

Third, the patterning of coping over time must also be examined. In a metanalysis, Suls and Fletcher (1985) evaluated the effects of two patterns over time (approach followed by avoidance, and avoidance followed by approach). They found that when studies were classified according to the temporal interval between stressor onset and measurement of adaptation, avoidance was more strongly associated with positive adaptation than was attention when the temporal interval was brief. However, as the interval between stressor onset and measurement of adaptation grew, attentional strategies tended to be the ones that were associated with more positive adaptation. Suls and Fletcher's findings point up the importance of looking at the sequence of coping over time (see also Horowitz, 1976, 1983; Lazarus, 1983) as well as the combination of coping strategies at any given time.

However, Suls and Fletcher's conceptualization of coping along approach–avoidance dimensions (see also Roth & Cohen, 1986) leads to the same problem of oversimplification that exists when we reduce coping to problem-focused and emotion-focused dimensions. In the studies my colleagues and I reported, for example, two types of avoidant coping, escape-avoidance and distancing, are differentially related to adaptive outcomes, and similarly two types of approach coping, planful problem-solving and confrontation, are also differentially related to adaptive outcomes (Folkman, Lazarus, Dunkel-Schetter, et al., 1986; Folkman, Lazarus, Gruen, et al., 1986). These important distinctions among different types of approach coping and different types of avoidant coping are lost, if all coping is reduced to the approach–avoidance dimension. Nevertheless, Suls and Fletcher's work shows the importance of considering temporal ordering of coping.

Selecting the Coping Outcome

In order to evaluate coping effects, coping has to be shown to have an effect on an outcome of interest. Too often, outcomes are chosen without much thought as to their appropriateness. The selection of an inappropriate outcome can lead either to an underestimation or overestimation of coping effects. The choice of outcomes should be informed by at least two considerations: proximity and relevance.

Proximity

In general, the more proximate an outcome is in relation to a specific coping process, the greater is our confidence in causal statements about the effects of coping. Let me illustrate this issue with affectively based outcomes, which a number of studies indicate are associated with stress processes. The ways a person copes with a problem with a spouse or child or a pressing deadline on the job should have a direct effect on his or her emotions at that time. This emotion response is a proximate affective outcome. Thus, for example, Folkman and Lazarus (1988b) found that coping accounted for changes in positive and negative emotions during stressful encounters that were reported by community residents. However, emotions that are experienced in specific stressful encounters are not necessarily informative with respect to long-term affective outcomes. Anxiety or sadness, for example, that are experienced with great intensity in the context of a specific encounter may be entirely appropriate to the encounter. Even when inappropriate, such expressions do not necessarily signify that the person is an anxious or distressed person. (See Thoits, 1984, for an excellent discussion of the meaning of emotion in coping processes.)

Distal outcomes would appear to be a logical alternative. However, distal outcomes also have their drawbacks. These drawbacks can be illustrated with mood. Mood is less immediate to a specific encounter than is emotion, and, thus, less proximate and more distal. Mood is a background affective state that is determined by multiple factors such as what went on during the previous week, other events of the day, or the anticipation of upcoming events. Thus, the way a person copes with a specific stressful encounter is but one determinant among many of the person's mood, which means that causal statements about coping in a given stressful encounter and mood cannot be made with great confidence.

Stone et al. (1988) described the problem in a study of 79 couples, who were followed for an average of 100 days. Questions were asked about how they coped with the day's most bothersome problem and daily mood. The investigators chose to look at next-day mood as an outcome of coping. However, they point out that what is defined as next-day mood is simultaneously the same-day mood for the next day and is, thus, likely to be influenced both by previous-day coping and present-day coping.

Outcomes such as depression and anxiety are even more distal from a particular stressful encounter than is mood. Establishing causality with them is even more difficult than with midrange distal outcomes such as mood. For example, several researchers have found a relationship between escape-avoidance and psychological distress (Billings & Moos, 1984; Coyne, Aldwin, & Lazarus, 1981; Felton & Revenson, 1984; Folkman & Lazarus, 1986; Folkman, Lazarus, Gruen et al., 1986; Manne & Sandler, 1984; Silver, Auerbach, Vishniavksy, & Kaplowitz, 1986; Vitaliano, Katon, Russo, & Maiuro, 1987). What cannot be determined from these findings is whether escape-avoidance is a symptom of psychological distress, causes psychological distress, or is in a recursive relationship with distress.

The problems inherent in distal outcomes can be managed to a certain extent. First, care must be taken to select an outcome variable that has the potential for changing during the period of study. Kasl (1983) illustrated the importance of this point:

> Taking a sample of blue collar workers (35 years and older) and following them for 5 years in order to discern the mental health impact of a boring, monotonous job may miss the phenomenon altogether: The casualties of inadequate adaptation may have disappeared from observation and the remainder have adapted "successfully" (e.g., giving up on expecting work to be a meaningful human activity), but the costs of such "successful" adaptation can no longer be reconstructed through the belated follow-up. (p. 90)

Second, repeated assessments of process-oriented variables will increase their reliability. The repeated assessment of proximal outcomes, for example, can increase their reliability as predictors of distal outcomes. Epstein (1979) wrote thoughtfully about this issue with respect to emotions. Kasl (1983) suggested that we use a rather intensive schedule of follow-up monitoring in order to detect the true causal sequence. In this regard, Kasl wrote: "In general, it is prudent to assume that many of our independent and dependent variables may be sensitive only when covering a specific span of time, and that covariation may not be detected when one is working outside of such time spans" (p. 90).

Relevance.   One of the key conditions for evaluating coping effects is that initially the predictor variable be independent of the outcome variable. Absence of independence results in confounding. However, in addition to being independent, an outcome must also be relevant, by which I mean that it has to be one that coping can theoretically be expected to affect. We would not, for example, expect the way a person copes with stressful events to directly affect political attitudes or occupational choice. Relevance applies to all variables, from the most proximal to the most distal.

Some investigators call for specifying the adaptive tasks that are associated with a particular stressful context. For an example, in a threat situation where one has little control over the outcome, such as awaiting news of a biopsy, a relevant outcome is the regulation of anxiety. In a situation of harm or loss, a relevant outcome is the restoration of morale or the formation of new goals and plans. In a highly charged decision-making situation, a relevant outcome is high-quality decision making, which also involves the management of distress emotions that might cause premature closure on the deliberative process. A number of investigators have made suggestions for specifying adaptive tasks including Hackman (1970), who stated that we must develop a classificatory system for describing task demands; Turk (1979), who suggested that we specify the adaptive tasks posed by an illness and the range of coping options that are available for accomplishing those tasks; and Hirsch (1981), who suggested that we specify particular coping objectives, adaptive tasks, and useful strategies according to criteria of social adaptation for particular subgroups (cited in Menaghan, 1982).

Specifying adaptive tasks in order to evaluate coping has several drawbacks, each of which can be addressed although probably not eliminated. At a practical level, the job of identifying adaptive tasks for diverse contexts is formidable. This drawback can be addressed by broadening the definition of adaptive tasks such that they apply to a category of contexts. For example, Cohen and Lazarus (1979) identified the following five adaptive tasks of illness:

(1) To reduce harmful environmental conditions and enhance prospects of recovery,
(2) to tolerate or adjust to negative events and realities,
(3) to maintain a positive self-image,
(4) to maintain emotional equilibrium, and
(5) to continue satisfying relationships with others. (p. 232)

Similarly Janis and Mann (1977) identified the conditions, or adaptive tasks, for making good decisions under stressful circumstances.

At a conceptual level, the strategy is based on an assumption that a given stressful event will have a normative set of adaptive tasks. However, individuals differ in their values, commitments, and goals. These differences can affect the person's appraisal of the adaptive tasks in a given encounter. Thus, the adaptive tasks involved in coping with not being invited to join a special group will differ for a person who places a high value on affiliation and a person who places a low value on affiliation. The fact that an individual's values, commitments, and goals can change over the life span further complicates the issue (see Lazarus & DeLongis, 1983). That adaptive tasks are not necessarily normative needs to be taken into consideration in the assessment process, perhaps by asking the individual to specify his or her own goals for that context.

A third drawback pertains to the potential that is inherent in this approach of equating effective coping with coping that solves problems and reduces distress. To do so is to equate effective coping with mastery. However, many situations of daily life can not be mastered. Problems are sometimes insoluble, and distress is sometimes intense and not easily regulated. To equate effective coping with mastery is to do a great disservice to the efforts that people make to cope with difficult, intractable, and unrelenting conditions of life. Indeed the presence of distress can indicate that adaptive coping processes are taking place, as when a person confronts a loss and tries to come to terms with it. This drawback can be addressed by carefully considering the controllability of the demands the person is coping with.

Focusing on the Process Rather Than the Outcome

An alternative approach to the outcome model for evaluating coping efficacy is to focus on the process, using what I call the goodness-of-fit approach. This approach is based on the idea that effective coping is a function of the fit between: (a) the person's appraisal of what is going on (primary appraisal) and what is actually going on, (b) the person's appraisal of coping options (secondary appraisal) and what the options actually are, and (c) the fit between the options for coping and actual coping processes (Folkman, 1984; Folkman, Schaefer, & Lazarus, 1979; Menaghan, 1982).

Notice that this approach to evaluating coping does not involve reference to outcomes. However, presumably effective coping (as defined in terms of goodness-of-fit) should more often than not have a positive influence on adaptational outcomes. Forsythe and Compas (1987) tested this hypothesis and found that level of psychological symptoms varied as a function of the match between appraisals of control and coping in life events. The use of relatively more problem-focused than emotion-focused coping in events that were appraised as controllable as compared to events that were uncontrollable was associated with an adaptive outcome, and conversely the use of relatively more emotion-focused than problem-focused coping was associated with an adaptive outcome for events that were appraised as uncontrollable as compared to controllable. Collins, Baum, and Singer (1983) evaluated the use of problem-focused and emotion-focused coping in residents of Three Mile Island following the nuclear accident there and found that problem-focused coping in dealing with the aftermath of the event (which was uncontrollable) was positively associated with psychological symptoms.

The advantage of the goodness-of-fit approach is that it does not rely on outcomes and thereby avoids some of the problems that are involved in their selection. Further, we have learned that the appropriateness of the coping strategy, given the appraised options for coping, can be evaluated by determining whether the use of problem-focused and emotion-focused forms varies according to the appraised controllability of the outcome (or some aspect of the outcome). However, determining the veridicality of appraisals poses problems. If the event or condition is one that is highly stressful or experienced by wide numbers of people, it may be possible to gather enough information to determine whether or not appraisals are reasonably veridical. However, many events of day-to-day living do not fall into these categories, and we may have to rely heavily on subject self-report for judgments as to what is going on and what the options for coping are.

Another approach that is similar to the goodness-of-fit model in that it focuses on processes rather than outcomes is suggested by homeostatic models of stress in which stress is seen as a discrepancy between environmental demands and individual capacities, or between environmental resources and individual needs and goals (cf. French, Rodgers, & Cobb, 1974; Menaghan, 1982). Effective coping reduces the discrepancy and restores homeostasis. I am not aware of a methodology that effectively measures the discrepancy.

SUMMARY

In some cases, the evaluation of coping efficacy may be best served by reliance on appropriate outcome measures. In other cases, especially those in which the designation of outcomes presents problems, the goodness-of-fit approach may be more appropriate. Until we have had more experience with each of these approaches, it is a good idea to use both to evaluate coping efficacy whenever possible. The use of two methods should increase our understanding of coping processes and increase our understanding of the strengths and weaknesses of both approaches.

Coping research is still in its own early stage of development. Its healthy growth depends on carefully reasoned research with people from all age groups. Ideally we would use longitudinal designs that span decades with the same measurements at every occasion. In reality, we are faced with constraints that limit the duration of individual projects such that we are more likely to have a series of minilongitudinal studies than a single, long-lasting study. Given this reality, it is all the more important that studies be designed with a full understanding of underlying theoretical models so that findings from one study can be meaningfully interpreted in the light of findings from other studies. By so doing, we increase the likelihood that we will come to understand how coping and coping effectiveness change over the life span.

REFERENCES

Aldwin, C., & Revenson, T. (1987). Does coping help? *Journal of Personality and Social Psychology, 53,* 337–348.

Billings, A. G., & Moos, R. H. (1981). The role of coping responses and social resources in attenuating the impact of stressful life events. *Journal of Behavioral Medicine, 4,* 139–157.

Billings, A. G., & Moos, R. H. (1982). Stressful life events and symptoms: A longitudinal model. *Health Psychology, 1,* 99–118.

Billings, A. G., & Moos, R. H. (1984). Coping, stress, and social resources among adults with unipolar depression. *Journal of Personality and Social Psychology, 46,* 877–891.

Cohen, F., & Lazarus, R. S. (1979). Coping with the stresses of illness. In G. C. Stone, F. Cohen, & N. E. Adler (Eds.), *Health Psychology* (pp. 217–254). San Francisco: Jossey Bass.

Collins, D. L., Baum, A., & Singer, J. E. (1983). Coping with chronic stress at Three Mile Island: Psychological and biochemical evidence. *Health Psychology, 2,* 149–166.

Compas, B. E. (1987). Coping with stress during childhood and adolescence. *Psychological Bulletin, 101,* 393–403.

Coyne, J. C., Aldwin, C., & Lazarus, R. S. (1981). Depression and coping in stressful episodes. *Journal of Abnormal Psychology, 90,* 439–447.

Epstein, S. (1979). The stability of behavior: I. On predicting most of the people most of the time. *Journal of Personality and Social Psychology, 37,* 1097–1126.

Felton, B. J., & Revenson, T. A. (1984). Coping with chronic illness: A study of illness controllability and the influence of coping strategies on psychological adjustment. *Journal of Consulting and Clinical Psychology, 52,* 343–353.

Felton, B. J., & Revenson, T. A (1987). Age differences in coping with chronic illness. *Psychology and Aging, 2,* 164–170.

Folkman, S. (1984). Personal control and stress and coping processes: A theoretical analysis. *Journal of Personality and Social Psychology, 46,* 839–852.

Folkman, S., & Lazarus, R. S. (1980). An analysis of coping in a middle-aged community sample. *Journal of Health and Social Behavior, 21,* 219–239.

Folkman, S., & Lazarus, R. S. (1985). If it changes it must be a process: Study of emotion and coping during three stages of a college examination. *Journal of Personality and Social Psychology, 48,* 150–170.

Folkman, S., & Lazarus, R. S. (1986). Stress processes and depressive symptomatology. *Journal of Abnormal Psychology, 95,* 107–113.

Folkman, S., & Lazarus, R. S. (1988a). The relationship between coping and emotion: Implications for theory and research. *Social Science and Medicine, 26,* 309–317.

Folkman, S., & Lazarus, R. S. (1988b). Coping as a mediator of emotion. *Journal of Personality and Social Psychology, 54,* 466–475.

Folkman, S., Lazarus, R. S., Dunkel-Schetter, C., DeLongis, A., & Gruen, R. (1986). The dynamics of a stressful encounter: Cognitive appraisal, coping, and encounter outcomes. *Journal of Personality and Social Psychology, 50,* 992–1003.

Folkman, S., Lazarus, R. S., Gruen, R., & DeLongis, A. (1986). Appraisal, coping, health status, and psychological symptoms. *Journal of Personality and Social Psychology, 50,* 571–579.

Folkman, S., Lazarus, R. S., Pimley, S., & Novacek, J. (1987). Age differences in stress and coping processes. *Psychology and Aging, 2,* 171–184.

Folkman, S., Schaefer, C., & Lazarus, R. S. (1979). Cognitive processes as mediators of stress and coping. In V. Hamilton & D. M. Warburton (Eds.), *Human stress and cognition: An information-processing approach* (pp. 265–298). London: Wiley.

Forsythe, C. J., & Compas, B. (1987). Interaction of cognitive appraisals of stressful events and coping. *Cognitive Behavior Therapy, 11,* 473–485.

French, J. R. P. Jr., Rodgers, W., & Cobbs, S. (1974). Adjustment as person–environment fit. In G. V. Coelho, D. A. Hamburg, & J. E. Adams (Eds.), *Coping and adaptation* (pp. 316–333). New York: Basic.

Garmezy, N., & Rutter, M. (Eds.). (1983). *Stress, coping, and development in children.* New York: McGraw-Hill.

Haan, N. (1977). *Coping and defending: Processes of self-environment organization.* New York: Academic Press.

Hackman, J. R. (1970). Tasks and task performance in research on stress. In J. E. McGrath (Ed.), *Social and psychological factors in stress* (pp. 202–237). New York: Holt, Rinehart & Winston.

Hirsch, B. (1981). Coping and adaptation in high risk populations: Toward an integrative model. *Schizophrenia Bulletin, 7,* 164–172.

Horowitz, M. J. (1976). *Stress response syndrome.* New York: Jason Aronson.

Horowitz, M. J. (1983). *Image formation and psychotherapy.* New York: Jason Aronson.

Janis, I. L., & Mann, L. (1977). *Decision making.* New York: Free Press.

Kahn, R. L., Wolfe, D. M., Quinn, R. P., Snoek, J. D., & Rosenthal, R. A. (1964). *Organizational stress: Studies in role conflict and ambiguity.* New York: Wiley.

Kasl, S. V. (1983). Pursuing the link between stressful life experiences and disease: A time for reappraisal. In C. L. Cooper (Ed.), *Stress research* (pp. 79–102). New York: Wiley.

LaBouvie-Vief, G., Hakim-Larson, J., & Hobart, C. J. (1987). Age, ego level, and the life-span development of coping and defense processes. *Psychology and Aging, 2*, 286–293.

Lazarus, R. S. (1966). *Psychological stress and the coping process.* New York: McGraw-Hill.

Lazarus, R. S. (1983). The costs and benefits of denial. In S. Breznitz (Ed.), *The denial of stress* (pp. 1–30). New York: International Universities Press.

Lazarus, R. S., & DeLongis, A. (1983). Psychological stress and coping in aging. *American Psychologist, 40*, 770–779.

Lazarus, R. S., & Folkman, S. (1984). *Stress, appraisal, and coping.* New York: Springer.

Manne, S., & Sandler, I. (1984). Coping and adjustment to genital herpes. *Journal of Behavioral Medicine, 7*, 391–410.

McCrae, R. R. (1982). Age differences in the use of coping mechanisms. *Journal of Gerontology, 37*, 454–560.

McCrae, R. R. (1984). Situational determinants of coping responses: Loss, threat, and challenge. *Journal of Personality and Social Psychology, 76*, 117–122.

Mechanic, D. (1962). *Students under stress; A study in the social psychology of adaptation.* New York: Free Press. (Reprinted in 1978 by the University of Wisconsin Press).

Meichenbaum, D., & Jaremko, M. E. (Eds.). (1983). *Stress reduction and prevention.* New York: Plenum.

Menaghan, E. G. (1982). Measuring coping effectiveness: A panel analysis of marital problems and efforts. *Journal of Health and Social Behavior, 23*, 220–234.

Menninger, K. (1963). *The vital balance: The life process in mental health and illness.* New York: Viking.

Murphy, L. B., & Moriarty, A. E. (1976). *Vulnerability, coping, & growth: From infancy to adolescence.* New Haven: Yale University Press.

Parkes, K. R. (1984). Locus of control, cognitive, appraisal, and coping in stressful episodes. *Journal of Personality and Social Psychology, 46*, 655–668.

Parkes, K. R. (1986). Coping in stressful episodes: The role of individual differences, environmental factors, and situational characteristics. *Journal of Personality and Social Psychology, 51*, 1277–1292.

Pearlin, L. I., & Schooler, C. (1978). The structure of coping. *Journal of Health and Social Behavior, 19*, 2–21.

Quayhagen, M. P., & Quayhagen, M. (1982). Coping with conflict: Measurement of age-related patterns. *Research on Aging, 4*, 364–377.

Roth, S., & Cohen, L. J. (1986). Approach, avoidance, and coping with stress. *American Psychologist, 41*, 813–819.

Silver, P. S., Auerbach, S. M. Vishniavsky, N., & Kaplowitz, L. G. (1986). *Journal of Psychosomatic Research, 30*, 153–171.

Stone, A. A., Helder, L., & Schneider, M. S. (1988). Coping with stressful events: Coping dimensions and issues. In L. Cohen (Ed.), *Stressful life events: Theoretical and methodological issues* (pp. 182–210).

Stone, A. A., & Neale, J. M. (1984). New measure of daily coping: Development and preliminary results. *Journal of Personality and Social Psychology, 46*, 892–906.

Suls, J., & Fletcher, B. (1985). The relative efficacy of avoidant and nonavoidant coping strategies: A meta-analysis. *Health Psychology, 4*, 249–288.

Thoits, P. A. (1984). Coping, social support, and psychological outcomes: The central role of emotion. In P. Shaver (Ed.), *Review of personality and social psychology* (Vol. 5, pp. 219–238). Beverly Hills, CA: Sage.

Thoits, P. A. (1986). Social support as coping assistance. *Journal of Consulting and Clinical Psychology, 54*, 416–423.

Thoits, P. A. (1987, October). *Gender differences in coping with emotional distress.* Paper presented at the American Public Health Association, New Orleans, Louisiana.

Turk, D. C. (1979). Factors influencing the adaptive process with chronic illness: Implications for intervention. In I. G. Sarason & C. D. Spielberger (Eds.), *Stress and anxiety*, (Vol. 6, pp. 291–311). New York: Hemisphere.

Vaillant, G. E. (1977). *Adaptation to life*. Boston: Little Brown.

Vitaliano, P. P., Katon, W., Russo, J., & Maiuro, R. D. (1987). Coping as an index of illness behavior in panic disorder. *Journal of Nervous and Mental Disease, 175,* 78–84.

Vitaliano, P. P., Maiuro, R. D., Russo, J., & Becker, J. (1987). Raw versus relative scores in the assessment of coping strategies. *Journal of Behavioral Medicine, 10,* 1–18.

A Diacritical Function Approach to Emotions and Coping

Karen Caplovitz Barrett
Colorado State University

Joseph J. Campos
University of California, Berkeley

In this chapter, we will discuss a developmental model of emotions and coping, which we call a diacritical function approach. According to Webster's Third New International Dictionary, "diacritical" is defined as "serving to separate or distinguish." A diacritical function, therefore is a function that serves to separate or distinguish one process, entity, or attribute from another. We will propose, in keeping with this idea, that by focusing on the functions implied both by particular organism–environment relationships and by the (coping) responses to those organism–environment relationships, one can distinguish among many different phenomena typically subsumed under the single rubric "stress." We submit that it is of great importance to make such distinctions because of potential differences among these categories in implications for coping, adaptation, and health.

Many of the principles we will present are speculative; the data needed to substantiate (or refute) them have not been obtained. We will present relevant evidence, when possible, as illustrations of how a more differentiated approach might have important implications for understanding the effects of stress. We hope, moreover, that our propositions will stimulate research that will validate our claims.

DEFINITIONS OF BASIC TERMS

Before discussing the model, it is important to define some terms that we will be using. First, given the focus of this chapter on phenomena typically described as stress, we will define our use of that term. We define stress as any organism–environment relationship that (a) is appreciated by the organism as having the potential for exceeding the organism's resources (cf. Lazarus & Folkman, 1984), and (b) serves to disorganize the organism's behavior and/or thought processes *in domains other than those relevant to the stressful organism–environment relationship*. Thus, we conceive of stress as a subordinate category within the category emotion—emotion sufficiently marked that it interferes with information processing and/or behavior in domains unrelated to the emotion-inducing encounter. If stress is sufficiently great, it may interfere with information processing and/or behavior that is relevant to the stressful encounter; however, under many circumstances, stress serves to organize adaptive responses to the encounter. Given our view of stress as a special case of emotion, it is important to explicate our conceptualization of emotion.

We conceive of emotions as members of families,* characterized by *intrinsic* but not *invariant* features: (a) particular action tendencies, (b) specific types of appreciations regarding the significance of ongoing event–organism encounters for the organism's functioning in that environment, (c) characteristic vocalic quality/intonation patterns, (d) (at least for certain families, termed "basic emotions" by many theorists) particular patterns of facial movement, (e) characteristic physiological patterns, and (f) particular adaptive functions.

By "intrinsic," we mean that one need not learn to associate the characteristic with the family. The universality of interpretation of certain facial expressions has been best documented (cf. Edman, 1980; Izard, 1971, but see Fridlund, in press for an alternative perspective); moreover, recent research and theory specifying emotion-specific physiological patterns (Ekman, Levensen, & Friesen, 1983), and vocalic patterns (Frick, 1985; Scherer, 1986) are quite promising. Much more research is needed to document these physiological and vocalic patterns and even more is needed to document the virtually unstudied "action tendencies" we propose.

Although we postulate an intrinsic relationship between these patterns and emotion families, we indicate that these features are not invariant. Although the emotion families typically are associated with these features, particular instances of an emotion (family members) may not be associated with one or more of them.

Before we outline patterns hypothesized for specific families, certain other notions should be clarified. One concept that is important to clarify is that of action tendencies. Action tendencies are defined as organisms' dispositions to perform behaviors that fulfill a particular function with respect to the environment. They are *dispositions* to act, which need not actually be realized in overt action.

---

*By a "family" of emotions, we mean a group of emotions that are very similar to one another, which often are viewed as variants of a single emotion—for example, anger at having one's arms restrained (for a baby), anger at being deceived (for an adult), anger at having one's opus plagiarized (for an adult), and fury at having one's candy taken away (for a child)—all would be considered members of the anger family).

Moreover, the meaning of any resultant overt behavior is defined by a *functional relationship between organism and environment*. Thus, an action tendency to approach need not literally lead to approach behavior, especially in older children and adults. A behavior that "brings one closer" to something may be utilized instead (e.g., reading or even thinking about that something). Similarly a baby's action tendency to avoid/protect itself from a fear-inducing event may be realized as a tendency to cling to the caregiver. Action tendencies are a particularly intriguing aspect of emotion in that they are *flexible* motor programs, impelling the organism toward a particular functional relationship with the animate and/or inanimate environment.

Another concept to clarify is that of the "appreciation"—a notion quite similar to many recent characterizations of "hot" cognitions (e.g., Ekman, 1984; Lazarus, 1985; Scherer, 1986). We use the term appreciation rather than "appraisal" to underscore the fact that the cognitive process need not be deliberative, conscious, or sophisticated. It may consist, for example, of simple detection that a substance is sweet, with the associated implications to a prewired, organismic goal. The important feature of an appreciation is that *significance* of an organism–event relationship is assessed; the sophistication of processing may range from sensation to abstraction.

Finally we wish to clarify how our emotion families relate to most theorists' notions of basic and complex emotions. Unlike theorists such as Izard and Malatesta (1987), we do not consider certain emotion families to be basic emotion building blocks out of which other "complex" emotions (or affective–cognitive structures) are constructed. We do think it is useful to make distinctions among several "fuzzy categories" of emotions; however, we do not consider any class more fundamental than any other. Furthermore, we acknowledge that there is overlap among the categories. A particular member of an emotion family may fall in one class, even though the majority of family members fall in a different class (e.g., pleasure is a primordial emotion, whereas joy is a concurrent-goal emotion (see following). Moreover, certain *families* (e.g., affection) fit most criteria for one class (primordial, in affection: see characteristics of primordial emotions, following) but are characterized by one or two criteria appropriate for a different class (social, in affection: Affection is communicated primarily by posture, demeanor, and touch rather than by specific facial patterns, and always involves an appreciation regarding another. (See criteria for social emotions, following).

We base our classification of emotion families on the following criteria: (a) the typical processes of attaining significance associated with an emotion family— process one (innately determined appreciation of survival value of stimuli), process two (socially communicated significance), or process three (ongoing goal-relevance); (b) the extent to which appreciations concern other organisms, as well as the organism itself; (c) the extent to which the *goals* with which the

TABLE 2.1
Characteristics of Some Emotion Families

Emotion Family	Goal	Appreciation re:Self	Appreciation re:Other	Action Tendency
Disgust	Avoiding contamination or illness	This stimulus may contaminate me, or cause illness	[a]	Active rejection
Fear	Maintaining integrity of the self (physical or psychological integrity)	This stimulus threatens my integrity	[a]	Flight; active withdrawal
Anger	Any end state that the organism currently is invested in achieving	There is an obstacle to my obtaining my goal	[a]	Active forward movement, especially to eliminate obstacles
Sadness	Any end state that the organism currently is invested in achieving	My goal is unattainable	[a]	Disengagement; passive withdrawal
Shame	Maintenance of others' respect and affection; preservation of self-esteem	I am bad (self-esteem is perceived to be impaired)	Someone/everyone notices how bad I am	Active or passive withdrawal; avoiding others; hiding of self
Guilt	Meeting one's own internalized standards	I have done something contrary to my standards	Someone has been injured by my act	Outward movement; inclination to make reparation, to inform others, and to punish oneself
Pride	Maintenance of the respect of oneself and others	I am good (I have respect for myself)	Someone/everyone thinks (or will think) I am good	Outward/upward movement; inclination to show/inform others about one's accomplishments

[a] No "appreciation re: other" is *central* to primordial or concurrent-goal emotions; however, certain particular family members might involve such an appreciation.
[b] These facial movements are adapted from Izard (1979).
[c] These physiological responses are adapted from Ekman et al. (1983).
[d] Ekman et al. (1983) found increased heart rate with sadness; however, *decreased* heart rate is consistent with our theoretical position on *sadness*. We think it possible that most subjects in Ekman et al.'s study experienced an agitated grief state rather than a sad, "giving-up" state.
[e] These vocalic responses are adapted from Scherer (1986).

emotion family is concerned have been developed through socialization; and (d) the extent to which the emotion family may be communicated socially via discrete facial expressions versus via posture and demeanor.

Class 1 (primordial emotion families) and Class 2 (concurrent-goal emotion families) are two classes that typically have been termed "basic" emotions by other theorists. Although we think it likely that the appreciations associated with each of these emotion families *may* attain significance via any of the three

TABLE 2.1
(Continued)

Adaptive Functions	Facial Expression[b]	Physiological Reaction[c]	Vocalic Pattern[e]
Avoid contamination and illness; learn about substances/ events/attributes to avoid; alert others re:contamination	Brows lowered, nose wrinkled, with widened nasal root; raised cheeks and upper lip	Low heart rate and skin temperature; increased skin resistance	Nasal, slightly tense, "very narrow," but fairly full and powerful voice
Avoid danger (physical and psychological); learn about events/ attributes that are dangerous; alert others re: danger	Brows raised and often pulled slightly together; eyes very wide and tense, rigidly fixated on stimulus	High, stable heart rate; low skin temperature; "gasping" respiration	"Narrow," extremely tense, very weak, thin, high voice
Attain difficult goals; learn to overcome obstacles and achieve goals; communicate power/dominance	Brows lowered and pulled together; mouth open and square *or* lips pressed tightly together	High heart rate and skin temperature; facial flushing	"Narrow," medium to very tense, medium to extremely full voice
Conserve energy; learn which goals are realizable; encourage nurturance of others	Inner corners of brows moved upward; corners of mouth pulled downward, often with middle of chin pulled upward	Low heart rate;[d] Low skin temperature and skin resistance	"Narrow," thin, lax, slow, or halting voice
Behave appropriately; learn/maintain social standards; communicate submission to others and to others' standards	—	Low heart rate; blushing	"Narrow," moderately lax, thin voice
Behave prosocially; learn/maintain moral and prosocial behavior; communicate contrition/good intentions	—	High heart rate and skin conductance; irregular respiration	"Narrow," tense, moderately full voice
Behave appropriately; learn/maintain social standards; communicate ability to meet standards	—	High heart rate	"Wide," medium tense, full voice

processes described earlier, each of these classes is most likely to employ particular processes. Class 1, which includes emotions like disgust and fear, usually involves innately determined appreciation of survival value of stimuli and/or socially communicated significance. Class 2, on the other hand, which includes families like anger and sadness, usually involves social communication and/or ongoing goal-relevance. The implication of this difference is that elicitation of primordial (Class 1) emotions is more closely tied to *particular stimulus parameters* than is elicitation of concurrent-goal (Class 2) emotions. Primordial and concurrent-goal families are similar to one another, however, in that each can be communicated socially by discrete, context-independent facial expressions.

A third group, Class 3 (the social emotions) includes families traditionally characterized as "complex," such as shame, guilt, pride, and envy. These families, like Class 2 families, involve the social communication of significance and/or ongoing goal-relevance. However, the *goals* with which we believe these emotions are concerned are developed through socialization (Barrett & Campos, 1987). In addition, each of these emotions seems associated not only with an appreciation regarding *the organism itself* but also an appreciation regarding *others* (see following). Third, these emotions seem to be communicated socially by voice, gesture, posture, and demeanor but not by discrete, context-free facial expressions.

Table 2.1 summarizes characteristics of some emotion families, as suggested by current research and theory. It lists the type of goals with which each family typically is concerned despite our realization that emotions induced via social communication may not concern these goals.

Note that appreciations are expressed in very general terms in Table 2.1. Thus, many different specific organism–environment encounters may be appreciated in each of the ways described in the table, and they may be appreciated at any level of cognitive sophistication.

Certain attributes of action tendencies also should be highlighted. Notice that approach tendencies accompany certain negative as well as certain positive emotions. In fact, inclination to inform others is predicted to accompany both guilt and pride—two emotions that some would consider opposites.

Note also that some emotion families are associated with *passive* tendencies and others with *active* tendencies. The active tendencies are predicted to be accompanied by tensing and activation, with accompanying hypertonic musculature. On the other hand, passive tendencies are predicted to be accompanied by deactivation and hypotonic musculature. This distinction between active and passive tendencies also has important implications for coping (see following).

Finally we wish to highlight the "adaptive functions" column. Note that three functions separated by semicolons, are listed for each family. The first function listed concerns behavior regulatory functions; the second concerns internal regulatory functions; and the third concerns social regulatory functions. We consider these three types of functions the hallmark of emotionality—these functions make emotions crucial forces in human development. Unlike language, emotions serve these functions from earliest infancy. Moreover, their functions are never replaced. Even while an individual communicates verbally, his/her vocalics, facial expressions, and body movements provide "metamessages" regarding the *true meaning* of the words and *relationship* between speaker and listener (Bateson, Jackson, Haley, & Weakland, 1956; Watzlawick, Beavin, & Jackson, 1967).

The previous definitions concern stress or emotion. For the purposes of the present chapter, another central construct is that of coping. Coping is defined as any response aimed at adaptive functioning in the face of a significant organism–environment relationship (whether or not the organism is aware of the aim of the response). Thus, the facial, vocalic, and physiological patterns defined previously, as well as the action tendencies (through their effects on gross motor behavior and/or posture) and appreciations (through their implications for reappraisal), all define potential coping responses. Our definition is much broader than that discussed by many others (e.g., Lazarus & Folkman, 1984) in that it includes nonvolitional acts. This is a useful definition for those interested in young babies, in whom volition is particularly difficult to assess. Moreover, this definition is consistent with our emphasis on social signals—facial, vocalic, or postural. Such social signals need not be volitional and are manifested by very young infants. Yet they clearly may affect a person's ability to cope with an event—through their impact on others.

WHY A DIFFERENTIATED MODEL OF EMOTIONS AND COPING IS RELEVANT TO STRESS

For at least the past two decades, there have been repeated challenges to the notion of a unitary, generalized stress response (e.g., Gunnar, 1987; Henry, 1980; Henry & Stephens, 1977; Mason, 1968). For example, recent research suggests that physiological responses to emotion are more differentiated then previously had been believed. Assessments of autonomic nervous system responses such as heart rate and skin temperature have indicated different patterns depending on the particular emotion being aroused (e.g., Ekman et al., 1983).

Neurochemical responses typically associated with stress seem differentiated as well (e.g., corticosterone and norepinephrine) (e.g., Henry, 1980). Elevated corticosterone appears to be associated with depression- and fear-related responses (e.g., giving up, submission), whereas elevated norepinephrine is associated with "goal-directed behavior and the fight aspect of the fight–flight response" (or what we would consider overt, anger-relevant responses) (cf. Henry, 1980). Moreover, when humans have control over an achievement task, they report more positive emotions and manifest an increment in catecholamines but a *decrement* in cortisol (Frankenhaeuser, 1980).

Henry (1980) submitted that the adrenal-cortical response (including release of corticosterone) is a recent evolutionary adaptation, which was "grafted onto the catecholamine fight or flight response" (p. 562). He held that this response is an adaptation in service of our advanced social system, allowing for deference to another's dominance to be utilized in lieu of the more direct coping strategies of fighting or fleeing. Thus, according to Henry (1980), there are subtypes of stress responses, each characterized by a specific pattern of physiological responses *subserving a particular adaptive-behavioral function* (i.e., fight–flight versus submission).

The observation that particular physiological patterns are associated with particular adaptive-behavior patterns is an important one. It supports the view that there is more than one form of stress response that, with each form having different implications for the person's coping with the environment. There also is evidence, moreover, that differentiating among forms of "stress" responses has implications for persons' overall adaptive functioning. One important area of research suggesting this is that regarding stress and health.

STRESS AND HEALTH

Stress has become a heavily discussed and increasingly researched topic in the psychological and medical literatures, and a major reason for this popularity is the implications of stress for mental and physical health of individuals under its influence. Although methodological flaws have compromised much of the research relating stressful Life Events Schedules to physical and mental health, a small relationship between stressful life events and health remains after correction for such methodological problems (cf. McCrae, 1984).

One way of improving the ability of Life Events surveys to predict negative health consequences has been to exclude events that the respondent views as *positive* life changes. In most studies, positive life changes are significantly related to very few physical or mental health outcomes. Moreover, those significant effects that are obtained usually imply *better* health of respondents with a large number of positive life changes. For example, positive life changes are associated with *less* depression in teenagers (Swearingen & Cohen, 1985).

It seems possible that an even stronger relationship between life events stress and health would be found, if the respondent characterized the *specific* emotional reaction they had to each stressful event. Perhaps health outcomes would be differentially associated with particular emotions (e.g., sadness/depression and/ or anger), and/or with the tendency to express freely versus suppressing particular emotions. In other words, even if all of these emotions were sufficiently disorganizing to be considered stress, some types of stress might have certain types of health consequences; others might have other types of health consequences; and others might actually innoculate the person against some type of health consequences.

Recent research is supportive of this suggestion. Stressful events that are associated with expression of depression (maternal separation, uncontrollable shock) also are associated with atypical immune responses (Kiecolt-Glaser, Garner, Speicher, Penn, Holliday, & Glaser, 1984; Kiecolt-Glaser, Ricker, George, Messick, Speicher, Garner, & Glaser, 1984; Laudenslager, Capitanio, & Reite, 1985; Laudenslager, Ryan, Drugan, Hyson, & Maier, 1983; Laudenslager & Reite, 1984). On the other hand, expressing *anger* openly and appropriately is associated with *longer* survival time among cancer patients, and constricted expressiveness of anger is more common in cancer and asthmatic patients than in normals (Cox & MacKay, 1982; Hallaender & Florin, 1983). Asthmatic children also have been found to constrict expression of joy and fear (Hollaender & Florin, 1983). Thus, although much more research is needed, it appears that expression of some emotions and *constriction* of expression of others is associated with poor immune system functioning and/or poor health.

Research on the effects of coping also illustrate the potential importance of differentiating among various stress emotions. For example, in one study (Folkman & Lazarus, 1988), strategies of "confrontive coping," and, to a slightly lesser extent, "distancing" (e.g., "didn't let it get to me") were positively related to being disgusted and/or angry at the end of the encounter and negatively related to being pleased, happy, and/or confident at the end of the encounter. On the other hand, "planful problem solving" and "positive reappraisal" were positively related to being pleased, happy, and/or confident and negatively related to being angry and/or disgusted at the end of the encounter. Unfortunately the authors do not report the relationship between specific emotions at the beginning of the encounter and coping methods; however, they do indicate a significant relationship between emotions at the beginning (taken as a group) and emotions at the end of the encounter (Folkman & Lazarus, 1988).

Thus, although extant data do not permit *confirmation* of the proposal that different emotions have different relationships to coping and adaptation, we believe that the evidence is highly suggestive that a differentiated approach to stress is needed. We propose the following principles to explicate our diacritical function approach to emotion and coping:

PRINCIPLES FOR A DIACRITICAL FUNCTION PERSPECTIVE ON EMOTIONS AND COPING

Principle I: In order to understand the implications of stressful situations for coping, one must determine the particular emotion family elicited by the stressor: Different emotion families should be associated with different forms of coping.

This principle follows from our definition of coping and our characterization of the features of each emotion family. As indicated previously, each family of emotion is associated with particular facial, vocalic, postural/behavioral, and/or physiological coping responses, which may significantly affect the adaptiveness of the person's interactions with the environment.

Principle II: Coping may take the form of a facial, vocalic, or physiological "expressive" response, of an overt gross motor behavior, or of cognitive restructuring/reappraisal.

Again, this follows from our definition of coping.

Corollary IIA. Facial, postural, vocalic, and physiological "expressive" responses are important forms of coping that often have been overlooked.

These responses serve important internal regulatory functions. Feedback from the facial musculature seems to lead the subject to experience the relevant emotion to some degree. Posed, "faked," "exaggerated," and "neutralized" expressions influence physiological arousal and self-reported phenomenology in accordance with their appearance (Ekman, Levenson, & Friesen, 1983; Laird, 1974; Zuckerman, Klorman, Larrance, & Spiegel, 1981). Postural cues following success or failure may affect future performance—subjects who are positioned in a "slump" following failure (by experimenter instruction) actually persisted longer at working insoluble puzzles than do those who are positioned in a "proud," chest-out demeanor (Riskind, 1984). Awareness and/or interpretation of physiological responses may lead one to change one's behavior (e.g., noting that one is trembling with fear may lead one to turn back rather than continuing to climb a mountain). As alluded to previously, physiological responses seem to be associated with particular forms of overt coping behaviors. Moreover, as has been discussed for many years, strong physiological arousal seems to be associated with a decrement in performance (e.g., Meng, Guo, Chen, & Lin, 1985; Yerkes & Dodson, 1908).

Furthermore, controlling one's emotional responses may help prevent extreme emotional arousal. Oster (1982) suggested that even young babies control their facial expressions, resulting in a distinctive "horseshoe mouth" expression.

Facial, behavioral/postural, vocalic, and even certain physiological responses serve important *social* regulatory functions as well: They may be utilized to elicit help from others, enabling the person to cope with a situation even when effective coping otherwise would have been beyond the individual's capabilities.

Several lines of research support the plausibility of this assertion. There is much evidence, first of all, that toddlers, children, and adults often help someone who manifests clear emotional signs of distress (e.g., Chapman, Zahn-Waxler, Cooperman, & Iannotti, 1987; Eisenberg, Cameron, Tryon, & Dodez, 1981; Regan, 1971; Thompson, Cowan, & Rosenhan, 1980; Zahn-Waxler, Radke-Yarrow, & King, 1979). Use of facial and/or vocalic and/or postural responses to enlist another's help need not to be purposeful or conscious, moreover. Babies' cries elicit helping responses from both adults and children, even though the young baby might not be crying *in order* to obtain help (Howes & Farver, 1987; Karraker, 1986; Wiesenfeld, Whitman, & Malatesta, 1984; Zahn-Waxler,

Friedman, & Cummings, 1983). It follows from this line of research that a victim's emotional signals may lead another to help him or her. Thus, nonvolitional emotional responses may help a person cope via their effects on others.

It is possible, moreover, that emotion signals may be used instrumentally to affect others' behavior as well. We hypothesize that emotion signals may be used instrumentally from early infancy. We do not mean to assert that the signals need be used purposefully in the strong sense of this term; the signals may be conveyed at an increased rate as a function of history of positive response to those signals in similar contexts. The empirical basis for this hypothesis is indirect and incomplete, but we will describe it later.

First, it is clear that the emotional signals of even young infants (3 and 6 months of age) systematically affect the responses of others. Malatesta and Haviland (1982), for example, presented evidence that the type of facial pattern mothers show during interaction with their babies is contingent upon the type of facial pattern the baby has just manifested. For example, if a baby showed a sad facial pattern, the mother was more likely to show a sad pattern within the second following it; if the baby smiled, the mother was systematically more likely to smile within a second of that baby's smile. Moreover, mothers' responses to infants' angry facial patterns were quite different from those to infants' sad patterns. Thus, it is clear that even young babies can emit discrete facial responses that differentially affect the responses of their mothers.

Second, recent research suggests that even young infants develop expectations regarding events to which they are exposed (e.g., Fagen & Ohr, 1985; Haith, Hazan, & Goodman, 1988). If one puts these two strands of research together, it seems quite possible that the baby learns to expect specific types of responses from the mother when he or she manifests particular facial patterns. Such expectations would provide a baby with a tool for improving negative situations.

Recent research on infants' responses to maternal (simulated) depression and to anger-elicitation are consistent with this possibility and, thus, illustrate the potential instrumental use of facial expressions to cope with stressful situations. One of the most interesting findings in Cohn and Tronick's (1983) study of three-month-old babies' reactions to their mothers "depression" was that babies increased their usage of a response labeled as "brief positive." Babies apparently would smile briefly at their mothers, as if they were trying to elicit a more positive response from their mothers, and would look away when the expected response did not occur. Certainly the data do not clearly indicate why the babies smiled when in this aversive situation. However, given that during naturalistic interactions with their babies mothers typically smile when their babies smile, it seems plausible that an expectation would be built that positive responses would ensue.

Another possible example of the instrumental use of facial responses to cope with a stressor is found in Stenberg (1982). In that study, four-month-old and seven-month-old babies were gently restrained by an experimenter. Both four-month-olds and seven-month-olds responded to this situation by displaying the prototypical angry facial pattern (Ekman & Friesen, 1978; Izard, 1979). However, whereas four-month-olds typically directed their angry face at the restraining hand, seven-month-olds directed their faces at the mother. This response could be due to increased understanding, with age, of how to use the angry signal instrumentally. Younger infants seemed not to realize at whom (or what) to direct their signal in order to obtain help with the situation. They directed their response at the immediate cause of the undesired situation, more frequently than at someone who could help them remedy the situation.

Children and adults may utilize emotional responses to cope with social expectations as well. There is much evidence that adults and children regulate their facial movements in accordance with social prescriptions and are aware of such regulation (e.g., Ekman & Friesen, 1978; Feldman, White, & Labato, 1982; Saarni, 1982; Shennum & Bugental, 1982). Presenting a desirable front, masking unacceptable feelings, may prevent secondary elicitation of social emotions such as shame/embarrassment. As noted earlier, however, it is possible that suppressing expression of some emotions (e.g., anger) on a long-term, pervasive basis, may have negative effects on ones health (Beutler, Engle, Oro'-Beutler, Daldrup, & Meredith, 1986).

Expression of emotions via mood contagion may inform/teach others about a situation so that the others avoid problems and/or better prepare themselves to cope with the situation. All of these are merely illustrations of the many ways in which emotional signals can help people cope with stressful situations.

Corollary IIB. Each emotion family is associated with a particular action tendency, which may or may not give rise to a relevant (coping) response.

As noted above, action tendencies prepare the individual to respond according to a particular *function*. Thus, they do not imply a fixed pattern of response. Even still, there are conditions under which it may be deemed undesirable or unnecessary to act upon an action tendency.

We propose that the likelihood that the relevant motor (coping) response will follow elicitation of an action tendency is affected by the class of emotion being elicited: (a) "Primordial" emotions, such as disgust and fear, involve the ability of the organism to survive. Thus, their action tendencies should be most closely associated with relevant overt action, especially in babies (or other relatively unsocialized organisms); (b) "concurrent goal" emotions, such as anger and sadness, may be dealt with via relinquishing or changing one's goals. As a result, action tendencies often might not give rise to associated actions; (c) "social" emotions, such as shame, guilt, and envy, may be dealt with by downplaying the importance of others' opinions (shame) and/or of the wrongdoing (guilt), and/or of the enviable person/possession (envy/jealousy). As a result, action tendencies often might not give rise to associated (coping) actions.

Principle III. Coping responses are divided into two categories—Intrinsic coping and Secondary coping.

Intrinsic coping is defined as responses in accordance with the facial, vocal, and/or physiological patterns and/or action tendencies associated with the emotion being aroused.

Secondary coping is defined as responses that an organism selects to deal with a situation if intrinsic coping is deemed inappropriate or undesirable. Most extant approaches to stress and coping make no distinction between intrinsic and secondary coping and make no mention of the possibility that certain forms of · coping flow naturally from the arousal of emotion. Although strong evidence does not exist, we hold that particular forms of coping are much more likely given the arousal of particular types of emotions. We are pursuing this question in our ongoing research efforts.

Principle IV. Coping responses also may be active or passive, and direct or indirect.

Active responses are those in which the organism engages in some new behavior aimed at affecting the ongoing organism–environment relationship in a fashion that is adaptive or desirable, or is viewed as adaptive or desirable.

Passive responses are those in which the organism, through inactivity and/or omission of a relevant behavior, affects an ongoing organism–environment relationship in a fashion that is adaptive or desirable, or is viewed as adaptive or desirable.

Direct responses are those in which the organisms emits an overt motor behavior (which might be a facial, vocalic, or gross motor response) so as to deal with or change the stressful event, without enlisting the help of a conspecific.

Indirect responses are those in which the organism responds to the stressful event by enlisting the aid of a conspecific or by changing its thoughts/appreciation about the stressful event. The research on infants' responses to anger-induction and maternal depression, cited previously, illustrates well indirect coping responses.

Principle V. Coping responses may function by changing the situation, one's goal for the situation, the focus of one's attention in the situation, one's arousal level, and so forth, and usually the emotion one experiences in that situation.

The class of emotion families to which an emotion belongs may influence the extent to which some of these coping response functions are useful. For example, changing one's goal for a situation is much more likely to be useful for concurrent-goal emotions than for primordial emotions in that, as Table 2.1 indicates, primordial emotions (fear and disgust, in the table) concern pervasive, always-important goals, whereas concurrent goals concern any situation-specific, immediate goal and, thus, could more easily be relinquished.

Principle VI. A particular coping response may or may not succeed in increasing the adaptiveness of one's functioning.

We, like others (e.g., Lazarus & Folkman, 1984), believe that coping should be defined on the basis of the *aim* of adaptation, rather than based on whether or not the coping is successful.

Principle VII. A coping response may or may not be intentional.

Many theorists (e.g., Lazarus & Folkman, 1984) have limited their definition of coping to *intentional* behaviors. In contrast, in keeping with our notion of *intrinsic* coping responses, we hold that some coping responses (especially intrinsic ones) are given by biology or automatized, and they may not be used intentionally. As alluded to earlier, there is a good deal of evidence that facial expressions, one form of intrinsic coping, are universally associated with certain emotion families (e.g., joy, sadness, anger) (cf. Ekman, 1980; Izard, 1971). In addition, there is some reason to believe that nonhuman primates display facial signals that are homologues of those manifested by humans (cf. van Hoof, 1962). On the basis of data such as these, most emotion theorists believe that there is a biological basis for the association of certain facial patterns with certain emotions (e.g., Campos, Barrett, Lamb, Goldsmith, & Stenberg, 1983; Ekman, 1980; Izard & Malatesta, 1987). It is quite plausible that there is a biological basis for other responses associated with emotions as well. Moreover, we do not believe that coping responses are restricted to *stressful* conditions, as we define stress, but may occur in response to elicitation of any degree of emotion (for an alternative position, see Lazarus & Folkman, 1984).

Principle VIII. Individuals differ in the types of coping reactions they manifest in the "same" situation.

Different individuals may focus on different aspects of the situation such that different emotions are elicited, and coping responses in keeping with the (different) aroused emotions ensue. Such differences in focus may (at times) be a function of differences in developmental level. For example, two-year-old children who are told to make a tower as quickly as possible and who obviously lag behind an experimenter in completing the tower still may express pride, because they focus on making the tower rather than on speed of performance. Older children are likely to express shame or embarrassment under the same circumstances, to the extent that they focus on speed (Halisch & Halisch, 1980).

Different individuals also may be affected differently by the same aspect of a situation (i.e., there still is a different organism–environment relationship despite the same environment). For example, in Zarbatany and Lamb's (1985) study of social referencing, children who reacted emotionally to a toy spider immediately upon seeing it were relatively unmoved by their mother's emotional reaction to the spider. On the other hand, children who did not have a strong initial response to the spider were more likely to approach it, if their mother signaled happiness than if their mother signaled fear. It seems likely that those without a strong initial reaction utilize their mother's response to guide their reactions, whereas those with a strong initial reaction do not.

In addition, different individuals manifest different coping responses to the same organism–environment relationship, due to differences in socialization, temperament, and skills of those individuals. For example, one person who is angry at his boss may storm into his boss' office and tell him so. Under the same circumstances, another person might write a hate note and tear it up, or might yell at a friend.

In many cases, it may be difficult to distinguish between these three sources of individual differences (focusing on different aspects of a situation, being affected differently by the same situation, or having different coping responses to the same emotion). For example, in a study still in progress, we have been investigating two different styles of coping responses to the infraction of a standard—Avoiders, who avoid the person that they "wronged," and Amenders, who do not avoid the "wronged" individual, but rather tell her about the mishap and quickly try to repair the problem. It is difficult to determine whether these two patterns represent different secondary coping responses to the same emotion, different emotional responses to the same situation (with the associated intrinsic coping patterns), or different emotional responses, resulting from focusing upon different aspects of the same situation (Barrett & Zahn-Waxler, 1988).

Principle IX. Even positive emotions have implications for coping.

There are several different types of conditions under which this principle holds. First, one's physical resources may become overwhelmed by an intense positive experience, causing that experience to become aversive and disorganizing. For example, a baby, while interacting with its mother, may express increasing delight, changing from showing interest, to smiling, to cooing, and then to laughing. Many have observed, however, that if stimulation continues, the baby is likely to avert its gaze from the mother or even to cry (Fogel, 1982; Sroufe & Waters, 1976). Most theorists have interpreted this observation as implying that the baby could not tolerate the continued arousal and, thus, became distressed and/or sought to "turn off" the arousing encounter. Similarly an adult may find exercise pleasurable until the point at which his/her physical resources are beginning to be depleted. After that point, continued exercise may be stressful.

A second condition under which positive emotion may become stressful is when social norms conflict with the act that induces pleasure. For example, teenagers, unmarried adults, or married adults "committing adultery" may feel stress while engaging in sexual intercourse, although they are enjoying the act as well.

Finally a third case in which positive emotion may become stressful is when euphoria becomes so great that is becomes disorganizing, leading to negative outcomes (e.g., an automobile accident).

Principle X. Although there are many aspects of emotions and coping that are similar across the lifespan (i.e., the characteristics of families and the basic principles described previously), emotions and coping skills do change with development, primarily as a function of cognitive development and socialization.

Influences of cognitive development.   Despite our conviction that emotional development is not *secondary* to cognitive development, we do believe that systematic changes in emotion families occur as a function of cognitive development. In particular, cognitive development increases (a) the number and variety of organism–environment interactions that can be appreciated as significant, (b) the number of aspects of complex organism–environment interactions that can be appreciated as significant (often with appreciations from several emotion families being provoked in the same situation), (c) the variety and number of *coping* responses with which the organism can enact an action tendency, and (d) the organism's ability to modulate consciously its emotional reactions, utilizing "display rules," "coping rules," and/or "feeling rules." Thus, cognitive development may make important contributions to the *breadth and complexity* of emotionality, *through its influence on one or more of the aspects of emotion families or the functions served by those aspects*. Cognitive developments are neither necessary nor sufficient for the developmental onset of particular emotion families; however, they are influential upon emotional development.

Socialization influences.   Perhaps even more influential on emotional development is socialization, and, in recent years, increasing attention has been devoted to this topic (e.g., Lewis & Saarni, 1985). When the typical theorist describes "socialization of emotion," s/he focuses on a very specific domain—the "disconnecting" of feeling from expression due to "display rules" (rules regarding socially acceptable expression.) (See Ekman & Friesen, 1978; Izard & Malatesta, 1987; Malatesta & Haviland, 1985.)

We agree that display rules exist and that they may importantly influence emotionality. However, display rules are not important because they disconnect expression from experience, but rather because they serve important social- and internal-regulatory functions.

Furthermore, we emphasize that these rules comprise only one effect of socialization on emotionality. Socialization does not merely change the way emotions *look and sound;* it changes the very nature of emotionality in later development. Although we would never claim that all emotionality is socially created, we believe that too little emphasis is placed on how *new members of emotion families may be socially constructed.*

It is beyond the scope of this chapter to fully explicate the ways in which socialization effects emotional development. In brief, we believe that new members of emotion families are constructed throughout development, via socialization influences on the following: (a) the ascription of *significance* to organism–environment relationships; (b) the "average expectable environment" the person faces (and, thus, the types of organism–environment relations that occur); (c) the ability to cope with organism–environment relationships and/or emotional phenomenology—to enact or counteract action tendencies; and (d) the tendency to display particular facial patterns, vocalic patterns, and/or physiological patterns under particular circumstances. We will focus on the final two influences, given their relevance to the present paper.

First, "appropriate" ways of enacting or counteracting action tendencies are socialized—both explicitly and implicitly—at the family level and at the societal level. A major function of childrearing is to guide children in coping with emotionally arousing situations in appropriate ways. Some families, subcultures, and cultures, for example, encourage overt aggression in response to anger, whereas others advise "turning the other cheek." Popular children's songs reflect such social prescriptions. For example, one song advises counteraction of defeat/depression action tendencies: "Hold out your chest, and lift up your chin. Half the battle is picking up the pieces and starting over again" (Michaelf, 1984). Interestingly, as mentioned earlier, it might actually be more adaptive to "give in" to the inclination to slump, in that persons who slump following failure seem to persist longer at an achievement task than those positioned in a "proud," chest-out demeanor (Riskind, 1984). Such findings highlight the complex internal-and behavior-regulatory impact of socialization of action tendencies.

Another effect of socialization on emotion is to regulate facial, vocalic, and physiological responses. We already alluded to the evidence that adults and children regulate their facial movements in accordance with social prescriptions (e.g., Ekman & Friesen, 1978; Feldman, White, & Labato, 1982; Saarni, 1982; Shennum & Bugental, 1982). Moreover, beginning in early infancy, parents respond differentially to their babies' various emotional signals (Izard & Malatesta, 1987; Malatesta & Haviland, 1982). There is less evidence regarding socialization of the other channels (voice and physiology), but such socialization seems to occur as well (cf. Malatesta & Haviland, 1985).

As alluded to earlier, we think that these display rules are important, not because they disconnect emotional expression from experience but because of the internal- and social-regulatory impact of these socialized responses. In fact, as also mentioned earlier, posed facial signals influence physiological arousal and self-reported phenomenology in accordance with their appearance (Ekman et al., 1983; Laird, 1974; Zuckerman, Klorman, Larrance, & Spiegel, 1981). Display rules, thus, *disconnect* facial movements only from the initial phenomenology and physiological responses to a particular organism–environment relationship. However, their end result may be to *blend* the original phenomenology and physiology with those appropriate to the posed emotion. To the extent that control of responses influences perceived stress, effects of stress on health, and choice of coping strategies, display rules are important developmental influences on stress and coping.

Moreover, virtually all social discourse relies on socialized emotional responses. As discussed earlier, emotion signals are important means of coping indirectly with events. "Inappropriate" signals change the communication and the receiver's evaluation of the communicator. In fact, extreme cases of inappropriateness can lead the receiver to question the communicator's sanity. We believe that these are the most important topics for research on display rule development: how the development of "appropriate" display rule usage versus *deficits* in display rule usage (in relationship to the norms for that age) impact social communication. We also think it important to study other instrumental uses of emotional responses and their effects on social communication and coping at various points in development.

In summary, we believe that every aspect of emotionality is influenced by socialization—including the important functions that emotions serve for the developing organism and the organism's ability to cope with stress. Many of the most important topics regarding emotion socialization have been neglected, leaving this as a very important area for future research.

CONCLUSION

In this chapter, we have presented only a skeletal proposal for a diacritical function approach to emotions and coping. We have discussed our definitions of stress and of coping, and have proposed ten principles to organize our approach. Persons' ability to cope with stress has widespread and significant implications for their concurrent and future well-being. We hope that many investigations will be spawned by our proposal and that our understanding of the effects of stress will be enhanced by those studies.

REFERENCES

Barrett, K., & Campos, J. (1987). Perspectives on emotional development II: A functionalist approach to emotions. In J. Osofsky (Ed.), *Handbook of Infant Development (2nd ed., pp. 555–578),* New York: Wiley.

Barrett, K., & Zahn-Waxler, C. (1988, August). *Toddlers' reactions to transgression: Avoiders versus Amenders.* Paper presented at the American Psychological Association meeting, Atlanta.

Bateson, G., Jackson, D., Haley, J., & Weakland, J. (1956). Toward a theory of schizophrenia. *Behavioral Science, 4,* 251–264.

Beutler, L., Engle, D., Oro'-Beutler, M. E., Daldrup, R., & Meredith, K. (1986). Inability to express intense affect: Common link between depression and pain? *Journal of Consulting and Clinical Psychology, 54,* 752–759.

Campos, J. J., Barrett, K. C., Lamb, M., Goldsmith, H. H., & Stenberg, C. (1983). Socioemotional development. In P. Mussen (Ed.), *Handbook of child psychology. Vol. II: and Infancy and developmental psychobiology* (pp. 783–916).

Chapman, M., Zahn-Waxler, C., Cooperman, G., & Iannotti, R., (1987). Empathy and responsibility in the motivation of children's helping. *Developmental Psychology, 23,* 140–145.

Cohn, J., & Tronick, J. (1983). Three-month-old infants' reaction to simulated maternal depression. *Child Development, 54,* 185–193.

Cox, T., & MacKay, C. (1982). Psychosocial factors and psychophysiological mechanisms in the etiology and development of cancer. *Social Science and Medicine, 16,* 381–396.

Eisenberg, N., Cameron, E., Tryon, K., & Dodez, R. (1981). Socialization of prosocial behavior in the preschool classroom. *Developmental Psychology, 17,* 773–782.

Ekman, P. (1980). Biological and cultural contributions to body and facial movement in the expression of emotions. In A. Rorty (Ed.), *Explaining emotions.* Berkeley: University of California Press.

Ekman, P. (1984). Expression and the nature of emotion. In K. Scherer & P. Ekman (Eds.), *Approaches to emotion* (pp. 319–344) Hillsdale, NJ: Lawrence Erlbaum Associates.

Ekman, P., & Friesen, W. (1978). *Facial action coding system.* Palo Alto, CA: Consulting Psychologists Press.

Ekman, P., Levenson, R., & Friesen, W. (1983). Autonomic nervous system activity distinguishes between emotions. *Science, 221,* 1208–1210.

Fagen, J., & Ohr, P. (1985). Temperament and crying in response to the violation of a learned expectancy in early infancy. *Infant Behavior and Development, 8,* 157–166.

Feldman, R., White, T., & Labato, D. (1982). Social skills and nonverbal behavior. In R. Feldman (Ed.), *Development of nonverbal behavior in children* (pp. 259–278). New York: Springer-Verlag.

Fogel, A. (1982). Affect dynamics in early infancy: Affective tolerance. In T. Field & A. Fogel (Eds.), *Emotion and early interaction* (pp. 25–56). Hillsdale, NJ: Lawrence Erlbaum Associates.

Folkman, S., & Lazarus, R. (1988). Coping as a mediator of emotion. *Journal of Personality and Social Psychology, 54,* 466–475.

Frankenhaeuser, M. (1980). Psychobiological aspects of life stress. In S. Levine & H. Ursin (Eds.), *Coping and health* (pp. 203–224). New York: Plenum.

Frick, R. (1985). Communicating emotion: The role of prosodic features. *Psychological Bulletin, 97,* 412–429.

Gunnar, M. (1987). Psychobiological studies of stress and coping: An introduction. *Child Development, 6,* 1403–1407.

Haith, M., Hazan, C., & Goodman, G. (1988). Expectation and anticipation of dynamic visual events by 3.5-month-old babies. *Child Development, 59,* 467–479.

Halisch, C., & Halisch, F. (1980). Kognitive voraussetzungen fruhkindlicher selbstbewertungsreaktionen nach erfolg und miberfolg. *zeitschrift fur Entwicklungspsychologie und Padagogische Psychologie, 12,* 193–212, cited in Geppert, U. (1986). (*A coding-system for analyzing behavioral expressions of self-evaluative emotions.* Unpublished manuscript, Max-Planck-Institute for Psychological Research.)

Henry, J. (1980). Present concept of stress theory. In E. Usdin, R. Kvetnansky, & I. Kopin (Eds.), *Catecholamines and stress* (pp. 557–572). New York: Elsevier.

Henry, J., & Stephens, P. (1977). *Stress, health, and the social environment: A sociobiologic approach to medicine.* New York: Springer-Verlag.

Hollaender, J., & Florin, I. (1983). Expressed emotion and airway conductance in children with bronchial asthma. *Journal of Psychosomatic Research, 27,* 307–311.

Howes, C., & Farver, J. (1987). Toddlers' responses to the distress of their peers. *Journal of Applied Developmental Psychology, 8,* 441–452.

Izard, C. (1971). *The face of emotion.* New York: Appleton-Century-Crofts.

Izard, C. (1979). *The maximally discriminative facial movement scoring system (Max.)* Unpublished manuscript, University of Delaware.

Izard, C., & Malatesta, C. (1987). Perspectives on emotional development I: Differential Emotions Theory of early emotional development. In J. Osofsky (Ed.), *Handbook of infant development (2nd edition, pp. 494–554).* New York: Wiley.

Karraker, K. (1986). Adult attention to infants in a newborn nursery. *Nursing Research, 35,* 358–363.

Kiecolt-Glaser, J., Garner, W., Speicher, C., Penn, G., Holliday, B., & Glaser, R. (1984). Psychosocial modifiers of immunocompetence in medical students. *Psychosomatic Medicine, 46,* 7–14.

Kiecolt-Glaser, J., Ricker, D., George, J., Messick, G., Speicher, C., Garner, W., & Glaser, R. (1984). Urinary cortisol levels, cellular immunocompetency, & loneliness in psychiatric inpatients. *Psychosomatic Medicine, 46,* 15–23.

Laird, J. (1974). Self-attribution of emotion: The effects of expressive behavior on the quality of emotional experience. *Journal of Personality & Social Psychology 29,* 475–486.

Laudenslager, M., Capitanio, J., & Reite, M. (1985). Possible effects of early separation experiences on subsequent immune function in adult macaque monkeys. *American Journal of Psychiatry, 142,* 862–864.

Laudenslager, M., & Reite, M. (1984). Losses and separations: Immunological consequences and health implications. *Review of Personality and Social Psychology, 5,* 285–312.

Laudenslager, M., Ryan, S., Drugan, R., Hyson, R., & Maier, S. (1983). Coping and immunosuppression: Inescapable but not escapable shock suppresses lymphocyte proliferation. *Science, 221,* 568–570.

Lazarus, R. (1985, August). *Classic issues about emotion from the perspective of a relational and cognitive theory.* Paper presented at the Summer Institute on Cognition–Emotion Relationships, Winter Park, CO.

Lazarus, R., & Folkman, S. (1984). *Stress, appraisal, and coping.* New York: Springer.

Lewis, M., & Saarni, C. (1985). *The socialization of emotions.* New York: Plenum.

Malatesta, C., & Haviland, J. (1982). Learning display rules: The socialization of emotion expression in infancy. *Child Development, 53,* 991–1003.

Malatesta, C., & Haviland, J. (1985). Signals, symbols, & socialization: The modification of emotional expression in human development. In M. Lewis & C. Saarni (Eds.), *The socialization of emotions* (pp. 89–116). New York: Plenum.

Mason, J. (1968). A review of psychoendocrine research on the pituitary-adrenal cortical system. *Psychosomatic Medicine, 30,* 576–608.

McCrae, R. (1984). Situational determinants of coping responses: Loss, threat, and challenge. *Journal of Personality and Social Psychology, 46,* 919–928.

Meng, Z., Guo, S., Chen, D., & Lin, J. (1985). The influence of different emotions on mental performance in infancy: II. *Information on Psychological Sciences, 2,* 7–13.

Michaelf, S. (1984). Half the battle. In *Ben Franklin in Paris.* New York: Morris.

Oster, H. (1982, March). *Pouts and horseshoe-mouth faces: Their determinants, affective meaning and signal value in infants.* Paper presented at the International Conference on Infant Studies, Austin.

Regan, J. (1971). Guilt, perceived injustice, and altruistic behavior. *Journal of Personality and Social Psychology, 18,* 124–132.

Riskind, J. (1984). They stoop to conquer: Guiding and self-regulatory functions of physical posture after success and failure. *Journal of Personality and Social Psychology, 47,* 479–493.

Saarni, C. (1982). Social and affective functions of nonverbal behavior. Developmental concerns. In R. Feldman (Ed.), *Development of nonverbal behavior in children* (pp. 123–148). New York: Springer-Verlag.

Scherer, K. (1986). Vocal affect expression: A review and a model for future research. *Psychological Bulletin, 99,* 143–165.

Shennum, W., & Bugental, D. (1982). The development of control over affective expression in nonverbal behavior. In R. Feldman (Ed.), *Development of nonverbal behavior in children* (pp. 102–122). New York: Springer-Verlag.

Sroufe, L. S., & Waters, E. (1976). The ontogenesis of smiling and laughter. *Psychological Review, 81,* 173–189.

Stenberg, C. (1982). *The development of anger facial expressions in infancy.* Unpublished doctoral dissertation, University of Denver.

Swearingen, E., & Cohen, L. (1985). Life events and psychological distress: A prospective study of young adolescents. *Developmental Psychology, 21,* 1045–1054.

Thompson, W., Cowan, C., & Rosenhan, D. (1980). Focus of attention mediates the impact of negative mood on altruism. *Journal of Personality and Social Psychology, 38,* 291–300.

van Hooff, J. (1962). Facial expression in higher primates. *Symposium of Zoological Society of London, 8,* 97–125.

Watzlawick, P., Beavin, J., & Jackson, D. (1967). *Pragmatics of human communication.* New York: Norton.

Wiesenfeld, A., Whitman, P., & Malatesta, C. (1984). Individual differences in adult women in responsivity to infants: Evidence in support of an empathy concept. *Journal of Personality and Social Psychology, 46,* 118–124.

Yerkes, R., & Dodson, J. (1908). The relation of strength of stimulus to rapidity of habit-formation. *Journal of Comparative and Neurological Psychology, 18,* 459–482.

Zahn-Waxler, C. Radke-Yarrow, M., & King, R. (1979). Child rearing and children's prosocial initiations toward victims of distress. *Child Development, 50,* 319–330.

Zuckerman, M., Klorman, R., Larrance, D., & Spiegel, N. (1981). Facial, autonomic and subjective components of emotion: The facial feedback hypothesis versus the externalizer-internalizer distinction. *Journal of Personality and Social Psychology, 41,* 929–944.

Zahn-Waxler, C., Friedman, S., & Cummings, E. M. (1983). Children's emotions and behaviors in response to infants' cries. *Child Development, 54,* 1522–1528.

Zarbabry, L., & Lamb, M. (1985). Social referencing as a function of information source: Mother versus strangers. *Infant Behavior and Development, 8,* 25–33.

II

INFANCY

Stress and Coping From Pregnancy Through the Postnatal Period

Tiffany Field
University of Miami Medical School Mailman Center for Child Development

The title "Stress and Coping across the Life Span" suggests that those processes start from birth. However, stress and coping probably start from the moment of conception. If stress and coping are thought to take place at the level of the individual as well as at the environmental level, then the fetal environment can be considered stressful, and the mother may cope in ways to alleviate that stress. We do not yet know the coping mechanisms of the fetus. In the same way, the neonate may experience many stressors and may cope insofar as he or she is able but rely more often on the coping resources of the caregiving environment.

This chapter is a review of research on stressors from pregnancy through the postnatal period and some of the ways infants naturally cope with those stressors as well as the ways caregivers can help infants cope. Included is a study on ultrasound feedback that helps the mother cope with anxiety, and by reducing pregnancy anxiety, diminishes fetal stress. In a second set of studies, nonnutritive sucking opportunities were presented to help the NICU infant cope with the stress of invasive procedures such as gavage feeding and heelsticks. Finally studies are reviewed on the provision of tactile stimulation and massage to help the ICU neonate cope with isolation and with the struggle for growth. All of these interventions are simple and inexpensive, because they capitalize on the infant's own coping mechanisms, or they involve procedures that are natural extensions of already existing medical procedures. Thus, some of the coping processes take place at the level of the infant (e.g., letting the infant suck on a pacifier to cope with pain), and others involve environmental change (e.g., reducing prenatal stress of the mother by ultrasound feedback). Most importantly, they seem to be effective at alleviating stressors experienced by the mother, fetus, or infant.

FETAL STRESS AND ULTRASOUND FEEDBACK

One of the first stressors is the effect of maternal anxiety on the fetus. Many studies have documented unusually high fetal activity and later irritability in newborns whose mothers experienced high levels of pregnancy anxiety (see Grossman, Eichler, & Winickoff, 1980, for a review). Presumably most of that anxiety is related to the woman's concern about whether the fetus is growing and developing normally. Many pregnant women are given ultrasound examinations to monitor the growth and development of their fetus. Thus, the ultrasound sessions can be used to effectively reassure the mother of normal growth and development. The ultrasonographer simply thinks out loud and points to those growth and development measures being assessed on the ultrasound monitor, including the activity of the fetus and its growth and developmental status. This feedback notably alleviated pregnancy anxiety.

For this study, 40 women who were prescribed to receive three ultrasound sessions during the last trimester of pregnancy were randomly assigned to a group who received ultrasound feedback and a group who were simply told that their fetus was developing normally (Field, Sandberg, Quetel, Garcia, & Rosario, 1985). For the feedback group, the ultrasonographer pointed to the body parts and features of the fetus as she measured them on the ultrasound video monitor and verbally elaborated her observations on growth and development throughout the session. Before these sessions, the mothers were administered the Spielberger State/Trait Anxiety Scale (Spielberger, Gorsuch, & Lushene, 1970). After the sessions, the mothers were given a time chart to take home for recording fetal activity and their own sleep. They were asked to record the number of hours of sleep they received on the night just prior to each visit to the clinic. On the same nights, they were also asked to record the number of minutes the fetus moved during a half-hour sit-down period just prior to their going to bed. In addition, the videotapes of the ultrasound sessions were coded for fetal trunk movements. As can be seen in Tables 3.1 and 3.2, positive effects of the feedback intervention were experienced by all mothers on some variables and by the primiparous mothers only on other variables. Among all mothers, the feedback group reported less fetal movement at times 2 and 3, and more sleep, more dreams, and fewer food aversions at time 3. Among the primiparous mothers only, the feedback group showed lower levels of state anxiety at times 2 and 3, although the trait anxiety levels of the two feedback groups did not differ. The primiparous feedback group also reported a shorter duration of fetal movements. In addition, the primiparous feedback mothers experienced fewer obstetric complications, and their infants were born at a greater birthweight and at a higher Ponderal index

TABLE 3.1
Means for Prenatal Measures (SDs in parentheses).
N = 10 per group. Adapted from Field et al. (1985).

	Groups				
	Feedback		No Feedback		Effect & Signif.
Measures	Primip	Multip	Primip	Multip	Level
Ultrasound 1					
State Anxiety	31(7.6)	36(9.1)	32(10.6)	31(7.4)	ns
Trait Anxiety	36(9.9)	46(8.2)	38(9.9)	40(5.9)	I*
Ultrasound Activity	17(12.0)	21(9.2)	18(9.9)	21(19.7)	ns
Food Aversion	.69(.5)	.75(.5)	.75(.5)	.57(.5)	ns
Ultrasound 2					
State Anxiety	30(6.5)	38(10.4)	37(7.2)	35(8.3)	I**
Trait Anxiety	36(10.8)	48(11.0)	37(6.9)	39(4.9)	I*
Ultrasound Activity	3(3.4)	4(2.6)	3(2.4)	4(3.0)	ns
Movements	6(5.9)	7(4.5)	13(7.6)	13(6.3)	F**
Movement Duration	5(4.0)	10(8.7)	5(2.9)	4(1.7)	I*
Sleep Difficulties	.62(.5)	.88(.4)	.25(.5)	.43(.5)	F**
Hours Sleep	8(1.0)	8(2.2)	8(1.1)	7(2.1)	ns
Dreams	1.2(.4)	1.3(.5)	1.3(.5)	1.3(.5)	ns
Ultrasound 3					
State Anxiety	31(5.8)	40(9.8)	38(5.5)	37(4.9)	I*
Trait Anxiety	38(10.7)	47(14.4)	39(8.3)	39(6.2)	I*
Ultrasound Activity	10(5.4)	8(6.7)	10(4.7)	7(3.1)	ns
Movements	10(6.9)	9(4.1)	13(7.2)	14(5.8)	F*
Movement Duration	4(2.0)	7(5.7)	8(4.7)	8(2.1)	I*
Sleep Difficulties	.23(.4)	.38(.5)	.25(.5)	.23(.4)	ns
Hours Sleep	9(1.2)	9(2.3)	8(1.2)	7(1.0)	F*
Dreams	1.8(.4)	1.8(.5)	1.2(.4)	1.0(.1)	F**
Food Aversion	.38(.5)	.38(.5)	.75(.5)	.86(.38)	F**

*p < .05   I = feedback by parity interaction effect
**p < .01   F = feedback effect

(weight for length index of growth deprivation). Their infants' Brazelton scores also were superior on three of seven dimensions.

Thus, by simply asking the ultrasonographer to think out loud throughout the ultrasound sessions and to highlight fetal features on the ultrasound monitor, we were able to reduce pregnancy anxiety as well as fetal activity, which in turn probably related to the mothers' ability to get more sleep. The reduced anxiety probably contributed to the better neonatal outcome both in terms of growth and developmental performance. There are no costs associated with the ultrasonographer verbalizing her evaluation, therefore this is a cost-effective intervention.

TABLE 3.2
Means for Prenatal Measures (SDs in parentheses).
N = 10 per group. Adapted from Field et al. (1985).

	Groups				
	Feedback		No Feedback		Effect & Signif.
Measures	Primip	Multip	Primip	Multip	Level
Obstetric Complications***	127(18)	106(22)	110(13)	117(17)	I*
Postnatal Complications***	154(16)	143(32)	146(21)	151(22)	ns
Birthweight	3462(186)	3133(348)	3229(485)	3108(202)	I*
Birthlength	51(1.5)	50(.9)	51(1.2)	50(1.8)	P*
Ponderal Index	2.61(.2)	2.51(.2)	2.43(.3)	2.49(.4)	I*
Brazelton Scores					
Habituation	5.9(.9)	5.1(.9)	4.6(.7)	5.2(.6)	I**
Orientation	5.4(.7)	5.7(.9)	5.4(.7)	5.6(.7)	ns
Motor	5.8(.6)	4.8(.7)	5.1(.4)	5.2(.6)	I**
Range of State	5.4(.5)	3.5(1.4)	4.3(.5)	4.6(.7)	I**
Regulation of State	5.0(1.0)	5.2(1.4)	4.7(1.5)	5.1(.7)	ns
Autonomic Stability	6.7(.3)	6.8(.7)	6.5(.3)	6.2(.1)	ns
Reflexes (#abnormal)	1.0(.9)	2.6(1.9)	1.3(.7)	1.7(1.0)	ns
Activity	7.1(4.8)	7.9(3.7)	7.4(2.2)	7.7(3.0)	ns

*p < .05
**p < .01
***higher number denotes fewer complications
I = feedback by parity interaction effect
F = feedback effect
P = parity effect

Unfortunately, many of the positive effects were limited to the primiparous women, possibly because the mothers were less knowledgeable about pregnancy and thereby more receptive to the ultrasound feedback.

INVASIVE PROCEDURES AS NICU STRESSORS

Gavage Feeding and Heelsticks

An unfortunate stressor experienced by some infants is prematurity and its attendant medical complications. Data on the stressors of the neonatal intensive care unit environment have filled volumes (see, for example, Gottfried & Gaiter, 1985). Although the preterm neonate appears to be bombarded by multiple and continuous medical procedures, many of the behavioral and physiological effects of these have not yet been studied. In those few studies that have researched the specific effects of invasive procedures on the preterm neonate, oxygen tension ($TCPO_2$) has been monitored as the primary measure of physiological stress.

Decreases in oxygen tension suggest a physiological imbalance and are, therefore, cause for clinical concern. Invasive procedures almost invariably contribute to decreases in oxygen tension. As part of a larger study on infant massage, we monitored oxygen tension during various invasive procedures (Morrow & Field, in press). For example, during the insertion of the tube for gavage or tube feeding (considered a necessary form of feeding by most neonatalogists), oxygen tension significantly decreased (on average 14 mm). Similarly during heelstick procedures (again, a necessary procedure for assaying bilirubin levels), oxygen tension again dropped 14 mm.

In a simple procedure to alleviate this problem, Long, Alistair, Phillip, and Lucey (1980) instructed the NICU nurses to use oxygen tension monitoring to modify these procedures and to limit those procedures that were considered to be "undesirable time," that is, procedural time that contributed to reduced oxygen tension. When the nurse monitored $TCPO_2$, the amount of undesirable time was reduced from 40 minutes to 6 minutes per 20 hours. Infants in the monitored group were handled less frequently and experienced less hypoxemia. Thus, simply alerting the nursing staff to monitor the physiology of the neonate during invasive procedures appears to attenuate the stress associated with those procedures. Presumably these procedures were accompanied by changes in neonatal behavior that may have attenuated the stress. However, behavior observations were not reported by Long et al.

Weaning From the Ventilator

Data from our lab and the lab of Long et al. highlight the physiological stress associated with the more obviously stressful ICU procedures such as gavage feeding and heelsticks. A less obvious stressor is the removal of the infant from live-saving procedures such as the incubator. The stressfulness of weaning was a serendipitous finding in our larger infant massage study (Field, 1987). That study included plasma sampling by heelsticks on days 1, 5, 9, and 10 of the stimulation study. The neonates were weaned from their ventilators one to two days prior to their recruitment for the stimulation study. The plasma was then assayed for levels of cortisol, a biochemical index of stress. As can be seen in Table 3.3, cortisol levels were significantly higher on day 1 (M = 61 ng/ml) than on day 5 (M = 41 ng/ml). The values of days 5, 9, and 10 were averaged, because there was no significant difference among the levels of cortisol on those days (suggesting stability of cortisol levels over that period), and the average was then compared to day 1. The percentage change from day 1 to the mean of days 5, 9, and 10 was a 25% ($p < .05$) decrease in cortisol values. In a future study, it would be important to investigate the difference between baseline levels taken prior to weaning from the ventilator and those taken subsequent to the procedure.

These findings suggest that the weaning process itself is stressful. These data are not surprising inasmuch as the infant has been dependent on this life support

TABLE 3.3
Plasma level of cortisol (ng/ml) at day 1 and day 5 (days 9 and 10
in parentheses) following weaning from ventilator.
Taken from Field (1987).

	Day 1	Day 5	Percentage Change From Day 1
Newborn			
1	60	39(41,37)	−35
2	47	25(25,25)	−47
3	90	64(68,61)	−29
4	33	32(29,35)	− 3
5	34	30(27,32)	−13
6	123	57(67,47)	−54
7	38	42(42,41)	+ 9

−25
S.E ± 7
$p < .05$

system to date and would quite expectedly experience an adjustment reaction. However, no apparent intervention, such as a gradual weaning process, is staged at this time to help the neonate make that adjustment. Unfortunately weaning from the life support system is as necessary as the life support system was at an earlier time, so this stressor is unavoidable. However, other stressors such as developmental assessments can be modified.

Developmental Assessments as Stressors

Simple newborn assessments such as the Brazelton Neonatal Behavior Assessment Scale (Brazelton, 1973) typically involve reflex testing and repositioning of the infant, handling that has been noted to be stressful for the preterm neonate. Although our oxygen tension monitoring of preterm neonates during the administration of the Brazelton examination (Morrow & Field, in press) yielded no substantial decreases in $TCPO_2$ (see Table 3.4), other indicators of stress such as elevations of cortisol and decreases in growth hormone following the Brazelton suggest that these assessments may be stressful. For example, data from a study by Gunnar and her colleagues (Gunnar, Isensee, & Fust, 1987) indicated that cortisol levels were elevated following the administration of the Brazelton to term neonates.

Data from our lab suggest that preterm neonates are also stressed when they are given the Brazelton at approximately term gestational age. Again, a serendipitous finding in our infant massage study (Field, 1987) suggests that preterm neonates are stressed during the Brazelton Assessment as manifested by a decrease in growth hormone levels. Until this study, growth hormone levels had not been

TABLE 3.4
Average TcPO$_2$ changes during Brazelton assessment items (N = 22). Taken from Morrow & Field (unpublished data, 1989).

Items	TcPO$_2$	
Flashlight	+ 1.4	
Rattle	+ 1.6	M = +1.7 (R = +1.4 to +2.0)
Bell	+ 2.0	
Pinprick	− 2.0	
Ankle clonus	− 2.9	
Plantar grasp	− 4.2	
Babinski	− 6.6	
Undress	− 6.3	
Passive arm movements	− 5.6	M = −4.3 (R = −2.0 to −6.6)
Passive leg movements	− 4.7	
Palmar grasp	− 3.2	
Pull-to-sit	−4.8	
Standing	− 6.0	
Walking	− 4.4	
Placing	− 4.7	
Incurvation	− 2.1	
Crawling	− 2.2	
Tonic neck deviation	+ 1.5	
Glabella	+ 1.0	
Rooting	+ .9	M = +1.4 (R = +.9 to +2.0)
Sucking	+ 2.0	
Inanimate visual	+ 5.3	
Inanimate auditory	+ 2.4	
Animate visual	+ 5.8	M = +3.1 (R = 0 to +5.8)
Animate auditory	+ 2.0	
Animate visual & auditory	0	
Cloth-on-face	+ .5	
TNR	+ .9	M = +1.1 (R = .5 to 1.8)
Moro	+ 1.8	

Note. Total mean change = −.7 (R = −6.6 to +5.8).

used as a physiological index of stress in preterm infants. In adults and children, growth hormone values typically increase during stress. In contrast, growth hormone levels decrease when infants are stressed (Stubbe & Wolf, 1971). Although we were assessing growth hormone levels for a different purpose (i.e., to determine the relationship between growth hormone and weight gain in the massage infants), we had inadvertently drawn blood samples following a stressful procedure (i.e., the Brazelton). At the time of the Brazelton assessment, the infants averaged 36 weeks postconceptional age and 1600 grams weight. The infants were given heelsticks for the plasma samples of growth hormone levels two hours following the Brazelton assessment and at the same time of day on the previous day. As can be seen in Table 3.5, the mean baseline value for plasma growth hormone was higher than the mean growth hormone value after the Brazelton (21.5 ng/ml vs. 14.4 ng/ml). The difference value (M = −7.1) was significant at $p < .02$. This 32% decrease in growth hormone following administration of the Brazelton suggests that neonatal assessments are stressful for preterm newborns even when they are given at approximately term age.

Thus, these stressful procedures are accompanied by distressed behavior and altered physiological and biochemical activity. Findings such as the ones we have just reviewed have contributed to the "minimal touch" policies adopted by many intensive care nurseries. This policy limits the number of stressful procedures and examinations as well as the periodicity of them. Newborn researchers are also designing less stressful assessments for the preterm neonate that involve less handling as well as shorter assessment protocols (Als, Lester, Ironick, & Brazelton, 1982; Korner, 1986).

Neonatal Coping and Caregiving Activities That Help Alleviate Stress

For those invasive procedures that are necessary, various forms of soothing stimulation can be applied during the procedures to alleviate their stressful effects. Spontaneous, self-comforting behavior by the infant, such as nonnutritive sucking, and natural caregiving stimulation, such as stroking the infant, are examples of how NICU stressors can be reduced.

TABLE 3.5
Plasma level of growth hormone (ng/ml) at baseline and post Brazelton assessment. Taken from Field (1987).

	Baseline	Post-Brazelton	Percentage Change
Newborn			
1	26.0(27,25)	19.0	−27
2	20.0(20,20)	12.0	−40
3	29.5(31,28)	14.0	−53
4	19.5(18,21)	9.0	−54
5	19.0(17,21)	9.0	−24
6	25.0(31,19)	19.0	− 4
7	13.5(12,15)	13.0	− 4
8	19.5(25,14)	19.0	− 5

−32
S.E. ± 7
p < .02

Nonnutritive Sucking as a Coping Mechanism

Various self-comforting, coping behaviors such as sucking are available as early as the neonatal stage. The infant can effectively alleviate stressful procedures by sucking. As was noted earlier, gavage or tube feeding is a stressful NICU procedure. Giving the NICU neonate a pacifier for nonnutritive sucking during the gavage feeding diminishes stress and facilitates faster recovery. In a study at our NICU (Field, Ignatoff, Stringer, Brennan, Greenberg, Widmayer & Anderson, 1982), a sample of 57 neonates were randomly assigned to nonnutritive sucking versus control conditions during gavage feedings. The two groups were equivalent on gestational age (M = 32 wks.), birthweight (M = 1300 gms.), and postnatal complications. Neonates in the nonnutritive sucking group were given a pacifier during all tube feedings, whereas the infants in the control group were not denied the pacifier at all times but at least did not receive it during gavage feeds. The follow-up data suggested that the treatment group required fewer tube feedings; their average weight gain per day was greater; they were hospitalized fewer days; and because of that, their hospital cost was significantly lower (see Table 3.6). Also, they were easier to feed during later bottle feedings, as evidenced by the nurses engaging in fewer stimulating behaviors such as bottle jiggling and feeding position changes. Thus, nonnutritive sucking not only diminished distress responses but also facilitated weight gain and a more rapid recovery process.

In another study of this kind, Bernbaum and her colleagues (Bernbaum, Pereira, Watkins, & Peckham, 1983) noted that the addition of nonnutritive sucking during gavage feedings accelerated the maturation of the sucking reflex, facilitating a more rapid transition from gavage to oral feedings. In addition, intestinal transit time (as measured by carmine dye) was decreased, and a more rapid weight gain was noted (despite a caloric intake comparable to the control group) resulting in a shorter hospital stay.

TABLE 3.6
Means for clinical outcome measures of treatment group receiving nonnutritive sucking stimulation and control group. Taken from Field and Goldson (1984).

Measures	Treatment	Control	p
Number of tube feedings	219.0	246.0	.05
Days of tube feeding	26.0	29.0	.01
Daily weight gain (gm)	19.3	16.5	.05
Number of hospital days	48.0	56.0	.05
Hospital cost	16,800.0	20,294.0	.01

Data from other groups suggest still other benefits of nonnutritive sucking during gavage feedings. For example, the decrease in oxygenation (oxygen tension) typically noted during routine gavage feeding is prevented by simultaneous nonnutritive sucking (Bernbaum, Pereira, Watkins, & Peckham, 1983). Moreover, an actual increase in $TCPO_2$ has been described during nonnutritive sucking in preterm infants (Burroughs, Asonye, & Anderson-Shanklin, 1978; Paludetto, Rauwitz, Hack, Shivpure, & Martin, 1984).

Nonnutritive sucking is apparently effective in calming neonates during gavage feedings; therefore, we conducted a study in which intensive and minimal care preterm neonates were given pacifiers during the heelstick procedure. Not surprisingly, because sucking and crying are somewhat incompatible, the infants who were given a pacifier showed less fussiness and crying both during and after the procedure than those not given a pacifier (Field & Goldson, 1984). The minimal-care neonates provided pacifiers were also less physiologically aroused by the heelstick procedure, as evidenced by lower heart rate and respiration rate (see Table 3.7). In contrast, the NICU neonates, despite less crying, showed no change in heart rate and respiration. The inconsistent effects on their behavior and physiological arousal were interpreted as a lack of cardiac-somatic coupling (linkage or integration of heart rate and behavior) in the very immature NICU neonates. Thus, nonnutritive sucking attenuated behavioral distress during heelsticks in all neonates and physiological arousal in more mature neonates with less severe neonatal complications. This is not surprising, considering that sucking is typically incompatible with crying. However, this simple, cost-effective procedure is rarely used during stressful procedures such as heelsticks.

Soothing Stimulation by Caregivers

Just as the infant can cope with invasive procedures in the NICU by his or her own self-comforting behaviors, caregivers have been noted to provide effective comforting behaviors such as stroking and body massage. One of the simplest of the caregiver interventions is the placing on of hands by nurses or volunteer grandmothers. In a study by Jay (1982), for example, a nurse simply placed her

TABLE 3.7
Means for measures taken during heelsticks for treatment (nonnutritive sucking) and control groups in minimal and intensive care nurseries. Taken from Field and Goldson (1984).

	Minimal Care			Intensive Care		
Measures	Treatment	Control	P	Treatment	Control	P
Crying (% Time)	25	41	.005	01	19	.001
Heart Rate (BPM)	172	187	.05	165	168	ns
Respiration Rate	81	72	.05	51	54	ns

hands on the infant's head and abdomen for 12 minutes at a time for four times daily. By scheduling this intervention at times other than invasive procedures, the intervention could provide the newborn gentle human touch without the infant experiencing simultaneous painful stimuli. This was an important feature of the design, because it is conceivable that newborns learn to associate these interventions (for example, nonnutritive sucking or stroking) with the painful invasive procedure they are supposed to alleviate. The results of Jay's study (1982) suggest that the simple placing of hands on the preterm neonate's head and abdomen was associated with a decreased need for mechanical ventilation, fewer startle responses, and fewer clenched fists in the stimulated infants.

In a more extensive touching intervention, we provided massage of preterm neonates (Field, et al., 1986). For 45 minutes per day (for 10 days) the neonates were given stroking and passive movements of the limbs. Based on a random stratification procedure, 40 preterm neonates were assigned to a treatment or a control condition at the time they entered the transitional "grower" nursery. The groups were comparable in gestational age (M = 31 wks.), birthweight (M = 1280 gms.), and duration of intensive care (M = 20 days). For 10 days, the treatment group received massage for three 15-minute periods during three con-secutive hours per day. Stimulation sessions were comprised of three 5-minute phases. During the first and third phases, tactile stimulation or massage-like stroking was provided. In a prone position, the neonate received body stroking of the head and face region, neck and shoulders, back, legs, and arms for five 1-minute segments. The chest/abdomen region was not massaged, because the neonates apparently found that aversive. We speculated that the neonates may have formed an association between pain and aversive procedures that typically affect that region and, thus, preferred not to be massaged on the chest or abdomen. The second 5-minute phase of the stimulation involved gentle flexing and ex-tending of the supine infant's limbs (as in bicycling motions). The final 5-minute phase was a repeat of the first massage phase. Each neonate was given the Brazelton scale, and his or her sleep/wake behavior was coded at the end of the 10-day treatment period. These behavior observations were conducted over a 45-minute period, during which sleep states were coded as well as behaviors such as limb movements and facial expressions.

The data analysis (Table 3.8) indicated that the stimulated infants: (a) averaged 47% greater weight gain per day, although the groups did not differ on average formula intake (volume or calories); (b) were awake and active a greater percent-age of the observation time; (c) showed more immature habituation, orientation, motor activity, and range of state behavior on the Brazelton; and (d) were hospitalized six days less than the control infants yielding an average hospital cost savings of $3,000 per infant.

Recently we conducted a replication of this study on 40 additional preterm infants (M = 30 wks. gestation; M = 1176 gms. birthweight) (Scafidi et al., 1989). As in the already described study, the treatment infants received the

TABLE 3.8
Means for measures differentiating tactile/kinesthetic stimulation
preterm neonates from controls. Taken from Field et al. (1986).

	Groups		
Measures	Stimulation	Control	p level
Feedings (#) per day	8.6	9.0	N.S.
Formula (ccs/kg/day)	171.0	166.0	N.S.
Calories/kg/day	114.0	112.0	N.S.
Calories/day	169.0	165.0	N.S.
Daily Weight Gain (grams)	25.0	17.0	.0005
% Time Awake	16.0	7.0	.04
% Time Movement	32.0	25.0	.04
Brazelton Scores			
Habituation	6.1	4.9	.02
Orientation	4.8	4.0	.02
Motor	4.7	4.2	.03
Range of State	4.6	3.9	.03

massage (tactile/kinesthetic stimulation) for three 15-minute periods during three consecutive hours of the day for a ten-day period. This study improved on the methodology of the previous study by scheduling sleep/wake behavior observations and Brazelton assessments at the beginning as well as at the end of the two-week treatment period. As in the previous study, the treatment infants averaged a greater weight gain per day (in this case 21%) despite similar formula intake. Once again, they were discharged five days earlier at a significant hospital cost savings. The massaged infants also engaged in less active sleep and showed less mouthing, facial grimaces, and clenched fists during sleep observations, suggesting that they were less stressed during sleep, and they showed superior habituation performance on the Brazelton Scale. In addition to the behavioral measures, plasma samples were collected for growth hormone and cortisol assays, and urine samples were collected for assaying catecholamines. These assays were performed to further explore the underlying mechanism for the massage/weight gain relationship. Preliminary analyses of urine catecholamine levels suggested that norepinephrine, epinephrine, and dopamine were more elevated in the massage versus the control group by the end of the treatment period. Although very little is known about the development of catecholamines in the early neonatal period, fitting these results into the context of the existing literature suggests that the treatment group is experiencing a more normal developmental increase in these catecholamines (see Table 3.9) (Lagercrantz & Slotkin, 1986).

The interventions that capitalize on the newborn's coping skills such as nonnutritive sucking are, of course, extremely cost-effective. In fact, they are free, because the pacifier is simply given to the infant. In contrast, the caregiving procedures just described (the placing on of hands and massage), although also

TABLE 3.9
Catecholamine and hormone changes over the massage treatment
period (days 1 and 10)

	Groups			
	Stimulation		Control	
	Day 1	Day 10	Day 1	Day 10
Measures				
Urine assays				
—Norepinephrine	44.2*	66.0	48.2	53.3
—Epinephrine	2.6**	4.1	3.1	3.3
—Dopamine	1175.7**	1447.8	1235.6	1433.4
—Cortisol	232.3**	274.0	248.0**	294.7
—Creatinine/vol wt.	9.7	7.5	7.0	6.1
—Creatinine/MgTVL	12.9	12.4	9.1	10.0
Plasma assays				
—Growth Hormone	19.5*	14.2	22.8*	15.4
—Cortisol	41.8	38.5	32.1	32.0

*p < .05 for adjacent means
**p < .01

cost-effective, do involve extra time spent by personnel at the infant's bedside. In some hospitals, these costs have been significantly reduced by employing volunteer grandmothers to provide these kinds of stimulation. As some have noted, this arrangement may be therapeutic for both the babies and the grand-mothers.

CONCLUSION

In summary, a simple intervention during the prenatal period reduced maternal anxiety as well as facilitated better neonatal outcome. The intervention procedure involved a simple component added onto a routine procedure, namely the ultraso-nographer thinking out loud during the ultrasound assessment for the mother's benefit. During the neonatal period, self-comforting stimulation such as nonnutri-tive sucking appeared to attenuate distressed behavior and physiology during invasive NICU procedures such as gavage feedings and heelsticks. Similarly although more expensive, natural caregiving stimulation such as the laying on of hands or gentle stroking also attenuated distressed behavior during the infant's NICU stay. Inasmuch as these interventions are readily provided at very minimal cost and given that they not only soothe the stressed infant but also have positive side effects such as increased weight gain and a shorter hospital stay, they would appear to be cost-effective forms of intervention. The intervention procedures in all cases involved a simple component added onto routine procedures. There are considerable costs typically associated with early interventions; therefore, investigations of simple adaptations for already existing procedures and further exploration of the newborn's own coping skills are bound to lead to more cost-effective ways of alleviating stress during the perinatal period.

ACKNOWLEDGMENTS

The author would like to thank the infants and mothers who participated in the studies. This research was supported by an NIMH Research Scientist Development Award #MH00331.

REFERENCES

Als, H., Lester, B. M., Tronick, E. Z., & Brazelton, T. B. (1982). Toward a research instrument for the assessment of preterm infants' behavior (APIB). In N. E. Fitzgerald, B. M. Lester, & M. W. Yogman (Eds.), *Theory and research in behavior pediatrics*. New York: Plenum.

Bernbaum, J., Pereira, G., Watkins, G., & Peckham, G. (1983). Nonnutritive sucking during gavage feeding enhances growth and maturation in premature infants. *Pediatrics, 71*, 41–45.

Brazelton, T. B. (1973). *Neonatal Behavior Assessment Scale*. Philadelphia: Lippincott.

Burroughs, A. K., Asonye, V. O., Anderson-Shanklin, G. C., & Vidyasagar, D. (1978). The effect of nonnutritive sucking or transcutaneous oxygen tension in noncrying preterm neonates. *Research in Nursing and Health, 1*, 69–75.

Field, T. (1987). Alleviating stress in NICU neonates. *Journal of the American Osteopathic Association, 87*, 646–650.

Field, T., & Goldson, E. (1984). Pacifying effects of nonnutritive sucking on term and preterm neonates during heelsticks. *Pediatrics, 74*, 1012–1015.

Field, T., Ignatoff, E., Stringer, S., Brennan, J., Greenberg, R., Widmayer, S., & Anderson, G. (1982). Nonnutritive sucking during tube feedings: Effects on preterm neonates in an ICU. *Pediatrics, 70*, 381–384.

Field, T., Sandberg, D., Quetel, T. A., Garcia, R., & Rosario, M. (1985). Effects of ultrasound feedback on pregnancy anxiety, fetal activity, and neonatal outcome. *Obstetrics and Gynecology, 66*, 525–528.

Field, T., Schanberg, S. M., Scafidi, F., Bauer, C. R., Vega-Lahr, N., Garcia, R., Nystrom, J., & Kuhn, C. M. (1986). Tactile/kinesthetic stimulation effects on preterm neonates. *Pediatrics, 77*(5), 654–658.

Gottfried, A. W., & Gaiter, J. L. (1985). *Infant stress under intensive care*. Baltimore: University Park Press.

Grossman, F., Eichler, L., & Winickoff, S. A. (1980). *Pregnancy, birth, and parenthood*. San Francisco: Jossey Bass.

Gunnar, M. R., Isensee, J., & Fust, S. (1987). Adrenocortical activity and the Brazelton neonatal Assessment Scale: Moderating effects of the newborn's biobehavioral status. *Child Development, 58*(6), 1448–1458.

Jay, S. (1982). The effects of gentle human touch on mechanically ventilated very short gestation infants. *Maternal–Child Nursing Journal, 11,* 199–256.

Korner, A. (1986). *Neurobehavioral maturity assessment for preterm infants.* Unpublished manual.

Lagercrantz, H., & Slotkin, T. A. (April, 1986). The "stress" of being born. *Scientific American, 20,* 100–107.

Long, J. G., Alistair, G. S., Phillip, A. G. S., & Lucey, J. F. (1980). Excessive handling as a cause of hypoxemia. *Pediatrics, 65,* 203–207.

Morrow, C., & Field, T. (in preparation). *Invasive procedures reduce oxygen tension.*

Paludetto, R., Robertson, S., Hack, M., Shivpuri, C., & Martin, R. (1984). Transcutaneous oxygen tension during nonnutritive sucking in preterm infants. *Pediatrics, 74,* 539–542.

Scafidi, F., Field, T., Schanberg, S., Bauer, C., Tucci, K., Roberts, J., Morrow, C. & Kuhn, C. M. (1990). Massage stimulates greater activity and growth in preterm infants. *Infant Behavior and Development, 13,* 167–188.

Spielberger, C. D., Gorsuch, R. L., & Lushene, R. E. (1970). *The State-Trait Anxiety Inventory.* Palo Alto: Consulting Psychologists Press.

Stubbe, P., & Wolf, M. (1971). The effect of stress on growth hormone, glucose and glyceral levels in newborn infants. *Hormone Metabolism Research, 3,* 175–179.

A Longitudinal Study of the Effects of Maternal Stress and Protective Factors on the Development of High-Risk Children

Byron Egeland
Terrie Kreutzer
University of Minnesota

The relationship between stressful life events experienced by the family (i.e., contextual stress) and the child's negotiation of salient developmental tasks has recently emerged as a major area of research in child development, particularly the field of developmental psychopathology (Beautrais, Fergusson, & Shannon, 1982; Garmezy, 1981; Madge, 1983; Masten et al., 1988; Pianta, Egeland, & Sroufe, 1990; Rutter, 1979; Wallerstein & Kelly, 1980). Research has demonstrated that this relationship between contextual stress and a child's development is not linear; that is, the absence of stress does not cause competence nor does the presence result in lack of competence. Rather the effects occur within a broader and infinitely more complex system that is mediated and affected by individual, developmental, relationship, and environmental variables (Pianta et al., 1990).

This chapter focuses on a series of interrelated studies that attempt to examine the complexity of the stress–outcome relationship. Focusing on the developmental outcomes of middle childhood, the relationship between stressful life events experienced by the child's mother (e.g., financial problems, divorce), and the child's school adjustment and academic success in first and third grade is examined.

First grade was chosen as one outcome point, because the beginning of full-time school involvement is a difficult period for young children. The transition to school is a significant and potentially stressful developmental progression for a child (Rutter, 1983). Research demonstrates that children do manifest behavioral problems related to school entry that typically dissipate after a short adjustment period (Hughes, Pinkerton, & Plewis, 1979). However, not all children's behavioral difficulties disappear following an adjustment period. Elizure (1986) had shown that parental support, coping, and cohesive family patterns are significantly related to improved adjustment in children who initially demonstrated behavioral difficulties at the beginning of first grade. Therefore, we have chosen two points of time to measure developmental outcomes: first grade and third grade. We are interested in examining the effects of stress experienced by the family on the child's adaptation during the difficult developmental period of beginning school (first grade) and during a more tranquil developmental period (third grade).

We are interested in the effects of stress assessed at different times during the child's life on his/her first- and third-grade school performance. We have found that concurrent stress may not affect developmental outcomes as much as stress experienced early in the child's development (Pianta et al., 1990). Thus, in examining the temporal effects of stress experienced by the family, *three* contextual stress periods were used to predict first and third grade developmental outcomes. The stress periods were: early stress (stress experienced by family prior to child's school entry); and contemporary stress experienced by family during child's first- and third-grade year. The relation between contextual stress and third-grade child outcomes involves stress scores obtained at three points in time: (a) contemporary stress (i.e., stress experienced by family during child's third-grade year); (b) first-grade contextual stress; (c) early contextual stress (i.e., stress experienced during the period from infancy through 64 months of age). Early contextual stress and first-grade contextual stress were used to predict child outcomes in the first grade. (Third-grade contextual stress was not used to predict first-grade outcomes.)

A second goal is to look at the child's past developmental history as a protective factor. In general, children entering first grade who are experiencing a high level of contextual stress appear at risk for acute or long-term school adjustment problems. However, it is clear that not all children who experience high levels of contextual stress will demonstrate poor school adjustment (Masten et al., 1988; Pianta et al., 1990). The second half of this chapter will examine the underlying factors that may account for successful adaptation in situations where poor school adjustment was anticipated. Researchers have examined numerous variables that may account for successful adaptation under distressing circumstances that include variables such as age, sex, self-esteem, IQ, constitutional and experiencial individual differences, environmental opportunity, and interpersonal relationships (Garmezy & Tellegen, 1983; Pianta et al., 1990; Rutter, 1979; Rutter, 1983; Wallerstein, 1983; Wallerstein & Kelly, 1980).

We hypothesized that the child's prior experience and success with the negotiation of developmental tasks may have given the child a foundation of success or failure from which he or she is launched into this new developmental task (school entry). We presumed that a sturdy foundation based on successful negotiation of prior tasks should mitigate the effects of stress and enhance continued competent functioning; that is, act as a protective factor (Sroufe, 1979).

This chapter is based on a longitudinal-developmental study of a high-risk poverty sample that allowed for examination of the relation between contextual stress and child outcomes as well as the investigation of child developmental history as a factor that may mediate the effects of stress on the child's successful negotiation of current developmental tasks. The sample consists of 267 primiparous women who were enrolled during the last trimester of pregnancy while patients at Public Health Clinics. The sample is at risk by virtue of their disadvantaged economic status as well as mothers' low educational level, age, lack of support, and a number of other factors related to poverty.

Maternal Stressful Life Events

Stressful life events were assessed using a scale adapted from Cochrane and Robertson's (1973) Life Event Inventory. Their 51-item scale was modified, because some of the items were inappropriate for a poverty sample (e.g., going on holiday), young parents (e.g., retirement), and primiparous women (e.g., son or daughter left home). A number of items were added in order to capture stressors specific to a poverty sample (e.g., trouble with welfare). The revised Stressful Life Events scale (SLE) consisted of 39 items.

The procedure for collecting the stressful life event data involved a semistructured interview with the mother, which was part of the assessments that occurred when the children were 12, 18, 24, 30, 42, 54, and 64 months of age and at the end of first, second, and third grade. The interviewer asked if a particular event or condition had occurred since the previous assessment or was ongoing at the time. The interviewer then elicited the mother's feelings about the experience and the extent to which it had had an effect on family functioning. This allowed the mothers to elaborate on each item and enabled us to make certain judgments about their subjective experiences.

Additional reasons for using the interview format as an alternative to the more commonly used checklist approach had to do with the accuracy of mothers' recall of events. We used a checklist in our first attempt to assess stress at the six-month assessment. We quickly learned that this approach resulted in unreliable and invalid data due to the mothers' misunderstanding of a particular event and poor recall.

During the first year of the child's life, we scheduled assessments each day in the hospital during the newborn period and at home on days 7 and 10. In addition, home or laboratory visits were done at 2, 3, 4, 6 (two visits), 9, and 12 months. We came to know the families well, and it became apparent that the mothers would often forget to endorse major life events with which we had become aware. The opposite was also true. Mothers would endorse items that were of minimal stress. For example, sickness in the family was often endorsed, even if the sickness involved a case of the flu. Totaling the number of endorsed items from a checklist of stressful life events did not accurately reflect the degree of stress

TABLE 4.1
Items in the Personal Stressor Scale

1. Trouble with superiors or continued tension at work
2. Quarrel with neighbors
3. Arguments about how money is spent
4. You or immediate family involved in physical fight
5. Immediate family member drinks heavily
6. Immediate family member attempts suicide
7. Death of immediate family member or close friend
8. Immediate family member seriously ill
9. Gain of new family member
10. Husband or boyfriend intoxicated frequently
11. Serious physical injury of mother, child, or father requiring hospitalization
12. Prolonged ill health of mother, child, or father requiring treatment by doctor
13. Miscarriage
14. Abortion
15. Pregnancy
16. Marriage
17. Boyfriend(s) moves out; Boyfriend(s) moves in
18. Other people moving in or out
19. Increase in number of arguments or severe arguments with spouse (or boyfriend/girlfriend)
20. Have you ever been frightened by your husband/boyfriend or other family member?
21. Increase in number of arguments or severe fights with close friend
22. Trouble with relatives
23. Marital separation or break-up
24. Divorce
25. Marital reconciliation
26. Custody, visitation problems
27. Separation of mother and child

experienced by many of the mothers in our poverty sample. We abandoned the checklist approach and began using an interview format at 12 months for determining stressful life events.

Using mothers' description of a stressful event, each SLE item was scored on a three-point scale reflecting the extent to which the stressful experience was disruptive to family functioning (Egeland, Breitenbucher, & Rosenberg, 1980). The ratings were based on the degree of disruptiveness, the frequency of the occurrence of the event since the previous assessment, and the extent to which it involved persons with whom the mother shared close relationships. A close relationship was defined as one which the mother shared with an immediate family member (e.g., a child, husband, boyfriend) or someone on whom the mother was financially or emotionally dependent (e.g., a close friend, parents, siblings). The reliability of this scoring technique was established through determining interrater agreement across several raters. The average interrater agreement was .86 (Pianta, 1986).

The SLE scale has been refined, and the score used in the analyses reported in this chapter are based on personal stress experienced by the mother. Pianta (1986) did a series of analyses, including a factor analysis of the 39-item scale. He found 27 items with loading greater than .30 that appeared to assess stressful experiences in the mother's interpersonal relationships. A scale based on these items was formed and was named Personal Stress. A list of the items is presented in Table 4.1.

In our earlier work examining the relation between maternal stress and child outcomes, we found that the Personal Stress score and certain subscales predicted outcomes better than the total score (Pianta et al., 1990). The reason that the total SLE score does not predict as well as the Personal Stress score is that endorsement of certain items are positively related to the mother's competence and as a consequence predicted positive child outcomes. For example, mothers who worked were likely to endorse stressful life event items having to do with their job (e.g., trouble with supervisor at work). The more competent mothers worked, and as a consequence of work, they often had higher SLE scores. The competent working mother would also likely have a competent child and, thus, a positive relation between stress associated with work and child outcomes. Four items on the scale pertained to work.

School Performance Measures

Ratings of the child's social-emotional development were obtained near the end of the child's first- and third-grade year in school from each child's teacher. The Child Behavior Checklist–Teacher Report Form (CBC–T) (Achenbach & Edelbrock, 1980) was used to assess classroom adjustment and behavior problems. Additionally teacher rankings of the child's emotional health and social competency/popularity as compared to other children in the class were also gathered. The child's classroom teacher was provided a short description of an emotionally healthy and popular/socially competent child, and was asked to rank each child in his or her class on these two dimensions. The child's score reflected his or her relative positive as compared with their classmates, and consisted of the child's rank divided by the number of students in the class.

Achievement testing was conducted in the child's home following completion of his or her first- or third-grade year using the Peabody Individual Achievement Test (PIAT) (Dunn & Markwardt, 1970). A total age standard score was obtained for each child on the following subtests: math, reading recognition, reading comprehension, spelling, and general information.

RESULTS: MATERNAL STRESSORS
AND SCHOOL ADAPTATION

Personal stress experienced by the mother at three different periods in the child's development were used to predict her child's adjustment and adaptation in first and third grade. An early cumulative personal stress score, which consisted of the total score from seven assessments during the period 18–64 months, was calculated. Two contemporary personal stress scores were determined based on stress experienced by the mother during the child's first- and third-grade years in school. Personal stress experienced by the mother during the child's early years (18–64 months), along with stress scores from the first- and third-grade period, were each used to predict child development outcomes.

Moderate correlations between maternal stress experienced prior to the child's first-grade year (18–64 months) and the child's school adjustment in first- and third-grade were found for both boys and girls. For boys, early stressors correlated moderately with four first-grade outcomes (r = .21 to .37): two Teacher Behavior Checklist scales, and teachers' ranking of social competence and emotional health (see Table 4.2). Early cumulative stress experienced by mother was not related to her son's academic achievement in the first or third grade, nor was it related to third-grade social and emotional outcomes except for the Self Destruction Scale from the Teacher Behavior Checklist.

For girls, early cumulative personal stressors experienced by mother correlated with teacher ratings on five scales from the Teacher Behavior Checklist given in the first grade (range .23 to .42, see Table 4.3). Early stress did not predict achievement in first or third grade except for first-grade Reading Recognition. The only significant correlation between early personal stressors and third-grade outcomes was the Unpopular Scale from the Teacher Behavior Checklist.

Using the contemporary scores, personal stress experienced by mother during her child's first-grade year was correlated with a number of scales from the Teacher Behavior Checklist and teacher rankings. For boys, first-grade maternal stressors correlated with five scales from the Teacher Behavior Checklist and both teacher rankings in the first grade (see Table 4.2). First-grade maternal stress was similarly correlated with third-grade outcomes (i.e., six Child Behavior Checklist scales were significantly correlated). First-grade maternal stressors did not, however, relate to achievement in first or third grade for boys.

For the girls, stress experienced by mother during the first grade year was correlated with both first- and third-grade outcomes. Stress experienced in first grade predicted four first-grade scales from the Teacher Behavior Checklist and both teacher ranking scales, five Teacher Behavior Checklist scales and both teacher rankings in the third grade (see Table 4.3). The correlation between maternal stressors and the Unpopular Scale in the first grade was moderate (r = .31) and by third grade was quite high (r = .45). Again, as with the boys, stressors experienced in the first grade did not predict first- or third-grade achievement for the girls.

TABLE 4.2
Significant Correlations Between Stress Experienced by Mothers
During 3 Time Periods (18–64 months, first grade, third grade)
and Their Sons' Performance in First and Third Grade

Outcomes	Grade	Early Stress (18–64 Mo.)		First-Grade Stress		Third-Grade Stress	
		Corr.	p	Corr.	p	Corr.	p
TBC*							
Unpopular	1			0.23	.014	N/A	
Unpopular	3			0.24	.013		
Self-Destructive	1	0.37	.002	0.29	.003	N/A	
Self-Destructive	3	0.21	.050	0.20	.032		
Obsessive/Compulsive	1					N/A	
Obsessive/Compulsive	3			0.18	.048		
Inattentive	1			0.19	.037	N/A	
Inattentive	3			0.23	.018		
Nervous Overactive	1					N/A	
Nervous Overactive	3						
Aggressive	1			0.22	.020	N/A	
Aggressive	3			0.30	.003		
Externalizing	1			0.22	.020	N/A	
Externalizing	3			0.30	.003		
Teacher Rankings							
Social Competence	1	−0.24	.038	−0.31	.003	N/A	
Social Competence	3						
Emotional Health	1	−0.27	.025	−0.30	.004	N/A	
Emotional Health	3					−0.20	.040

Note: N/A—third-grade stress was not correlated with first-grade outcomes.
*Achenbach & Edelbrock's Child Behavior Checklist–Teacher Form

Personal stress experienced by the mothers during their child's third-grade year related to few third-grade child outcomes. For both boys and girls, maternal stress in third grade only predicted one outcome variable, emotional health ranking (−.20) for boys and the Self Destructive Scale from the Teacher Behavior Checklist (r = .21) for girls.

Summary and Conclusions

The relation between personal stressful life events experienced by the mother and her child's adjustment and adaptation to school were moderate. The correlations were consistent with the findings from similar investigations (Sandler & Block, 1979). The data supported Compas' (1987) conclusion that the research findings

TABLE 4.3
Significant Correlations Between Stress Experienced by Mothers
During 3 Time Periods (18–64 months, first grade, third grade)
and Their Daughters' Performance in First and Third Grade

Outcomes	Grade	Early Stress (18–64 Mo.)		First-Grade Stress		Third-Grade Stress	
		Corr.	p	Corr.	p	Corr.	p
TBC*							
Depressed	1	0.42	.001			N/A	
Depressed	3						
Social Withdrawal	1					N/A	
Social Withdrawal	3			0.21	.034		
Unpopular	1	0.38	.002	0.31	.003	N/A	
Unpopular	3	0.28	.022	0.45	.001		
Nervous Overactive	1	0.23	.049			N/A	
Nervous Overactive	3					N/A	
Self-Destructive	1					N/A	
Self-Destructive	3					0.21	.030
Inattentive	1	0.28	.021	0.22	.029	N/A	
Inattentive	3			0.20	.043		
Aggressive	1	0.25	.039	0.23	.024	N/A	
Aggressive	3			0.20	.041		
Externalizing	1			0.25	.017	N/A	
Externalizing	3			0.23	.025		
Teacher Rankings							
Social Competence	1	−0.42	.001	−0.35	.001	N/A	
Social Competence	3			−0.35	.001		
Emotional Health	1	−0.31	.014	−0.28	.009	N/A	
Emotional Health	3			−0.29	.005		
PIAT Reading Recognition	1	−0.24	.046				
PIAT Reading Recognition	3						

Note: N/A—third-grade stress was not correlated with first-grade outcomes.
*Achenbach & Edelbrock's Child Behavior Checklist–Teacher Form

in this area provide weak evidence to support stressful events as an etiological factor in the development of disorder.

In this study, the relationship between personal stressors and child outcomes depended on the age at which stress was assessed, sex of the child, grade, and outcome measure. Contemporary stressors experienced by mother during the child's year in first grade predicted first- and third-grade outcomes, whereas personal stressors experienced in the third grade did not predict third-grade outcomes. Overall, child outcomes assessed in the first grade were easier to predict than outcomes assessed in the third grade. Early cumulative personal stressors predicted only first-grade outcomes.

There are a number of possible reasons for the differential prediction of first- and third-grade outcomes. First grade represents a crucial developmental task for the child in that it is the beginning of full-time school experience. (All of the children attended half-day kindergartens.) It may be that children are more sensitive to the effects of family stress during this difficult period. In addition, many of the children from this poverty sample have limited resources for coping and adapting to the demands of school. Mothers experiencing high levels of stress may be less available to provide emotional support and help for their children. For these children, the effects of family stressors, lack of family support and availability, and limited resources make it difficult for the child to adapt to the demands of school.

A child goes through many developmental phases that represent periods of increased vulnerability to the effects of stress. Leaving home for the first time, becoming involved in a structured academic setting, and responding to the limits and demands of an unfamiliar authority figure are experiences that may increase vulnerability. In addition, the mother–child relationship may be more vulnerable to the effects of stress in this period. Some mothers may not have had a positive experience when they were in school, which may make it difficult for them to provide adequate support for the child as he or she enters school. Others may view their child's entrance to school as a separation and react with feelings of melancholy and loss. As we will discuss in a subsequent section, many of these mothers report that they need and long for attention and affection. Providing their child with the necessary emotional support and care during the child's transition to school may be difficult for the mother who craves attention and affection. Increased amounts of stress during this period further exacerbates the problem.

Interestingly not only were first-grade outcomes predicted by first-grade contextual stress but so were third-grade outcomes. The same areas of social and emotional functioning that were affected by high first-grade stress continued to be affected in third grade. This appeared to represent a complex relationship in which development had been affected at a crucial point in time, and rather than the child rebounding after an adjustment period, he or she remains "off track" in subsequent years. For instance, the child who experienced high contextual stress and subsequently had difficulty with developing appropriate peer relationships continued to have difficulty with peer relationships. We do not assume that stress in first grade caused third-grade maladaptation but rather that first-grade adaptation was influenced by stress severely enough to alter future development.

Contextual stressors experienced by the child in third grade were not, however, related to third-grade outcomes. It appeared that maternal stressors have less of an impact on the child's school adjustment and adaptation, if they occurred in later years. Perhaps school provides the structure and activities through which the child can, with additional adult support and guidance, develop the self-control, self-esteem, humor, and problem-solving skills that have been shown to be related to coping abilities (Maccoby, 1983; Masten, 1982; Wallerstein, 1983). In school, the child also has the opportunity to succeed academically, socially, and/or athletically, and these opportunities may serve as a protective factor. Rutter (1985a) found that school success differentiated well-functioning and nonwell-functioning women who had been institutionalized as children. A good school experience may act as a buffer for family stress. Additionally maturation may mediate this process. Older children may be able to employ more sophisticated mediational skills due to cognitive maturity and thereby be better able to adapt to stress, especially if they themselves are not being stressed by development (Schultz & Heuchert, 1983).

Finally, regarding sex differences, the magnitude of the correlations between early stressful events experienced by mother and her child's school adjustment was about the same for boys and girls; however, different developmental outcomes were predicted. For girls, the highest correlations were with depression, unpopular, and social competence rankings. Poor peer competence and unpopularity at this age have been shown to place the child at risk for pathology and behavior problems at a later age (Cowen, Pederson, Babigan, Izzo, & Frost, 1973; Green, Forehand, Beck, & Vosk, 1980; Hartup, 1983).

For boys, the only consistent finding in first and third grade was early personal stress and the Self Destructive scale. This scale seems to indicate significant maladaptation and, like poor social competence, has been related to pathology at a later age (Pattison & Kahan, 1983). Thus, for boys and girls, personal stressors predict somewhat different social and emotional outcomes. However, the outcomes are similar in that they reflect severe maladaptation that is related to later psychopathology.

Protective Factors

In the previous section, we reported that there were relations between maternal stress prior, during, and after the child's first-grade year in school and the child's school adjustment and academic success. We found in earlier work that characteristics of the individuals, quality of relationship with parents, and characteristics of the home environment affect the relation between stress and school outcomes (Pianta et al., 1990). We have seen that children affected by stress during their first-grade year are still influenced two years later in third grade. However, it is clear that not all children were negatively affected in first grade nor continued to be in third grade. The question addressed in the second part of this chapter is whether the child's prior history of competence acts as a protective factor for the negative effects of stress. Specifically are children who have a history of competence during the infancy, toddler, and preschool periods less vulnerable to the effects of maternal stressors during the early school years?

History of Child Competence.   Determination of the history of early competency for each child was based on five assessments conducted at 12, 18, 24, and 42 months (two testing sessions at this age). Children were observed in tasks designed to assess competence and adaptation as defined by the salient developmental issues of that particular age.

At each of the five assessments, the children were placed in one of three groups, depending on their competence. A score of one, two, or three was assigned for each assessment: the least competent received a score of 1, average competent a score of 2, and most competent a score of 3. The scores were summed across the five assessments. Children who attended less than three assessments were not included in the analysis. For purposes of statistical analysis, the division of most competent and least competent classification was based on a median split of the average history of competence score of their same-sex constituents.

Assessment of competence at 12 and 18 months involved the determination of the quality of mother–infant attachment as assessed by means of the Strange Situation (Ainsworth, Blehar, Waters, & Wall, 1978). Infants were classified into three major groups (A, B, C), primarily based on their behavior during the reunion episodes following separation from the mother. Securely attached infants (Group B) greeted and interacted with their mothers positively, displaying few, if any, negative behaviors toward her. The infants demonstrating secure attachments received a most competent rating (3), whereas infants who exhibited substantially negative behaviors toward the mother and were classified as anxiously attached (Groups A and C) received a least competent rating (1). Although no child received an average competence rating (score = 2) for either the 12- or 18-month assessment, an average rating would be obtained over the two assessment periods by children who were secure at one assessment and insecure at another (score total = 3 + 1 = 4) as opposed to insecure–insecure (1 + 1 = 2) or secure–secure (3 + 3 = 6).

The assessment at 24 months involved a series of tool-using/problem-solving tasks of increasing difficulty. In each task, a small toy or candy was visible inside a clear plexiglass container but was accessible to the child only if he or she used the tool in a specific way to retrieve the prize. The first two problems were simple and not included in the scoring. The last two problems, however, were too difficult for two-year-olds to solve without assistance from their caregiver. Children were rated on the following variables that reflected developmentally salient issues for two-year-olds: dependency on mother, noncompliance with maternal directions and suggestions, anger and frustration, persistence, strategies for coping with challenges and frustration within the situation, and enthusiasm for the task.

A similar age-appropriate, mother–child interaction activity was designed at 42 months that involved a series of teaching tasks. The tasks were difficult enough to require that the mother use some teaching strategies to enable the child to complete the tasks. Children were rated on their persistence, enthusiasm, anger/negativity, compliance with mothers' directions, reliance on mothers for help, affection for mothers, avoidance of mothers, and general quality of their experience in the session.

The final assessment at 42 months, the Barrier Box task, was the only session in which mother–child interaction was not involved. The Barrier Box was designed to assess the child's reaction to frustration. The child was allowed to play with a variety of attractive toys for one minute prior to a project assistant removing the toys, telling the child they belonged in another room. In the center of the room was a large plexiglass box containing a set of toys identical to the ones that had been removed; however, the box was latched so that the child could not open it. A few unattractive toys were available on the floor. For ten minutes, the child was allowed to try to open the box, play with the few available toys, or wander around the room. The child was rated on the following variables: self-esteem, ego control, apathy/withdrawal, flexibility, creativity, agency, hyperactivity-distractibility, dependency on the project assistant, directness, intensity of help seeking, and positive and negative affect.

In order to determine the child's competency for the three assessments at 24 and 42 months, a hierarchical cluster analysis was conducted involving the child variables for each assessment. The cluster analyses were conducted for each assessment by sex (i.e., six separate analyses). For each assessment by sex, a three-, four-, or five-group cluster solution best fit the data. Determination as to the competency of each cluster group was made by relative comparisons of the profile of that group to the profiles of the remaining groups in that analysis. Assignments of most competent, average competent, and least competent were made for each group. Each child received a competency assignment based on the cluster solution in which s/he was located (cf. Pianta et al., 1990).

Procedure.   Using a double median split procedure, children were divided into high and low maternal stress groups and high and low history of competence groups. The maternal personal stress score was based on the assessment that occurred at the end of the child's first-grade year. Four groups were formed: high-stress/high-competence (N = 28), high-stress/low-competence (N = 41), low-stress/high-competence (N = 41), and low-stress/low-competence (N = 32). We were most interested in the role of history of competence in outcomes for the two high-stress groups. A series of ANOVAs were conducted comparing the mean scores on the teacher ratings, rankings, and achievement test scores. If history of competence is a protective factor, then the high stress/high competence group should show more positive outcomes in the first and third grades than the high-stress/low-competence group. This particular comparison involves groups 3 and 4 from Tables 4.4 and 4.5.

RESULTS: HISTORY OF COMPETENCE
AS A PROTECTIVE FACTOR

A history of early competence acted as a protective factor against the negative effects of maternal personal stress, especially for the boys. As can be seen from Table 4.4, there were a number of differences between the least and most competent groups who experienced high stress (Groups 3 vs 4). Compared to Group 3, boys in Group 4 scored lower on the Child Behavior Checklist–Teacher Report Form self-destructive, obsessive–compulsive, inattentive, and externalizing scales in the first grade and on teacher rankings of social competence/popularity. This indicated that, for those first-grade school outcomes, a history of competence during earlier developmental periods did serve as a protective factor against the effects of maternal personal stress. For boys in the third grade, the only variable for which past developmental history served as a protective factor was teacher ranking of social competence/popularity.

A number of the comparisons in the third grade involving history of least competence (groups 1 and 3) versus most competence (groups 2 and 4) were significant. It should also be noted that there are numerous differences between Groups 1 and 2 (see Table 4.4). Within the low-stress group, boys with a history of high competence were doing much better in the first and third grade on a number of scales from the Teacher Behavior Checklist, teacher ranking and total achievement score than boys with a history of least competence. Not surprisingly, the low-stress/history-of-competence group did the best of the four groups in both the first and third grades.

Although the high-stress/high-competence group was doing quite well in the first grade, they showed a substantial decline in functioning between first and third grades; on every scale, boys in this group showed a decline in functioning (see Table 4.4). Thus, history of competence acted as a protective factor in the first grade but not in the third grade. The high-stress/most-competent boys continued to do better than the high-stress/least-competent boys in the third grade, but the differences were no longer significant except for the social competence/popularity ranking in the third grade.

Surprisingly the findings for girls were quite different (see Table 4.5). History of competence during the infancy through preschool period did not serve as a protective factor for girls except on the unpopular scale and social competency/popularity rankings. These two variables are important, however, because social competence and relationship success are highly predictive of later developmental outcomes, including psychopathology (Hartup, 1983).

By accounting for the prior developmental history of the child, the stress outcome model was broadened. The results indicate that the child's prior history of competence, especially for boys, acts as a buffer or protective factor against the negative effects of maternal stress. If the child had successfully met challenges

TABLE 4.4

History of Competence as a Protective Factor: Differences on First- and Third-Grade Outcomes for Boys Whose Mothers Experienced High or Low Personal Stress (First-Grade Year)

School Outcomes	Grade	Low Stress (1st Grade)		High Stress (1st Grade)		p value	Significant Contrasts
		Group 1 Least Comp (N=28)	Group 2 Most Comp (N=20)	Group 3 Least Comp (N=16)	Group 4 Most Comp (N=16)		
TBC Unpopular	1	3.25 (3.53)	1.05 (1.76)	5.94 (5.22)	2.94 (3.45)	.00	1/2<3/4; 1/3>2/4; 1>2
	3	3.43 (3.51)	1.58 (1.77)	5.20 (3.99)	3.67 (4.51)	.03	1/2<3/4; 1>2
Self-Destructive	1	2.07 (2.49)	0.45 (1.39)	4.25 (4.06)	1.25 (1.69)	.00	1/2<3/4; 1/3>2/4; 3>4; 1>2
	3	2.29 (2.43)	0.32 (0.75)	2.53 (2.33)	2.13 (2.88)	.01	2<4; 1/3>2/4; 1>2
Obsessive/Compulsive	1	2.96 (3.43)	1.10 (1.71)	4.00 (3.48)	1.50 (1.83)	.01	1/3<2/4; 3>4; 1>2
	3	2.46 (2.92)	0.89 (1.33)	3.60 (3.20)	2.53 (2.92)	.04	1/2<3/4; 1/3>2/4; 1>2
Inattentive	1	14.89 (11.10)	7.65 (8.49)	19.25 (11.78)	10.75 (7.16)	.00	1/3>2/4; 3>4; 1>2
	3	14.39 (10.49)	10.00 (6.41)	18.07 (10.23)	15.27 (9.79)	.10	

Aggressive	1	16.04 (14.84)	6.45 (6.72)	22.88 (18.61)	13.75 (11.91)	.01	2<4; 1/2<3/4; 1/3>2/4; 1>2
	3	16.54 (14.79)	10.21 (11.09)	24.93 (19.70)	21.20 (20.75)	.06	
Externalize	1	30.29 (23.35)	13.75 (13.52)	41.25 (28.30)	23.25 (17.18)	.00	1/2<3/4; 1/3>2/4; 3>4; 1>2
	3	30.29 (22.30)	20.05 (15.28)	42.13 (25.87)	35.60 (28.33)	.04	2<4; 1/2<3/4
Teacher Rankings Emotional Health	1	42.75 (28.73)	53.89 (21.55)	24.38 (27.16)	41.07 (28.64)	.03	1<3; 1/2>3/4; 1/3<2/4
	3	35.21 (27.22)	49.37 (27.22)	24.47 (26.87)	38.33 (24.37)	.06	
Social Competence	1	47.44 (28.99)	54.26 (22.66)	24.92 (33.06)	35.20 (27.05)	.02	1>3; 2>4; 1/2>3/4
	3	39.50 (29.48)	53.58 (26.47)	18.40 (24.06)	45.07 (26.61)	.00	1>3; 1/2>3/4; 1/3<2/4; 3<4
Achievement PIAT TOTAL	1	95.57 (14.28)	102.95 (9.96)	98.53 (11.38)	105.19 (8.89)	.04	1/3<2/4; 1<2
	3	96.86 (15.85)	104.63 (9.89)	100.33 (11.57)	102.56 (9.85)	.27	

TABLE 4.5

History of Competence as a Protective Factor: Differences on First- and Third-Grade Outcomes for Girls Whose Mothers Experienced High or Low Personal Stress (First-Grade Year)

School Outcomes	Grade	Low Stress (1st Grade)		High Stress (1st Grade)		p value	Significant Contrasts
		Group 1 Least Comp (N=15)	Group 2 Most Comp (N=20)	Group 3 Least Comp (N=22)	Group 4 Most Comp (N=11)		
TBC Unpopular	1	1.00 (1.69)	0.70 (1.30)	1.27 (1.63)	1.45 (1.69)	.54	
	3	0.93 (1.39)	1.15 (1.09)	2.50 (2.82)	1.00 (1.41)	.04	1<3; 3>4
Teacher Rankings Social Competence	1	54.33 (29.10)	57.42 (24.96)	30.05 (21.88)	52.36 (27.22)	.00	1>3; 1/2>3/4; 1/3<2/4; 3<4
	3	53.53 (21.04)	59.10 (20.56)	38.45 (24.73)	47.45 (24.13)	.03	1>3; 1/2>3/4

on earlier developmental tasks, he or she was more likely to meet with success on a task despite high levels of maternal stress.

DISCUSSION

In the past 20 years, starting with Holmes and Rahe (1967), a number of life event scales/checklists have been constructed and used within prospective-risk research designs as well as concurrent or retrospective designs. Stressful events have been found to relate to a number of outcomes. Data from prospective designs have been used to make inferences regarding the causal nature of stressors and developmental outcomes. The field of developmental psychopathology has given considerable emphasis to the importance of the effects of stress on a child's development (Garmezy, 1981; Garmezy, Masten, & Tellegen, 1984).

Within our study, we found a relation between personal stress experienced by the mother and child outcomes; however, the magnitude of the correlations were relatively small, and the nature of relationship was complex. The few investigations, such as Beautrais, Fergusson, and Shannon (1982), which report higher correlations, have used parents to provide both the stressful life event data and child outcome data. In the present investigation, the child outcome data was based on teacher ratings and hopefully not biased by family circumstances and stress. Furthermore, we found little evidence to support the idea that stress experienced by the family causes child psychopathology and nonstress causes competence. Stress experienced by mother is one of many factors to consider in understanding the causes of developmental outcomes—it is not functionally responsible for psychopathology or competence.

In order to better understand the role of family stressors in early development, we need to move beyond a linear model and toward a strategy that takes into account patterns of caretaking, family functioning, and home environment. The relation between stressors and child outcomes is mediated through the care the mother provides the child and her emotional availability and responsiveness. A large number of interpersonal stressful events may tax the mother's emotional and psychological resources to the extent that she is less able to provide appropriate support for her child. This hypothesis has been suggested for divorce as a stressor (Hetherington, 1979) and has found support in the stressful life event literature. Zelkowitz, Saunders, Longfellow, and Belle (1979) reported that stressors resulted in less supportive behavior from mothers, which in turn led to poor adjustment in their children. Patterson (1983) noted that mothers under stress were more likely to use disapproval, negativism and yelling, and less likely to use talk, laughter and approval.

The relation between stress experienced by the family and child developmental outcomes is mediated by the parents, particularly as the stress may directly affect the parents' caregiving capabilities. How parents filter and give meaning to stressful life events depends on a number of factors, including the broader home environment, availability of support, family dynamics, as well as the parents' personal vulnerabilities, resources, and characteristics. For our sample, stressors must be viewed within the sociocultural context of poverty. Poverty is a major variable to consider in attempting to understand the mediational process.

Many of our mothers were psychologically vulnerable to the effects of stress, poverty, and other environmental risk factors. The experience of poverty results in a sense of powerlessness, helplessness, and lack of confidence in the ability to adequately manage one's life. We and others (Musick, Bernstein, Percansky, & Stott, 1987; Musick & Stott, 1990) found many poverty mothers, particularly the teen mothers, to be lonely, needy, and longing for attention and affection. The teen mothers particularly have not successfully negotiated the developmental issues around autonomy and individuation, separation, and loss. Left vulnerable by unresolved childhood issues, they are not prepared to negotiate the developmental tasks of adolescence and early adulthood. Instead of becoming more detached from their own mothers and individuating in a developmentally appropriate and competent fashion, many of these mothers remain dependent and hunger for attention and affection that they did not receive as a child. Without adequate physical resources and social support, these personal issues often do not get resolved, particularly if the psychologically vulnerable individual has to deal with the demands and conflicts involved in taking care of a young child.

A number of parents themselves have histories of insufficient nurturance, frequent separations, multiple caretakers, and multiple surrogate fathers (Musick & Halpern, 1989). Often there were many siblings sharing a mother's limited resources, which may result in premature demands for adult responsibility. Chronic exposure to violence and disorganization was common, and in our sample approximately 25% of all mothers report having been physically or sexually abused as children (Egeland, Jacobvitz, & Papatola, 1987). The effects of family stressors within the context of poverty is further exacerbated by the parents' lack of a healthy experience in the caregiving role.

Certainly not all parents living in poverty are psychologically vulnerable in the manner we have described. Over the past 13 years that we have followed this sample, we have been gratified by the number of mothers who are competent and successful in their work/school, relationships, and particularly in caring for their children. As with any sample, regardless of socioeconomic status, we see a range of psychological vulnerabilities and resources. Unfortunately too few have the support, physical and psychological resources, and level of maturity to cope with stress within the sociocultural context of poverty. For young, poor, single mothers to cope with life stresses, meet their own needs, and provide adequate child care requires a level of maturity found in too few of our mothers.

The past history, unmet needs, expectations, and feelings of inadequacy of the typical mother living in poverty are a few of the factors that influence the way they negotiate and filter stressful life events and the experience of poverty.

Their psychological resources and vulnerabilities determine the way they interpret and respond to poverty and stress. Elder (1974) and Werner and Smith (1982) noted that these environmental risk factors do not act directly to harm the child in any simple comprehensible way. These researchers and others note that parents filter these experiences, and it is the meaning that they give to these experiences that affects the quality of care provided for their children. How the parents transmit these experiences to the young child or protect the child has not received much attention from researchers.

In an earlier investigation, we attempted to account for good caretaking outcomes among a group of high-stressed mothers (Egeland et al., 1980). We compared a group of parents who experienced high family stress and provided inadequate care for their children with a similar group experiencing high stress who provided adequate care. There was no difference between the two groups on the type of life stress event experienced (e.g., financial, work related, sickness, interpersonal, etc.). High-stressed mothers who provided adequate care were found to be less aggressive, anxious, defensive and suspicious, more open and seeking of support, and had higher self-esteem scores as compared to those providing inadequate care. The mothers in the high stress/inadequate care group had anxiety levels beyond the 90th percentile, which, according to the test authors, is certain to have adverse effects on work and one's ability to carry out routine activities (Cattell & Scheier, 1976). The high anxiety level is likely due to the cumulative effect of stressful events as well as psychological dynamics having to do with her past developmental history.

We have discussed psychological vulnerabilities and resources of the parents as the primary mediator of stress, poverty, and environmental risk. Clearly conditions other than these influence mediational process. Werner and Smith (1982), Garmezy (1987), and Rutter (1985b) viewed attributes of the child as making a substantial contribution to resiliency in the face of adversity. Our data indicates that history of competence makes the child less vulnerable to dangers of adverse life circumstances. Despite highly stressful life events, children with a history of competence functioned well in the first grade, but unfortunately as these children progressed through school, their performance deteriorated. At the third-grade year, none of the children in our sample appear invulnerable to the effects of poverty, stress, and a host of other environmental risk factors.

Pianta et al. (1990) found that the structure, organization, and stimulation provided in the home environment was a major protective factor for boys. These protective factors were quite different from those reported for girls. It appeared that, for girls, personal characteristics of the mother translated into an attitude and set of expectations. Mothers who were able to communicate positive attitudes and expectations to their child protected their child from stress, whereas mothers who communication an attitude of pessimism, doom, and despair exacerbated the negative effects of stress. Sex differences in children are an important consideration in attempting to understand the mediators of stress.

CONCLUSION

Perhaps the only conclusion we can make from our data and the work of others is that the relation between stressors and child developmental outcomes is complex. We and others have oversimplified this complex relationship by examining the linear relation between stress and outcome, then searching for protective factors by examining exceptions to predicted outcomes. Although this approach has yielded many important and significant findings, it has also implied that stress is the major causal variable in psychopathology and developmental outcomes. The search for protective factors to account for exceptions to predicted outcomes implies that these variables are only important in their preventive role and that they are of lesser importance within the broader context of understanding development. Does a stressful life event score that consists of a summary description of highly complex environmental conditions deserve a central role as a major causal variable in the study of child outcomes, particularly child psychopathology? Our answer would be that stressors are important as long as they are considered within the complex interaction of the broader sociocultural context, quality of care the children receive, families' life circumstances, and children's past developmental history.

In looking at the effects of stress experienced by the family on child outcomes, we have emphasized the importance of the parents' psychological vulnerabilities and resources in mediating this relationship. The parents also play a role in mediating the effects of stressors that more directly affect the child (e.g., problems with peers, school, etc.). Research examining the effects of stress experienced directly by the child and child outcomes needs to consider the factors mediating this relationship, particularly the child's psychological vulnerabilities and resources. In Chandler's (1985) earlier studies of children under stress, he viewed the role of stressful life events as exacerbating existing anxieties in the individual. As we described earlier, this seemed to be the case with many of our mothers, who experienced a number of stressors. Most of the research on the effects of stressful life events on children leave out of the equation preexisting anxieties and other personal vulnerabilities. At best, child characteristics are considered as protective factors and stressors have achieved the status of dynamic entities in their own right. Behavioral and dynamic theories of development must be incorporated into any theory of stressful life events as a cause of child outcomes and psychopathology.

Sameroff and Seifer (1983) noted that the study of environmental risk factors has moved the field of child development from a primary interest in the process of development, such as basic work in the areas of language and perception, to a greater interest in the context of development. Obviously one cannot study child development without including contextual variables; however, in the area of stressful life events, the pendulum seems to have swung too far. We would argue for a return to the study of the individual and the process of development.

ACKNOWLEDGMENTS

This research was supported by a grant from the Maternal and Child Health Service of the Department of Health, Education and Welfare (MC–R–270416–01–0). This research is currently supported by a grant from the Office of Special Education, Department of Education (G008300029), and the William T. Grant Foundation, New York, NY.

REFERENCES

Achenbach, T. M., & Edelbrock, C. S. (1980). *The Child Behavior Checklist.* Burlington, VT: Department of Psychiatry, University of Vermont.

Ainsworth, M., Blehar, M., Waters, E., & Wall, S. (1978). *Patterns of attachment.* Hillsdale, NJ: Lawrence Erlbaum Associates.

Beautrais, A. L., Fergusson, D. B., & Shannon, F. T. (1982). Family life events and behavioral problems in preschool-aged children. *Pediatrics, 70* (5), 774–779.

Cattell, R. B., & Scheier, I. H. (1976). *Anxiety scale questionnaire.* Champaign, IL: Institute for Personality and Ability Testing.

Chandler, L. (1985). *Children under stress: Understanding emotional adjustment reactions* (2nd ed.). Springfield, IL: Thomas.

Cochrane, R., & Robertson, A. (1973). The life events inventory: A measure of the relative severity of psycho-social stressors. *Journal of Psychosomatic Research, 17,* 135–139.

Compas, B. E. (1987). Stress and life events during childhood and adolescence. *Child Psychology Review, 7,* 1–28.

Cowen, E. L., Pederson, A., Babigan, M., Izzo, L. D., & Frost, M. A. (1973). Long-term follow up of early detected vulnerable children. *Journal of Consulting and Clinical Psychology, 41,* 438–446.

Dunn, L. M., & Markwardt, F. C. (1970). *Peabody Individual Achievement Test.* Circle Pines, MN: American Guidance Service.

Egeland, B., Breitenbucher, M., & Rosenberg, D. (1980). Prospective study of the etiology of child abuse. *Journal of Consulting and Clinical Psychology, 48,* 195–205.

Egeland, B., Jacobvitz, D., & Papatola, K. (1987). Intergenerational continuity of abuse. In R. Gelles & J. Lancaster (Eds.), *Child abuse and neglect: Biosocial dimensions.* pp. 255–276. New York: Aldine de Gruyter.

Elder, G. (1974). *Children of the great depression.* Chicago: University of Chicago Press.

Elizure, J. (1986). The stress of school entry: Parental coping behaviors and children's adjustment to school. *Journal of Child Psychology and Psychiatry, 27,* 625–638.

Garmezy, N. (1981). Children under stress: Perspectives on antecedents and correlates of vulnerability and resistance to psychopathology. In A. I. Rabin, J. Aronoff, A. M. Barclay, & R. A. Zucker (Eds.), *Further explorations in personality* (pp. 196–269). New York: Wiley Interscience.

Garmezy, N. (1987, April). Stress, competence, and development: Continuities in the study of schizophrenic adults, children vulnerable to psychopathology, and the search for stress-resistant children. *American Journal of Orthopsychiatry, 57* (2), 159–174.

Garmezy, N., Masten, A., & Tellegen, A. (1984). The study of stress and competing in children: A building block for developmental psychopathology. *Child Development, 55* (1), 97–111.

Garmezy, N., & Tellegen, A. (1983). Studies of stress-resistant children: Methods, variables, and preliminary findings. *Applied Developmental Psychology, 1,* 231–287.

Green, K. D., Forehand, R., Beck, J., & Vosk, B. (1980). An assessment of the relationship among measures of children's social competence and children's academic achievement. *Child Development, 51,* 1149–1159.

Hartup, W. W. (1983). Peer relations. In E. M. Hetherington (Ed.), P. H. Mussen (Series Ed.), *Handbook of child psychology: Socialization, personality and social development* (vol. 4, pp. 103–196). New York: Wiley.

Hetherington, E. M. (1979). Divorce: A child's perspective. *American Psychologist, 34,* 851–858.

Holmes, T. H., & Rahe, R. H. (1967). The social readjustment rating scale. *Journal of Psychosomatic Research, 11,* 213–218.

Hughes, M., Pinkerton, G., & Plewis, I. (1979). Children's difficulties on starting infant school. *Journal of Child Psychology and Psychiatry, 20,* 187–196.

Maccoby, E. E. (1983). Social-emotional development and response to stressors. In N. Garmezy & M. Rutter (Eds.), *Stress, coping, and development in children* (pp. 217–234). McGraw-Hill.

Madge, N. (1983). Unemployment and its effect on children. *Journal of Child Psychology and Psychiatry, 24,* 311–319.

Masten, A. (1982). *Humor and creative thinking in stress-resistant children.* Unpublished doctoral dissertation, University of Minnesota.

Masten, A., Garmezy, N., Tellegen, A., Pellegrini, D., Larkin, K., & Larsen, A. (1988). Competence and stress in school children: The moderating effects of individual and family qualities. *Journal of Child Psychology and Psychiatry, 29,* 745–764.

Musick, J. S., Bernstein, V., Percansky, C., & Stott, F. (1987). A chain of enablement: Using community-based programs to strengthen relationships between teen parents and their infants. Using community-based programs to strengthen relationships between teen parents and their infants. *Zero to Three, 8* (2), 1–6.

Musick, J. S., & Halpern, R. (1989). Giving children a chance: What role community-based early parenting interventions? In S. Meisels & J. Shonkoff (Eds.), *Handbook of early intervention* (pp. 177–194). Cambridge, England: Cambridge University Press.

Musick, J. S., & Stott, F. M. (1990). Paraprofessionals, parenting and child development: Understanding the problems and seeking solutions. In S. Meisels & J. Shonkoff (Eds.), *Handbook of early intervention* (pp. 651–667). Cambridge, England: Cambridge University Press.

Patterson, G. (1983). *Coercive family process.* Eugene, OR: Catalena.

Pianta, R. C. (1986). *The longitudinal effects of maternal life stress on the developmental outcomes of first grade children in a high risk sample.* Unpublished doctoral dissertation, University of Minnesota.

Pianta, R. C., Egeland, B., & Sroufe, L. A. (1990). Maternal stress and children's development: Prediction of school outcomes and identification of protective factors. In J. Rolf, A. Masten, D. Cicchetti, K. Nuechterlein, & S. Weintraub (Eds.), *Risk and protective factors in the development of psychopathology* (pp. 215–235). New York: Cambridge University Press.

Rutter, M. (1979). Protective factors in children's responses to stress and disadvantage. In M. W. Kent & J. E. Rolf (Eds.), *Primary prevention of psychopathology: Social competence in children* (vol. 3, pp. 49–74). Hanover, NH: University Press of New England.

Rutter, M. (1983). Stress, coping and development: Some issues and some questions. In N. Garmezy & M. Rutter (Eds.), *Stress, coping, and development in children* (pp. 1–41). New York: McGraw-Hill.

Rutter, M. (1985a). Family and school influences: Meanings, mechanisms and implications. In A. R. Nicol (Ed.), *Longitudinal studies in child psychology and psychiatry: Practical lessons from research experience* (pp. 357–403). Chicester, England: Wiley.

Rutter, M. (1985b). Resilience in the face of adversity: Protective factors and resistance to psychiatric disorder. *British Journal of Psychiatry, 147,* 598–611.

Sameroff, A. J., & Seifer, R. (1983). Familial risk and child competence. *Child Development, 54,* 1254–1268.

Sandler, I., & Block, M. (1979). Life stress and maladaptation of children. *American Journal of Community Psychology, 7* (4), 425–440.

Schultz, E. W., & Heuchert, C. M. (1983). *Child stress and the school experience*. New York: Human Science Press.

Sroufe, L. A. (1979). Socioemotional development. In J. Osofsky (Ed.), *Handbook of infant development* (pp. 462–516). New York: Wiley.

Wallerstein, J. S. (1983). Children of divorce: Stress and development. In N. Garmezy & M. Rutter (Eds.), *Stress, coping and development in children* (pp. 265–302). New York: McGraw-Hill.

Wallerstein, J. S., & Kelly, J. B. (1980). *Surviving the breakup: How children and parents cope with divorce*. New York: Basic.

Werner, E. E., & Smith, R. S. (1982). *Vulnerable but invincible: A study of resilient children*. San Francisco: McGraw-Hill.

Zelkowitz, P., Saunders, E., Longfellow, C., & Belle, D. (1979, March). *The impact of stress on the mother–child relationship*. Paper presented at the biennial meeting of the Society for Research in Child Development, San Francisco, CA.

Normative Stress and Coping Processes in Infancy

Katherine Hildebrandt Karraker
Margaret A. Lake
West Virginia University

A truly life-span perspective on stress and coping requires an understanding of the processes of stress and coping at all ages as well as an understanding of changes in these processes with age. A large literature exists on stress and coping in adulthood (e.g., Goldberger & Breznitz, 1982; Hamilton & Warburton, 1979; Kutash & Schlesinger, 1980; Lazarus & Folkman, 1984), and a small but rapidly growing literature exists on stress and coping in childhood (e.g., Compas, 1987; Field, McCabe, & Schneiderman, 1988; Garmezy & Rutter, 1983; Murphy & Moriarty, 1976). However, very little has been written that deals directly with stress and coping during infancy. For example, the recently published second edition of the *Handbook of Infant Development* (Osofsky, 1987) contains only three listings for stress and no listings for coping in the index. Only a few chapters and articles have been published elsewhere on general aspects of stress and coping in infancy (e.g., Kagan, 1983; Lerner & East, 1984; Lipsitt, 1983) or on specific stressors and coping responses in infancy (e.g., Field, 1985; Gianino & Tronick, 1988; Gunnar, Malone, & Fisch, 1985; Schanberg & Field, 1988).

This seeming neglect of the concepts of stress and coping in the infancy literature may be more a matter of semantics than reality. Although the terms "stress" and "coping" are infrequently used in discussions of infant behavior, much research on infant behavior can be interpreted as evidence for stress or coping. The primary purpose of this chapter is to apply what is known about stress and coping processes in adults and children to what is already known about infant development. Basic social psychological principles concerning stress and coping (primarily as represented by Lazarus & Folkman, 1984) will serve as a framework for reinterpreting aspects of our knowledge about infant development.

The present chapter will focus on normative stressors and coping strategies.

These are events and behaviors that typical infants in typical environments may encounter or display. A major portion of the chapter is devoted to development of a taxonomy of stressors and coping responses that are common in infancy. The chapter also evaluates evidence for cognitive appraisal processes during infancy, discusses individual differences in infant stress and coping processes, and considers developmental changes in these processes that occur during infancy and later.

STRESS IN INFANCY

Definitions

Lazarus and Folkman (1984) defined psychological stress as "a particular relationship between the person and the environment that is appraised by the person as taxing or exceeding his or her resources and endangering his or her well-being" (p. 19). Given that we cannot ask infants about their appraisal of a particular environmental event, how do we know if the event is stressful? The most intuitively appealing answer to this question is that an infant who displays signs of distress is experiencing stress. Signs of distress may include negative emotional expressions, disruptions of sleeping or eating, behavioral inhibition, avoidance or withdrawal, illness, or certain physiological responses (Gianino & Tronick, 1988; Gunnar, 1987; Lipsitt, 1983). The most basic emotional expressions that convey that the infant is experiencing stress are vocal distress such as crying and fussing. Various facial expressions, such as anger, sadness, and fear also can indicate stress (Campos, Barrett, Lamb, Goldsmith, & Stenberg, 1983). For the purposes of this chapter, a stimulus will be assumed to be a common stressor, if it frequently produces any of these signs of distress in infants.

Several issues must be considered when using this approach to identifying stressors. For example, some behaviors identified as stress indicators can also serve as coping behaviors (Compas, 1987). Effective coping may eliminate the signs of stress, making it difficult to determine if an event was initially stressful. Infants who do not show distress may either appraise an event as nonstressful or may be coping quickly and successfully with the stress.

Another issue in using this approach relates to the high frequency at which infants (especially young infants) display distress. Many of the events that elicit frequent distress in infants are expectable and even necessary, and could probably be labeled "daily hassles" (Lazarus & Folkman, 1984) rather than stressors. No such distinction is made here but may prove fruitful in future consideration of infant stressors.

Using signs of distress to identify stressors also focuses almost exclusively on infants' typical responses to an event. Although a particular occurrence may lead to stress reactions in the majority of infants, variations among infants in both the appraisal process and the intensity or type of reaction to appraised stress will result in variations in infants' responses to the same presumed stressor. Such individual differences in reactions to some of the common stressors detailed below will be highlighted, and the general issue of individual differences in stress and coping processes will be discussed later in the chapter.

Finally, the possible imposition of cultural values and an adult perspective in determining what is stressful for an infant must be recognized. Adults may base their judgment of the stressfulness of an event more on the nature of the event than on the degree of distress shown by an infant experiencing the event. For example, most parents are more concerned with the stress produced by leaving an infant at a day care center than with the stress produced by leaving an infant with a familiar relative or alone in his or her bedroom at night. Researchers have similarly focused more on mother–infant separations resulting from employment than on other separations (Suwalsky, Klein, Zaslow, Rabinovich, & Gist, 1987). The taxonomy of stressors provided here likely reflects some of these biases, as emphasis is placed on potential stressors that have received attention in the research literature.

Taxonomy of Common Stressors

Common stressors in infancy are first divided into the categories of physiological and psychological stressors. Although the emphasis in this chapter is on psychological stressors, physiological stressors are mentioned briefly, because they occur commonly during infancy, and individual differences in the appraisal of their stressfulness are evident. Psychological stressors are then divided into the categories of interpersonal stressors (stress related to the behavior of another person) and environmental stressors (stress related to changes in the social, temporal, or physical environment). Further subcategories of stressors included in this taxonomy are listed in Table 5.1. Common characteristics of many infant stressors are detailed in a final section.

Physiological Stressors

A variety of physical events or stimuli produce bodily harm or discomfort, leading to the expression of distress by infants. Mild distress is produced by physical discomforts such as hunger, wet diapers, and cold temperatures. More extreme distress is produced by painful stimulation, such as inoculations, falls, and circumcision (Gunnar, Malone, & Fisch, 1985; Izard, Hembree, & Heubner, 1987). Multiple other physical stimuli cause distress reactions: loud noises, falling, respiratory occlusion, bright lights, and unpleasant smells and tastes (Lipsitt, 1983).

Individual differences in infants' responses to these physiological stressors are evident in parents' ratings of their infants on temperament questionnaires (e.g., Carey & McDevitt, 1978). Some infants react quickly and intensely to physiologi-

TABLE 5.1
Taxonomy of Common Stressors and Coping Responses in Infancy

Stressors
Physiological stressors
Psychological stressors
Interpersonal stressors
Separations from attachment figures
Exposure to unfamiliar persons
Distressing interactions
Environmental stressors

Coping responses
Physiological coping
Psychological coping
Emotion-focused coping
Independent coping
Aided coping
Problem-focused coping
Independent coping
Aided coping
Anticipatory coping

cal stressors, whereas others react more slowly and dispassionately. Parents also report by anecdote that infants' responses to these stressors vary according to the social context. For example, toddlers often are described as more likely to cry following a fall in the presence of adults than when the toddlers are alone. These variations in infant reactions represent differences in infants' appraisals of the stressfulness of physiological stressors.

Psychological Stressors

Interpersonal Stressors

Interpersonal stressors include interactions with other people that infants appraise as distressing. The major categories of interpersonal stressors are separations from attachment figures, exposure to unfamiliar persons, and distressing interactions. Developmental changes in and contextual influences on infants' appraisals of these events are particularly evident; some events produce little or no stress, and perhaps even pleasure at some times, whereas the same events can produce mild to extreme distress reactions at other times (Campos et al., 1983).

Separations from attachment figures. Young infants often react negatively to the termination of an ongoing pleasant social interaction, regardless of whom the interaction is with (Fogel, 1980). Starting around 7–8 months, however, infants react most negatively to separation from an attachment figure (Ainsworth, Blehar, Waters, & Wall, 1978). Brief separations from the mother (the usual primary attachment figure) are common during infancy (Suwalsky et al., 1987), and some infants also experience longer separations due to infant hospitalization, maternal hospitalization for the birth of another child, or maternal vacations (Field, 1985; Rutter, 1983; Suwalsky et al., 1987). Although separation from attachment figures appears to be the most stressful separation for infants, even separation from familiar peers (such as when changing classes or schools) can produce stress in infants and young children (Field, Vega-Lahr, & Jagadish, 1984).

Characteristics of the separation influence the degree of distress shown by an infant, indicating the operation of cognitive appraisal. For example, briefer preparations for separation produce less stress (Adams & Passman, 1981). Stress also is lessened when separations take place in a familiar environment (Rinkoff & Corter, 1980) and when infants can either see their mother (Corter, 1976) or have access to their mother through an open door (Rinkoff & Corter, 1980).

Individual differences in infants' responses to brief separations from their mothers have been studied most systematically in the context of the Strange Situation paradigm (Ainsworth et al., 1978). This procedure entails observation of infants' reactions to a series of events that are intended to be mildly stressful, including two brief separations from and reunions with their mothers. Individual differences are evident in infants' behavior during these separations and reunions, and three major categories of responses, which are thought to relate to the quality of the attachment relationship, have been identified. Compas (1987) further proposed that these differences in infant behavior during separation and reunion indicate variations in infants' appraisals of the stress of separation and their ability to cope with that stress. Compas suggested that securely attached infants, who typically show moderate distress at separation plus greeting behavior and rapid calming at mother's return, experience the separation as mildly stressful. Ambivalent or resistant infants, who protest intensely at separation and who continue to show distress and combined approach and resistance when the mother returns, are seen as experiencing high levels of stress. Avoidant infants, who show little distress at separation and ignore or avoid the mother when she returns, are thought to assess the separation as nonstressful.

An alternative interpretation of the stress appraisal of avoidant infants is provided by Main and Weston (1982). They suggested that avoidant infants are highly stressed by separation from their mothers. Evidence showing accelerated heart rates of avoidant infants during separations and reunions (Sroufe & Waters, 1977) also supports this interpretation. Main and Weston (1982) further proposed that avoidant infants have learned to cope with their stress through avoidance of the mother and overcontrol of their emotions. This coping response results from the mother's rejecting behavior toward the infant, which derives from her aversion to physical contact with the infant and restricted emotional expression.

The controversy concerning the meaning of avoidant behavior in the Strange

Situation illustrates some of the problems in determining the stress experienced by nonverbal infants. This particular controversy has significant contemporary relevance because of recent reports that infants exposed to early day care are more likely than home-reared infants to demonstrate avoidant behavior in the Strange Situation (Belsky, 1984). These reports have created concern because of evidence that avoidant (as well as resistant) home-reared infants manifest less optimal developmental outcomes than do more securely attached infants (see review by Campos et al., 1983). However, researchers do not agree about the meaning of avoidance in the Strange Situation by day care infants. Some researchers suggest that avoidance by day care infants indicates high stress produced by maternal separation; other researchers suggest that day care infants experience little stress and show greater maturity and more effective coping with separation than do home-reared infants (Belsky, 1984; Clarke-Stewart, 1989).

Exposure to unfamiliar persons.   Another category of interpersonal stress involves encounters with unfamiliar people. Again, age is relevant; infants do not typically show distress to strangers prior to about eight months (Sroufe, 1977). Even after that age, distress is not an inevitable reaction. Many infants will react positively to strangers under certain conditions (Bretherton, 1978), although all infants react negatively at some point (Gaensbauer, Emde, & Campos, 1976).

Infants appear to evaluate the potential danger of a particular confrontation with a stranger based on such variables as the physical characteristics and behavior of the stranger, the environmental circumstances, and their own state (Clarke-Stewart, 1978; Feinman, 1980; Skarin, 1977; Trause, 1977). These findings suggest that infants appraise the stressfulness of an encounter with a stranger in relation to their assessment of the likelihood of harm from the stranger.

Distressing interactions.   A final category of interpersonal stress includes social interactions that produce stress. Gianino and Tronick (1988) discussed both minor and major interactive stresses that can impinge upon the young infant during face-to-face interaction. During a normal interaction, the infant experiences mild stress whenever the behavior of the infant and adult are mismatched. This stress is quickly dissipated through the infant's effective use of coping behaviors, such as signaling, self-comforting, or withdrawal. More intense stress is produced by "prolonged, exaggerated, and/or aberrant forms of interactive stress" (Gianino & Tronick, 1988, p. 51). The most frequently studied intense interactional stressors are adult still-face behavior (when an interacting adult suddenly terminates all behavior) and either simulated or real adult depressive behavior.

The infant's typical response to adult still-face behavior is to first attempt to re-engage the adult in interaction and then to show avoidance, distraction, and elevated heart rate (Field, 1981; Tronick, Als, & Adamson, 1979; Trevarthen, 1977). When the adult resumes normal interaction, infant agitated motor activity, distress brow, and crying remain elevated (Field, Vega-Lahr, Scafidi, &

Goldstein, 1986). Still-face leads to greater distress for the infant than brief separation (Field et al., 1986) and interruptions of mother–infant interaction by a third person (Trevarthen, 1977).

Depressed maternal behavior during face-to-face interaction also produces signs of interactive stress in infants. Cohn and Tronick (1983) reported that 3-month-old infants showed heightened levels of protest and wary behavior when their normal mothers simulated depressed affect. Infants interacting with clinically depressed mothers showed even greater distress and disengagement (Gianino & Tronick, 1988). Other characteristics of adult face-to-face interaction that infants appear to find stressful are noncontingent adult behavior, overstimulating adult behavior, lack of rhythm modulation by an adult, and limited adult response repertoires (Field, 1978, 1987).

Older infants and toddlers are stressed by interactions that interfere with their ongoing behaviors or desires. For example, Stenberg, Campos, and Emde (1983) observed increasing anger and distress in 7-month-old infants when a teething biscuit was repeatedly taken away from them. Toddlers sometimes show direct defiance accompanied by negative affect when their mothers attempt to control their behaviors (Kuczynski, Kochanska, Radke-Yarrow, & Girnius-Brown, 1987). Toddlers also are sometimes stressed by parent limit setting and restrictions (Lester, 1985; Wenar, 1982). Interactions with siblings and peers also can create stress through altercations and disagreements (Abramovitch, Corter, & Pepler, 1980; Brownlee & Bakeman, 1981; Hay & Ross, 1982; Kavenaugh & McCall, 1983).

Environmental Stressors

Changes in an infant's physical, temporal, or social environment often produce temporary distress. Simply moving an infant from an accustomed to a novel environment can result in sleep disturbances and fussiness (Field et al., 1984). Similarly, changes in routines or changes in the family configuration (caused by such events as the birth of a sibling or a divorce) can disrupt infants (Kagan, 1983; Kendrick & Dunn, 1980; Rutter, 1983). Environmental instability can be stressful (Vaughn, Egeland, Sroufe, & Waters, 1979), as can encounters with unfamiliar or frightening environmental events, such as an alarming toy (Gunnar, Leighton, & Peleaux, 1984; Gunnar-von Gnechten, 1978). Noncontingent events can produce stress, especially when they follow or are mixed with contingent experiences (Fagen & Ohr, 1985; Lewis, Sullivan, & Brooks-Gunn, 1985; Watson, 1972). Physical obstructions to goals also frequently produce stress reactions (Van Lieshout, 1976).

Infants' social environments can indirectly cause stress as well. Infants may suffer stress reactions when other members of the family are undergoing stress. Interpersonal anger, lack of social support, and life event stresses that do not directly impact the infant can all be stressful for an infant (Crnic, Greenberg,

Robinson, & Ragozin, 1984; Cummings, Zahn-Waxler, & Radke-Yarrow, 1981; Thompson, Lamb, & Estes, 1982). Finally, specific environments such as hospitals (Gottfried & Gaiter, 1985; Leiderman, 1983; Rutter, 1983) and poor quality day care (Belsky, 1984) may directly or indirectly stress infants.

Common Characteristics of Stressful Events

Events that induce stress in infants often appear innocuous to adults. Some common cognitive features of these events, rather than the objective content of the events, help to explain why infants appraise these events as stressful. These features include unassimilable discrepancy (when a stimulus is so different from what is already known that it cannot be understood), unpredictability of events, violation of expectancies, loss or lack of control, and uncertainty (Field et al., 1986; Gunnar, 1980; Kagan, 1983). Events characterized by these features tend to be stressful for infants as well as for older individuals (although see the discussion by Folkman, 1984, of the complex relationship between personal control and stress in adults). However, different events will be appraised as possessing these features at different ages. Lipsitt (1983) suggested that such cognitively induced stressors are more likely in older than younger infants, because older infants have a greater base of experience and knowledge with which to compare events. The importance of these cognitive features in determining stress appraisals prevents the development of a comprehensive list of specific stress-inducing events in infancy and provides support for the operation of cognitive appraisal processes (Lazarus & Folkman, 1984) in infants' reactions to stress.

COPING IN INFANCY

Definitions

Lazarus and Folkman (1984) defined coping as "constantly changing cognitive and behavioral efforts to manage specific external and/or internal demands that are appraised as taxing or exceeding the resources of the person" (p. 141). This definition considers coping to be an effortful process designed to reduce stress rather than a specific outcome whereby stress necessarily is reduced. The coping process may include both cognitions and behaviors, and the process is likely to change continually as the appraised demands or stressfulness of a specific situation change.

One consideration in identifying coping processes in infants is determining if behaviors are truly effortful attempts to reduce stress. Conclusions about the effortful nature of infant behaviors may be biased by both our adult perspective and our observations of outcome (i.e., reductions in infant distress). A converse tendency is to assume that every response in a stressful or even nonstressful situation is a coping response (e.g., Zeitlin, Williamson, & Szczepanski, 1984).

Behaviors selected for discussion in the following taxonomy are likely to occur in response to the types of stressors previously identified and appear to have the goal of stress management.

Lazarus and Folkman's (1984) description of the coping process emphasizes individual differences that result from variations in cognitive appraisal processes, availability of coping resources, and coping styles. Individual differences in infant coping are discussed in detail in a later section. The coping behaviors listed here are generally available to normal infants but may be utilized differently and in different combinations in stressful situations by individual infants.

Taxonomy of Coping Responses

Although physiological reactions to stressors do not fit Lazarus and Folkman's (1984) definition of coping, they are briefly mentioned here because they are often used by researchers as indicators of infant coping. The major categories of psychological coping are based on Lazarus and Folkman's (1984) identification of the two primary functions of coping. Emotion-focused coping responses are designed to reduce the emotional response to a stressor, whereas problem-focused coping responses are designed to deal directly with the problem or event that is causing the stress. Each of these forms of coping is further divided here into independent coping (i.e., coping that the infant can accomplish alone) and aided coping (i.e., coping that requires assistance from another person). A final form of psychological coping, anticipatory coping, is also briefly described. Table 5.1 presents the categories of coping included in this taxonomy.

Physiological Coping

Physiological changes that occur simultaneously with or immediately following a stressful experience are often seen as attempts by the body to cope with the stressor. Most studied in infancy are hormonal changes and changes in sleep patterns that follow stressful (particularly physically stressful) events (e.g., Field, 1985; Gunnar, Malone, & Fisch, 1985). For example, Gunnar, Malone, Vance, and Fisch (1985) observed healthy male newborns' recovery from circumcision. The infants showed heightened adrenocortisol levels immediately following the procedure, but levels rapidly returned to baseline. The infants also exhibited increased amounts of quiet sleep following the procedure. Gunnar, Malone, Vance, and Fisch (1985) interpreted these physiological responses as effective mechanisms for coping with the stress of circumcision.

Psychological Coping

Emotion-Focused Coping

Independent coping. Infants can independently modulate their negative emotional responses to a stressful event through self-soothing techniques or through avoidance of or withdrawal from the stressful situation. Even neonates have some capacity for self-soothing, typically through sucking on their hands or fingers

(Brazelton, 1984). Young infants exposed to stressful social interactions will attempt to comfort themselves through sucking on parts of their bodies, sucking on an available object, clasping their hands together, or rocking (Gianino & Tronick, 1988). Some older infants can pacify themselves through thumb sucking or physical contact with an attachment object such as a blanket or soft toy (Passman, 1976, 1977; Passman & Weisberg, 1975).

Infants also may control their emotional responses to stressful situations by avoidance or withdrawal. For example, young infants may direct their attention away from their mothers during stressful face-to-face interaction (Gianino & Tronick, 1988), and older infants may focus on toys during separations from their mothers or avoid looking at a frightening stranger. Prolonged stresses may lead to more complete infant withdrawal (Field, 1985; Gianino & Tronick, 1988).

Aided coping. Emotion-focused coping in infancy is often accomplished through the assistance of an adult. Crying and other negative emotional signals are typically very effective means of soliciting soothing interventions from a responsive adult (Lester & Boukydis, 1985; Lipsitt, 1983). Communicative gestures, such as raising the arms to request being picked up and verbal requests for comfort also can be effective means of obtaining assistance with emotion-focused coping.

Infants who have established an attachment relationship can use the constellation of behaviors that serve the attachment behavioral system (described by Ainsworth et al., 1978) to seek or obtain proximity to their attachment figure. This proximity facilitates "felt security" in the infant, thereby reducing the distress of stressful situations. A variety of behaviors can serve the attachment behavioral system; some examples include both negative and positive signaling, searching, following, and clinging. These behaviors can be seen as emotion-focused coping behaviors because their goal is proximity to the attachment figure and the concomitant felt security that accompanies this proximity.

Problem-Focused Coping

Independent coping. Infants can at times directly cope with a stressor by avoiding or removing the source of stress. The young infant is generally limited to avoidance of the stressor and can be seen to do so in response to distressing social interactions (Gianino & Tronick, 1988). The older infant has motor skills available and can, therefore, leave a stressful situation—as in moving away from a frightening stranger, a hitting peer, or an alarming toy—or physically master the stressor—as in removing a barrier (Garrity & Weisman, 1982), pushing a peer away, or turning off a noisy toy. Older infants may also be able to terminate some stressors (such as parental commands or punishments) through inhibiting their own behavior (Kopp, 1982). Cognitive skills, such as assimilation, recognition, and memory, also may aid an infant in coping directly with a stressful situation through problem solving (Kagan, 1983) and reappraisal.

Aided coping.   Infants can also cope with a stressor by seeking help from another person. Infant communicative signals in the presence of a stressor often serve to solicit assistance from an adult in coping directly with the stressor. Caregiving adults quickly learn that removing an identifiable stressor (e.g., wet diapers, hunger, a sibling wearing a Halloween mask) is often more effective at calming a distressed infant than providing soothing (Lester, 1985). Infants learn that particular communicative actions may signal an adult to help eliminate a stressor. Some examples observed in the Strange Situation include infants pointing at the door or pulling the stranger over to the door in an attempt to get the stranger to open the door for them, and infants waving bye-bye or saying "home" after the mother's return in an attempt to convince their mother to remove them from the Strange Situation environment.

Anticipatory Coping

Infants, like older individuals (Lazarus & Folkman, 1984), learn that certain events indicate the subsequent onset of a stressful event. This knowledge allows an infant to cope with the event either by trying to avoid the emotional stress of the event or by trying to prevent the event itself. An example is infants' recognition that the arrival of a babysitter and parental donning of coats signals imminent separation from the parents. Infants may show anticipatory coping by either attempting to prevent their own distress (by going and getting their security blanket or ignoring their parents, for example) or by attempting to prevent the onset of the departure (by crying loudly and plaintively, clinging to the parents, trying to get the parents to play a game with them, or blocking the door, for example). Anticipatory coping reveals the importance of cognitive mechanisms (including memory and appraisal) to the understanding of infants' coping efforts.

THE ROLE OF COGNITIVE APPRAISAL

Lazarus and Folkman (1984) emphasized the importance of cognitive appraisal in understanding stress and coping processes. They proposed that the stressfulness of an event is determined by individuals' evaluations of the significance of that event for their own well-being and that these evaluations influence the nature of the individuals' coping responses. Recognition of cognitive appraisal processes is necessary to understand individual differences in reactions to similar potentially stressful events. Infants also differ in their stress and coping responses to similar events; therefore, consideration of evidence for infant cognitive appraisal processes is warranted.

Three steps are involved in the appraisal process, according to Lazarus and Folkman (1984). Primary appraisal involves evaluation of the significance of an event for the individual's well-being. Although other evaluations are possible, our concern is with appraisals of stressfulness. Secondary appraisal involves evaluation of an individual's resources and options for coping with an appraised stressor. Finally, reappraisal involves changing an initial appraisal of the stressfulness of a situation based on new information. Direct and indirect evidence suggests that infants engage in rudimentary forms of these processes.

Primary Appraisal and Reappraisal

The lack of uniformity in individual infants' responses to potentially stressful events implies that infants engage in primary appraisal. A good example of this process is seen in infants' responses to strangers. Negative responses are more or less pronounced depending on characteristics of the stranger such as height, gender, and behavior (Clarke-Stewart, 1978). Apparently infants judge the potential danger of a stranger based on these (and other) aspects of the situation. Reappraisal is evident in infants' changing reactions to strangers as a function of familiarity and stranger friendliness (Ross, 1975; Trause, 1977).

Studies of social referencing also indicate that infants can seek information in order to appraise the stressfulness of an event (primary appraisal) and that they may change their appraisal (reappraisal) as a function of new or additional information (Campos & Stenberg, 1981; Feinman, 1982; Klinnert, Campos, Sorce, Emde, & Svejda, 1983). These studies demonstrate that infants older than about 9 months will look to an adult for information when exposed to an ambiguous but potentially frightening stimulus. The mere act of looking for information implies that the process of appraisal is occurring. Infants frequently respond differentially based on the information provided by the adult they socially reference, implying that this information is successfully used for appraisal or reappraisal of the stressfulness of the event.

Secondary Appraisal

Piagetian theory (Ginsburg & Opper, 1978) suggests that infants' abilities to cognitively assess available means of coping with a stressful event are quite limited until the end of the sensorimotor period. Infant problem solving is generally restricted to trial and error, and the infant appears incapable of foresight in considering available options for tackling problems.

Despite this argument against the availability of secondary appraisal processes at the cognitive level in infancy, infant behaviors in some stressful situations suggest that infants do search for available options and resources when first encountering a stressor. Most prominent are visual and locomotor search. For example, infants commonly look alternately at a stranger and at their mother (Campos & Stenberg, 1981). Looking at the mother probably functions both as an aid to primary appraisal (i.e., determining the stressfulness of the event) and as a check on one possible resource for coping with the stressor (i.e., emotion-focused or problem-focused aided coping). Another example can be seen during separations from the mother during the Strange Situation. Infants often search the room visually and motorically for coping options such as toys to focus on or methods of escape from the room.

Other components of the secondary appraisal process, such as evaluation of the potential effectiveness of a coping response and evaluation of the individual's ability to use the strategy, are difficult to directly assess in infants. The infant's learning history probably determines the likelihood that the infant will use a particular coping strategy and expect it to be effective. More general experientially based constructs, such as security of attachment (Ainsworth et al., 1978) and a sense of effectance (Lamb, 1981; White, 1959), probably also affect an infant's aspirations concerning the outcome resulting from coping attempts. For example, an infant with a secure attachment will be more likely than an infant with an insecure attachment to assume that the attachment figure will be available to effectively assist with coping efforts. Similarly, an infant who has acquired a sense of effectance through repeated successful attempts to control the environment will be more likely than an infant who has not acquired this sense to expect independent coping endeavors to be successful.

INDIVIDUAL DIFFERENCES IN STRESS AND COPING PROCESSES IN INFANCY

Many factors influence the degree of stress an individual experiences and how effectively an individual copes with that stress. Much of the adult research has examined these influences on individual differences in stress and coping processes (Lazarus & Folkman, 1984). Individual differences in infants' reactions to specific stressors and exhibition of coping responses, as well as the general influence of cognitive appraisal processes on individual differences in infant stress and coping processes, have been discussed previously. Several other influences on variations in infant stress and coping processes, including temperament, the availability of coping resources, resistance to stress, adaptive and maladaptive coping behaviors, and coping styles, will be described here.

Temperament

Temperament refers to an individual's enduring behavioral style (Thomas & Chess, 1977). Lerner and East (1984) discussed in detail the role of temperament in early stress, coping, and self-regulatory processes. They propose that infant temperamental differences, as well as differences in the fit between an infant's temperament and his or her environment, strongly influence infants' reactions to stressors and ability to cope effectively with stress. For example, they suggested that infants with easier temperaments can more effectively use information from social referencing and can more easily obtain appropriate care and assistance with coping from the environment. These benefits to easy infants presumably derive from the better fit between the infants' temperament and their environment than is the case with difficult infants. More specific aspects of temperament also can influence infants' appraisals of stress and ability to use particular coping strategies. For example, an infant with a low threshold of reactivity would be more easily stressed by a low intensity stimulus than would an infant with a high threshold of reactivity. A more active and persistent infant might be more effective at problem-focused coping, because more solutions to the problem are attempted. Compas (1987) and Kagan (1983) also emphasized the relevance of temperament to individual differences in stress appraisal and coping effectiveness.

Coping Resources

Individual differences in the assessment of one's ability to cope with an appraised stressor (secondary appraisal) as well as in the effectiveness of actual coping responses depends in large measure on certain resources an individual has available (Lazarus & Folkman, 1984). Adults vary enormously in the extent to which they have or are able to access these coping resources. Similar variations can be identified among infants. Lazarus and Folkman (1984) proposed that the major categories of adult coping resources include health and energy, positive beliefs, problem-solving skills, social skills, social support, and material resources. Evidence indicating individual differences in infants' access to resources in each of these categories and influences of these resources on infant stress and coping will be described.

Health and Energy

Chronic health problems (such as those associated with prematurity) act as stressors as well as detrimental influences on infants' tolerance of stress and ability to cope with stress (Field, 1987; Garrity & Weisman, 1982; Leiderman, 1983). Field (1987) noted that face-to-face interaction appears to be more stressful for high-risk than for normal infants, indicating deficits in the high-risk infants' coping skills. Leiderman (1983) emphasized that infant prematurity can stress the entire family system, limiting both infant independent coping and the ability of family members to assist the infant's coping efforts.

In normal infants, acute conditions such as fatigue, hunger, minor illness, and general irritability can increase the potency of stressors and decrease the effectiveness of infant coping. Most parents are well aware that their infants cope less well and require more soothing interventions when faced with such stressors as parental separations and encounters with strangers when the infants are tired, hungry, or ill.

Positive Beliefs

Positive beliefs cannot be measured directly in infants, but a variety of researchers and theorists have suggested that individual differences exist in the extent to which infants acquire a sense of effectance, mastery motivation, or contingency awareness (e.g., Lamb, 1981; Lewis, 1978; Messer, McCarthy, McQuiston, MacTurk, Yarrow, & Vietze, 1986; Watson, 1966; White 1959). Regardless of the term used, this construct generally refers to infants' perceptions of their ability to control and influence the environment. This positive belief has been found to be related to various measures of infant competence (e.g., Lamb, 1981; Messer et al., 1986) and is likely to influence stress and coping processes as well.

Problem-Solving and Social Skills

Problem-solving skills increase the options available to infants for problem-focused coping. Infants generally acquire more problem-solving skills with age but also show individual differences in the rate at which they acquire these skills (Bayley, 1969; Uzgiris & Hunt, 1975). Infants with more advanced problem-solving skills should cope more effectively with environmental demands. Similarly, social skills can serve as coping mechanisms (Gianino & Tronick, 1988) or can increase the likelihood that the infant can gain assistance with coping. Relevant social skills include verbal and nonverbal communication abilities, sociability with adults and peers, and the ability to express and perceive a wide range of emotions. Infants vary in their social skills, and these variations may be associated with variations in problem-solving skills (e.g., Lamb, 1982), making it difficult to separate the effects on coping of these two competencies.

Social Support

Although some research has focused on documenting the nature and extent of infants' social networks (Lewis, 1987), more attention has been paid to the effects of social support networks on parents' coping than on infants' coping (e.g., Crockenberg, 1981; Crnic et al., 1984). Research on the quality of infants' attachments provides the best evidence for the contribution of social support (typically from the mother) to infants' coping and competence. Infants with secure attachments (i.e., more and better social support from the mother) exhibit generally more effective coping skills and higher intellectual and social competence than infants with insecure attachments (e.g., Easterbrooks & Lamb, 1979; Hazen & Durrett, 1982; Matas, Arend, & Sroufe, 1978; Thompson & Lamb, 1983).

Material Resources

Familial monetary resources clearly increase the coping options of adults (Lazarus & Folkman, 1984) and probably indirectly influence the coping options of infants. Infants in families with more money are likely to have more toys, more stable care, less stressed parents, and fewer siblings. These factors and others likely contribute to optimal infant development both by reducing stresses and providing more coping resources.

Resistance to Stress

Much has been written about individual differences in children's invulnerability and resilience in the face of stress (Anthony & Cohler, 1987; Garmezy, 1985; Werner & Smith, 1982). This research has identified several factors in addition to the specific coping resources described previously that seem to determine whether or not a child will be adversely affected by exposure to chronic, serious stress. Some of these factors have their origins in infancy (Werner & Smith, 1982).

Garmezy (1983) listed three general factors that contribute to stress resistance. The first factor is the child's dispositional attributes (or temperament). Children with positive socioemotional characteristics, such as a positive mood, friendliness, and an internal locus of control (Garmezy, 1983), seem to cope better than others with high stress levels. Werner and Smith (1982) found that infants who were active and socially responsive were most likely to show resistance to stress in childhood and adulthood. Lerner and East (1984) suggested that these temperamental attributes contribute to stress resistance because they contribute to the goodness of fit between the infant and his or her social environment.

A second factor that Garmezy (1983) identified as having a buffering effect on stress reactions in childhood is family cohesion and warmth. Similarly, the physical and psychological environment of the home in infancy (Bradley, 1982; Gottfried, 1984) has been associated with infant competence. Two items from the Home Observation of the Environment, Organization of the Environment and Provision of Appropriate Play Materials, have been found to correlate significantly with mental scores on the Bayley Scales of Infant Development (Bradley, 1982).

Finally, the availability of strong social support has been associated with resilience in the face of stress in childhood (Garmezy, 1983). Infants who have a strong support figure, in the form of someone to whom they are securely attached, also show greater competence. This attachment figure may not need to be the mother; attachments to fathers, siblings, and child care workers have been reported (Lewis, 1987). Especially when the mother is unavailable or incapable of providing adequate emotional support for an infant, the availability of an alternate attachment figure can provide an infant with important resources for coping with stress.

Adaptive and Maladaptive Coping

The terms "adaptive and maladaptive coping" and "effective and ineffective coping" are sometimes used in discussions of infant stress and coping, but little empirical research has been conducted in this area. Some infants are described as coping maladaptively, which suggests that their coping attempts either are ineffective or are effective but utilize undesirable behaviors. Gianino and Tronick (1988) described the acquisition of defensive behaviors (which could also be characterized as maladaptive coping strategies) in young infants repeatedly exposed to interactive stress. These infants learn to use behaviors such as disengagement to avoid interactions with their stress-inducing mothers as well as with other individuals who may not interact in a stressful manner. Such behaviors are maladaptive because they are used automatically, inflexibly, and indiscriminately. Note that although these behaviors may be maladaptive because they prevent the infant from having the opportunity to experience normal interaction, such behaviors also are effective in helping the infant avoid overly stressful interactions.

Several other infant coping behaviors can be regarded as maladaptive. Potentially self-injurious behaviors such as tantrums, regurgitation, or head banging (Lipsitt, 1983) may be temporarily effective coping strategies but will limit coping in the future. Similarly, the discontinuation of active coping efforts by withdrawing from a stressful situation may be both effective and adaptive in the short term (Field, 1985) but may be maladaptive if continued for long periods. Any inflexible or persistent use of a coping strategy without modification according to the contextual features of the stressor might also be considered maladaptive (Compas, 1987). Finally, habitual use of ineffective coping strategies (i.e., behaviors that do not reduce infant distress) could also be regarded as maladaptive.

Care must be taken in labeling infant coping efforts as maladaptive. Behavior that appears maladaptive in one context may be adaptive in other contexts. Alternately, behavior that is adaptive in an atypical environment may be maladaptive in relation to the broad context of development. Finally, some behaviors that psychologists initially label as maladaptive (such as avoidant attachment behavior in day care infants) may actually be mature, adaptive coping responses or an indication that a presumed stressor is not actually stressful for certain infants (Compas, 1987). Lazarus and Folkman (1984) emphasized the value of studying coping as a process rather than focusing on coping outcomes. A similar focus in the study of infant coping may be more enlightening than attempting to assess the adaptiveness of specific infant coping behaviors.

Coping Styles

Lazarus and Folkman (1984) and Compas (1987) discussed many of the problems encountered in efforts to characterize the coping styles of children and adults. Although there is general agreement that individuals differ in overall coping style (or the patterning of coping behaviors), little agreement exists as to how to describe these stylistic differences. Identifying consistencies in behavior across all stressful encounters or across stressful encounters sharing particular features is a necessary first step in the study of coping styles. Gianino and Tronick (1988) and Hock and Clinger (1981) reported evidence of consistencies in infants' coping behaviors.

Gianino and Tronick (1988) reported that 6-month-old infants' styles of coping with a still-face interaction were stable over a 1-week period. In addition, one component of coping with a still-face interaction at 6 months, signaling, was significantly related to the security of attachment at 12 months. Hock and Clinger (1981) found that 12-month-old infants' coping patterns (defined as the degree to which infants made use of resources such as toys and a stranger) were consistent across three stressful episodes of the Strange Situation. These findings suggest that infants acquire individualized styles of coping that are at least somewhat stable, but further research is needed to more explicitly and fully describe infant coping styles.

DEVELOPMENTAL CHANGES IN STRESS
AND COPING PROCESSES

Dramatic changes in skills during infancy result in constantly changing stress and coping processes. Improvements in cognitive abilities, social skills and knowledge, motor skills, and communication skills, and the acquisition of a learning history all are likely to influence infants' appraisals of what is stressful and infants' abilities to cope with appraised stressors. These changes also increase the range of resources infants have available for coping. Two cross-sectional studies of infant coping provide evidence of changes with age in stress and coping processes. Gianino and Tronick (1988) reported a comparison of 3-, 6-, and 9-month-old infants' responses to still-face interactions. Older infants displayed more coping behaviors, more frequent transitions between coping behaviors, more effective self-soothing activity, and generally more organized behavior. Hyson (1983) observed the stress and coping responses of infants, toddlers, and preschool-age children during visits to the doctor for well-child checkups. Younger children displayed more overt negative emotion and protest. Older children showed more anticipatory and goal-directed coping. These investigations provide evidence of expected changes in stress and coping processes with increasing age.

The relationship between stress and coping processes in infancy and those processes in later life has not been studied systematically. In general, stress and coping processes have been studied only at specific ages, and little is known about changes across major age periods. Maccoby (1983) provided an intriguing yet speculative series of hypotheses about how reactions to stress might change across childhood and adolescence. Most relevant to the infancy period are her following suggestions: (a) vulnerability to stress does not change with age, although the types of events that produce stress change dramatically; (b) environmental structure is more important in aiding coping with stress for younger children; (c) younger children are more likely to show behavioral disorganization in response to stress; and (d) the range of coping behaviors increases with age, with decreasing dependence on attachment figures as coping resources. Careful longitudinal research will be needed to test these hypotheses.

A final series of interesting questions concerns the long-term effects of exposure to high levels or particular types of stress during infancy. A fascinating cross-cultural analysis by Landauer and Whiting (1981) suggests that early exposure to stress can in some cases enhance later development. In particular, they report a positive relationship between physical stress in early infancy (such as circumcision, vaccination, and exposure to extreme temperatures) and adult stature. Rutter (1983) proposed mechanisms by which early exposure to stress can positively or negatively affect later development. Early stressful experiences can interfere with ongoing development, create physical changes in the child, alter the child's environment, or change the child's sensitivity to stress or ability to cope with subsequent stress. Several authors (Gianino & Tronick 1988; Lipsitt, 1983; Rutter, 1983) suggested that coping strategies and styles acquired early in life set the stage for later development of coping skills. Obviously much work is needed to address these issues.

CONCLUSIONS

Lipsitt (1983) described infancy as survival training, both from a physical and psychological perspective. Many rudimentary skills are acquired during infancy, although much elaboration and development remains to be accomplished. Optimal development is likely to result when an infant experiences a normative amount and normative types of stress and when the infant learns a variety of appropriate coping strategies. Overprotection of an infant may compromise development by preventing the infant from experiencing stress and learning to cope. Alternately, excess exposure to stress in early life may overwhelm an infant's coping and learning capacities and prevent the acquisition of effective coping skills. The perspectives on stress and coping during infancy advanced in this chapter will hopefully contribute to a life-span view of the processes underlying stress and coping.

REFERENCES

Abramovitch, R., Corter, C., & Pepler, D. J. (1980). Observations of mixed-sex sibling dyads. *Child Development, 51,* 1268–1271.

Adams, R. E., Jr., & Passman, R. H. (1981). The effects of preparing two-year-olds for brief separations from their mothers. *Child Development, 52,* 1068–1070.

Ainsworth, M., Blehar, M., Waters, E., & Wall, S. (1978). *Patterns of attachment.* Hillsdale, NJ: Lawrence Erlbaum Associates.

Anthony, E. J., & Cohler, B. J. (Eds.). (1987). *The invulnerable child.* New York: Guilford.

Bayley, N. (1969). *Manual for the Bayley Scales of Infant Development.* New York: Psychological Corporation.

Belsky, J. (1984). Two waves of day care research: Developmental effects and conditions of quality. In R. C. Ainslie (Ed.), *The child and the day care setting* (pp. 1–34). New York: Praeger.

Bradley, R. H. (1982). The HOME Inventory: A review of the first fifteen years. In N. J. Anastasiow, W. Frankenburg, & A. W. Fandal (Eds.), *Identifying the developmentally delayed child* (pp. 87–100). Baltimore: University Park Press.

Brazelton, T. B. (1984). *Neonatal Behavioral Assessment Scale* (2nd ed.). London: Blackwell Scientific.

Bretherton, I. (1978). Making friends with one-year-olds: An experimental study of infant–stranger interaction. *Merrill-Palmer Quarterly, 24,* 29–51.

Brownlee, J. R., & Bakeman, R. (1981). Hitting in toddler–peer interaction. *Child Development, 52,* 1076–1079.

Campos, J. J., Barrett, K. C., Lamb, M. E., Goldsmith, H. H., & Stenberg, C. (1983). Socioemotional development. In J. J. Campos & M. M. Haith (Eds.), *Handbook of child psychology: Volume II. Infancy and developmental psychobiology* (pp. 783–916). New York: Wiley.

Campos, J. J., & Stenberg, C. R. (1981). Perception, appraisal, and emotion: The onset of social referencing. In M. E. Lamb & L. R. Sherrod (Eds.), *Infant social cognition: Empirical and theoretical considerations* (pp. 273–314). Hillsdale, NJ: Lawrence Erlbaum Associates.

Carey, W. B., & McDevitt, S. C. (1978). Revision of the Infant Temperament Questionnaire. *Pediatrics, 61,* 735–739.

Clarke-Stewart, K. A. (1978). Recasting the lone stranger. In Glick & K. A. Clarke-Stewart (Eds.), *The development of social understanding* (pp. 109–176). New York: Gardner.

Clarke-Stewart, K. A. (1989). Infant day care: Maligned or malignant? *American Psychologist, 44,* 266–273.

Cohn, J. F., & Tronick, E. Z. (1983). Three-month-old infants' reaction to simulated maternal depression. *Child Development, 54,* 185–193.

Compas, B. E. (1987). Coping with stress during childhood and adolescence. *Psychological Bulletin, 101,* 393–403.

Corter, C. M. (1976). The nature of the mother's absence and the infant's response to brief separations. *Developmental Psychology, 12,* 428–434.

Crnic, K. A., Greenberg, M. T., Robinson, N. M., & Ragozin, A. S. (1984). Maternal stress and social support: Effects on the mother – infant relationship from birth to eighteen months. *American Journal of Orthopsychiatry, 54,* 224–235.

Crockenberg, S. B. (1981). Infant irritability, mother responsiveness, and social support influences on the security of infant–mother attachment. *Child Development, 52,* 857–865.

Cummings, E. M., Zahn-Waxler, C., & Radke-Yarrow, M. (1981). Young children's responses to expressions of anger and affection by others in the family. *Child Development, 52,* 1274–1282.

Easterbrooks, M. A., & Lamb, M. E. (1979). The relationship between quality of infant–mother attachment and infant competence in initial encounters with peers. *Child Development, 50,* 380–387.

Fagen, J. W., & Ohr, P. S. (1985). Temperament and crying in response to the violation of a learned expectancy in early infancy. *Infant Behavior and Development, 8,* 157–166.

Feinman, S. (1980). Infant response to race, size, proximity, and movement of strangers. *Infant Behavior and Development, 3*, 187–204.

Feinman, S. (1982). Social referencing in infancy. *Merrill-Palmer Quarterly, 28*, 445–470.

Field, T. M. (1978). The three Rs of infant–adult interactions: Rhythms, repertoires, and responsivity. *Journal of Pediatric Psychology, 3*, 131–136.

Field, T. (1981). Infant gaze aversion and heart rate during face-to-face interactions. *Infant Behavior and Development, 4*, 307–315.

Field, T. (1985). Coping with separation stress by infants and young children. In T. M. Field, P. McCabe, & N. Schneiderman (Eds.), *Stress and coping* (pp. 197–219). Hillsdale, NJ: Lawrence Erlbaum Associates.

Field, T. (1987). Affective and interactive disturbances in infants. In J. D. Osofsky (Ed.), *Handbook of infant development* (2nd ed., pp. 972–1005). New York: Wiley.

Field, T. M., McCabe, P. M., & Schneiderman, N. (Eds.). (1988). *Stress and coping across development*. Hillsdale, NJ: Lawrence Erlbaum Associates.

Field, T. M., Vega-Lahr, N., & Jagadish, S. (1984). Separation stress of nursery school infants and toddlers graduating to new classes. *Infant Behavior and Development, 7*, 277–284.

Field, T., Vega-Lahr, N., Scafidi, F., & Goldstein, S. (1986). Effects of maternal unavailability on mother–infant interaction. *Infant Behavior and Development, 9*, 473–478.

Fogel, A. (1980). The effect of brief separations on 2-month-old infants. *Infant Behavior and Development, 3*, 315–330.

Folkman, S. (1984). Personal control and stress and coping processes: A theoretical analysis. *Journal of Personality and Social Psychology, 46*, 839–852.

Gaensbauer, T. J., Emde, R. N., & Campos, J. (1976). Stranger distress: Confirmation of a developmental shift in a longitudinal sample. *Perceptual and Motor Skills, 43*, 99–106.

Garmezy, N. (1983). Stressors of childhood. In N. Garmezy & M. Rutter (Eds.), *Stress, coping, and development in children* (pp. 43–84). New York: McGraw-Hill.

Garmezy, N. (1985). Stress-resistant children: The search for protective factors. In J. E. Stevenson (Ed.), *Recent research in developmental psychopathology* (pp. 213–233). Oxford: Pergamon.

Garmezy, N., & Rutter, M. (Eds.). (1983). *Stress, coping, and development in children*. New York: McGraw-Hill.

Garrity, L., & Weisman, B. (1982). Coping behavior: Differences in barrier performance in full-term and premature infants. *Journal of Child Psychology and Psychiatry and Allied Disciplines, 23*, 159–168.

Gianino, A., & Tronick, E. (1988). The mutual regulation model: The infant's self and interactive regulation and coping and defensive capacities. In T. M. Field, P. M. McCabe, & N. Schneiderman (Eds.), *Stress and coping across development* (pp. 47–68). Hillsdale, NJ: Lawrence Erlbaum Associates.

Ginsburg, H., & Opper, S. (1978). *Piaget's theory of intellectual development* (2nd ed.). Englewood Cliffs, NJ: Prentice-Hall.

Goldberger, L., & Breznitz, S. (Eds.). (1982). *Handbook of stress: Theoretical and clinical aspects*. New York: Free Press.

Gottfried, A. W. (Ed.). (1984). *Home environment and early cognitive development*. Orlando, FL: Academic Press.

Gottfried, A. W., & Gaiter, J. J. (1985). *Infant stress under intensive care*. Baltimore: University Park Press.

Gunnar, M. R. (1980). Control, warning signals, and distress in infancy. *Developmental Psychology, 16*, 281–289.

Gunnar, M. R. (1987). Psychobiological studies of stress and coping: An introduction. *Child Development, 58*, 1403–1407.

Gunnar, M. R., & Leighton, K., & Peleaux, R. (1984). Effects of temporal predictability on the reactions of 1-year-olds to potentially frightening toys. *Developmental Psychology, 20*, 449–458.

Gunnar, M. R., Malone, S., & Fisch, R. O. (1985). The psychobiology of stress and coping in the human neonate: Studies of adrenocortical activity in response to aversive stimulation. In T. M.

Field, P. McCabe, & N. Schneiderman (Eds.), *Stress and coping* (pp. 179–196). Hillsdale, NJ: Lawrence Erlbaum Associates.

Gunnar, M. R., Malone, S., Vance, G., & Fisch, R. O. (1985). Coping with aversive stimulation in the neonatal period: Quiet sleep and plasma cortisol levels during recovery from circumcision. *Child Development, 56,* 824–834.

Gunnar-von Gnechten, M. R. (1978). Changing a frightening toy into a pleasant toy by allowing the infant to control its action. *Developmental Psychology, 14,* 157–162.

Hamilton, V., & Warburton, D. M. (Eds.). (1979). *Human stress and cognition: An information processing approach.* New York: Wiley.

Hay, D. F., & Ross, H. S. (1982). The social nature of early conflict. *Child Development, 53,* 105–113.

Hazen, N. L., & Durrett, M. E. (1982). Relationship of security of attachment to exploration and cognitive mapping abilities in 2-year-olds. *Developmental Psychology, 18,* 751–759.

Hock, E., & Clinger, J. B. (1981). Infant coping behaviors: Their assessment and their relationship to maternal attributes. *Journal of Genetic Psychology, 138,* 231–243.

Hyson, M. C. (1983). Going to the doctor: A developmental study of stress and coping. *Journal of Child Psychology and Psychiatry and Allied Disciplines, 24,* 247–259.

Izard, C. E., Hembree, E. A., & Heubner, R. R. (1987). Infants' emotion expressions to acute pain: Developmental change and stability of individual differences. *Developmental Psychology, 23,* 105–113.

Kagan, J. (1983). Stress and coping in early development. In N. Garmezy & M. Rutter (Eds.), *Stress, coping, and development in children* (pp. 191–217). New York: McGraw-Hill.

Kavenaugh, R. D., & McCall, R. B. (1983). Social influencing among two-year-olds: The role of affiliative and antagonistic behavior. *Infant Behavior and Development, 6,* 39–52.

Kendrick, C., & Dunn, J. (1980). Caring for a second baby: Effects on interaction between mother and firstborn. *Developmental Psychology, 16,* 303–311.

Klinnert, M. D., Campos, J. J., Sorce, J. F., Emde, R. N., & Svejda, M. (1983). Emotions as behavior regulators: Social referencing in infancy. In R. Plutchik & H. Kellerman (Eds.), *Emotion, theory, research, and experience: Volume 2. Emotions in early development* (pp. 57–86). New York: Academic Press.

Kopp, C. B. (1982). Antecedents of self-regulation: A developmental perspective. *Developmental Psychology, 18,* 199–214.

Kuczynski, L., Kochanska, G., Radke-Yarrow, M., & Girnius-Brown, O. (1987). A developmental interpretation of young children's noncompliance. *Developmental Psychology, 23,* 799–806.

Kutash, I. L., & Schlesinger, L. B. (Eds.). (1980). *Handbook on stress and anxiety.* San Francisco: Jossey-Bass.

Lamb, M. E. (1981). The development of social expectations in the first year of life. In M. E. Lamb & L. R. Sherrod (Eds.), *Infant social cognition* (pp. 155–175). Hillsdale, NJ: Lawrence Erlbaum Associates.

Lamb, M. E. (1982). Individual differences in infant sociability: Their origins and implications for cognitive development. In H. W. Reese & L. P. Lipsitt (Eds.), *Advances in child development and behavior* (vol. 16, pp. 213–239). New York: Academic Press.

Landauer, T. K., & Whiting, J. W. (1981). Correlates and consequences of stress in infancy. In R. Monroe, R. Monroe, & B. Whiting (Eds.), *Handbook of cross-cultural development* (pp. 355–375). New York: Garland.

Lazarus, R. S., & Folkman S. (1984). *Stress, appraisal, and coping.* New York: Springer.

Leiderman, P. H. (1983). Social ecology and childbirth: The newborn nursery as environmental stressor. In N. Garmezy & M. Rutter (Eds.), *Stress, coping, and development in children* (pp. 133–159). New York: McGraw-Hill.

Lerner, R. M., & East, P. L. (1984). The role of temperament in stress, coping, and socioemotional functioning in early development. *Infant Mental Health Journal, 5,* 148 – 159.

Lester, B. M. (1985). There's more to crying than meets the ear. In B. M. Lester & C. F. Z. Boukydis (Eds.), *Infant crying: Theoretical and research perspectives* (pp. 1–28). New York: Plenum.

Lester, B. M., & Boukydis, C. F. Z. (Eds.). (1985). *Infant crying: Theoretical and research perspectives*. New York: Plenum.

Lewis, M. (1978). The infant and its caregiver: The role of contingency. *Allied Health and Behavioral Sciences, 1,* 469–492.

Lewis, M. (1987). Social development in infancy and early childhood. In J. D. Osofsky (Ed.). *Handbook of infant development* (2nd ed., pp. 419–493). New York: Wiley.

Lewis, M., Sullivan, M., & Brooks-Gunn, J. (1985). Emotional behaviour during the learning of a contingency in early infancy. *British Journal of Developmental Psychology, 3,* 307–316.

Lipsitt, L. (1983). Stress in infancy: Toward understanding the origins of coping behavior. In N. Garmezy & M. Rutter (Eds.). *Stress, coping, and development in children* (pp. 161–190). New York: McGraw-Hill.

Maccoby, E. E. (1983). Social-emotional development and response to stressors. In N. Garmezy & M. Rutter (Eds.), *Stress, coping, and development in children* (pp. 217–234). New York: McGraw-Hill.

Main, M., & Weston, D. R. (1982). Avoidance of the attachment figure in infancy: Descriptions and interpretations. In C. M. Parkes & J. Stevenson-Hinde (Eds.), *The place of attachment in human behavior* (pp. 31–59). New York: Basic.

Matas, L., Arend, R. A., & Sroufe, L. A. (1978). Continuity of adaptation in the second year: The relationship between quality of attachment and later competence. *Child Development, 49,* 547–556.

Messer, D. J., McCarthy, M. E., McQuiston, S., MacTurk, R. H., Yarrow, L. J., & Vietze, P. M. (1986). Relationship between mastery behavior in infancy and competence in early childhood. *Developmental Psychology, 22,* 366–372.

Murphy, L. B., & Moriarty, A. E. (1976). *Vulnerability, coping, and growth: From infancy to adolescence*. New Haven: Yale University Press.

Osofsky, J. D. (Ed.). (1987). *Handbook of infant development* (2nd ed.). New York: Wiley.

Passman, R. H. (1976). Arousal reducing properties of attachment objects: Testing the functional limits of the security blanket relative to the mother. *Developmental Psychology, 12,* 468–469.

Passman, R. H. (1977). Providing attachment objects to facilitate learning and reduce distress: Effects of mothers and security blankets. *Developmental Psychology, 13,* 25–28.

Passman, R. H., & Weisberg, P. (1975). Mothers and blankets as agents for promoting play and exploration by young children in a novel environment: The effects of social and nonsocial attachment objects. *Developmental Psychology, 11,* 170–177.

Rinkoff, R. F., & Corter, C. M. (1980). Effects of setting and maternal accessibility on the infant's response to brief separation. *Child Development, 51,* 603–606.

Ross, H. S. (1975). The effects of increasing familiarity on infants' reactions to adult strangers. *Journal of Experimental Child Psychology, 20,* 226–239.

Rutter, M. (1983). Stress, coping, and development: Some issues and some questions. In N. Garmezy & M. Rutter (Eds.), *Stress, coping, and development in children* (pp. 1–41). New York: McGraw-Hill.

Schanberg, S. M. & Field, T. M. (1988). Maternal deprivation and supplemental stimulation. In T. M. Field, P. M. McCabe, & N. Schneiderman (Eds.), *Stress and coping across development* (pp. 3–25). Hillsdale, NJ: Lawrence Erlbaum Associates.

Skarin, K. (1977). Cognitive and contextual determinants of stranger fear in 6- and 11-month-old infants. *Child Development, 48,* 537–544.

Sroufe, L. A. (1977). Wariness of strangers and the study of infant development. *Child Development, 48,* 731–746.

Sroufe, L. A., & Waters, E. (1977). Heart rate as a convergent measure in clinical and developmental research. *Merrill-Palmer Quarterly, 23,* 3–27.

Stenberg, C. R., Campos, J. J., & Emde, R. N. (1983). The facial expression of anger in seven-month-old infants. *Child Development, 54,* 178–184.

Suwalsky, J. T. D., Klein, R. P., Zaslow, M. J., Rabinovich, B. A., & Gist, N. F. (1987).

Dimensions of naturally occurring mother–infant separations during the first year of life. *Infant Mental Health Journal, 8,* 3–18.

Thomas, A., & Chess, S. (1977). *Temperament and development.* New York: Brunner/Mazel.

Thompson, R. A., & Lamb, M. E. (1983). Security of attachment and stranger sociability in infancy. *Developmental Psychology, 19,* 184–191.

Thompson, R. A., Lamb, M. E., & Estes, D. (1982). Stability of infant–mother attachment and its relationship to changing life circumstances in an unselected middle-class sample. *Child Development, 53,* 144–148.

Trause, M. A. (1977). Stranger responses: Effects of familiarity, stranger's approach, and sex of infant. *Child Development, 48,* 1657–1661.

Trevarthen, C. (1977). Descriptive analysis of infant communicative behaviour. In H. R. Schaffer (Ed.), *Studies in mother–infant interaction* (pp. 227–270). London: Academic Press.

Tronick, E., Als, H., & Adamson, L. (1979). Structure of early face-to-face communicative interactions. In M. Bullowa (Ed.), *Before speech: The beginnings of interpersonal communication* (pp. 349–372). Cambridge: Cambridge University Press.

Uzgiris, I. C., & Hunt, J. McV. (1975). *Assessment in infancy.* Urbana: University of Illinois Press.

Vaughn, B., Egeland, B., Sroufe, L. A., & Waters, E. (1979). Individual differences in infant–mother attachment at twelve and eighteen months: Stability and change in families under stress. *Child Development, 50,* 971–975.

Van Lieshout, C. F. (1976). Young children's reactions to barriers placed by their mothers. *Child Development, 46,* 879–886.

Watson, J. S. (1966). The development and generalization of contingency awareness in early infancy: Some hypotheses. *Merrill-Palmer Quarterly, 12,* 123–135.

Watson, J. S. (1972). Smiling, cooing, and "the game." *Merrill-Palmer Quarterly, 18,* 323–339.

Wenar, C. (1982). On negativism. *Human Development, 25,* 1–23.

Werner, E. E., & Smith, R. S. (1982). *Vulnerable, but invincible: A study of resilient children.* New York: McGraw-Hill.

White, R. W. (1959). Motivation reconsidered: The concept of competence. *Psychological Review, 66,* 297–333.

Zeitlin, S., Williamson, G. G., & Szczepanski, M. (1984). *Early coping inventory (research edition): A measure of adaptive behavior.* Edison, NJ: John F. Kennedy Medical Center.

III

CHILDHOOD

6

Stress During Childhood and Adolescence: Sources of Risk and Vulnerability

Bruce E. Compas
Vicky Phares
University of Vermont

An important task facing the field of developmental psychopathology is the identification of factors that predict an increased probability for emotional and behavioral problems in children and adolescents. Although a wide range of social and biological factors may play a role in child and adolescent maladjustment, research indicating a consistent association between stressful events and psychological disorder in adults suggests that stress[1] may be an important construct to investigate in younger populations. Stressful experiences occurring early in development may contribute to emotional/behavioral problems and disrupt positive development. Further, early events may alter the course of later development either directly or transactionally. Stressful events and maladjustment may be reciprocally related, each contributing to the etiology and maintenance of the other. Thus, stressful events during childhood and adolescence may set in motion a process in which stress and emotional/behavioral problems contribute to one another in a self-perpetuating cycle.

In spite of the potential importance of studying stressful events in childhood

---

[1]The field of stress research has been soundly and appropriately criticized for its failure to adequately define the concept of central interest, stress. As a result of this confusion around the definition of stress, it is difficult to decide what areas of research are appropriate to include in a review of this area. Our thinking has been guided by the work of Lazarus and Folkman, who defined (1984) psychological stress as "a particular relationship between the person and the environment that is appraised by the person as taxing or exceeding his or her resources and endangering his or her well being" (p. 19). From this framework, stress can be the result of either discrete events of major or minor magnitude or ongoing, chronic aspects of the person–environment relationship. Therefore, we focus our discussion on studies of the cumulative effects of both major and minor stressful events and processes.

and adolescence, relatively little empirical research has been carried out in this area. The purposes of this chapter are to review recent studies that have examined psychosocial stress as a source of risk for emotional/behavioral problems in childhood and adolescence, to identify sources of individual differences in vulnerability to stress in children and adolescents, and to address the issues that arise from the use of multiple informants to define and measure emotional/behavioral problems in children and adolescents in stress research. First, we define the concepts of risk and vulnerability as they relate to stress and maladjustment in childhood and adolescence. Second, we review research concerning stress as a risk factor, emphasizing prospective, longitudinal studies with children and adolescents. In the third section, we discuss some of the factors that have been found to moderate the effects of stress, leading some youths to be vulnerable and others to be resistant to the effects of stress. Fourth, we discuss the different findings that have been obtained when children's and adolescents' self-reports, rather than the reports of other informants such as parents, have been used to assess the criterion variable of emotional/behavioral problems. Finally directions for future research in this area are outlined. Throughout this chapter, we draw extensively on work carried out by our research group, the Vermont Stress, Coping, and Development Project, over the past five years.

RISK AND VULNERABILITY

Although the terms risk and vulnerability are often used interchangeably in the developmental psychopathology literature, there is good reason to make a clear distinction between them (Masten & Garmezy, 1985). With regard to the notion of risk, Masten and Garmezy (1985) stated, "The presence of *risk factors* assumes that there exists a higher probability for the development of a disorder; as such, these factors are statistically associated with higher incidence rates" (p. 3). They described the roots of the concept of risk in the field of epidemiology with its emphasis on statistical patterns of disease in *populations*. In contrast, Masten and Garmezy (1985) wrote that *vulnerability* refers to "the *susceptibility or predisposition of an individual to negative outcomes*" (p. 8). They noted that in relation to psychopathology, vulnerability has typically referred to an *individual's* predisposition to either a particular disorder or a general susceptibility to stress. As such, they make a distinction between an emphasis on a group or population (risk) as opposed to an individual (vulnerability).

These two concepts are useful in defining the central tasks for researchers interested in the role of stress in developmental psychopathology. First, it must be established that stress operates as a risk factor in children and adolescents at the population level. This will require data from prospective longitudinal studies in which stressful events are shown to contribute to increases emotional/behavioral problems in children and adolescents after controlling for the tendency for these problems to persist over time. (See Cohen, 1988; Depue & Monroe, 1986; Monroe, 1982b; Monroe & Peterman, 1988, for discussions of issues on research design related to stress and psychopathology.) Once stress has been established as a risk factor for children and adolescents at the group level, investigators need to determine those factors that predispose certain individuals and not others to experience emotional/behavioral problems in association with stressful events. That is, if stress and disorder are only modestly to moderately correlated in the population, there must be substantial individual differences in responses to stress. It is, therefore, the task of researchers concerned with vulnerability to identify sources of these individual differences. In the following sections, we review research concerning psychosocial stress as a source of risk and individual differences in vulnerability to stress in children and adolescents.

STRESS AS A RISK FACTOR FOR EMOTIONAL/ BEHAVIORAL PROBLEMS IN CHILDREN AND ADOLESCENTS

Much like research with adults, investigations of stressful events in children and adolescents have emphasized the role of discrete major life events (e.g., parental divorce, moving to a new home) rather than the role of minor, daily stressors (e.g., homework, chores and responsibilities at home, restrictions by parents). The majority of the early studies in this area were cross-sectional in design and found a modest association between major life events and a variety of types of psychological and physical maladjustment (see Compas, 1987b, and Johnson, 1986, for reviews). Correlations between self-reports or maternal reports of stressful events and emotional/behavioral problems typically were found in the range from .20 to .40. This pattern of findings is quite similar to those reported in early studies of major life events in adults (Rabkin & Struening, 1976; Sarason, deMonchaux, & Hunt, 1975; Thoits, 1983).

Although these early studies were useful in providing a foundation for research on child and adolescent stress, cross-sectional studies cannot be used as evidence that stressful events are a risk factor for emotional/behavioral problems (i.e., these studies cannot test whether stressful events are predictive of changes in emotional/behavioral problems over time). The emphasis in risk research is on establishing a link between a possible risk factor and *subsequent* disorder, and this requires the use of one of two prospective longitudinal research designs.

One approach is to test the concurrent association between stress and maladjustment after controlling for prior levels of maladjustment. This design allows for a sensitive test of the contribution of recent stressful events to changes in emotional/ behavioral problems over time but is subject to problems of confounding between measures of stress and maladjustment obtained concurrently. When stressful events and maladjustment are assessed concurrently, it is difficult to determine the temporal sequence of these two factors. Further, it is possible that reports of both variables might be affected by another factor, such as a negative response bias.

A second design used in prospective studies of stress and maladjustment is to test the prediction of maladjustment at one point in time from indicators of stress obtained at a prior point in time, again controlling for prior levels of maladjustment. This approach is less affected by possible confounds between stress and maladjustment than when they are assessed concurrently. However, when the time lag between the assessment of the two variables is quite long (several months or more), this design will not be sensitive to possible associations between stressful events and disorder.

Although neither of these designs can rule out the effects of other variables that may be causing both stressful events and emotional/behavioral problems (and, therefore, cannot be used to test true causal relations between stress and maladjustment), they are useful in meeting the criteria necessary for risk research by establishing a *predictive* relation between stress and maladjustment. Studies using each of these designs have found a prospective longitudinal relation between stress and symptoms in older adolescents (e.g., Compas, Wagner, Slavin, & Vannatta, 1986; Wagner, Compas, & Howell, 1988), college students (e.g., Hammen, Mayol, deMayo, & Marks, 1986; Monroe, Imhoff, Wise, & Harris, 1983; Nelson & Cohen, 1983), and adults (e.g., Billings & Moos, 1982; Monroe, 1982a).

In contrast to research with adults and older adolescents, prospective studies of stress and emotional/behavioral problems in children and young adolescents have been rare and have only recently begun to provide support for the role of stress as a risk factor (Cohen, Burt, & Bjork, 1987; Compas, Howell, Phares, Williams, & Giunta, 1989; Gersten, Langner, Eisenberg, & Simcha-Fagan, 1977; Glyshaw, Cohen, & Towbes, 1988; Siegel & Brown, 1988; Swearingen & Cohen, 1985). In the first prospective study in this area, Gertsten et al. (1977) examined the association between mothers' reports of major life events in their children's lives and maternal reports of their children's behavior problems at two points in time over five years. They found that life events did not explain any of the variance in behavior problems after parental and family variables were accounted for. Cohen et al. (1987) and Swearingen and Cohen (1985) also did not find an association between young adolescents' initial self-reports of major life events and self-reported anxiety and depression five months later after controlling for initial levels of anxiety and depression. However, Cohen et al. (1987) found that self-reports of negative events at the second point in time accounted for a small (5%) but significant portion of the variance in depression and anxiety at the second time point after controlling for initial self-reports of depression and anxiety obtained five months earlier.

More recently, three studies have provided stronger support for the role of stress as a risk factor in children and young adolescents. Siegel and Brown (1988) examined the association of minor or daily stressors with self-reported depressed mood and physical illness in a sample of 10- to 17-year-old adolescent girls at two points in time nine months apart. Stressful events at the first time predicted later depressed mood for the younger adolescents, and for the whole sample, stressful events predicted depression in interaction with positive events; negative events predicted physical symptoms only in interaction with positive events. That is, negative events were predictive of maladjustment only in the presence of low levels of positive events. Glyshaw et al. (1988) found that young adolescents' self-reports of stressful life events predicted self-reported anxiety and depression five months later, after controlling for initial levels of these symptoms. These findings were in contrast to earlier findings by Cohen and his colleagues, and Glyshaw et al. (1988) noted that the prospective effects of stress in their study may be a result of their sample reporting higher than expected levels of stressful events and symptoms.

A recent investigation by our research group examined several issues regarding stress as a risk factor in young adolescents (Compas, Howell, Phares, Williams, & Giunta, 1989). First, the role of major stressful events as opposed to minor or daily stressors had not been directly compared in prospective studies in this age group. These two factors had been studied independently (e.g., Cohen et al., 1987, Siegel & Brown, 1988), but a comprehensive model of stress should include both of these sources of stress (Rowlison & Felner, 1988; Wagner et al., 1988). Second, prospective studies have focused on internalizing problems such as depression and anxiety to the exclusion of externalizing problems (e.g., conduct disorder, delinquency). Cross-sectional studies have shown an association between stressful events and both internalizing and externalizing problems, therefore, it seems important to examine both types of problems in prospective analyses. Third, the relation between stress and maladjustment may not be linear, as suggested by findings reported by Cohen and colleagues that anxiety and depression are predictive of later stressful events in young adolescents (Cohen et al., 1987; Swearingen & Cohen, 1985). It is possible that stress and disorder are reciprocally related, each contributing to the etiology and maintenance of the other (Compas et al., 1986). Fourth, the strength of child and adolescent reports of stress as a predictor of maladjustment may vary depending on the source of information on these two variables. That is, the role of stress may appear different when children's self-reports as opposed to the reports of other informants (e.g., parents, teachers) are used to assess stress and maladjustment. The use of different informants' reports of maladjustment had not been compared directly.

To examine these issues, young adolescents' self-reports of major and daily stressors and internalizing and externalizing emotional/behavioral problems, along with mothers' reports of their children's emotional/behavioral problems, were assessed twice, nine months apart (Compas, Howell, Phares, Williams, & Giunta, 1989). The concurrent association between self-reported stressful events and self-reports of emotional/behavioral problems was significant at the second time point, with stress accounting for 11% of the variance in emotional/behavioral problems after controlling for initial levels of problems. Further, stressful events at the initial time predicted emotional/behavioral problems nine months later (accounting for 2% of the variance), again controlling for initial emotional/behavioral problems. Analyses of data at the second point in time indicated that daily but not major stressors were predictive of emotional/behavioral problems; a similar pattern emerged in the prediction of problems at the second time point from initial levels of stress. Stressful events predicted self-reports of both internalizing and externalizing problems, although there was a trend for a stronger association with internalizing problems. Further, both internalizing and externalizing problems at the first time point predicted daily stressors nine months later. However, adolescents' self-reports of stress were *not* predictive of mothers' reports of their children's emotional/behavioral problems in any of the cross-sectional or prospective analyses, an issue that we discuss in detail following.

In summary, several recent studies have established stressful events, particularly minor or daily stressors, as a risk factor for self-reported emotional/behavioral problems in older children and young adolescents. That is, stressful events are predictive of maladjustment over time even after controlling for persistence in emotional/behavioral problems. However, the association of stress and maladjustment at the group level has been modest. This suggests that there may be substantial individual differences in the association between stressful events and maladjustment. The search for factors that may moderate this association has been the focus of research on individual differences in vulnerability to stress.

FACTORS ASSOCIATED WITH VULNERABILITY TO STRESS IN CHILDREN AND ADOLESCENTS

As discussed previously, the concept of vulnerability is concerned with factors that predispose individuals toward disorder when those individuals have been exposed to known risk factors. Identification of individual differences in responses to stress may clarify *how* and *why* stressful events contribute to emotional/behavioral problems in younger age groups. Sources of vulnerability can lie either in the individual or in the environment and may operate independently or in an additive or interactive fashion. In examining the notion of vulnerability, it is important to attend also to the related concept of resilience or stress resistance (Anthony & Cohler, 1987; Cowen & Work, 1988; Masten & Garmezy, 1985). That is, in the process of identifying a group of youngsters who are adversely affected by stress, researchers will simultaneously identify a group who are less negatively affected by stress. For any given aspect of the individual or the environment, one extreme of this variable may represent a source of vulnerability, whereas the other extreme may represent a source of protection from or resistance to stress.

Research concerned with vulnerability to stress has examined a wide range of factors, including the effects of poverty (e.g., Pianta, Egeland, & Sroufe, in press; Rutter & Madge, 1976), psychopathology of a parent (e.g., Beardslee, Bemporad, Keller, & Klerman, 1983; Cytryn, McKnew, Zahn-Waxler, & Gershon, 1986), parental abuse (e.g., Egeland, Breitenbucher, & Rosenberg, 1980; Pianta, Egeland, & Erickson, in press), children's temperament (e.g., Chess & Thomas, 1984), and biological predisposition to a particular disorder (e.g., Gottesman, 1985). In our own work, we have focused on five possible sources of vulnerability: (a) coping strategies and styles, (b) age or developmental level, (c) gender and gender-related personal characteristics, (d) social-cognitive factors, including perceptions of personal competence, and (e) stress and symptoms experienced by family members. We have discussed coping processes in children and adolescents in detail elsewhere (Compas, 1987a; Compas, Malcarne, & Banez, in press; Compas, Malcarne & Fondacaro, 1988); therefore, we will focus here on the remaining four factors.

Developmental Level and Gender

In a cross-sectional study, we examined the frequency and intensity of stressful events as well as their association with emotional/behavioral problems as a function of age, gender, and the gender-related traits of instrumentality and expressiveness[2] (Wagner & Compas, in press). Self-reports of several subtypes of major and daily stressors and emotional/behavioral problems were obtained from samples of adolescents in junior high school (11- to 14-years-old), high school (14- to 18-years-old), and college (17- to 20-years-old). Females in all three samples reported more overall negative events than males. Further, early adolescent girls reported more negative events of an interpersonal nature than boys, including stressful events affecting others in their social network (network events) and stressors involving family, peer, and intimate relationships. Middle-adolescent females reported more network and intimacy stressors than males, and a trend was found for late adolescent females to report more network stress than males.

With regard to the perceived stressfulness of events, young adolescent females rated all types of interpersonal stressors as more stressful overall than did males. There was not an overall difference in middle adolescents' ratings of the stressfulness of events, although there was a moderating effect for expressiveness, with middle adolescents who were higher in expressiveness reporting events as more stressful. Among the older adolescents, females rated network and peer events

---

[2]In this study, we drew on the work of Spence and Helmreich (1978, 1980) in assessing self-reports of instrumentality and expressivity. Using the Personal Attributes Questionnaire (Spence & Helmreich, 1978), instrumentality was characterized by personal attributes such as independence and self-confidence, and expressivity was reflected in traits such as kindness and awareness of others' feelings.

as more stressful than males, but no differences were found as a function of expressiveness or instrumentality.

Although separate regression analyses indicated that a number of different types of stress were related to emotional/behavioral problems in each age group, stepwise analyses, in which the various types of stress were entered within a single equation, showed that different types of stressors were related to emotional/behavioral problems in the three age groups. Family stressors were the only significant predictor of maladjustment among young adolescents; peer stressors were the only significant predictor among middle adolescents, and academic stressors were the only significant predictor among older adolescents. These associations were not moderated by gender or levels of instrumentality or expressiveness.

Evidence regarding the role of expressiveness and instrumentality as sources of vulnerability and resilience during adolescence has also been reported by Towbes, Cohen, and Glyshaw (1988). Instrumentality was directly and inversely related to psychological distress in male and female junior high and high school students. Further, in a high school sample, instrumentality served a protective function against stress only for females, specifically in relation to interpersonal stressors. In contrast, instrumentality was a source of vulnerability to stress in junior high school girls, again in relation to interpersonal stress. These findings indicate that the role of gender-related traits as a source of vulnerability or resistance to stress may change with development.

Although research on the roles of gender and developmental level as sources of vulnerability to stress is at an early stage, the results of these two studies suggest that the number, intensity, and effects of stressful events may vary with age, gender, and the traits of instrumentality and expressiveness. The finding that junior and senior high school females reported more interpersonal stressful events than did males is consistent with the idea that adolescent females have a greater investment in interpersonal relationships than males (e.g., Marcia, 1981; Montemayor, 1982). Further, this suggests that the greater susceptibility of adult females (compared with males) to be adversely affected by network events (Kessler & McLeod, 1984) may have its roots in adolescence. Further, gender differences in perceptions of the stressfulness of events indicate that early adolescence may be a period in which females experience interpersonal events as especially stressful. The possibility that a single characteristic (e.g., instrumentality) may serve as a source of vulnerability in one age group and a source of protection in another age group is a particularly important focus for future research.

Social-Cognitive Factors

Cognitive models of stress and coping emphasize the importance of self-referent thoughts as important sources of vulnerability and resistance to stress. Specifically self-perceptions of competence may reflect the degree to which individuals believe they can successfully manage stressful events and the degree to which an event is experienced as stressful at all. Further, perceptions of competence in different life domains may result in different patterns of vulnerability to various types of stress across individuals.

To examine these possibilities, we analyzed the association between two types of stress, interpersonal and academic achievement stressors, and emotional/behavioral problems as a function of self-perceptions of social and academic competence in a sample of 10- to 14-year-olds (Compas & Banez, 1989). When children's self-reports of stress and emotional/behavioral problems were analyzed, the findings supported the role of domain-specific perceptions of competence as sources of vulnerability and resilience. Children who were vulnerable to only interpersonal stress (those who reported high emotional/behavior problems, high interpersonal stress but low academic stress) reported lower self-perceptions of social competence than children resistant to social stress (those who reported low emotional/behavioral problems, high social stress but low academic stress). Similarly children vulnerable only to academic stress (those who reported high emotional/behavioral problems, high academic stress but low interpersonal stress) reported lower self-perceptions of academic competence than children resistant to academic stress (those who reported low emotional/behavioral problems, high academic stress but low interpersonal stress). Further, children who were vulnerable to both interpersonal and academic stress reported lower self-perceptions of their global self-worth than children who were resistant to both types of stress. However, self-perceptions of competence did not distinguish systematically between vulnerable and resistant children when mothers' reports of children's emotional/behavioral problems were used to classify children as vulnerable or resistant.

These findings suggest that, at least with regard to children's self-reports of emotional/behavioral problems, children who experience high levels of behavior problems in association with high levels of stressful events in a particular domain are likely to feel less competent in that domain than children who experience similarly high levels of stress but who do not report high levels of emotional/behavioral problems. This pattern is consistent with the model of stress proposed by Lazarus and Folkman (1984) in which events will be experienced as stressful, if the individual believes that the event exceeds her on his personal abilities to cope; low levels of perceived competence appear to be reflective of the belief that one is incapable of managing stressful experiences in a life domain. Further, the finding that children who were vulnerable to both types of stress reported low levels of global self-worth is consistent with previous research indicating that vulnerable children are distinguished by, among other factors, low levels of self-esteem (Garmezy, 1985, 1987). Low levels of perceived competence may be associated with a tendency to perceive events as more threatening or stressful as well as with the use of less effective efforts at coping with stressful events. For example, children who perceive themselves as low in interpersonal competence may fail to use active problem-solving efforts in coping with interpersonal stress.

The use of problem-focused coping with interpersonal stressors has been shown to be associated with lower levels of maladjustment in children (Compas et al., 1988); therefore, the failure to use this type of coping may be related to increased maladjustment in children who perceive themselves as low in interpersonal competence. These factors warrant attention in future research.

Family Factors

The studies discussed previously are useful in identifying characteristics of children and adolescents that predispose them to be vulnerable or resistant to stress. However, reflective of stress research in general, these studies have examined individuals' stressful experiences independent of stress and maladjustment in the lives of others in their social environment. A comprehensive model of stress needs to include the broader social context, particularly interpersonal relationships, in which individuals encounter and attempt to cope with stressful events. The family represents an especially important context for understanding stress in children and adolescents.

Whether and how parents' stressful events and psychological symptoms are related to children's adjustment has been the focus of considerable research. However, prior studies have been quite mixed in their findings, some finding an association between parents' stress and symptoms and levels of maladjustment in their children (e.g., Hammen, Adrian, Gordon, Burge, Jaenicke, & Hiroto, 1987; Holahan & Moos, 1987; Pianta, Egeland, & Sroufe, in press), and others failing to find support for these associations (e.g., Cohen, Burt, & Bjork, 1987). We concentrate here on two recent studies by our group that have addressed these issues (Compas, Howell, Phares, Williams, & Ledoux, 1989; Compas, Howell, Phares, Williams, & Giunta, 1989).

We first used cross-sectional data from a sample of 211 young adolescents and their parents in two-parent families to test a model of stress and symptom processes in families (Compas, Howell, Phares, Williams, & Ledoux, 1989). We hypothesized that children would be indirectly affected by stressful events in their parents' lives. That is, a stressful event experienced by a parent should be related to a child's level of distress, if the event implies a significant level of threat to the child's personal well being and/or the functioning of the family as a whole. This level of meaning may not be apparent in the occurrence of the event but may depend on the parent's response to the stressor. If the parent displays little or no distress in response to the stressor, the child may perceive the event as relatively benign. However, if the parent displays symptoms of depression, anxiety, or other signs of psychological distress in association with the stressor, this may convey a high degree of threat to the child.

To test this hypothesis, we used structural equation analyses to examine the paths from mothers' and fathers' self-reported daily stressors and psychological symptoms to their children's self-reported emotional/behavioral problems. As hypothesized, both mothers' and fathers' daily stressors were related to their own psychological symptoms, but parents' stressors were not directly associated with their children's maladjustment. Partial support was found for the hypothesis that parents' symptoms would mediate the association of their stress with their children's adjustment, as fathers' but not mothers' psychological symptoms were related to children's self-reported emotional/behavioral problems. This pattern was consistent when separate analyses were conducted for boys and girls.

Associations of parents' stress and symptoms with their children's maladjustment were examined with this sample, again in both cross-sectional and prospective analyses, after additional data were collected on these families nine months later (Compas, Howell, Phares, Williams, & Giunta, 1989). Multiple regression analyses were used to test the significance of parental stress and symptoms as predictors of children's emotional/behavioral problems in cross-sectional analyses within both points in time, within the second point in time controlling for initial levels of maladjustment, and from the initial data collection to follow-up, again controlling for initial maladjustment. In all analyses, the predictor variables, in this case mothers' and fathers' daily stressors and psychological symptoms, were entered last in the regression equations to obtain the most conservative estimate of the unique variance accounted for by each predictor. In cross-sectional analyses at both time 1 and time 2, fathers' but not mothers' symptoms were a significant predictor of children's self-reports of internalizing behavior problems, explaining approximately 4% of the variance. Fathers' symptoms were also a significant predictor of total behavior problems at time 1 but were not related to externalizing problems at either time point. Further, neither fathers' daily stressors nor mothers' daily stressors or symptoms were significant predictors of children's self-reported problems in the prospective analyses within time 2 or from time 1 to time 2 after controlling for children's initial self-reports of maladjustment.

The consistent effects associated with fathers' but not mothers' symptoms was unexpected. These findings suggest that symptoms of fathers' psychological distress carried a different meaning than mothers' symptoms for children in this sample. Although mothers reported more psychological symptoms than fathers, mothers' symptoms may have been discounted in these families due to their higher frequency or lower "status" given to mothers within the family. In alternative, mothers may not have expressed their symptoms in a way that was as readily observable to their children as fathers. These findings differ from the results of studies of maladjustment in children of mothers with problems in the clinical range (e.g., Hammen et al., 1987). It is possible that mothers' symptoms must reach a higher threshold than fathers' symptoms before children are affected. Thus, in this nonclinical sample, mothers' symptoms failed to reach this threshold, whereas fathers' symptoms attained a lower necessary threshold to adversely affect their children.

When mothers' reports of their children's emotional/behavioral problems were used as the criterion, only mothers' self-reports of their own psychological symptoms were a significant predictor of children's maladjustment in the cross-sectional analyses, explaining from 3% to 7% of the variance. In the analyses at time 2 controlling for initial reports of child maladjustment, mothers' symptoms remained a significant predictor of both internalizing and externalizing problems, accounting for 3% of the variance. However, no parental variables were significantly related to mothers' ratings of children's maladjustment in the analyses from time 1 to time 2.

Other studies that have found an association between parental stress and symptoms and children's maladjustment have typically relied on adult informants for information about both the parent and child variables. For example, Holahan and Moos (1987) obtained reports from mothers on their own stress and symptoms as well as judgments of their children's maladjustment. Pianta, Egeland, and Sroufe (in press) found an association between maternal reports of stressful events and teachers reports of child behavior problems. However, associations between parental stress and symptoms and children's self-reports of emotional/behavioral problems have been rare, with the exception of cross-sectional data reported by Hammen et al. (1987) in a sample of children of depressed mothers. The differences in findings from studies using adult versus child reports of child maladjustment is a topic that we now address in greater depth.

IDENTIFYING RISK AND VULNERABILITY FACTORS IN CHILDREN AND ADOLESCENTS: IT DEPENDS ON WHO YOU ASK

The research reviewed previously indicates that understanding the role of psychosocial stress as a source of risk and vulnerability for emotional/behavioral problems is an important task for the field of developmental psychopathology. However, identification and measurement of the criterion variable of children's and adolescents' emotional/behavioral problems is not as simple as it may initially appear. There is no single, objective measure of childhood and adolescent emotional/behavioral problems that can be seen as representing the true indicator of maladjustment. Whether using the reports of children and adolescents, parents, observers, or clinicians, the definition of problematic behavior and, therefore, the types of behaviors that are reported depends on who you ask.

In order to comprehensively review the many individual studies that look at this issue, Achenbach, McConaughy, and Howell (1987) completed a metaanalysis of studies that obtained multiple perspectives on child and adolescent emotional/behavioral problems (e.g., ratings by parents, teachers, clinicians, observers, and children and adolescents themselves). They found that the mean correlation of ratings between similar informants (e.g., pairs of parents) was .60, between different types of informants (e.g., parent and teacher) was .28, and between children or adolescents and other informants was .22. Although all of these mean correlations were significant, this pattern suggested that informants in the same role tended to rate child and adolescent emotional/behavioral problems more similarly than informants in different roles, and more similarly than child or adolescent self-reports with other informants. There were also small but significant differences when type of problems and age of the child were analyzed. Associations between all types of informants were significantly higher for externalizing than internalizing problems, and correlations were significantly higher for 6- to 11-year-olds than for adolescents. This metaanalysis suggests that, although there are significant relations between different informants, there may be wide variations in their reports of child and adolescent emotional/behavioral problems.

In order to further delineate the associations between multiple informants of child and adolescent emotional/behavioral problems, we completed two studies that investigated the influence of situational specificity on informants in different situations and the role of parents' psychological symptoms on the association between parents' and children's reports of children's maladjustment (Phares, Compas, & Howell, 1989). In the first study, we found that teachers' and mothers' reports were modestly and independently associated with children's self-reported emotional/behavioral problems. This suggests that children's self-reports represent an independent perspective on their own behavior that is not a simple compilation of the reports of adults who observe them in different situations. In the second study, we found that mothers' and fathers' reports of their children's emotional/behavioral problems were moderately associated with parents' self-reports of their own psychological symptoms as well as with their children's self-reports of their emotional/behavioral problems. These findings were consistent with previous studies (e.g., Brody & Forehand, 1986; Schaughency & Lahey, 1985) that showed that parental perceptions of child behavior are a function of the combined influence of parental symptoms and child behavior. Additionally in both of these studies, high rates of disagreement were found when patterns of clinical identification were assessed (i.e., whether the ratings by each informant identified the child in the "clinical range"). These studies suggest that all types of informants, including children and adolescents, have an important and unique perspective in the assessment of child and adolescent emotional/behavioral problems.

Until relatively recently, there were few, standardized self-report measures of child and adolescent emotional/behavioral problems. In the area of stress research as well as in most other areas, reports by adult informants (e.g., parents) were most often used to assess children's and adolescents' maladjustment (e.g., Gersten et al., 1977). However, with the emerging trend toward multiaxial assessment of child and adolescent behavior problems (Achenbach, 1985), many stress researchers have begun utilizing child and adolescent self-reports of their emotional/behavioral problems (e.g., Cohen et al., 1987; Glyshaw et al., 1988; Siegel & Brown, 1988).

In general, it appears that in prospective studies, child and adolescent self-reports of stressful events are associated with their self-reports of emotional/behavioral problems, but they are not related to parents' or teachers' reports of childrens' maladjustment. Further, parents' reports of their own stress and psychological symptoms are more often associated with their reports of their children's maladjustment than with children's self-reports of distress. Although there have been exceptions in which parent and child stress and maladjustment measures have been associated across informants (e.g., Compas, Howell, Phares, Williams, & Giunta, 1989; Hammen et al., 1986), these have typically been in cross-sectional analyses.

This pattern of findings has led some researchers to call for the use of more objective indicators of child and adolescent maladjustment in studying stress, based on concerns about the effects of common method variance when children or parents are relied on for information about both stress and emotional/behavioral problems. We agree that it is essential to determine the extent to which the association between stress and maladjustment is due to methodological confounding between measures of these two variables. Failure to address this concern leaves open the possibility that stress-maladjustment relations are merely the result of individuals' response sets or that measures of stress and maladjustment actually reflect a single variable.

However, we do not believe that identifying more objective measures of either stress or emotional/behavioral problems is the answer to this problem. Although parents', teachers', and children's self-reports of child maladjustment are not highly related, this does not mean that these measures are invalid indicators of children's emotional/behavioral problems. Rather if reports from each of these respondents have been assessed with reliable measures, then they can be viewed as potentially valid reports of different individuals' *perspectives* of children's problems. In fact, it should come as no surprise that parents, teachers, and children have different perspectives on the types of emotions and behaviors that are experienced by children or that they differ on the degree to which certain behaviors are perceived as problematic. The perspective of each informant has substantial clinical importance and represents a target for change in preventive and remedial interventions. Therefore, risk and vulnerability researchers need to identify the variables that are significant predictors of each of these perspectives on child and adolescent maladjustment, with the expectation that a different set of predictors will be identified for each perspective.

If we are to accept the reports of parents, teachers, and children as important perspectives on stress and maladjustment, it is essential that our measures of each are validated against meaningful external criteria. However, it is unlikely that this will be accomplished by comparing reports of parents, teachers, and children with one another. Instead, we must use different methods to assess the perspectives of each informant and separate the portion of variance in each informant's report that is due to a particular assessment method. For example, assessment of

child and adolescent emotional/behavioral problems via questionnaires could be compared with the results of structured interviews concerning these problems. Similar methods could be compared in the assessment of stressful events. Comparisons of interview and questionnaire assessment of stressful events in college students and adults has indicated that they produce different findings, and this has not been examined in the assessment of child and adolescent stress (Hammen, Marks, Mayol, & deMayo, 1985).

A final issue of concern involves the types of problems that are assessed in our measures of emotional/behavioral problems. In a review and critique of studies of stress and disorder in adults, Depue and Monroe (1986) argued that most studies of adults have used broad measures of chronic distress and disturbance as the criterion rather than measures of specific disorders. They raise the concern that this has taken the field of stress research far away from its original focus (i.e., the prediction of specific disorders). Similarly the identification of individual differences in susceptibility to specific disorders has been a focus of research on vulnerability to stress in children (Masten & Garmezy, 1985). Thus, the use of measures of broad factors such as internalizing and externalizing behavior problems will result in a similar problem in younger age groups as well. However, the assessment of symptoms of more specific problems such as anxiety and depression in children and adolescents may prove to be problematic, as recent research has indicated that children's self-reports of these symptoms may reflect a more general factor of negative affectivity (e.g., Wolfe, Finch, Saylor, Blount, Pallmeyer, & Carek, 1987).

The prediction of specific disorders in any age group depends on consensus regarding the presence or absence of a disorder. In the assessment of child and adolescent disorders, there is not only disagreement among informants on whether a particular individual's problems are in the clinical range, but there is more fundamental disagreement on the types of disorders manifested by children and adolescents. For example, the narrow-band problem types identified on the three forms of the Child Behavior Checklist (CBCL, Achenbach & Edelbrock, 1983; Teacher Report Form, Achenbach & Edlebrock, 1986; Youth Self-Report, Achenbach & Edelbrock, 1987) vary across the different informants who complete the measures. This indicates that the nature and structure of disorder will vary as function of whose perspective is used. Thus, a different set of predictors are likely to be identified for parents', teachers', and children's self-reports of maladjustment, whether broad-band measures of chronic disturbance or indicators of specific disorders are used as the criteria.

The use of multiple criteria to define child and adolescent emotional/behavioral problems has certain implications for intervention programs designed to reduce risk and vulnerability associated with stress. Those programs that teach children to cope effectively with stress (Compas, Phares, & Ledoux, 1989) are likely to produce positive outcomes in children's self-reports of maladjustment but may not affect parent and teacher reports. In contrast, programs that enhance parents' coping skills are likely to show beneficial effects on parents' reports of children's problems but may not impact on children's self-reports. Comprehensive programs designed to affect children and those in their social environment may be needed to achieve broad effects in measures of children's maladjustment.

CONCLUSIONS

The research summarized previous indicates that stressful life events and chronic, minor stressful events and processes are important factors in the development and maintenance of emotional/behavioral problems in children and adolescents. Prospective longitudinal studies have shown that stress is a risk factor for subsequent maladjustment in younger age groups, and a number of characteristics of children and their environments have been found to moderate the association between stress and maladjustment, leading some children to be vulnerable to stress and others to display patterns of resilience when faced with high levels of stress.

These findings indicate that stressful events play a similar role during childhood and adolescence as they do at other points in the life span. Longitudinal research is needed to further delineate the developmental continuities and changes in the relation between stress and maladjustment. When attempting to identify risk and vulnerability factors in childhood and adolescence, it is particularly important for researchers to be cognizant of whose perspective is being used to identify sources of risk and vulnerability as well as the presence and degree of maladjustment in the individual. Different children and adolescents may appear to be at risk or vulnerable to emotional/behavioral problems when different informants are used. It is our belief that all of these perspectives are important to consider, as they may all lead us to the end goal of prevention of child and adolescent emotional/ behavioral problems, albeit through different avenues.

ACKNOWLEDGMENTS

Preparation of this chapter was supported in part by funds from the William T. Grant Foundation and National Institute of Mental Health Grant 1 R01 MH438919–01.

REFERENCES

Achenbach, T. M. (1985). *Assessment and taxonomy of child and adolescent psychopathology.* Beverly Hills, CA: Sage.
Achenbach, T. M., & Edelbrock, C. (1983). *Manual for the Child Behavior Checklist and Revised Child Behavior Profile.* Burlington, VT: Department of Psychiatry, University of Vermont.
Achenbach, T. M., & Edelbrock, C. (1986). *Manual for the Teacher's Report Form and Teacher*

Version of the Child Behavior Profile. Burlington, VT: Department of Psychiatry, University of Vermont.

Achenbach, T. M., & Edelbrock, C. (1987). *Manual for the Youth Self-Report.* Burlington, VT: Department of Psychiatry, University of Vermont.

Achenbach, T. M., McConaughy, S. H., & Howell, C. T. (1987). Child/adolescent behavioral and emotional problems: Implications of cross-informant correlations for situational specificity. *Psychological Bulletin, 101,* 213–232.

Anthony, E. J., & Cohler, B. J. (Eds.). (1987). *The invulnerable child.* New York: Guilford.

Beardslee, W. R., Bemporad, J., Keller, M., & Klerman, G. L. (1983). Children of parents with major affective disorder: A review. *American Journal of Psychiatry, 140,* 825–832.

Billings, A. C., & Moos, R. H. (1982). Stressful life events and symptoms: A longitudinal model. *Health Psychology, 1,* 99–117.

Brody, G. H., & Forehand, R. (1986). Maternal perceptions of child maladjustment as a function of the combined influence of child behavior and maternal depression. *Journal of Consulting and Clinical Psychology, 54,* 237–240.

Chess, S., & Thomas, A. (1984). *Origins and evolution of behavior disorders: From infancy to adult life.* New York: Brunner/Mazel.

Cohen, L. H. (1988). Measurement of life events. In L. H. Cohen (Ed.), *Life events and psychological functioning: Theoretical and methodological issues* (pp. 11–30). Newbury Park, CA: Sage.

Cohen, L. H., Burt, C. E., & Bjork, J. P. (1987). Effects of life events experienced by young adolescents and their parents. *Developmental Psychology, 23,* 583–592.

Compas, B. E. (1987a). Coping with stress during childhood and adolescence. *Psychological Bulletin, 101,* 393–403.

Compas, B. E. (1987b). Stress and life events during childhood and adolescence. *Clinical Psychology Review, 7,* 275–302.

Compas, B. E., & Banez, G. A. (1989). *Social-cognitive factors in vulnerability to stress in children and adolescents: The role of perceived competence and personal importance.* Unpublished manuscript, University of Vermont.

Compas, B. E., Howell, D. C., Phares, V., Williams, R. A., & Giunta, C. T. (1989). Risk factors for emotional/behavioral problems in young adolescents: A prospective analysis of adolescent and parental stress and symptoms. *Journal of Consulting and Clinical Psychology, 57,* 732–740.

Compas, B. E., Howell, D. C., Phares, V., Williams, R., & Ledoux, N. (1989). Parent and child stress and symptoms: An integrative analysis. *Developmental Psychology, 25,* 550–559.

Compas, B. E., Malcarne, V. L., & Banez, G. A. (in press). Coping with psychosocial stress: A developmental perspective. In B. Carpenter (Ed.), *Personal coping: Theory, research and application.* New York: Praeger.

Compas, B. E., Malcarne, V. L., & Fondacaro, K. M. (1988). Coping with stressful events in older children and young adolescents. *Journal of Consulting and Clinical Psychology, 56,* 401–411.

Compas, B. E., Phares, V., & Ledoux, N. (1989). Stress and coping preventive interventions with children and adolescents. In L. A. Bond, & B. E. Compas (Eds.), *Primary prevention in the schools* (pp. 319–340). Newbury Park, CA: Sage.

Compas, B. E., Wagner, B. M., Slavin, L. A., & Vannatta, K. (1986). A prospective study of life events, social support, and psychological symptomatology during the transition from high school to college. *American Journal of Community Psychology, 14,* 241–258.

Cowen, E. L., & Work, W. C. (1988). Resilient children, psychological wellness, and primary prevention. *American Journal of Community Psychology, 16,* 591–607.

Cytryn, L., McKnew, D. H., Zahn-Waxler, C., & Gershon, E. S. (1986). Developmental issues in risk research: The offspring of affectively ill parents. In M. Rutter, C. E. Izard, & P. B. Read (Eds.), *Depression in young people: Developmental and clinical perspectives* (pp. 163–188). New York: Guilford.

Depue, R. A., & Monroe, S. M. (1986). Conceptualization and measurement of human disorder in life stress research: The problem of chronic disturbance. *Psychological Bulletin, 99,* 36–51.

Egeland, B., Breitenbucher, M., & Rosenberg, D. (1980). Prospective study of the etiology of child abuse. *Journal of Consulting and Clinical Psychology, 48*, 195–205.

Garmezy, N. (1985). Stress-resistant children: The search for protective factors. In J. E. Steveson (Ed.), *Recent research in developmental psychopathology. Journal of Child Psychology and Psychiatry Book Supplement No. 4* (pp. 213–233). Oxford: Pergamon.

Garmezy, N. (1987). Stress, competence, and development: Continuities in the study of schizophrenic adults, children vulnerable to psychopathology, and the search for stress-resistant children. *American Journal of Orthopsychiatry, 57*, 159–174.

Gersten, J. C., Langner, T. S., Eisenberg, J. G., & Simcha-Fagan, O. (1977). An evaluation of the etiologic role of stressful life-change events in psychological disorders. *Journal of Health and Social Behavior, 18*, 228–244.

Glyshaw, K., Cohen, L. H., & Towbes, L. C. (1988). *Coping strategies and psychological distress: Longitudinal analyses of early and middle adolescents.* Manuscript submitted for publication.

Gottesman, I. I. (1985). The contribution of genetic factors to the common psychopathologies. In *The prevention of mental-emotional disabilities.* Resource papers to the Report of the National Mental Health Association Commission on the Prevention of Mental-Emotional Disabilities. Alexandria, VA: The National Mental Health Association.

Hammen, C., Adrian, C., Gordon, D., Burge, D., Jaenicke, C., & Hiroto, D. (1987). Children of depressed mothers: Maternal strain and symptom predictors of dysfunction. *Journal of Abnormal Psychology, 96*, 190–198.

Hammen, C., Marks, T., Mayol, A., & deMayo, R. (1985). Depressive self-schemas, life stress, and vulnerability to depression. *Journal of Abnormal Psychology, 94*, 308–319.

Hammen, C., Mayol, A., deMayo, R., & Marks, T. (1986). Initial symptom levels and the life–event–depression relationship. *Journal of Abnormal Psychology, 95*, 114–122.

Holahan, C. J., & Moos, R. H. (1987). Risk, resistance, and psychological distress: A longitudinal analysis with adults and children. *Journal of Abnormal Psychology, 96*, 3–13.

Johnson, J. H. (1986). *Life events as stressors in childhood and adolescence.* Beverly Hills, CA: Sage.

Kessler, R. C., & McLeod, J. D. (1984). Sex differences in vulnerability to undesirable life events. *American Sociological Review, 49*, 620–631.

Lazarus, R. S., & Folkman, S. (1984). *Stress, appraisal and coping.* New York: Springer.

Marcia, J. E. (1981). Identity in adolescence. In J. Adelson (Ed.), *Handbook of adolescent psychology* (pp. 159–187). New York: Wiley.

Masten, A. S., & Garmezy, N. (1985). Risk, vulnerability, and protective factors in developmental psychopathology. In B. B. Lahey & A. E. Kazdin (Eds.), *Advances in clinical child psychology* (vol. 8, pp. 1–52). New York: Plenum.

Monroe, S. M. (1982a). Life events and disorder: Event–symptom associations and the course of disorder. *Journal of Abnormal Psychology, 91*, 14–24.

Monroe, S. M. (1982b). Life events assessment: Current practices, emerging trends. *Clinical Psychology Review, 2*, 435–453.

Monroe, S. M., Imhoff, D. F., Wise, B. D., & Harris, J. E. (1983). Prediction of psychological symptoms under high-risk psychosocial circumstances: Life events, social support, and symptom specificity. *Journal of Abnormal Psychology, 92*, 338–350.

Monroe, S. M., & Peterman, A. M. (1988). Life stress and psychopathology. In L. H. Cohen (Ed.), *Life events and psychological functioning: Theoretical and methodological issues* (pp. 11–30). Newbury Park, CA: Sage.

Montemayor, R. (1982). The relationship between parent–adolescent conflict and the amount of time adolescents spend with parents and peers. *Child Development, 53*, 1512–1519.

Nelson, D., & Cohen, L. H. (1983). Locus of control and control perceptions and the relationship between life stress and psychological disorder. *American Journal of Community Psychology, 11*, 705–722.

Phares, V., Compas, B. E., & Howell, D. C. (1989). Perspectives on child behavior problems:

Comparisons of children's self-reports with parents' and teachers' reports. *Psychological Assessment: A Journal of Consulting and Clinical Psychology, 1,* 68–71.

Pianta, R., Egeland, B., & Erickson, M. (in press). The antecedents of child maltreatment: The results of the Mother–Child Interaction Research Project. In D. Cicchetti & V. Carlson (Eds.), *Developmental perspectives on theory and research in child maltreatment.* London: Cambridge University Press.

Pianta, R. C., Egeland, B., & Stroufe, L. A. (in press). Maternal stress and children's development: Prediction of school outcomes and identification of protective factors. In J. Rolf, A. Masten, D. Cicchetti, K. Neuchterlein, & S. Wentraub (Eds.). *Risk and protective factors in the development of psychopathology.* New York: Cambridge University Press.

Rabkin, J. G., & Struening, E. L. (1976). Life events, stress, and illness. *Science, 194,* 1013–1020.

Rowlinson, R. T., & Felner, R. D. (1988). Major life events, hassles, and adaptation in adolescence: Confounding in the conceptualization and measurement of life stress and adjustment revisited. *Journal of Personality and Social Psychology, 55,* 432–444.

Rutter, M., & Madge, N. (1976). *Cycles of disadvantage.* London: Heinemann.

Sarason, I. G., deMonchaux, C., & Hunt, T. (1975). Methodological issues in the assessment of life stress. In L. Levi (Ed.), *Emotions: Their parameters and measurement.* New York: Raven.

Schaughency, E. A., & Lahey, B. B. (1985). Mothers' and fathers' perceptions of child deviance: Roles of child behavior, parental depression and marital satisfaction. *Journal of Consulting and Clinical Psychology, 53,* 718–723.

Siegel, J. M., & Brown, J. D. (1988). A prospective study of stressful circumstances, illness symptoms, and depressed mood among adolescents. *Developmental Psychology, 24,* 715–721.

Spence, J. T., & Helmreich, R. L. (1978). *Masculinity and femininity: Their psychological dimensions, correlates and antecedents.* Austin, TX: University of Texas Press.

Spence, J. T., & Helmreich, R. L. (1980). Masculine instrumentality and feminine expressiveness: Their relationships with sex role attitudes and behavior. *Psychology of Women Quarterly, 5,* 147–163.

Swearingen, E. M., & Cohen, L. H. (1985). Life events and psychological distress: A prospective study of young adolescents. *Developmental Psychology, 21,* 1045–1054.

Thoits, P. A. (1983). Dimensions of life events that influence psychological distress: An evaluation and synthesis of the literature. In H. B. Kaplan (Ed.), *Psychosocial stress: Trends in theory and research* (pp. 33–103). New York: Academic Press.

Towbes, L. C., Cohen, L. H., & Glyshaw, K. (1988). *Instrumentality as a life stress moderator for early vs. middle adolescents.* Manuscript submitted for publication.

Wagner, B. M., & Compas, B. E. (in press). Gender, instrumentality, and expressivity: Moderators of the relation between stress and psychological symptoms. *American Journal of Community Psychology.*

Wagner, B. M., Compas, B. E., & Howell, D. C. (1988). Daily and major life events: A test of an integrative model of psychosocial stress. *American Journal of Community Psychology, 16,* 189–205.

Wolfe, V. V., Finch, A. J., Saylor, C. F., Blount, R. L., Pallmeyer, T. P., & Carek, D. J. (1987). Negative affectivity in children: A multitrait-multimethod investigation. *Journal of Consulting and Clinical Psychology, 55,* 245–250.

Children's Coping With Angry Environments: A Process-Oriented Approach

E. Mark Cummings
Mona El-Sheikh
West Virginia University

There is increasing interest in the application of a stress and coping perspective to research on children. Garmezy and Rutter's (1983) landmark volume called attention to this issue, and there has been increasing interest in this topic over the past several years. One approach to this issue uses questionnaires or more occasionally interviews to assess the effects of major life events and daily hassles in the family on parents and children. This research strategy has its origins in the adult literature on stress and coping (e.g., Folkman, chap. 1 in this volume) and is now being productively applied to research on adolescents and children and their families (Compas and Phares, chap. 6 in this volume; Compas, Howell, Phares, Williams, & Ledoux, 1989; Crnic & Greenberg, in press).

Relations between stressful events and negative outcomes have been found in children and adolescents (e.g., anxiety, suicide attempts, depression, and physical illness) (Compas, 1987; Compas & Phares, chap. 6 in this volume). A key finding is that everyday negative events, sometimes called daily hassles, appear to mediate the effects of major life events on psychological outcomes. For example, Compas and his colleagues (Compas et al., 1989; Wagner, Compas, & Howell, 1988) reported that, for adolescents, the correlations between daily stressors and psychological symptomatology were much larger than the correlations between major life events and psychological symptomatology. In addition, follow-up path analyses indicated that minor daily stressors mediated the observed relations between major life stressors and psychological symptomatology.

The demonstrated importance of daily stressors to child development outcomes suggests the value of approaches to the study of stress and coping that are relatively fine-grained and process-oriented. Another tradition in the study of stress and coping has focused on the effects of specific stressors. The actual responses of children to real stress events are frequently reported. Studies have examined children's responses to hospital admissions (Rutter, 1981), birth of a sibling (Dunn & Munn, 1985), separation from the mother (Garcia-Coll, Kagan, & Reznick, 1984), angry adult behavior (Cummings, Zahn-Waxler, & Radke-Yarrow, 1981), and achievement tasks (Diener & Dweck, 1980). A long history in research on infants and children has been concerned with children's responses to specific stressors (e.g., the attachment literature), although this work has only infrequently and recently been viewed as research on stress and coping per se.

There are exciting possibilities for the cross-fertilization of concepts, methods, and theory from these different approaches to stress and coping. Research based on global survey instruments can be integrative and may be particularly useful for clinical-outcome and developmental-outcome studies (Wagner et al., 1988). Studies of responses to specific stressors can yield more fine-grained and process-oriented analyses of the effects of stressors on children and should prove to be a useful complement to approaches based on more general analyses of daily hassles or major life events, particularly when these more global characterizations of stress and coping leave significant questions unanswered about the precise processes involved in child development outcomes. Certainly the development of instruments to assess daily hassles or major life events should be informed by studies of responses to important everyday stressors.

This paper focuses on an important and specific everyday stressor in the lives of most children: anger and discord within the social environment. Angry social exchanges are an important category of emotional expression within the family that may go a long way towards defining the child's perception of the emotional climate in the home. Other emotions may occur more often, but perhaps no other emotion has the potential to be so highly influential in shaping the child's perception of family life. There is emerging evidence that anger between adults, regardless of how it is expressed (e.g., verbally, the silent treatment, physically), remains a stressor for children throughout the age span of childhood and, thus, constitutes a significant category of stressful event in the lives of children. The focus of the present work is on discordant emotional climates or environments as background events initiated between adults and children's role in such social or family systems.

ADULTS' ANGRY BEHAVIOR AS A STRESSOR

Angry home environments are a common fact of American life. In 1984, over nine million minors were living in one-parent families due to divorce or separation (U.S. Bureau of the Census, 1985). Estimates suggest that as many as 20% of intact marriages can be classified as "distressed." Further, even in the most harmonious of marriages, there are moments of anger between parents. Thus, virtually all children are exposed to angry behavior between adults at times, and it is likely to be an everyday reality of family life for some children.

Studies from the last six decades indicate that children from angry home environments are at risk for the development of psychopathology, including behavior problems of aggressiveness and acting out and emotional disorders of depression and withdrawal (Baruch & Wilcox, 1944; Emery & O'Leary, 1984; Gassner & Murray, 1969; Hubbard & Adams, 1936; Johnson & Lobitz, 1974; Porter & O'Leary, 1980; Rutter, 1970; Towle, 1931; Wallace, 1935). Discordant conditions surrounding divorce, rather than the breakup of parents per se, appear to primarily account for certain adverse effects on children, particularly behavior problems and acting out disorders (Emery, 1988; Rutter, 1979). Although the issue is a complex one and not subject to easy answers, there is reason to believe that children may be better off in some cases after divorce, if the parents' breakup decreases the rate of exposure to anger and discord in the home (Hetherington & Camara, 1984). Family discord may also be a contributor to psychopathology in populations considered to be vulnerable primarily for other reasons. For example, exposure to high rates of anger and discord may be a factor underlying risk in children of parents with affective disorders (Emery, Weintraub, & Neale, 1982) and in children of alcoholic parents (West & Prinz, 1987).

Cummings and his associates have conducted a series of studies of children's responses to discord in the home and laboratory. Specifically this research has focused on children's responses to "background anger," that is, angry interactions between adults to which the child is initially a bystander. These studies of children's responses to adults' angry behavior provide direct evidence that adults' angry behavior stresses children. When confronted with angry interactions between adults, children respond behaviorally with distress (e.g., Cummings et al., 1981), identify these events as eliciting negative emotions (Cummings, 1987), show increased aggressiveness in subsequent play with friends (Cummings, Iannotti, & Zahn-Waxler, 1985), and evidence physiological responses indicative of heightened stress (El-Sheikh, Cummings, & Goetsch, 1989). Responses to anger are not uniform; pronounced age and sex differences in coping strategies and emotional response have been reported (Crockenberg, 1985; Vuchinich, Emery, & Cassidy, 1988), and there are also significant individual differences in styles of coping (Cummings, 1987).

Thus, evidence is accumulating to indicate that adults' angry behavior is a stressor for children and that exposure to high rates of anger has implications for children's development of styles of coping with stress. For example, Cummings, Pellegrini, Notarius, and Cummings (1989) found that children from homes in which there was a history of physical aggression between the parents displayed more distress and became more involved in angry interactions involving the mother than children that did not have a history of exposure to interparent physical aggression. In addition, marital dissatisfaction, without regard to parents' conflict tactics, was linked with greater preoccupation and concern/support seeking in response to anger.

In an effort to organize the complex array of results pertaining to children's responses to anger, Cummings and Cummings (1988) presented a framework for viewing children's processes of coping with adults' angry behavior. Specifically they proposed that children's coping with adults' angry behavior was a function of the following: (a) children's personal and social characteristics and their family history or background (e.g., sex, age, relative aggressiveness, history of exposure to marital conflict); (b) the context and stimulus characteristics of exposure to anger (e.g., relationship of the child to the angry adults, the form of expression of anger); (c) the type of stress and coping processes that were assessed (e.g., the level of analysis, the forms of responding assessed); and (d) the context in which outcomes occurred (the relative adaptiveness of responding within a particular social context).

In the next portion of this chapter, we consider several of the themes that underlie what Cummings and Cummings referred to as a process-oriented approach to the study of children's stress and coping with angry environments. Our hope is that the present treatment will further stimulate thinking towards more sophisticated methodologies and approaches for studying children's coping with marital and family discord. Following this we present a study examining the relations between children's styles of coping with anger and their styles of coping with another significant everyday stressor, separation from the mother. Research on everyday stressors has tended to focus on only one stressor at a time; this study offers an analysis of responding to two everyday and significant stressors in family life. The chapter closes with the consideration of several important directions for future research on children's coping with angry environments.

GUIDING THEMES FOR A PROCESS-ORIENTED STRATEGY

Although research has established that children from angry homes are at risk for certain negative socioemotional outcomes, there were, until recently, clear limits on what else could be concluded. In part, this reflects the inherent limitations of the research strategies that have been employed. Studies of discord and development have typically relied on global assessments of correlations between family background and child outcome, usually in clinic samples (Emery, 1982). This research strategy has significant, well-documented limitations (Atkeson, Forehand, & Richard, 1982; Hetherington & Camara, 1984; Kurdek, 1986). Only a relative handful of studies have used rigorous multimethod approaches to study relations between family development and the development of psychopathology in children (Belsky & Pensky, 1988; Cummings & Cummings, 1988). There is a need for further development of process-oriented approaches to the study of the effects of angry environments on children.

One step in this direction is to explicitly outline themes that describe a process-oriented model to research. There is no claim that what follows is exhaustive in this regard; the purpose is simply to convey more of a sense of this orientation to research and also to review recent findings as they pertain to a process-oriented perspective on children's coping with anger.

A Process-Oriented Focus

First, our work focuses on the study of complex processes of response as opposed simply to the study of global or "diagnostic" end results of exposure to anger (e.g., classifications of children as depressed, conduct disorderd, etc.). Specifically we are interested in examining multiple dimensions of responding: both different response dimensions and different levels of analysis. This includes emotional and social responses in observable behavior, self-reported emotional responses and behavioral dispositions, physiological responses of heart rate, blood pressure, and other such domains. We are also interested in the study of responding extended in time; this is likely to be of particular concern for clinical outcome studies. For example, are children more aggressive throughout the day following exposure to interparent anger? At another level, we are concerned with the meaning and interpretation of coherent patterns of responding, not just isolated response domains, which can give a limited if not distorted picture of response processes.

This approach contrasts with the focus on global outcomes that has historically characterized much research discord and child development. Diagnoses on standardized clinical instruments (e.g., the Achenbach Child Behavior Checklist) certainly identify that there is a problem but shed limited light on the how or why of children's difficulties. By now, it is well established that marital discord (e.g., Emery, 1982) and violence (e.g., Emery, 1989) are linked with behavioral and emotional problems in children. The next step is to trace the etiology and understand the mechanisms behind this association, and to specify the precise nature and characteristics of the response patterns that are affected. This can only come from a fine-grained consideration of response processes and their development.

Stress and coping research, pioneered by Susan Folkman and Richard Lazarus (e.g., Folkman & Lazarus, 1985), provides models for studying process as opposed to outcome (also see Folkman, chap. 1 in this volume). Folkman, Lazarus, Dunkel-Schetter, DeLongis, & Gruen (1986) defined a *process-oriented* strategy as focusing "on what the person actually thinks and does in a specific stressful encounter, and how this changes as the encounter unfolds" (p. 993). They further stated that "our concern with the process of coping contrasts with trait approaches, which are concerned with what the person usually does, and hence emphasize stability rather than change" (p. 993). Folkman, Lazarus, Gruen,

& DeLongis (1986) wrote that *coping* refers "to the person's cognitive and behavioral efforts to manage (reduce, minimize, master, or tolerate) the internal and external demands of the person–environment transaction that is appraised as taxing or exceeding the person's resources" (p. 572). Thus, coping is not a single response but a dynamic and extended-in-time part of the pattern of experiencing and responding to stress that includes multiple covert and overt responses of cognition, feelings, and behavior. Although some of these elements may correspond, they may also define independent aspects of response.

Responding may also be viewed at different *levels* of analysis, that is, in terms of strategies or higher-order coping styles (Fleming, Baum, & Singer, 1984). The message or goal that underlies complex response patterns may be a better predictor of general functioning than any discrete reaction or response. For example, although distress response to separation from parents in an unfamiliar setting exhibits neither test–retest stability nor predictive power, classification of attachment based on *patterns* of response to separation and reunion shows stability over time and predicts other aspects of social and emotional functioning (Bretherton, 1985; Sroufe & Waters, 1977).

Thus, stress and coping can be viewed in terms of multidimensional and multilevel aspects of responding. Integrating sometimes disparate information poses a challenge for research, but failing to note multiple aspects of response may lead to misleading results. For example, children who show no overt emotional response to anger actually report *feeling* angry during these incidents; in fact, these children are more likely to report anger than those who appear upset behaviorally during anger (Cummings, 1987). The fact that different sources of information conflict does not invalidate one or another source (Achenbach, McConaughy, & Howell, 1987). Instead, the inclusion of multiple sources of information offers the opportunity for more sophisticated characterizations of coping processes and individual organizations of these processes.

Developmental Time Course

Developmental continuity and change are fundamental issues for a developmental psychology of the effects of exposure to angry environments. Virtually every developmental study of children's response to background anger to date has reported age changes in responding (Cummings & Cummings, 1988). Aside from normative age changes in responding, trajectories of individual continuity and change of responding also must be considered, particularly for a developmental psychopathology of angry environments. The form of expression of psychopathology may change with age. Further, risk patterns may precede and be systematically related to later-developing psychopathology but may not be explicitly classified as abnormal responses at early ages (e.g., the case of depression, Rutter, Izard, & Read, 1986).

Typically very young children, that is, 1- to 3-year-olds, engage in what might be termed emotion-focused coping when confronted with anger between others; they appear almost entirely concerned with their own emotional response. Beginning at approximately age 5 children are much more likely to show problem-focused coping, which includes mediating or intervening in others disputes. The emergence of problem-focused coping is not strictly a stage-related issue, however. Although much less common in very young children, examples of certain problem-focused coping responses (e.g., distraction of the fighting parents or comforting distressed parents) have been reported in children as young as 1 year of age (Cummings et al., 1981). Further, children's history of exposure to anger in the home appears to interact with age in determining when responses emerge in development. Children with a history of exposure to physical expressions of anger between the parents (e.g., hitting, pushing) show a markedly higher incidence of problem-focused coping responses than other children starting at approximately 5 years of age (J. S. Cummings, et al., 1989); before this age, problem-focused is relatively uncommon regardless of family background.

A recent study of the responses of children as bystanders to others' conflicts found that children's problem-focused involvements in others' conflicts peaked at 13–15 years of age, declining notably at 17–19 years (Cummings, Ballard, El-Sheikh, & Lake, 1989). Middle adolescence may be a time of maximal intervention in the disputes of others, both in the family and elsewhere. This issue merits further study.

Individual Adaptation/Maladaptation

Another, related focus is on study at the level of individual adaptation and maladaptation. We found that individual differences in affective responsivity to anger in the home show stability even with a 5-year span between testings (Cummings et al., 1981; Cummings, Zahn-Waxler, & Radke-Yarrow, 1984). Cummings et al. (1985) found stability in affective responsivity to anger in the laboratory. These results suggest that individual differences in responding to anger may be robust but leave many questions unanswered about how these differences might be best characterized.

When looking for broad coherences in responding across multiple response dimensions, a difficult issue is where to enter the system. Where does one start to look for patterns of responding? We reasoned that emotional responses would provide an entree into broader organizations of coping processes, based on the assumption that emotions serve a primary organizing function for behavior and, therefore, should reflect broader organizations or patterns of coping with anger. We, thus, started with individual differences in basic characteristics of emotional response to anger and examined what other aspects of responding were associated with these differences in emotional response.

This approach has its foundation in a functionalist approach to emotions that has been cogently outlined by Campos (Barrett & Campos, chap. 2 in this volume) and by Bretherton (Bretherton, Fritz, Zahn-Waxler, & Ridgeway, 1986) and their colleagues. As Bretherton (Bretherton et al., 1986) wrote: "Emotions are conceptualized as important internal monitoring and guidance systems, designed to appraise events and motivate human action. . . . This view emphasizes emotions as organizers of personal and interpersonal life and of development itself" (p. 530).

Cummings (1987) identified three styles of coping with anger based on 4- to 5-year-old children's behavioral emotional responses to live simulations of anger between strangers. The basic groups of behavioral emotional response were distressed emotion, ambivalent emotion, and no emotional response. These patterns were further developed by examining links between basic emotional responses and aspects of self-reported response and social responses with peers, resulting in broader category descriptions. *Concerned* emotional responders showed distress during anger and said in later interviews that they wanted to intervene. They were most likely to report sadness, which might be seen as a form of empathy or alternatively could indicate that the child got caught up in the emotional flow of what s/he was witnessing. *Ambivalent* responders showed both positive and negative affect during exposure to anger. In later interviews, they reported strong feelings of emotional and behavioral arousal and showed increased social aggression towards peers in a subsequent play period. *Unresponsive* children showed no behavioral evidence of emotional response but later reported that they felt angry while the fight was going on. Cummings speculated that these patterns may correspond to more general styles of overresponding, underresponding and appropriate responding, and they may be associated with broader patterns of adaptive and maladaptive responding (see further discussion in Cummings & Cummings, 1988). Elements of these styles were also evident in responses to anger among these children three years earlier as toddlers. For example, ambivalent responders at age 5 had also showed the most post-anger aggression at age 2.

In an extension and replication of Cummings (1987), El-Sheikh et al. (1989) again examined behavioral and self-reported responses of 4–5-year-olds to anger between adult strangers and also collected data on aspects of physiological responding. Behavioral and self-reported responses of distress in reaction to adults' angry behavior were again found, and systolic blood pressure also increased. As in Cummings (1987), children's behavioral emotional responses to anger predicted other aspects of responding. The ambivalent group (actually more precisely an angry/ambivalent group, because some children evidenced anger as well as distress and positive effect in this instance) showed a complex heart rate pattern, including a decrease in heart rate with the onset of anger. Concerned children, on the other hand, showed a heart rate increase in response to anger. Both groups reported more emotional distress (mostly anger) than unresponsive children, and ambivalent children again verbalized the most behavioral arousal.

These results provide support for the existence of discrete patterns of responding to anger across multiple social, emotional, and physiological response dimensions and also some evidence for stability over time in response organization. Our speculation is that the ambivalent style, which is a style of high behavioral and emotional arousal coupled with increased aggressiveness immediately following exposure to anger, is linked with greatest risk for the development of behavior disorders at a clinical level, but this remains for future research to examine.

Context and Environment

Marital discord and anger are often treated in both professional and popular publications as if they were single response entities. In fact, anger and discord are not homogeneous stimuli but can vary on a variety of dimensions and domains. For example, there are differences in the mode of expression of anger. Anger may be expressed nonverbally, verbally, or physically. There are also differences in how angry exchanges are resolved or at least ended. From the child's perspective, the *way* parents fight or how they act towards each other *after* the fight is over may be just as important or more important as the frequency of conflict. The issue of the effects of the form and the social context of anger expression on children's responding to anger has been largely neglected in the marital discord literature but surely is of great importance.

In a first examination of children's responses to different modes of expression of anger, Cummings, Vogel, Cummings and El-Sheikh (1989) examined the responses of children between 4 and 9 years of age to videotaped segments of different forms of angry and friendly interactions between adults. The forms of expression of anger presented to children included nonverbal anger, verbal anger, hostile anger (anger with physical contact), unresolved anger (based on an interaction that began on a positive note but ended with anger between the adults), and resolved anger (based on an interaction that began with anger but ended with reconciliation and friendly overtures between the adults).

The results indicated that *all* forms of anger expression were perceived as negative events by children and elicited negative emotions in children; contrasts with control conditions of friendly interactions following the same themes and modes of expression of affect (e.g., nonverbal, verbal, verbal-physical) were consistently significant. Nonverbal anger was seen as just as negative as overt verbal expressions of anger and was noticed as such by children of all ages in this study. Anger involving physical contact, however, was clearly judged to be the most negative form of anger expression. A striking finding was that unresolved anger was perceived as a far more negative event than resolved anger and induced far greater feelings of anger and distress in children. In fact, resolution of anger seemed to largely ameliorate any negative impact of anger exposure.

Although this study showed that children do make distinctions between angry interactions as a function of the form of expression of anger, children were clearly far more affected by whether or not anger was resolved than by the manner in which it was expressed. This aspect of the context of exposure to anger clearly had a very strong influence on children's responses to anger and merited further study.

Cummings, Ballard, El-Sheikh, and Lake (1990) replicated and extended the previous study by conducting a more extensive analysis of the role of resolution in children's responses to adults' anger in a sample of 5- to 19-year-olds. Children were again presented with videotaped segments of angry and friendly interactions and asked questions concerning their responses. In Cummings, Vogel, Cummings, and El-Sheikh (1989), adults resolved their disputes through compromise. Other tactics for ending disputes are possible, including endings that are intermediate between resolution and nonresolution. In the present study, children's responses to conflicts with the following endings were contrasted: compromise, apology, letting the other adult win, changing the topic, continuing to fight, and the silent treatment.

Children's reactions to adults' conflicts were highly influenced by the extent of resolution of anger; responses were typically an inverse function of the degree of resolution of anger. Unresolved anger (continuing to fight, the silent treatment) was perceived as a more negative form of interaction, elicited more anger and distress, and was seen as requiring more additional involvement by both arguing adults and bystanders than resolved anger (compromise, apology). Partially resolved anger (letting the other adult win, changing the topic) typically resulted in responses within the range of those elicited by resolved and unresolved anger.

Little anger or distress was induced in children by conflicts when they ended with either compromise or apology, but children perceived that compromise more completely settled the substantive issues of the conflict than apology. In fact, apology was seen as a relatively "unfinished" resolution of the issues; the perceived need for additional adult and bystander involvement was comparable to that found for partial resolution conditions.

Adults were perceived as angrier when one adult won than when they changed topics, but in most other respects responses to the two partial resolution conditions were remarkably similar. One interpretation is that the level of resolution indicated by interactions, in this instance both endings indicated partial resolution, may in some cases outweigh the perceived negativity of events in determining children's *own* emotional and behavioral reactions. Similarly whereas adults' interactions were seen as somewhat more negative when they continued to fight than when they lapsed into the silent treatment, there were no differences in other response dimensions.

Cummings, Ballard, and El-Sheikh (1990) examined responses to different forms of expression of anger in children between 9 and 19 years of age. Categories of anger with destructiveness towards property and anger that was expressed as criticism of others but was not a direct verbal attack were added to the three categories studied by Cummings et al. All unresolved expressions of anger were perceived as negative events and elicited negative emotional responses. Further, the addition of physical contact again increased negative response; negative response was heightened when *either* people or property were the objects of physical aggression. Finally criticism elicited less negative response than other forms of expression of anger. One possibility is that children view indirect expressions of anger, such as criticism, as less threatening than direct attacks. In alternative, criticism may be seen as less intense or reacted to as constructive or true, in part.

The social relevance and implications of these findings for parents and others concerned with childrearing merit consideration. An instructive and perhaps hopeful message for parents is that, at least for verbal conflicts, the negative effects of exposure to adults' angry behavior appear to be almost completely ameliorated by a following resolution. Even partial resolutions as endings to conflict had significant beneficial effects and were clearly preferable to unresolved endings. Given that conflicts between parents are inevitable in some form (they are likely to be expressed nonverbally, if parents abstain from verbal expression) and may even be necessary to some extent for effective family functioning, the message would appear to be that parents should be more concerned about ensuring that they openly resolve their conflicts afterwards than with attempting the impossible and undesirable feat of avoiding all conflict. In fact, verbalized conflicts might be preferable to nonverbal or "held in" anger, because verbal anger allows for far more opportunity for the subsequent resolution of issues than anger expressed nonverbally. Another clear message for parents is that they should avoid physical expressions of anger. Children of all ages find such expressions of anger especially disturbing.

Consideration of the nature of anger expression in the home needs to be incorporated into research on the long-term effects of exposure to marital discord on children. Clearly habitual modes of expression of marital discord differ between families, and the implications of these differences for child development outcomes may be quite significant. For example, is aggressiveness in children most strongly induced by exposure to overt, hostile anger in the home? Do children respond differently to marital anger as a function of whether or not they have reason from past experience to expect a later apology between the parents after the fight is over? Do children show sensitization in families where yelling is the norm; that is, do reactions found in the laboratory persist over time in family settings? Issues pertaining to the context and environment of children's exposure to anger are significant concerns for future research consistent with a process-oriented approach.

Risk Groups and Normal Samples

The study of both risk groups and normal samples is a useful strategy for understanding the full range of effects of anger on children. Response to anger is transactional in the sense that the classes of persons as well as the classes of environmental events need to be defined before response tendencies can be predicted. The full range of response will only become evident when a range of populations or samples are studied, including children that might be expected to show atypical response patterns.

This point is vividly illustrated by recent research on responses to Ainsworth's Strange Situation paradigm (Ainsworth, Blehar, Waters, & Wall, 1978). A tripartite system for classifying response to separation and reunion in this context long seemed adequate until researchers examined the responses to this situation of children who had abusing/neglecting or depressed parents (Cummings, 1990). The study of these non-normal populations has made it clear that quite a range of responses to the Strange Situation other than the classic A, B, and C patterns could occur and that taking these other patterns into account could improve prediction of child development outcomes (e.g., Radke-Yarrow, Cummings, Kuczynski, & Chapman, 1985).

Individual differences among children in temperament, personality, or family background have been shown to predict differences in patterns of coping with angry adult behavior. For example, Zahn-Waxler, Cummings, McKnew, & Radke-Yarrow (1984) found that children of bipolar depressed parents were more likely than children of nondepressed parents to show affective disregulation as a result of exposure to adults' anger. Ballard and Cummings (1990) reported that children of alcoholic parents more often indicated a desire to intervene in the disputes of angry adult actors than children of nonalcoholic parents. Several studies have found that aggressive children are more reactive behaviorally and emotionally to anger (Cummings et al., 1985; Cummings, Vogel, Cummings, & El-Sheikh, 1989). For example, Klaczynski and Cummings (1989) compared the responses of aggressive and nonaggressive first- to third-grade boys to background anger. Aggressive boys reported feeling more highly aroused than nonaggressive boys and indicated that they would mete out more punishment to children in hypothetical stories. Finally discordant family backgrounds have consistently been associated with greater emotional and behavioral reactivity to anger (Cummings et al., 1981; J. S. Cummings et al., 1989; Cummings, Vogel, Cummings, & El-Sheikh, 1989).

Comparing the responses of risk and normal groups to adults' anger may also shed light upon the coping processes that mediate the occurrence and development of problematic behaviors. Further, the study of specific coping patterns may help discriminate between children at high risk for later disorder from those not at high risk, even within samples relatively likely to have difficulty in development (e.g., children of abusing/neglecting parents).

Buffers and Resilience Factors

Finally the concern with anger and discord as sources of difficulty for children should not cause researchers to neglect the existence and important role of buffers and resilience factors in even the most angry homes. Garmezy (Garmezy & Masten, chapter 8 in this volume) has lead the way in articulating this general issue for developmental and clinical research. In fact, Garmezy has argued that the notion of stress and coping focuses too much attention on psychopathology and negative outcomes in childhood, when typically children are successful in overcoming the challenges and stresses with which they are faced. As described elsewhere in this volume, Garmezy contends that the concept of "competence" may be more useful than stress and coping concepts that are more narrowly conceptualized for prediction of childhood outcomes as well as provide a more encompassing descriptor of the nature of children's response processes.

Relatively little work has been directed towards identifying factors that might buffer or protect children against the effects of background anger; this is surely an important domain for future research that merits emphasis. The quality of children's relationships or attachments to parents may figure in child outcomes in homes in which there are high levels of marital discord. If parents can maintain a secure relationship with their children, even when they are not getting along with each other, such relationships may buffer children to some extent from the negative impact of familial stresses (see reviews in Emery, 1982, 1988). Second, some patterns of coping with the stress of family discord may be more adaptive developmentally than others and, thus, might be viewed as a resilience factor. For example, children who respond with appropriate concern, without overresponding with aggressiveness or underresponding with denial and covert anger, might constitute one resilience group. A problem here, of course, is that our research suggests that appropriate levels of responding are less likely when there is a history of marital conflict; thus, resilient coping styles may be least likely when they are most needed.

PRESCHOOLERS' COPING INTERADULT ANGER AND SEPARATION

The study reported here, which is an extension of our concern with coping styles, is concerned with whether styles of responding to anger are related to classifications of responding to separation from the mother. The larger question is whether styles of coping with stress show consistencies or associations across multiple stress stimuli. Another interest was to compare the relative stressfulness of two important stressors of early childhood: adult's anger and separation.

Although the Strange Situation is typically thought of as a measure of the quality of mother–child attachment, it may also be viewed as a context for the observation of coping with stress (Compas, 1987). The stresses are the unfamiliar laboratory setting, interaction with a stranger, and, most importantly, separation from the parent.

Three main attachment or coping patterns have been identified: secure (B), insecure-avoidant (A), and insecure-resistant (C) (Ainsworth et al., 1978). The secure pattern is characterized by proximity seeking towards the mother upon reunion and may reflect successful emotional control (Compas 1987). The inse-cure-avoidant pattern is characterized by avoidance of the parent upon reunion and a seeming lack of concern regarding the mothers' absence during separation. The insecure-resistant pattern is characterized by high levels of distress during the parent's departure and angry resistance upon reunion.

In the absence of other work on this issue, this study should be regarded as exploratory. We expected that the children who exhibited what we regarded as the most appropriate response to anger (the concerned pattern) would also show the most appropriate response to separation/reunion (the B pattern), and that what we regarded as less adaptive responses to anger (ambivalent and unresponsive patterns) would be linked with less adaptive responses to separation/reunion (the A and C patterns).

Method

Thirty-four 4- to 5-year-olds (17 boys and 17 girls) and their mothers participated. For the separation/reunion procedure, the child and mother were seen in a labora-tory room. Toys were available for the child's play. After a 5-minute familiari-zation period, the mother left the child alone in the room. Three minutes later the mother returned.

For the background anger procedure, the mother and child were seen again in the same room. Social interactions were enacted by two female assistants follow-ing a rehearsed script with emphasis on projecting the desired emotions. The sequence of conditions was as follows: (a) no interaction, (b) friendly interaction, (c) no interaction, (d) angry argument, (e) no interaction, (f) reconciliatory interaction, and (g) no interaction. The background anger simulation, thus, lasted three minutes. These conditions are described in detail in El-Sheikh et al. (1989).

Following each procedure, children were interviewed. The first question con-cerned their emotional responses to conditions. Children were asked to point to a picture (identified sad, mad, happy, scared, or okay) that best represented their feelings during either the mother's departure or the angry interaction. The second question concerned what they wanted to do during conditions. The question was open-ended for the separation procedure and followed a multiple choice format for the anger condition (the child picked among cards showing responses of crying, playing, yelling at actors, hitting the actors, ignoring the actors, leaving the room, and having the actors make up).

Responses were time sampled every 30 sec. Virtually the same category system was used for each condition. Behaviors were coded by observers who were blind to the child's group classification in the other procedure. Interrater reliabilities for behaviors and pattern classification ranged from 80% to 100%. The negative emotional responses that were scored were: (a) Freezing—the child is tense and motionless for five or more seconds; (b) facial distress—the child's facial expression reflects anxiety and/or fear; (c) postural distress—"odd" bodily movement that may reflect anxiety (e.g., stereotypic movements or postural slumping); (d) verbal concern—the child expresses concern regarding the mother's departure (e.g., "Where were you mom?"); (e) crying or whining; (f) aggression—the child hammers a toy or throws objects; (g) searching—the child searches for mother after her departure (coded only for the separation procedure); (h) escape—the child tries to escape the actors' interactions (e.g., leaving the room) (coded only for the background anger procedure); (i) anger expression—the child looks mad while looking at actors (coded only for the background anger procedure).

For the separation/reunion procedure, children who greeted the mother and interacted positively with her during reunion were categorized *secure* (n = 16). Children who avoided the mother upon reunion were classified as *avoidant* (n = 16). Two children in the avoidant group also showed strong resistance and controlling behavior. All children in the avoidant group received at least a 4 on Ainsworth et al.'s 7-point avoidance scale (mean = 5.29, SD = 1.03). Patterns of response to anger were coded based on Cummings' (1987) system. The *angry/ambivalent* group (n = 15) included subjects who exhibited both distressed and positive emotional responses and/or anger. The *concerned* group (n=11) included subjects who only exhibited distress or concern. The *unresponsive* group (n=7) consisted of subjects who did not exhibit any emotional response.

Results

Patterns of responding to anger and separation/reunion were associated, X^2 (2) = 9.97, p < .01. Children who responded to anger with concern showed the highest incidence of secure responding in reunion (90% secure, 10% insecure-avoidant), followed by angry/ambivalent responders (47% secure, 53% insecure-avoidant) and unresponsive children (14% secure; 86% insecure-avoidant).

A MANOVA comparing negative emotional responses to conditions yielded a significant condition main effect, F (2,27) = 12.31, p = .0001. Anger elicited greater distress responding (mean—6.16, SD = 5.2) than separation (mean = 1.59, SD = 3.57). ANOVAs for individual categories of distress responding indicated that freezing, facial distress, and postural distress were significantly greater in reaction in anger than in reaction to separation (see Table 7.1).

A MANOVA performed for self-reported emotional responses also yielded a condition main effect, F (2,27) = 13.15, p < .0001. Planned comparisons indicated that children were more likely to report feeling mad in reaction to others' anger (mean = .53, SD = .51) than during separation from the mother (mean = .06, SD = .25), F (1,28) = 27.27, p < .0001. Differences in self-reported distress responding were not significant.

Finally an ANOVA compared the incidences of children reporting behavioral impulses indicative of arousal in response to the two stressors. The condition main effect was again significant, F (1,18) = 13.17, p < .005. Children were more likely to say that they wanted to yell, leave, hit others, and engage in other

TABLE 7.1
Responses to Separation and Adults' Angry Behavior

| Behavior | Separation | | Anger | | |
	Mean	SD	Mean	SD	F(1,28)
Freezing	.12	.55	1.41	1.95	11.99**
Facial Distress	.19	.64	2.63	2.58	29.14***
Postural Distress	.00	.00	1.22	1.88	12.82***
Verbal Concern	.34	1.13	.41	.50	.09
Crying	.22	.94	.03	.17	1.10
Aggression	.25	.80	.16	.63	.39
Escape/Search	.47	1.14	.31	1.18	.73

behaviors indicative of arousal in response to anger (mean = .68, SD = .48) than during separation (mean = .18, SD = .39).

Discussion

The main finding of this exploratory study was that children who showed what we view as the appropriate response to anger, that is, the concerned pattern, were significantly more likely to evidence secure response to reunion. Further, those who evidenced what we regard as relatively inappropriate responses to anger, either the angry/ambivalent or unresponsive patterns, showed a significantly greater incidence of avoidant response to reunion following separation.

These results suggest that appropriate styles of responding to stress may generalize across stress contests. However, responses to anger and separation were quite different in their organization, and the correspondences we observed were at the level of what we *interpreted* as optimal or not optimal responding. Further, there is currently not a widely accepted system for classifying responses to separation in 4- to 5-year-olds. Although it seems reasonable to expect avoidance to remain a problematic response to reunion at 4 to 5 years, this has not yet been firmly established.

Finally other's anger emerged, based on analyses of both behavioral and self-reported responses, as more stressful, for 4 to 5-year-olds than separation and was also more likely to induce aroused behavioral impulses. A methodological consideration is that self-reports of behavioral arousal may have been more difficult to obtain for separation because of the use of an open-ended procedure, in contrast to the multiple-choice format use for response to anger.

NEW DIRECTIONS FOR RESEARCH

In closing, I would like to identify several additional promising directions for future research:

1. Response to adults' angry behavior needs to be studied within the context of a broader family systems model. Multiple parameters may operate in angry environments and may have additive or interactive effects. Further, it is important to understand the relative significance of anger directed at the child and expressed by the child, as well as the role of angry events that the child observes between adults.

2. Research should be targeted towards identifying the mechanisms through which anger affects children (e.g., modeling, stress-induction, or sensitization). The processes through which children are buffered against the negative effects of angry environments and stress resilience are other important elements of a process model.

3. A long-term goal for research is to shed light upon bases for relations between marital and family discord and psychopathology in children. The research thus far suggests that sensitization to anger and perhaps stress more generally may underlie risk for the development of psychopathology as a result of chronic exposure to angry environments. Exposure to a family background of anger may have its greatest impact by increasing children's level of experienced distress and arousal, particularly in those already disposed towards high response. Specifically repeated exposure to anger may lead to lower thresholds for emotional disregulation and an undercontrolling pattern of coping with anger. If anger is a frequent occurrence in the home, this response pattern may become a salient segment of the child's behavior, particularly if an undercontrolling style becomes a part of the child's repertoire for coping with other stresses (see also Gottman & Fainsilber, 1989). A consequence over time of repeated exposure may be a gradual altering of coping strategies and styles towards overreactivity to anger in others and perhaps to stress in general. This in turn may set in motion a pattern of responding from others that increases the likelihood of aggression and persistent aggressive response. Repeated exposure to anger is unlikely in itself to lead to behavior problems but may act in concert with other factors to increase risk for later disorder. Although relatively little is known of the role of the context and stimulus characteristics of anger in this development, evidence suggests that physical anger between parents is particularly stressful; its occurrence in the home may, therefore, be especially significant in the development of undercontrolling response patterns. An important next step in this research is to get back into the home, where this line of research began initially, to further develop and examine the hypotheses suggested by recent laboratory-based findings.

Finally it is a natural part of life that individuals, including parents and family members, become angry. Within certain ill-defined bounds, exposure to anger between parents and others is unlikely to create difficulty for children and may even be a necessary experience in the development of adequate coping skills and abilities. However, cause for concern increases when these conflicts are frequent, very hostile, and are associated with the dissolution of marriages. Research on children's patterns of adaptive and maladaptive coping with anger should illuminate the development of children's abilities for coping with this common and naturally occurring event and increase understanding of the border between normal and pathogenic levels of anger in the home.

REFERENCES

Ainsworth, M. D., Blehar, M. C., Waters, E., & Wall, S. (1978). *Patterns of attachment: A psychological study of the Strange Situation*. Hillsdale, NJ: Lawrence Erlbaum Associates.

Achenbach, T. M., McConaughy, S. A., & Howell, C. T. (1987). Child/adolescent behavioral and emotional problems: Implications of cross-informant correlations for situational specificity. *Psychological Bulletin, 101*, 213–232.

Atkeson, B. M., Forehand, R. L., & Rickard, K. M. (1982). The effects of divorce on children. In B. Lahey (Ed.), *Advances in clinical child psychology* (pp. 255–281). New York: Academic Press.

Ballard, M., & Cummings, E. M. (1990). Response to adults' angry behavior in children of alcoholic and non-alcoholic parents. *Journal of Genetic Psychology, 151*, 165–173.

Baruch, D. W., & Wilcox, J. A. (1944). A study of sex differences in preschool children's adjustment coexistent with interparental tensions. *Journal of Genetic Psychology, 64*, 281–303.

Belsky, J., & Pensky, E. (1988). Developmental history, personality, and family relationships: Towards an emergent family system. In R. Hinde & J. Stevenson-Hinde (Eds.), *The interrelation of family relationships* (pp. 193–217). Oxford: Oxford University Press.

Bretherton, I. (1985). Attachment theory: Retrospect and prospect. In I. Bretherton and E. Waters (Eds.), *Growing points in attachment theory and research* (Society for Research in Child Development Monographs Series), *50*, 3–38.

Bretherton, I., Fritz, J., Zahn-Waxler, C., & Ridgeway, D. (1986). Learning to talk about emotions: A functionalist perspective. *Child Development, 57*, 529–548.

Compas, B. E. (1987). Coping with stress during childhood and adolescence. *Psychological Bulletin, 101*, 393–403.

Compas, B. E., Howell, D. C., Phares, V., Williams, R. A., & Ledoux, N. (1989). Parent and child stress and symptoms: An integrative analysis. *Developmental Psychology, 25*, 550–559.

Crnic, K., & Greenberg, M. T. (in press). Minor parenting stresses with young children. *Child Development*.

Crockenberg, S. (1985). Toddlers' reactions to maternal anger. *Merrill-Palmer Quarterly, 31*, 361–373.

Cummings, E. M. (1987). Coping with background anger in early childhood. *Child Development, 58*, 976–984.

Cummings, E. M. (1990). Classification of attachment on a continuum of felt-security: Illustrations from the study of children of depressed parents. In M. Greenberg, D. Cicchetti, & E. M. Cummings (Eds.), *Attachment during the preschool years: Theory, research and intervention* (pp. 311–337). Chicago and London: The University of Chicago Press.

Cummings, E. M., Ballard, M., El-Sheikh, M., & Lake, M. (1990). *Resolution and children's responses to interadult anger*. Manuscript submitted for publication.

Cummings, E. M., Ballard, M., & El-Sheikh, M. (1990). *Preadolescents' and adolescents' responding to different modes of expression of interadult anger*. Manuscript submitted for publication.

Cummings, E. M., & Cummings, J. S. (1988). A process-oriented approach to children's coping with adults' angry behavior. *Developmental Review, 8,* 296–321.

Cummings, E. M., Iannotti, R. J., & Zahn-Waxler, C. (1985). Influence of conflict between adults on the emotions and aggression of young children. *Developmental Psychology, 21,* 495–507.

Cummings, E. M., Vogel, D., Cummings, J. S., & El-Sheikh, M. (1989). Children's responses to different forms of expression of anger between adults. *Child Development, 60,* 1392–1404.

Cummings, E. M., Zahn-Waxler, C., & Radke-Yarrow, M. (1981). Young children's responses to expressions of anger and affection by others in the family. *Child Development, 52,* 1274–1282.

Cummings, E. M., Zahn-Waxler, C., & Radke-Yarrow, M. (1984). Developmental changes in children's reactions to anger in the home. *Journal of Child Psychology and Psychiatry, 25,* 63–74.

Cummings, J. S., Pellegrini, D., Notarius, C., & Cummings, E. M. (1989). Children's responses to angry adult behavior as a function of marital distress and history of interparent hostility. *Child Development, 60,* 1035–1043.

Diener, C. I., & Dweck, C. S. (1980). An analysis of learned helplessness: II. The processing of success. *Journal of Personality and Social Psychology, 39,* 940–952.

Dunn, J., & Munn, P. (1985). Becoming a family member: Family conflict and the development of social understanding in the second year. *Child Development, 56,* 480–492.

El-Sheikh, M., Cummings, E. M., & Goetsch, V. (1989). Coping with adults' angry behavior: Behavioral, physiological, and verbal responses in preschoolers. *Developmental Psychology, 25,* 490–498.

Emery, R. E. (1982). Interparental conflict and the children of discord and divorce. *Psychological Bulletin, 92,* 310–330.

Emery, R. E. (1988). *Marriage, divorce, and children's adjustment.* London: Sage Publications.

Emery, R. E. (1989). Family violence. *American Psychologist, 44,* 321–328.

Emery, R. E., & O'Leary, K. D. (1984). Marital discord and child behavior problems in a nonclinic sample. *Journal of Abnormal Child Psychology, 12,* 411–420.

Emery, R. E., Weintraub, S., & Neale, J. M. (1982). Effects of marital discord on the school behavior of children of schizophrenic, affectively disordered, and normal parents. *Journal of Abnormal Child Psychology, 10,* 11–24.

Fleming, R., Baum, A., & Singer, J. E. (1984). Toward an integrative approach to the study of stress. *Journal of Personality and Social Psychology, 46,* 939–949.

Folkman, S., & Lazarus, R. S. (1985). If it changes it must be a process; Study of emotion and coping during three stages of a college examination. *Journal of Personality and Social Psychology, 48,* 150–170.

Folkman, S., Lazarus, R., Dunkel-Schetter, C., DeLongis, A., & Gruen, R. J. (1986). Dynamics of stressful encounter: Cognitive appraisal, coping, and encounter outcomes. *Journal of Personality and Social Psychology, 50,* 992–1003.

Folkman, S., Lazarus, R. S., Gruen, R., & DeLongis, A. (1986). Appraisal, coping, health status, and psychological symptoms. *Journal of Personality and Social Psychology, 50,* 571–579.

Garcia-Coll, C., Kagan, J., & Reznick, J. S. (1984). Behavioral inhibition in young children. *Child Development, 55,* 1005–1019.

Garmezy, N., & Rutter, M. (1983). *Stress, coping, and development in children.* New York: McGraw-Hill.

Gassner, S., & Murray, F. J. (1969). Dominance and conflict in the interactions between parents of normal and neurotic children. *Journal of Abnormal Psychology, 74,* 33–41.

Gottman, J. M., & Fainsilber, L. (1989). Effects of marital discord on young children's peer interaction and health. *Developmental Psychology, 25,* 373–381.

Hetherington, E. M., & Camara, K. A. (1984). Families in transition: The processes of dissolution and reconstruction. In R. D. Parke (Ed.), *Review of child development research* (vol. 7, pp. 398–440). Chicago: University of Chicago Press.

Hubbard, R. M., & Adams, C. F. (1936). Factors affecting the success of child guidance clinic treatment. *American Journal of Orthopsychiatry, 6,* 81–103.

Johnson, S. M., & Lobitz, C. K. (1974). The personal and marital adjustment of parents as related to observed child deviance and parenting behavior. *Journal of Abnormal Child Psychology, 2,* 193–207.

Klaczynski, P., & Cummings, E. M. (1989). Responding to anger in aggressive and non-aggressive boys: A research note. *Journal of Child Psychology and Psychiatry, 30,* 309–314.

Kurdek, L. A. (1986). Children's reasoning about parental divorce. In R. D. Ashmore & D. M. Borzinsky (Eds.) *Thinking about the family: Views of parents and children* (pp. 233–276). Hillsdale, NJ: Lawrence Erlbaum Associates.

Porter, B., & O'Leary, K. D. (1980). Marital discord and childhood behavior problems. *Journal of Abnormal Child Psychology, 8,* 287–295.

Radke-Yarrow, M., Cummings, E. M., Kuczynski, L., & Chapman, M. (1985). Patterns of attachment in two- and three-year-olds in normal families and families with parental depression. *Child Development, 56,* 884–893.

Rutter, M. (1970). Sex differences in response to family stress. In E. J. Anthony & C. Koupernik (Eds.), *The child in his family* (pp. 165–196). New York: Wiley.

Rutter, M. (1979). Maternal deprivation, 1972–1978: New findings, new concepts, new approaches. *Child Development, 50,* 283–305.

Rutter, M. (1981). Stress, coping, and development: Some issues and some questions. *Journal of Child Psychology and Psychiatry, 22,* 323–356.

Rutter, M., Izard, C., & Read, P. (1986). *Depression in young people.* London: Guilford.

Sroufe, L. A., & Waters, E. (1977). Attachment as an organizational construct. *Child Development, 48,* 1184–1199.

Towle, C. (1931). The evaluation and management of marital status in foster homes. *American Journal of Orthopsychiatry, 1,* 271–284.

U.S. Bureau of the Census. (1985). *Current population reports,* Series P–23, No. 141. Child support and alimony: 1983. Washington, DC: U.S. Government Printing Office.

Vuchinich, S., Emery, R., & Cassidy, J. (1988). Family members as third parties in dyadic family conflict: Strategies, alliances, and outcomes. *Child Development, 59,* 1293–1302.

Wagner, B. M., Compas, B. E., & Howell, D. C. (1988). Daily and major life events: A test of an integrative model of psychosocial stress. *American Journal of Community Psychology, 16,* 189–205.

Wallace, R. (1935). A study of relationship between emotional tone of the home and adjustment status in cases referred to a travelling child guidance clinic. *Journal of Juvenile Research, 19,* 205–220.

West, M. O., & Prinz, R. J. (1987). Parental alcoholism and childhood psychopathology. *Psychological Bulletin, 102,* 204–218.

Zahn-Waxler, C., Cummings, E. M., McKnew, D. H., & Radke-Yarrow, M. (1984). Altruism, aggression, and social interactions in young children with a manic-depressive parent. *Child Development, 55,* 112–122.

8

The Protective Role of Competence Indicators in Children at Risk

Norman Garmezy
Ann S. Masten
University of Minnesota

Competence, coping, and *stress* have been viewed as interrelated constructs that enhance our understanding of the genesis and maintenance of adaptive or disordered behavior. Nevertheless, the frequency of their copairings vary markedly in the psychological and psychiatric literature. Over the past decade, "stress and coping" have achieved almost a paired associate status in book, chapter, and journal titles (e.g., Antonovsky, 1979; Holroyd & Lazarus, 1982; Lazarus & Folkman, 1984; Milgram, 1986; Roth & Cohen, 1986). In contrast, the linkage of "stress and competence," or "competence and coping" is far less common, an infrequency that suggests competence is the odd construct out and presumably of limited power in predicting adaptation to challenging circumstances.

In this chapter, we focus on competence as the central predictor of resilient behavior in children exposed to stressful events and trauma. We view levels of achieved competence as a powerful marker of resistance or vulnerability as well as a marker of development and prognosis for various psychopathological disorders. In order to support this position, we have divided this chapter into four segments: The first section examines the nature of competence and the efforts of several noted contributors to clarify the concept and its usage; the second segment describes the linkage of competence to adaptive functioning in children in the presence of severe stressful life events, with an emphasis on pervasive and chronic poverty; the third segment examines the relationship of competence to the prediction of recovery from psychopathology; and the fourth and final segment offers a comparison of the concepts of competence and coping and their comparative utility for *predicting* effective performance under stress.

Although not yet a large literature, there are an increasing number of studies that support the view that competence itself has a protective function, facilitating positive outcomes in children despite their exposure to markedly disadvantaging environments and events. Diverse studies attest to the potential power of competence, defined in terms of cognitive functioning, work, social exchange, and supportive familial patterns, as a predictor of resilience under stress. These studies include wide-ranging stressors such as poverty, foster home placement of minority children, escape from delinquent subcultures, the trauma of separation and loss, child abuse, divorce, parental psychopathology, the vicissitudes of war, the Holocaust, and so forth (see Garmezy, 1985; Garmezy & Rutter, 1985).

THE NATURE OF COMPETENCE

More than a half century ago, Jersild and Holmes (1935), in their classic monograph on children's fears, demonstrated the interrelatedness of stress responsivity and competence by engaging children in a variety of procedures designed to reduce their fearfulness in multiple emotion-evoking situations. Jersild (1946) later noted that the most effective procedures were those that "helped the child to gain increased competence and skill, aiding him in finding practical methods of his own for dealing with the feared situation, and helped him by degrees to have active experience with, or successful direct participation in the feared situation" (p. 768).

Specifically in these early studies, enhanced competence was the gateway for reducing children's fearfulness. Bandura's (1982) contemporary formulation of self-efficacy posits a mechanism by which this may occur: Perceived self-efficacy is enhanced by the successful execution of courses of action, which in turn heightens the probability of continued effective (i.e., competent) performance.

The Jersild study had an intervention cast. It left unanswered the broader question of how children of greater competence approach fearful situations: Are such children more adventuresome? More evaluative? Are they more prone to use different and varied problem-solving strategies? Do they tend to be more socially engaged? More achievement oriented? Do they recover more rapidly from fear-evoking situations? Studies analyzing children's behaviors in stressful situations may serve to answer such questions while revealing those substrates of competence that could facilitate prediction of survivorship in children confronted with highly trying circumstances.

One step in this direction is the growth of attention to the development of competence across the life span. Volumes have been published on the competence attributes of infants (Stone, Smith, & Murphy, 1973), toddlers (White, Kaban, & Attanucci, 1979), children (Connolly & Bruner, 1974; Kohn, 1977; Rathjen & Foreyt, 1980), adolescents (Dragastin & Elder, 1975), and adults (Holliday & Chandler, 1986; Wine & Smye, 1981), including the aged (Lieberman & Tobin, 1983; Schaie & Willis, 1986; Siegler, 1980; Windley & Scheidt, 1980). The accelerated growth curve of competence-related articles was documented in a 50-

year survey of the Psychological Abstracts (Garmezy, Masten, Nordstrom, & Ferrarese, 1979). In that earlier review, competence had to be subsumed under a variety of related terms; another mark of this surge is that now it stands alone as an ascriptor term in the Abstracts.

Measuring Competence

Competence is most broadly defined as the process of effectively dealing with the environment (adapting) so as to further the continued development of the individual, the family, or society. Over the years, different aspects of this process have been emphasized in theory and research. Competence has referred variously to the following: (a) manifest effectiveness of adaptation; (b) the *capacity* for effective adaptation, a trait-like concept (often inferred from a); (c) the motivational system underlying efforts to achieve effective interaction with the environment; (d) perceptions and evaluations by a person of their own effectiveness; and (e) knowledge or skills associated with effective adaptation (Ford, 1985, 1987; Garmezy et al., 1979; Phillips, 1968; Walters & Sroufe, 1983; White, 1959, 1960, 1979, 1987; Wine & Smye, 1981; Zigler & Glick, 1986).

Competence also has been subdivided by the domain or context in which it occurs and by more specific types of performance. Thus, over the decades, there have been treatises on *interpersonal competence* (Spitzberg & Cupach, 1989), *social competence* (Wine & Smye, 1981), *cognitive competence* (Carey, 1973), *communication competence* (McDevitt & Ford, 1987), *affective competence* (Harter, 1982), and *moral reasoning competence* (Trevethen & Walker, 1989).

Harter (1983) argued that children judge their own competence in general distinct domains including cognitive competence, physical competence, social competence, and the quality of self-esteem reflected in "general self worth." Further, Minton (cited by Harter, 1983) demonstrated that children use different sources of information to make judgments of other children in specific areas of competence. For example, physical competence can be inferred from the following: (a) peer preference to play on one's team, (b) evaluations of adult teachers and coaches, and (c) concrete abilities. In contrast, general self worth is often defined by children in the following terms: (a) parental relationships (being obedient and receiving parental approval), (b) the control of anger, (c) self-acceptance, (d) being able to get along with others, and (e) being helpful and good in school.

Studies of competent children have revealed a striking congruence of qualities associated with this construct across a diversity of children. Digman & Digman (1980) studied a cohort of children, broadly representative of Hawaii's ethnic mixture and principally drawn from a working and lower middle-class background, who were first seen in grades one and two. Teachers' judgments of the competence of the children revealed 11 factor scores: (a) friendliness; (b) intelligence; (c) ego-strength as reflected in adaptability, perceptiveness, and positive emotionality; (d) activity level; (e) dominance; (f) planful, purposeful, responsible behavior; (g) gregariousness; (h) relational insecurity (i.e., concern about acceptance); (i) compliance; (j) creativity; and (k) tension. These 11 factors were subsumed under three broad dimensions: Successful vs. Unsuccessful Socialization; Freedom vs. Restraint; and Emotionality—positive ("warm") versus negative ("cold").

These same authors examined specific competencies in college studies and identified "seven paths in competence development":

1. Heterosexual competence (dated occasionally or regularly)
2. Educational competence (had desired grades in high school)
3. Group membership (belongs to clubs and/or organizations)
4. Work skills (job history, earned money through work)
5. Social skills (invited to parties, elected leaders)
6. Intimacy (has friends including a "best friend")
7. Marriage and family (married, parent status)

These findings are similar to the research findings related to premorbid competence as predictors of recovery from psychopathology. In studies of mental patients, these included such life-history factors as prehospitalization social competence, marital status, achieved occupational level, employment history, intelligence, and education (Phillips, 1953; Zigler & Glick, 1986; Zigler & Phillips, 1961).

These paths reflect what other investigators identify as the developmental tasks of adolescence (Masten, 1988). Waters and Sroufe (1983), who defined the competent individual as "one who is able to make use of environmental and personal resources to achieve a good developmental outcome" (p. 81), suggested that to measure competence in a given developmental period, salient tasks for that period must be assessed by broad and multiple measures. The characteristics of the competent person and criteria for assessing competence may recur in study after study, because these criteria are closely linked to developmental tasks and expectations, values, and goals shared by many peoples in many cultures.

One cannot engage in a discussion of the concept of competence and efficacy without paying tribute to the contributions of Robert White that have extended over three decades (White, 1959, 1960, 1963, 1964, 1966, 1972). Recently, in *A Memoir*, White (1987) summed up these early contributions and his implicit life span developmental/motivational view of the construct of competence.

> In ordinary usage competence means fitness, capacity, skill. As a broad biological concept I intended it to refer to all those actions, at first playful and exploratory, later more serious and focalized, which tend to increase fitness, capacity, and skill in dealing with the environment. This includes behavior all the way from eye-hand

coordination, locomotion, (and) physical skills, to thinking, planning, building, and changing the world, a long curriculum in what can and cannot be done to our surroundings. To account for the persistence of such activity I considered that competence must be a motivational concept. (p. 52)

Beyond the underlying assumption of the biological bases for competence and the time trajectory of its relevance ("from eye–hand coordination . . . to building and changing the world"), White has emphasized two consequences that attend competent functioning in the course of development. One, *effectance,* is focused on the impact of the individual's actions on the environment; the other, *a sense of efficacy,* emphasizes the personal growth that followed upon repeated effectiveness in successfully meeting life's challenges. The latter, cumulative over time, provided the basis for the evolution of an individual's development of a sense of mastery and self-esteem.

Increasingly evident and repeatedly affirmed is the critical role for competence played by the child-rearing practices of parents, the familial attributes of the home in which the child is reared, and the opportunity structure of the broader environment. These constitute background variables that can foster or inhibit (in White's words) "the cumulative product of one's history of efficacies and inefficacies" that can serve as a "set" in meeting the demands of new situations.

White's views suggest that skills and self-beliefs are powerful contributors to one's actions and to probable outcomes, a point that Bandura (1986) made but with a somewhat greater emphasis on the role played by one's self-perception of personal efficacy:

Successful functioning requires both the skills and the self-beliefs that ensure optimal use of these capabilities. Because most efforts do not bring quick results, success requires robust self-assurance. Optimistic self-reports of efficacy reduce stress reactions in taxing situations, as well as enhance motivation. This affective benefit not only spares wear and tear on the viscera, but it lessens the likelihood that performances will be impaired by disruptive arousal. (p. 226)

For Bandura, there are four principal sources of self-efficacy: (a) *performance attainments,* (b) *the vicarious experiences derived from observing others,* (c) *verbal persuasion,* and (d) *the existent physiological state of the individual.* In our view, the least equivocal of these are performance attainments; success raises efficacy appraisals, failures diminish them. Vicarious experiences provide only limited certainties as to one's comparative abilities; "pursuasory means" are unlikely to induce long-term boosts in self-efficacy, and one's physiological status can provide mixed messages about the readiness to succeed or fail in meeting necessary performance standards. It would appear that evidence of actual *attainments* provide the most powerful source for judgments of one's self-efficacy, just as others often infer the capacity for competence from behavioral evidence.

In our own research program, we have focused on manifest competence in relation to resources, stressors, and vulnerability or protective factors. We have defined competence in terms of effective functioning in the environment as reflected in developmental tasks and in the judgments of observers (such as parents, teachers, and peers) in salient contexts for adjustment of school-aged American children (Garmezy, 1987; Garmezy, Masten, & Tellegen, 1984; Masten, 1989; Masten, Garmezy, Tellegen, Pellegrini, Larkin, & Larsen, 1988; Pellegrini, Masten, Garmezy, & Ferrarese, 1987).

COMPETENCE AND POVERTY

The evidence of competence as a favorable prognostic sign for adaptation under conditions of risk is supported by its power in predicting outcomes under adverse living conditions, either in terms of responsiveness to stressful life experiences or disadvantaged socioeconomic status. Detailed evidence has been summarized elsewhere (Garmezy, 1985, 1987, 1989; Garmezy & Rutter, 1985). What follows are examples from studies of poverty and its consequences that support this contention.

One of the foremost examples of positive adult outcomes of children reared in poverty is provided by the longitudinal study of a cohort of children born on the Hawaiian island of Kauai in 1955, which has been documented in a series of books and articles by Werner and her colleagues (Werner, Bierman, & French, 1971; Werner & Smith, 1977, 1982). This investigation began in 1954 and has extended over more than three decades. The risk status of the Kauai cohort is best expressed in the authors' own words in the first volume (1971) of the study, *The Children of Kauai:*

> During the span of the months of pregnancy and the first decade of life, the reproductive and environmental casualties in this community amounted to about one-half of those conceived and about one-third of the live born. (p. 132–133)

In the second volume (*Kauai's Children Come of Age*), Werner and Smith (1977) wrote:

> A low standard of living, especially at birth, increased the likelihood of exposure to the infant to both early biological stress and early family instability. But it was the interaction of early biological stress and early family instability that led to a high risk of developing serious and persistent learning and behavior problems in both lower- and middle-class children. (p. 219)

The title of the third volume in the Kauai series, *Vulnerable but Invincible: A Study of Resilient Children,* best illustrates the thrust of the current chapter. These resilient children, constituting some 10% of the sample, had also been exposed to chronic poverty, high rates of prematurity and perinatal stress, and had parents of limited education—all factors that have been implicated in the lives of a majority of the original cohort who had subsequently developed serious learning and behavior problems. Despite their risk status, these children emerged in late adolescence and early adulthood as competent, able, and autonomous people. What characterized their histories?

Werner reported that this able subset had better relationships with their parents who were less frequently absent from the home, were supportive of their offspring, set rules and exerted discipline, and respected their children's individuality. Their patterns of family life were marked by cohesion and stability. The children, in turn, had better health histories, recuperated more rapidly when they were ill, and in childhood were more active, sociable, responsive, and autonomous. Among the girls, there were fewer teenage pregnancies and accidents. The resilient children were skilled in identifying and selecting positive models and were able to seek support from peers, older friends, teachers, ministers, and so forth.

In elementary school, they had better reading and reasoning skills, and used these effectively. Their interests were many as were their activities and hobbies. Werner stated (1989) that these skills provided a sense of pride and achievement that were helpful in adversity. Girls were more assertive and independent achievers. Personality measures of this subset of males and females reflected more nurturant, responsible, and achievement-oriented attitudes. All of these factors are indices of competence that may have served as protective factors when stressful circumstances, such as family conflict, arose.

When these resilient children grew to adulthood and married, as parents many have continued a transgenerational cycle of competence. Werner noted that the primary goal of these mothers for their children has been "the acquisition of personal competencies and skills." High achievement has been expected and independence stressed. Based on her preliminary analysis of her 30-year span of interview data, Werner found evidence of a continuity of competence; most individuals who had coped successfully with adversity in childhood and adolescence retained their competence in meeting adult responsibilities.

In a summary of the findings, Werner confirmed the results of other studies that detail the attributes of resilient children grown to adulthood: (a) dispositional qualities of intelligence, sociability, activity, and effective school-related skills; (b) cohesion and warmth of their families, and the supportive qualities of their parents and siblings; (c) the availability of external support housed in societal institutions, and in friends and family members who appreciated and reinforced the resilient child's and the adult's responsible behaviors.

These observations of competent children in poverty is a welcome antidote to the concept of a "permanent underclass." The latter suggests a hopelessness about the fate of children reared under very difficult conditions of economic and social disadvantage. In contrast, a recent ethnographic study (Williams & Kornblum, 1985) of children in poverty provides a chapter on "superkids" who have been reared by parents who have engaged in a long-term struggle to survive, yet have remained fully cognizant of their responsibility to provide as stable a home and as good an education for their children as possible.

The ethnographer's method is the case study, and in the (1985) passage following, many of Werner's resiliency factors are repeated by a young man of the black ghetto who speaks of his family:

> My family is great, they praise me when I do something right and let me hear it when I do something wrong. My father always expects the best from me and if I didn't do that, don't come home. My father, who was ready to graduate when he had to drop out to take care of his family, tells me, "The only way to make it is to get a good education!" Everyone in this house listens to what he says because he's right. My father always says, "Don't come home if you get left back." I never knew and nobody else knew what was going to happen if they got left back because nobody in this house ever got left back. He demands respect and gets it from all of us. He always told me, "Education first, basketball second," and still says that today. My father is one in a million because he treats me the same way I treat him, with respect and pride. (p. 17)

The small *N* studies of ethnography have a partial counterpart in the economically deprived backgrounds of a large sample of children reared in foster homes from early childhood to adulthood. The study is detailed in a volume titled *No One Ever Asked Us* (Festinger, 1983) that describes the outcomes in adulthood of 277 persons who, early in childhood, were placed in foster care in New York City and released when they were 18–21 years of age. Most of the group had received home placements ($N = 201$), but a substantial portion ($N = 76$) were placed in group settings. Further, placement instability and discontinuity was the lot of many of the children in the group. Of the home placement group, 68% had had three or more placements, typically between the ages of three and four. The group setting children had on average placement between 9–10 years of age. The primary reasons for placement included neglect (24%), mental illness of the primary care-giver (20%), parental inability to cope (12%), abandonment and desertion (12%), physical illness (8%), and death (6%). Only 2.5% of the cases of initial placement was due to the child's behavior. Most children, other than the sample who were placed in foster care during the same time period, were either adopted or returned to their homes. Unfortunately the available records did not indicate why similar placements were not achieved for these 277 children. For the most part, these children were neither physically nor cognitively handicapped. However, the time period of placement did coincide with New York State laws that deterred freeing children for adoption unless there was definitive proof of abandonment.

Festinger tracked these 277 children and "roughly" compared their adult accomplishments with those based on the results of a national survey of a subset of respondents of a similar age and the same sex conducted by the Institute of Social Research of the University of Michigan. (The limited ISR sampling of Blacks and Hispanics precluded ethnicity comparisons.)

Comparisons of the groups yielded levels of young, adult-age achievements, accomplishments, and education that were partially equivalent to that of young adults in the United States. This similarity extended to the number and degree of satisfaction with their friendships. The foster care group showed lower scholastic achievement, the employment rates of the two groups of males were similar for white respondents, lower for Blacks in the fostered group (with the larger contribution coming from the group home-reared males). No differences were evident between the group in their assessments of their health and symptoms status (e.g., headaches, loss of appetite, sleep difficulties, dizziness, nightmares, etc.). Self-evaluations were essentially similar, as were reports of a "sense of happiness." Their hopes and feelings were akin to their same-age counterparts.

Summing up her observations, Festinger questioned the assumptions and dread expectations that surround foster-cared children. Her cohort did not become "problem-ridden" adults; there has been no evidence of a generational repetition of foster care placement, no excessive dependence on welfare and public support. A recurrent theme heard by Festinger was their sense of never having been consulted, of never having been asked for their views—hence the title of the volume, *No One Ever Asked Us*. What these young men and women did exhibit was the generosity of reply, their willingness to cite their experiences, and to open themselves up to a study of their lives. In doing so, they hoped that their experiences and lives might prove to be of help to others.

To return to the prevailing viewpoint of presumed incompetence of those who have known poverty and stressful separations, Festinger (1983) contributed this closing appeal:

> In view of these results it behooves one to ask: Why do people tend to make dire predictions about those who have spent many years in foster care? Why is it when I casually inquired of others, the most common response was not positive, or even an "I don't know," but something on the order of "they're probably all a mess." In response I must pose some questions of my own. Is such a negative view tied to people's tendency to ascribe to all what may describe but a few? Is such a view bound to beliefs about the overriding import of blood relations for people's development? Is there a tendency to blame offspring for the inabilities and role-failing of biological parents? Why such a singular emphasis on vulnerability? Is there so little confidence in young people's capacities to come to grips with the reality that no one's world is perfect? Is there so little faith in the strength and resilience of children? (p. 253)

Finally a comment on the variations among families within the lower socioeconomic group. Long and Vaillant (1984) reported the results of a follow-up study of the Glueck and Glueck (1950) investigations conducted during the 1940s. The Gluecks' effort was a search to unravel the causes of delinquency in America. Their studies involved groups of white children whose families lived in the poorest sections of Boston. From this common disadvantaged economic background, they selected two groups of junior high school students (aged 12–16), one group already known to the police who had been sent to reform school; the other group had no police record. Both groups were matched for IQ, ethnicity, and resilience in high-crime neighborhoods.

When the group was approximately 47-years-old, a follow-up study was initiated, and data were collected from 87% of the original group of children. On follow-up, the adults in both groups were rated on socioeconomic measures, criminality indicators, and global mental health. In addition, the early family patterns provided for four categories reflected in the following: (a) *chronically dependent;* (b) *multiproblem;* (c) *nondependent, nonproblem;* and (d) *Class V* (lowest SES group) but *nondependent, nonproblem.*

By age 47, some men, who as children had been in the chronically dependent, multiproblem group, were similar in terms of income, employment, and global mental health to their counterparts whose families, when they were children, were categorized as nondependent and nonproblem. What factors distinguished those who had escaped the pattern of their families from those who failed to do so? Both childhood IQ and a measure of social, family, and school integration correlated with upward social mobility. Intelligence is an index of cognitive competence, and familial integration a protective factor against delinquent behavior and an evident correlate of competence.

Factors that led to Class V status of some families point to those risk factors that are negatively correlated with competence. These included alcoholism, antisocial personality disorder, schizophrenia, IQ below 80, and disabling physical illness. These are some of the correlates of later incompetence.

THE INTERRELATEDNESS OF COMPETENCE AND PSYCHOPATHOLOGY

It may seem somewhat anachronistic to examine the relation of competence and psychopathology, yet there exists a rather sturdy literature that relates levels of premorbid adjustment to onset or resistance to various forms of psychopathology, to patterns of symptomatology, and to the nature of outcomes (positive or negative) over the course of the disorder. Moreover, past and current competence data continues to be an important element in the diagnosis and classification of some mental disorders.

In the sense of long-term negative outcomes, schizophrenia dominates the psychiatric scene. Prior to the advent of effective drug intervention in the 1950s, long-term hospitalization for the disorder was an almost inevitable outcome.

Spontaneous remission was a rarity, intervention efforts were largely ineffectual, and the average stay in mental institutions for schizophrenic patients approximated 13 years.

Yet even prior to the development of effective pharmacotherapeutics (see the interesting story of *Chlorpromazine in Psychiatry,* Swazey, 1974), a curious variability in outcome was to be found in cohorts of diagnosed schizophrenics. These variations led to categorizations that distinguished cases of poor prognosis as *chronic, nonremitting, process,* or *nuclear,* from others marked by more positive outcomes as *acute, remitting, reactive,* or *schizophreniform* (Goodwin & Guze, 1979).

This variability long had been noted (Bleuler, 1924, Jaspers, 1913) and takes form today by distinguishing schizophrenia from schizophreniform as described in the current Diagnostic and Statistical Manual of Mental Disorders (DSMIII–R; American Psychiatric Association, 1987). More than outcome is implicated in the distinction. DSMIII–R cites "good premorbid social and occupational functioning" as one of four patient features to consider in making the diagnosis of "schizophreniform." Zigler and Glick (1986) recently summarized (see Table 8.1) aspects of earlier research findings that differentiated so-called "process" versus "reactive" cases. The interesting aspect of these variations lies in the longitudinal consistency of competence trajectories that culminates in the segregation of the two groups of patients. In the premorbid phase, the differentiation resided in markedly different levels of competence (Zigler & Phillips, 1961). The contents of this differentiation were based on six biographical variables: age prior to onset of the disorder, intelligence, education, occupation, employment history, and marital status. Zigler and Phillips perceived social competence to be a reflection of the individual's developmental-maturational level as adduced from the age-related tasks that had been successfully completed. The link to competent

TABLE 8.1
Distinguishing Features of the Process–Reactive Distinction
in Schizophrenia (From Zigler & Glick, 1986)

Criterion	Process Type	Reactive Type
1. Premorbid Adjustment	Poor; marked sexual, social, and occupational inadequacy	Relatively adequate prepsychotic social, sexual, and occupational adjustment
2. Onset of the Disorder	Gradual, with no identifiable precipitating stress	Sudden, with clear-cut precipitating stress
3. Age of Onset	Frequently in late adolescence	Generally later in life
4. Course and Outcome	Deteriorating course; poor prognosis	Good prognosis

functioning was viewed as one of being able either to successfully resolve life's problems or to successfully undo life problems that previously had been ineffectively solved (Zigler & Phillips, 1961). Such capabilities were reflected in the reactive patients by comparatively brief periods of hospitalization and a successful return to spouse, family, community, and employment.

By contrast, outcome for the typical process patient had a different cast. Although the prior course of deterioration that earlier characterized the process schizophrenic patient currently has been partially contained by effective pharmacotherapy, the blossoming of competent behaviors has not followed. The current pattern of rapid hospital discharge of chronic schizophrenic patients has not led to enhanced social, intellective, and work competence. Indeed such rapid discharge has contributed to the presence of the homeless on the streets of our great urban centers.

Interestingly even the expression of symptoms in the two groups of schizophrenic patients (not listed in Table 8.1) may convey different qualities of residual competencies. Recent studies have focused on distinguishing between *positive* and *negative* symptoms in the disorder (Andreasen & Olsen, 1982; Harvey & Walker, 1987). The former reflects a more florid and active cast as evidenced by delusions, hallucinations, bizarre behavior, and formal thought disorder. In contrast, negative symptoms seem to reflect a defect and deficit state as recorded by flattened affect, attentional impairment, poverty of speech, an absence of motivation, and a lack of pleasure and desire.

Evidence suggests that in keeping with the defect emphasis, negative symptom patients have made poorer premorbid adjustments (i.e., a lowered level of functional competence), have a poorer prognosis, and have more frequent and lengthier periods of hospitalization. Even younger and as yet nonchronic schizophrenic patients demonstrate a linkage of negative symptoms with poor social and instrumental functioning prior to hospitalization (Pogue-Geile & Harrow, 1987).

This relationship of premorbid functioning and recovery or escape from disorder is not confined to schizophrenia. Studies of other disorders, both child and adult, substantiate the power of this linkage. Higher competence levels tend to characterize those affectively laden disorders once specified as neurotic disorders such as anxiety neurosis, phobic neurosis, depressive neurosis, and so on. (American Psychiatric Association, 1968). Lower competence levels marked the schizophrenias and personality disorders (Phillips, 1968; Phillips & Rabinovitch, 1958; Zigler & Phillips, 1961). This differentiation is attributed, in part, to the higher developmental levels achieved by individuals as reflected in the internalization of societal rules and standards of conduct, and the arousal of social guilt when these are violated (Zigler & Glick, 1986).

Among the severe psychopathologies, as noted, the predictive power of premorbid competence is most striking in schizophrenia and its variants (i.e., process–reactive; schizophrenia–schizophreniform). Efforts at a similar diagnostic differentiation within the affective disorder cluster have proved less successful. An "endogenous–reactive" dichotomy has been formulated with the endogenous disorder marked by terminal sleep disturbance, severe depressed mood, psycho-motor retardation, weight loss, concentration difficulties, and unresponsiveness to positive environmental changes. By contrast, reactive (or neurotic) depression has been assigned to those conditions marked by an onset that follows an acutely stressful life event, which when terminated presumably is followed by a lifting of the depression (Andreason, 1982). However, the distinction has been found wanting. Endogenous depression can also occur in conjunction with stressful life events; distinct differences in symptomatology for endogenous and reactive depression are clouded, and reactive depression has lacked the degree of validity that has accrued to endogenous depression.

How then to evaluate the role of competence in the affective disorders? Here the comparisons are best made between depressed and nondepressed groups. There is a substantial literature that supports the hypothesis that measures of social skill do discriminate between depressed versus nondepressed adults (Lewisohn, 1974). Depressed children also show deficient social skills, impaired peer relation-ships, and reduced interpersonal problem-solving ability (Kennedy, Spence, & Hensley, 1989). Such children tend to show reduced assertiveness and heightened submissiveness, accompanied by a greater degree of isolation from peers and rejection by them. Puig-Antich and his colleagues (Puig-Antich, Lukens, Davies, Goetz, Brennan-Quattrock, & Todak, 1985) also reported social impairment in depressed children, with only a partial improvement in social competence follow-ing recovery from the depressive symptomatology. Wierzbicki and McCabe (1988) provided supportive data showing that even within a normal population, depressive symptoms are significantly related both to the parents' judgment of their children's social skills as well as to the self-ratings of perceived skills by other children.

Related to depression is the acute problem of adolescent suidicidality. Rubin-stein et al. (Rubinstein, Heeren, Housman, Rubin, & Stechler, 1989) evaluated risk and protective factors in a sample of potentially suicidal and nonsuicidal high school students. Risk factors included life stressors, environmental changes, family conflicts and emotional disorders, family and peer loss. Protective factors were reflected in positive family and peer relationships, family cohesion, flexible family rules, and so forth. Depression, even of a moderate degree, proved to be a significant risk factor. Problems of sexuality, loss, achievement pressures, and family suicidality increased thoughts of suicide and raised the risk of a suicide attempt. On the side of protectiveness were family support, peer friendship, and being integrated within the peer group. Reports of positive peer relationships (i.e., social competence) proved to be negatively related to suicidality.

Competence, defined in terms of academic achievement, social skills or peer acceptance, and adult ratings of good conduct, has been consistently linked to feelings of psychological well-being versus distress or depression, fewer symptoms on problem checklists, and more positive self-evaluations, as well as social skills and various cognitive assets (Blechman, Tinsley, Carella, & McEnroe, 1985; Ford, 1985; Masten, 1989; Pellegrini et al., 1987).

Cole (1990) submitted for publication an intriguing study of some 1400 elementary school children, linking together such competency domains as academic achievement, social behavior, physical attractiveness, positive conduct, and availability of support figures, with self-reports of depression and peer nomination measures. His findings suggest: (a) that competency in these various domains is negatively related to depression (as measured by the Children's Depression Inventory), (b) multiple incompetencies when cumulated are related to an increasingly high probability of depression, (c) conversely, cumulation of competencies has a beneficial effect in terms of reduced depression, and (d) incompetency is a more powerful indicator of depression scores than is competency.

Further, the relation of competence indicators to symptoms and prognosis suggests that processes underlying competence may be *protective* with regard to psychopathology. In the area of child abuse, Walker, Downey, and Bergman (1989) reported that children exposed to parental maltreatment in families of lower socioeconomic status were nevertheless aggressive and less likely to experience peer rejection, if they gave evidence of adequate interpersonal problem-solving competence. These findings, the author noted, suggest that adequacy of social cognition can modify risk for maladaptation in identifiable high-risk groups, although social problem solving may be an index of a broader protective mechanism, than one indexed by IQ scores alone (Pellegrini et al., 1987).

There is increasing evidence that IQ is a protective factor in regard to prognosis for conduct problem behaviors and delinquency. Masten et al. (1988) found that children with high IQ scores and exposed to high stress showed significantly less disruptive/aggressive behavior than did low-IQ/high-stress exposed children. However, if stress exposure was low, IQ level failed to predict disruptiveness. Huesmann, Eron, and Yarmel (1987) hypothesized, based on their 22-year study of aggression in three generations, that low intelligence increases the risk of aggressive behavior in early childhood and that subsequently aggressive behavior interferes with future intellectual development.

Consistent with these findings, Kandel et al. (1988), in a study of a Danish birth cohort, reported that children of severely criminal fathers who had avoided crime careers had, as adults, significantly higher IQ scores when compared with a similar high-risk group that had developed criminal behavior. Their scores were also higher when contrasted with those achieved by both criminal and noncriminal low-risk groups. White Moffitt, and Silva (1989) recently confirmed the findings of Kandel et al. (1988) in a prospective study of a New Zealand birth cohort. They found for both boys and girls that higher IQ was associated with less delinquency in adolescence for both high- and low-risk children and that a very high IQ may particularly help high-risk boys avoid delinquency.

Several protective mechanisms might be postulated to underlie the IQ factor.

School success may mediate this effect, yielding higher self-efficacy and self-esteem or better teacher and peer reputation, any of which in turn mitigate against antisocial behavior. On the other hand, IQ may be a marker of more ability to evaluate the consequences of one's behavior, to delay gratification, to contain impulses, and so on, an array of cognitive processes that may serve to contain aggression or to find smarter ways to deal with problems. Thus, intelligence and its underlying competence-related processes may reduce the risk of subsequent conduct disorders.

Significantly studies of young people who desist from delinquent behavior also suggest a powerful role for competence. Mulvey and Aber (1988), as well as other investigators (Blumstein, Farrington, & Moitro, 1985; Loeber & Dishion, 1983) noted the pattern of comparative inattention to the subgroup of delinquents who cease their antisocial behavior.

These "false positives" with respect to continuity to criminal behavior suggest that competence and deterrence are correlated. "Desisters" have been found to utilize greater resources including current job experience, work involvement, planning for future employment, accompanied by strategies for achieving these goals. Further, the social network for this group was marked by the presence of a small number of good friends and a sense of personal efficacy. Such positive qualities can be compared to early predictors of male delinquency as indexed by such risk factors as educational underachievement, lack of parental discipline, poor child-rearing practices, family criminality, and low family SES status accompanied by the low-competence attributes of the offspring (see Loeber & Dishion's, 1983, excellent review).

COMPETENCE, COPING, AND PROTECTIVE MECHANISMS

The studies cited previously attest to the stability and predictive power of work, social, interpersonal, and cognitive competence in predicting adaptation to stressors and recovery from episodes of mental illness. *Coping* variously refers to a particular subclass of individual behavior manifested under certain conditions (e.g., threat) or with certain functions (e.g., restoration of equilibrium, reduction of anxiety or fear, or reestablishing effective functioning in the environment). Coping usually refers to purposeful efforts by an individual to preserve or restore either the integrated functioning of the self or the quality of adaptation to the environment in the face of a significant challenge to survival (Coelho, 1980; Coelho, Hamburg, & Adams, 1974; Compas, 1987; Murphy & Moriarty, 1976). Thus, coping refers to a subclass of processes ultimately directed at attaining or regaining competence when adaptation has in some way been threatened. Unfortunately the origins and evaluation of the processes underlying such adaptation have been neglected in favor of the description and categorization of postevent coping behaviors.

Coping behaviors have been broadly and narrowly described. Adaptational processes are always contextually defined, therefore, specific responses usually derive from studies of specific threats. Wirtz and Harrell (1987), for example, studied the coping responses of crime victims, including such activities as "changed phone," "stayed home more," "don't go out alone," "bolt locks more," "carry or purchased a weapon," and so forth. Similar efforts have been made to identify coping strategies for doctor or dental visits in children (Curry & Russ, 1985; Hyson, 1983).

Such specific event-related categories can be contrasted with category sets of more generalized and presumably more transituational responses, such as coping aimed at altering the environment versus the self, or styles of coping (Band & Weisz, 1988; Compas, 1987; Lazarus & Folkman, 1984). Moos and Schaefer (1986) provided a tripartite set of behaviors termed appraisal-focused coping, problem-solving coping, and emotion-focused coping. Problem-focused coping, for example, is presumed to have three components: *seeking information and support, taking problem-solving actions, and identifying alternative rewards*.

Yet it is difficult to distinguish these components from any other type of instrumental behavior leading to more or less effective adaptation. Similarly appraisal-focused coping also has components clearly reflective of intellectual abilities underlying other classes of competent behavior, including *logical analysis and mental preparation, cognitive redefinition,* and *cognitive avoidance or denial*.

Moos (1974) also described the multiform psychological techniques that are available to assess adaptive behavior and the manner in which people handle major life crises and every day stressors ("hassles" in Lazarus's terminology). Moos asked three questions of these techniques:

1. How complex and how true to life is the stimulus situation confronting the subject?
2. What type of response must the subject make? How complex and "real" is it?
3. How complex and difficult is the analysis of the data required by the investigator? (p. 337).

These questions parallel the inquiries one makes of laboratory analogues in relation to real-life situations. Laboratory analogues can take the form of *subject analogues, stimulus analogues,* and *response analogues*. If all three appear to be veridical with real-life situations to which these generalizations are to be applied, then the laboratory and the real-world situation are in juxtaposition, and the generalization is capable of being sustained. If all three are essentially distant and artificial analogues, then any generalization from the obtained data must be appraised with the greatest caution. Thus, as is the case in some of the literature on coping, if hypothetical situations are used (a stimulus analogue), accompanied by multiple choice response categories (a response analogue), with individuals recreating the presumed stressor (a subject analogue), then (to use baseball parlance) the researcher has swung futilely generating three strikes, and the study should be retired.

Similarly dichotomizing coping responses made to situations and described as problem-focused versus emotion-focused, or categorizing social support as "emotional," "tangible," or "informational," may presume more precision than warranted or justified by these hypothetical divisions. The issue does not rest on the act of forming hypothetical categories but rather on the need to consider behavior under stress as a continuum that ranges from adaptability to maladaptability. The placement of an individual somewhere on such a continuum will require knowledge of the individual's history, the processes activated by numerous stressors, and the adequacy of the assessment methods intended to reflect such processes, and so on.

Additional problems are posed by current methods for measuring coping, among which is the issue of continuity and discontinuity in an individual's response to a stressor. Discontinuities can be a function of many variables: age changes, patterns of growth and development, transition points in development, cumulative stress experiences, shifts in economic or social danger, environmental or individual constraints at a given point in time, and so forth. These and other factors can and do alter the behavioral responses of individuals under stress and affect the reliability of systems presumed to categorize, in some fixed format, coping styles or methods.

Another criticism of the coping construct, as it is currently described in the literature, is its measurement as an after-the-event response. Research on the power of coping indicators in one stressful situation to predict responses in other stress situations is in short supply. In contrast, the competence/incompetence construct is a powerful predictor of the degree of efficacy with which one deals with stressful events, even prior to their occurrence. In this sense, coping is evanescent, whereas competence is stable. The former invites discontinuity by its unreliability and its lack of transituational generality; the latter ensures a reasonable likelihood of successfully measuring continuities or discontinuities in adaptation over time.

Of course, it is possible that the image of disagreement between coping and competence is more apparent than real. What Lazarus and Folkman (1984) described as coping *resources,* such as health and energy, positive self-regard, problem-solving skills, social skills, social support, and material resources, others would label as the correlates or the substrate of competence. Moreover, "coping," "stress resistance," and "protective mechanisms" are closely related ideas. Although coping focuses on the individual, the two latter terms refer more broadly to attributes, behaviors, or processes that yield better adaptation. Protective mechanisms are the processes by which threat to an individual is avoided, reduced, or ameliorated in its effect and subsumes actions that may be external and uncontrollable to the individual child (e.g., school changes that provide a new and effective teacher for the classroom, or removes a bully and reduces threat or foreboding in a child), or individual attributes (e.g., flexible or creative thinking in challenging new situations) and relationships (e.g., parental comforting of a child). The concept of protective factors and mechanisms may prove more useful than coping for identifying adaptational patterns in children, precisely because it accommodates a broader set of processes. Coping in a young child often may consist of signaling the caregiver who then steps into action; the child has triggered a protective process. The *parent* may be the agent of "coping strategies" on behalf of the child.

When Antonovsky (1979) wrote of "generalized resistance resources" (GRR), he referred initially to the following: (a) adaptability on the physiological, bio-chemical, psychological, cultural, and social levels; (b) profound ties to concrete, immediate others; and (c) commitment of the individual to institutional ties between the self and the total community. Here one cannot make the case for competence as *the* embracing construct, for the definition is too broad and encompassing. However, in that same volume (1979) on *Health, stress, and coping,* those GRRs, as Antonovsky identified them, appeared to be markedly similar to the resources and protective factors hypothesized to support competence under adversity in research on stress: (a) a preventive health orientation (i.e., the wisdom to avoid dangerous situations that can be debilitating); (b) the availability of material resources that accompanies higher social status (often as an antecedent or consequent of manifest competence); (c) good interpersonal relations including power, status, and the utilization of available services; (d) knowledge-intelligence; (e) ego identity. "Knowledge-intelligence," wrote Antonovsky (1979), "is the decisive GRR in coping with stress." Ego identity, for Antonovsky, is comparable to the Eriksonian composite of good mental health: constitutional quality, manifest capabilities, consistent roles, effective defenses, significant identification. In this elaboration, Antonovsky moved far beyond the coping construct to perceive a composite of those very elements that constitute the basis of efficacy and self-esteem.

Finally when Antonovsky evaluated good coping strategies, the tie to competence as the underlying substrate becomes evident. Rationality, flexibility, and farsightedness become the definition attributes, each of which reflects aspects of cognitive competence: Rationality implies accurate and objective assessments; flexibility, the ability to generate alternative solutions; farsightedness is the anticipation of consequences, and planful behavior on a longer-term basis. Such defining attributes bring us full-circle to the integrating construct of competence.

CONCLUSIONS

In this chapter, we review only a small portion of the evidence supporting the power of *competence* both as an integrative construct, as a marker of adaptational status, and as providing potential for recovery from the vicissitudes of development. Yet the adaptational and developmental processes underlying competence have not been well delineated. We believe this task, which will require the attention of many investigators, is a central one for developmental psychopathology (Cicchetti, 1990; Masten & Braswell, in press) and one that will yield better strategies of intervention and prevention.

The study of perturbations in competence, associated with stressful life events or normative developmental transitions, may provide a window to observe the processes of adaptation that underly competence. Recent attention to the long-neglected phenomenon of resilience in children at risk due to psychosocial disadvantage, ongoing disorder, or exposure to severe stressors has already yielded new insights and ideas on the processes that foster better adaptation in development (Garmezy, 1985; Masten, 1989; Rutter, 1990).

The linkage of competence to other constructs may also provide important avenues for inquiry about the interrelation of processes underlying adaptation. Coping, self-efficacy, perceived competence, and mastery motivation, for example, are constructs frequently related to competence. Rather than debate definitional differences, it might prove enlightening to examine more carefully the possible adaptational mechanisms underlying the linkage of these constructs in the competence family. Investigators such as Bandura (1977, 1982), Skinner (1990), and Harter (1985) carefully examined, both conceptually and empirically, subsystems of the competence process, in illuminating attempts to identify some of these mechanisms.

Evidence was discussed in this chapter linking competence to better premorbid functioning and recovery from psychopathology. There is a great deal to be learned about the relations of competence to psychopathology and to possible mechanisms that may underly this linkage. For example firstly, the constructs may be confounded. Definitions of mental disorder usually include either signs of internal adaptational problems as reflected in symptoms of distress, such as anxiety or depression, or significant problems with work, interpersonal relations, or other areas of expected social competence. Thus, some mental disorders might also be described as disorders of competence.

Secondly, a stable trajectory of competence may be temporarily disrupted by illness. If and when the mental disorder abates, recovery to a previous level of functioning may be possible, although some symptoms may produce other events that have lasting consequences for future adaptation (e.g., the destruction of a marriage or financial security, or the loss of a job with attendant financial insecurity).

Thirdly, in some cases, more competent children (or adults) may have bioge-netic, personality, and psychosocial attributes that provide the base for resistance to mental diseases or disorder. Alternative cases with better premorbid histories may simply be less genetically vulnerable to some of the most serious mental disorders such as schizophrenia or bipolar disorder.

Fourthly, psychopathology may also be related to lowered social competence through a disease process that impairs adaptational behavior. This may become evident early in childhood (e.g., autism) or at a later point in life (e.g., schizo-phrenia).

Finally we suggest that the study of protective mechanisms may be a broader approach to understanding processes that serve to buffer psychological adaptation or facilitate recovery than are traditional coping studies. Delineating these pro-cesses offers hope for improvements in programs and policies aimed at advancing the well-being of children deemed to be at risk.

ACKNOWLEDGMENTS

Preparation of this chapter was facilitated by grants from the William T. Grant Foundation, the National Institute of Mental Health, the University of Minnesota, a Research Career Award to N. Garmezy, and a McKnight–Land Grant Professo-rial Appointment of the University of Minnesota to A. S. Masten. Appreciation is expressed to Dr. Auke Tellegen, Coprincipal Investigator of Project Competence.

REFERENCES

American Psychiatric Association. (1968). *Diagnostic statistical manual of mental disorders, (3rd ed., DSM-II)*. Washington, DC: American Psychiatric Association.

American Psychiatric Association. (1987). *Diagnostic statistical manual of mental disorders (DSM-III-R)*. Washington, DC: American Psychiatric Association.

Andreasen, N. C. (1982). Concepts, diagnosis and classification. In E S. Paykel (Ed.), *Handbook of affective disorders* (pp. 3–11). New York: Guilford.

Andreasen, N. C., & Olsen, S. (1982). Negative vs. positive schizophrenia. *Archives of General Psychiatry, 39,* 784–788.

Antonovsky, A. (1979). *Health, stress, and coping.* San Francisco, Jossey-Bass.

Band, E. B., & Weisz, J. R. (1988). How to feel better when it feels bad: Children's perspectives on coping with everyday stress. *Developmental Psychology, 24,* 247–253.

Bandura, A. (1977). Self-efficacy: Toward a unifying theory of behavioral change. *Psychological Review, 84* (2), 191–215.

Bandura, A. (1982). Self-efficacy mechanisms in human agency. *American Psychologist, 37,* 122–147.

Bandura, A. (1986). *Social foundations of thought and action.* Englewood Cliffs, NJ: Prentice Hall.

Blechman, E. A., Tinsley, B., Carella, E. T., & McEnroe, M. J. (1985). Childhood competence and behavior problems. *Journal of Abnormal Psychology, 94,* 70–77.

Bleuler, E. (1924). *Textbook of psychiatry.* New York: Macmillan.

Blumstein, A. Farrington, D., & Moitro, S. (1985). Delinquency careers: Innocents, desisters, and persisters. In M. Tonry & N. Morris (Eds.), *Crime and justice: An annual review of research* (Vol. 6), Chicago: University of Chicago Press.

Carey, S. (1973). Cognitive competence. In K. J. Connolly & J. S. Bruner (Eds.), *The growth of competence* (pp. 169–193). London: Academic Press.

Cicchetti, D. (1990). A historical perspective on the discipline of developmental psychopathology. In J. Rolf, A. S. Masten, D. Cicchetti, K. Nuechterlein, & S. Weintraub (Eds.), *Risk and protective factors in the development of psychopathology* (pp. 2–28). New York: Cambridge University Press.

Coelho, G. V. (1980). Environmental stress and adolescent coping behavior: Key ecological factors in college student adaptation. In I. G. Sarason & C. D. Spielberger, (Eds.) *Stress and anxiety* (vol. 7, pp. 247–263). Washington, DC: Hemisphere.

Coelho, G. V., Hamburg, D. A., & Adams, J. E. (Eds.). (1974). Coping and adaptation. New York: Basic.

Cole, D. A. (1990). *Empirical support for a competency-based model of child depression*. Manuscript submitted for publication.

Compas, B. E. (1987). Coping with stress during childhood and adolescence. *Psychological Bulletin, 101,* 393–403.

Connolly, K. J., & Bruner, J. S. (Eds.). (1974). *The growth of competence*. London: Academic Press.

Curry, S. L., & Russ, S. W. (1985). Identifying coping strategies in children. *Journal of Clinical Child Psychology, 14,* 61–69.

Digman, J. M., & Digman, K. C. (1980). Stress and competence in longitudinal perspective. In S. B. Sells, R. Crandall, M. Roff, J. S. Strauss, & W. Pollin (Eds.), *Human functioning in longitudinal perspective* (pp. 219–229). Baltimore: Williams & Wilkins.

Dragastin, S. E., & Elder, G. H., Jr. (Eds.). (1975). *Adolescence in the life cycle: Psychological change and social context*. Washington, DC: Hemisphere.

Festinger, T. (1983). *No one ever asked us*. New York: Columbia University Press.

Ford, M. E. (1985). The concept of competence: Themes and variations. In H. A. Marlowe, Jr. & R. B. Weinberg (Eds.), *Competence development: Theory and practice in special populations* (pp. 3–49). Springfield, IL: Thomas.

Ford, M. E. (1987). Processes contributing to adolescent social competence. In M. E. Ford & D. H. Ford (Eds.), *Humans as self-constructing living systems* (pp. 199–233). Hillsdale, NJ: Lawrence Erlbaum Associates.

Garmezy, N. (1985). Stress-resistant children. The search for protective factors. In J. E. Stevenson (Ed.), *Recent research in developmental psychopathology: Journal of Child Psychology and Psychiatry Book Supplement No. 4* (pp. 213–233). Oxford: Pergamon.

Garmezy, N. (1987). Stress, competence and development: Continuities in the study of schizophrenic adults, children vulnerable to psychopathology, and the search for stress-resistant children. *American Journal of Orthopsychiatry, 57* (2), 159–174.

Garmezy, N. (1989). The role of competence in the study of children and adolescents under stress. In B. Schneider, G. Attili, J. Nadel, & R. P. Weissberg (Eds.), *Social competence in developmental perspective* (pp. 25–39). Dordrecht, The Netherlands: Kluwer.

Garmezy, N., Masten, A., Nordstrom, L., & Ferrarese, M. (1979). The nature of competence in normal and deviant children. In M. W. Kent & J. E. Rolf (Eds.), *The primary prevention of psychopathology: Promoting social competence and coping in children* (vol. 3, pp. 23–43). Hanover, NH: University Press of New England.

Garmezy, N., Masten, A. S., & Tellegen, A. (1984). The study of stress and competence in children: A building block for developmental psychology. *Child Development, 55,* 97–111.

Garmezy, N., & Rutter, M. (1985). Acute reactions to stress. In M. Rutter & L. Hersov (Eds.), *Child and adolescent psychiatry: Modern approaches* (2nd ed., pp. 152–176). Oxford, UK: Blackwell.

Glueck, S., & Glueck, E. (1950). *Unraveling juvenile delinquency*. New York: The Commonwealth Fund.

Goodwin, D. W., & Guze, S. B. (1979). *Psychiatric diagnosis* (2nd ed.). New York: Oxford University Press.

Harter, S. (1982). A cognitive-developmental approach to children's understanding of affect and trait labels. In F. C. Serafica (Ed.), *Social-cognitive development in context* (pp. 27–61). New York: Guilford.

Harter, S. (1983). Developmental perspectives on the self-system. In E. M. Hetherington (Ed.), *Handbook of child psychology: Vol. 4. Socialization, personality and social development* (pp. 275–385). New York: Wiley.

Harter, S. (1985). Competence as a dimension of self-evaluation. Toward a comprehensive model of self-worth. In R. L. Leahy (Ed.), *The development of the self* (pp. 55–121). New York: Academic Press.

Harvey, P. D., & Walker, E. E. (Eds.). (1987). *Positive and negative symptoms in psychosis: Description, research and future directions.* Hillsdale, NJ: Lawrence Erlbaum Associates.

Holliday, S. G., & Chandler, M. J. (1986). *Wisdom: Explorations in adult competence.* Basel: Karger.

Holroyd, K. A., & Lazarus, R. S. (1982). Stress, coping, and somatic adaptation. In L. Goldberger & S. Breznitz, (Eds.), *Handbook of stress: Theoretical and clinical aspects* (pp. 21–35). New York: The Free Press.

Huesmann, L. R., Eron, L. D., & Yarmel, P. W. (1987). Intellectual functioning and aggression. *Journal of Personality and Social Psychology, 52* (1), 232–240.

Hyson, M. C. (1983). Going to the doctor: A developmental study of stress and coping. *Journal of Child Psychology and Psychiatry, 24,* 247–259.

Jaspers, K. (1913). Kansale und verständliche zusammenhange zwischen schichksal und der psychose bei der demential praecox [Causal and rational connection between life experience and psychosis in dementia praecox]. *Zeitschrift für Neurologie und Psychiatrie, 14,* 158.

Jersild, A. T. (1946). Emotional development. In L. Carmichael (Ed.), *Manual of child psychology* (pp. 752–790). New York: Wiley.

Jersild, A. T., & Holmes, F. B. (1935). Children's fears. *Child Development Monographs, No. 20.*

Kandel, E., Mednick, S. A., Kirkegaard-Sorensen, L., Hutchings, B., Knop, J., Rosenberg, R., & Schulsinger, F. (1988). IQ as a protective factor for subjects at high risk for antisocial behavior. *Journal of Consulting and Clinical Psychology, 56* (2), 224–226.

Kennedy, E., Spence, S. H., & Hensley, R. (1989). An examination of the relationship between childhood depression and social competence amongst primary school children. *Journal of Child Psychology and Psychiatry, 30,* 561–573.

Kohn, M. (1977). *Social competence, symptoms and underachievement in childhood: A longitudinal perspective.* Washington, DC: Winston.

Lazarus, R. S., & Folkman, S. (1984). *Stress, appraisal and coping.* New York: Springer.

Lewisohn, P. M. (1974). A behavioral approach to depression. In R. J. Friedman & M. M. Katz (Eds.), *The psychology of depression: Contemporary theory and research* (pp. 157–178). Washington, DC: Winston.

Lieberman, M. A., & Tobin. S. S. (1983). *The experience of old age.* New York: Basic.

Loeber, R., & Dishion, T. (1983). Early predictors of male delinquency: A review. *Psychological Bulletin, 94,* 68–99.

Long, J. V. F., & Vaillant, G. E. (1984). Natural history of male psychological health. XI: Escape from the underclass: *The American Journal of Psychiatry, 141,* 341–346.

Masten, A. S. (1988). Toward a developmental psychopathology of early adolescence. In M. D. Levine & E. R. McAnarney (Eds.), *Early adolescent transitions* (pp. 261–278). Lexington, MA: Heath.

Masten, A. S. (1989). Resilience in development: Implications of the study of successful adaptation for developmental psychopathology. In D. Cicchetti, (Ed.), *The emergence of a discipline: Rochester Symposium on Developmental Psychopathology* (Vol. 1, pp. 261–294). Hillsdale, NJ: Lawrence Erlbaum Associates.

Masten, A. S., & Braswell, L. (in press). Developmental psychopathology: An integrative framework for understanding behavior problems in children and adolescents. In P. R. Martin (Ed.), *Handbook of behavior therapy and psychosocial science: An integrative approach.* New York: Pergamon.

Masten, A. S., Garmezy, N., Tellegen, A., Pellegrini, D. S., Larkin, K., & Larsen, A. (1988). Competence and stress in school children: The moderating effects of individual and family qualities. *Journal of Child Psychology and Psychiatry. 29* (6), 745–764.

McDevitt, T. M., & Ford, M. E. (1987). Processes in young children's communicative functioning and development. In M. E. Ford & D. H. Ford (Eds.), *Humans as self-constructing living systems* (pp. 145–175). Hillsdale, NJ: Lawrence Erlbaum Associates.

Milgram, N. A. (Ed.). (1986). *Stress and coping in time of war.* New York: Brunner/Mazel.

Moos, R. H. (1974). Psychological techniques in the assessment of adaptive behavior. In G. V. Coehlo, D. A. Hamburg, & J. E. Adams (Eds.), *Coping and adaptation* (pp. 334–399). New York: Basic.

Moos, R. H., & Schaefer, J. A. (1986). Life transitions and crises: A conceptual overview. In R. H. Moos (Ed.), *Coping with life crises* (pp. 3–28). New York: Plenum.

Mulvey, E. P., & Aber, M. (1988). Growing out of delinquency. In R. L. Jenkins & W. K. Brown (Eds.), *The abandonment of delinquent behavior: Promoting the turnaround* (pp. 99–116). New York: Praeger.

Murphy, L. B., & Moriarty, A. E. (1976). *Vulnerability, coping, and growth: From infancy to adolescence.* New Haven: Yale University Press.

Pellegrini, D. S., Masten, A. S., Garmezy, N., & Ferrarese, M. J. (1987). Correlates of social and academic competence in middle childhood. *Journal of Child Psychology and Psychiatry, 28* (5), 699–714.

Phillips, L. (1953). Case history data and prognosis in schizophrenia. *Journal of Nervous and Mental Disease, 117,* 515–525.

Phillips, L. (1968). *Human adaptation and its failures.* New York: Academic Press.

Phillips, L., & Rabinovitch, M. S. (1958). Social role and patterns of symptomatic behavior. *Journal of Abnormal and Social Psychology, 57,* 181–186.

Pogue-Geile, M. F., & Harrow, M. (1987). Negative symptoms in schizophrenia: Longitudinal characteristics and etiological hypotheses. In P. D. Harvey & E. Walker (Eds.), *Positive and negative symptoms of psychoses* (pp. 94–123). Hillsdale, NJ: Lawrence Erlbaum Associates.

Puig-Antich, J., Lukens, E., Davies, M., Goetz, D., Brennan-Quattrock, J., & Todak, G. (1985). Psychosocial functioning in prepubertal major depressive disorders. *Archives of General Psychiatry, 42,* 500–517.

Rathjen, D. P., & Foreyt, J. P. (Eds.). (1980). *Social competence.* New York: Pergamon.

Roth, S., & Cohen, L. J. (1986). Approach, avoidance, and coping with stress. *American Psychologist, 41,* 813–819.

Rubinstein, J. L., Heeren, T., Housman, D., Rubin, C., & Stechler, G. (1989). Suicidal behavior in "normal" adolescents; Risk and protective factors. *American Journal of Orthopsychiatry, 59,* 59–71.

Rutter, M. (1990). Psychosocial resilience and protective mechanisms. In J. Rolf, A. S. Masten, D. Cicchetti, K. Nuechterlein, & S. Weintraub (Eds.) *Risk and protective factors in the development of psychopathology* (pp. 181–214). New York: Cambridge University Press.

Schaie, K. W., & Willis, S. L. (1986). *Adult development and aging* (2nd ed.). Boston: Little Brown.

Siegler, I. C. (1980). The psychology of adult development and aging. In E. W. Busse & D. G. Blazer (Eds.), *Handbook of geriatric psychiatry* (pp. 169–221). New York: Van Nostrand Reinhold.

Skinner, E. A. (1990). Development and perceived control: A dynamic model action in context. In M. Gunnar (Ed.), *Self-processes in development. Minnesota Symposia on Child Psychology* (vol. 23), pp. 167–216. Hillsdale, NJ: Lawrence Erlbaum Associates.

Spitzberg, B. H., & Cupach, W. R. (1989). *Handbook of interpersonal competence research.* New York: Springer-Verlag.

Stone, L. J., Smith, H. T., & Murphy, L. B. (Eds.). (1973). *The competent infant.* New York: Basic Books.

Swazey, J. P. (1974). *Chlorpromazine in psychiatry: A study of therapeutic innovation*. Cambridge, MA: MIT Press.

Trevethen, S. D., & Walker, L. J. (1989). Hypothetical versus real-life moral reasoning among psychopathic and delinquent youth. *Development and Psychopathology. 1*, 91–103.

Walker, E., & Downey, G., & Bergman, A. (1989). The effects of parental psychopathology and maltreatment on child behavior: A test of the diathesis-stress model. *Child Development, 60*, 15–24.

Waters, E., & Sroufe, L. A. (1983). A developmental perspective on competence. *Developmental Review, 1*, 59–79.

Werner, E. E. (1989). High-risk children in young adulthood: A longitudinal study from birth to 32 years. *American Journal of Orthopsychiatry, 59*, 72–81.

Werner, E. E., Bierman, J. M., & French, F. E. (1971). *The children of Kauai*. Honolulu: University of Hawaii Press.

Werner, E. E., & Smith, R. S. (1977). *Kauai's children come of age*. Honolulu: The University Press of Hawaii.

Werner, E. E., & Smith, R. S. (1982). *Vulnerable but invincible: A study of resilient children*. New York: McGraw-Hill.

White, J. L., Moffitt, T. E., & Silva, P. A. (1989). A prospective replication of the protective effects of IQ in subjects at high risk for juvenile delinquency. *Journal of Consulting and Clinical Psychology, 57* (6), 719–724.

White, R. W. (1959). Motivation reconsidered: The concept of competence. *Psychological Review, 66*, 297–333.

White, R. W. (1960). Competence and the psychosexual stages of development. In M. R. Jones (Ed.), *Nebraska Symposium on Motivation* (pp. 97–141). Lincoln, NE: University of Nebraska Press.

White, R. W. (1963). Sense of interpersonal competence: Two case studies and some reflections on origins. In R. W. White (Ed.), *The study of lives* (pp. 72–93). New York: Atherton.

White, R. W. (1964). *The abnormal personality*. New York: Ronald.

White, R. W. (1966). *Lives in progress*. New York: Holt, Rinehart & Winston.

White, R. W. (1972). *The enterprise of living*. New York: Holt, Rinehart & Winston.

White, R. W. (1979). Competence as an aspect of personal growth. In M. W. Kent & J. E. Rolf (Eds.), *Primary prevention of psychopathology. Volume III: Social competence in children* (pp. 5–22). Hanover, NH: University Press of New England.

White, R. W. (1987). *Seeking the shape of personality: A memoir*. Marlborough, NH: Homestead Press.

White, B. L., Kaban, B. T., & Attanucci, J. S. (1979). *The origins of human competence*. Lexington, MA: Lexington.

Wierzbicki, M., & McCabe, M. (1988). Social skills and subsequent depressive symptomatology in children. *Journal of Clinical Child Psychology, 17*, 203–208.

Williams, T., & Kornblum, W. (1985). *Growing up poor*. Lexington, MA: Lexington.

Windley, P. G., & Scheidt, R. U. J. (1980). Person–environment dialectics: Implications for competent functioning in old age. In L. W. Poon (Ed.), *Aging in the 1980s* (pp. 407–423). Washington, DC: American Psychological Association.

Wine, J. D., & Smye, M. D. (Eds.). (1981). *Social competence*. New York: Guilford.

Wirtz, P. W., & Harrell, A. V. (1987). Victim and crime characteristics, coping responses, and short- and long-term recovery from victimization. *Journal of Consulting and Clinical Psychology, 55*, 866–871.

Zigler, E., & Glick, M. (1986). *A developmental approach to adult psychopathology*. New York: Wiley.

Zigler, E., & Phillips, L. (1961). Social competence and outcome in psychiatric disorder. *Journal of Abnormal and Social Psychology, 63*, 264–271.

IV

ADOLESCENCE

9

Understanding Coping Within Adolescence: Ego Development and Coping Strategies

Stuart T. Hauser
Harvard Medical School

Emily H. Borman
Harvard Medical School

Mary K. Bowlds

Sally I. Powers
University of Massachusetts, Amherst

Alan M. Jacobson
Harvard Medical School

Gil G. Noam
Harvard Medical School

Kristen Knoebber
Virginia Commonwealth University

The adolescent phase of the life cycle refers to a complex terrain of intersecting biological, intrapsychic, and social forces that together contribute to significant transformations in individual development. These varied forces lead to a *diversity* of developmental paths and coping patterns in adolescence. As numerous investigators have pointed out, significant biological changes usually occur during the early years of adolescence, often influencing other aspects of adolescent development (Brooks-Gunn, Petersen, & Eichorn, 1985; Petersen, 1988; Petersen & Spiga, 1982). Our vantage point is that besides these biologically defined aspects of adolescence, another way to understand this developmental era is with respect to individual differences among adolescents along the lines of impulse control, as well as cognitive and interpersonal style, dimensions representing components of ego development (Loevinger, 1976).

We examine broad questions about ego development and coping during adolescence. How do levels and paths of adolescents' ego development influence their ways of coping during this phase of the life cycle? To what extent does adolescent coping, in early years, anticipate subsequent developmental paths. In this chapter, drawing from our ongoing study of individual development and family context in adolescence, we present conceptualizations and findings germane to these questions, as we focus on links between adolescent ego development and adolescent coping.

Adolescence can be disturbing for both the youth and his or her family, as new dialogues, tensions, and dilemmas surface, sometimes unexpectedly. Established familial patterns may shift under the influence of a spectrum of factors, including cognitive, biological, and social changes. Cognitive transformations are salient, as many adolescents engage more readily in abstract thought and delight in new logical analyses, opening the way to intricate reflections and questions regarding family relationships and traditions. Biological changes are often associated with body and self-image conflicts,[1] leading to new or intensified demands for parental assistance. Parental responses to these bodily and intellectual changes may reflect ambivalence or conflict.[2] Finally adolescent confusion over new social opportunities and competing or inconsistent sexual norms and behaviors is frequently expressed in terms of struggles over family rules and limits. When teenagers handle these changes successfully, they experience increasing clarity about themselves and future directions. We know that adolescents vary dramatically in how they cope with these powerful changes. The psychiatric literature abounds with examples of difficult passages from child to adult status.[3] However, there is evidence of *diversity* beyond labeled psychiatric patients. For many years, students of normal adolescents, such as Jack Block (1971) and Daniel Offer (1969), have drawn our attention to the striking variations in development during the teenage years. They have described a rich landscape of patterns, a landscape defined by important variations in impulse control, autonomy, and relationships with family and peers.[4]

The diverse ways that adolescents cope with these many-sided biological and contextual demands are shaped by individual and contextual factors. Among the most significant are: (a) the adolescent's level and path of socioemotional developmental and, (b) the family setting, including continuing relationships with parents, availability of parents, past identifications with parents, and the presence of parents as role models, in dyadic and familial interactions. In this chapter, we consider how adolescents' ego development may influence their coping style. Subsequent reports deal with the influences of parental ego development and family interactions upon adolescent coping.

THEORETICAL PERSPECTIVES
AND EMPIRICAL APPROACHES

Adolescent Ego Development

Our perspective on adolescent socioemotional development, based on the extensive theoretical and empirical work of Loevinger and her associates (Loevinger, 1976, 1985; Loevinger & Wessler, 1970), construes ego development as involving a series of qualitatively differing stages. Loevinger's approach is best charac-

---

[1]cf. Blos (1962), Petersen and Spiga (1982), Brooks-Gunn, Petersen, & Eicharn (1985).
[2]cf. Steinberg (1981), Steinberg and Hill (1978), Hill (1987).
[3]cf. Weiner (1970), Blos (1962, 1979).
[4]cf. Block (1971), Offer (1969), Blos (1962).

terized as one that takes account of the individual's integrative processes and overall frame of reference. Her conception of ego development assumes that each person has a customary orientation to himself and to the world, and that there is a continuum (ego development) along which these frames of reference can be arrayed. As Candee (1974) wrote: "In general, development is marked by a more differentiated perception of one's self, of the social world, and the relations of one's feelings and thoughts to those of others" (p. 621). Trends in ego development can be discerned in terms of increases in internalization of rules of social intercourse, cognitive complexity, tolerance of ambiguity, and objectivity. In addition, the individual's impulse control becomes progressively guided by self-chosen, long-term intentions, accompanied by an enhanced respect for individual autonomy and an interest in genuine mutuality.

Early studies of ego development using the Washington University sentence completion test (Loevinger & Wessler, 1970) involved normal samples and addressed basic psychometric questions of reliability and validity (cf. Hauser, 1976; Loevinger, 1979). Recently a number of research groups, including our own, reported findings from clinical samples (e.g., Browning, 1987; Frank & Quinlan, 1976; Hauser et al., in press; Kirshner, 1988; Noam et al., 1984; Rosznafsky, 1981). These extensions from healthy populations to those with psychiatric and medical conditions are not surprising, in light of the fact that ego development refers to clinically relevant dimensions, such as impulse control, anticipation, responsibility taking, and social judgment. These are the very features highlighted in analyses of impaired individual functioning. With respect to adaptive functioning, previous reports have described connections between adolescent ego development and self-esteem (Hauser et al., 1979; Isberg et al., 1989; Jacobson, Hauser, Powers, & Noam, 1985) as well as interpersonal style (Hauser, 1978). A number of theoretical and empirical considerations, therefore, point to links between adolescent ego development and psychopathology as well as varied patterns of adaptive functioning.

Ego Development Trajectories

Until now, studies relevant to questions about adolescent ego development and coping have been based on cross-sectional observations. Although valuable in generating questions and leads about relations between ego development and adaptation, they do not examine actual developmental paths and associated patterns of coping, or transformations in coping processes. Vaillant and McCullough (1987) and Helson and Wink (1987) addressed the development of coping in adulthood. However, we have minimal information about how coping changes or remains stable during the adolescent years and in the transition to adulthood. Through our longitudinally collected ego development observations, we can explore relations between paths of ego development and varying patterns of coping expressed at different points in adolescence. For instance, in this chapter, we identify the coping strategies utilized at one point in middle adolescence by teenagers who subsequently follow varied developmental paths. These first coping observations, thus, represent "markers" of these paths.

In the past two years (Hauser, Powers, Noam, & Bowlds, 1987; Hauser et al., in preparation), we have advanced the argument that another way to think about ego development is with respect to individual patterns of change, patterns that can be identified from underlying theoretical considerations. Through this conceptual step, we can generate an array of developmental paths. The form of development that each individual shows represents his or her developmental curve, or ego development *trajectory*. Each trajectory type identifies the base level of ego development for subjects in early adolescence and characterizes their change or stability in development throughout high school. These trajectories represent the form of development, the profile of stages, that the adolescent follows over a period of several years (shown schematically in Fig. 9.1). Some boys and girls begin their adolescent years in the early stages of ego development, continuing to be highly dependent on their parents, almost unaware of differences between themselves and others, and relating to peers and adults through largely exploitative styles. In addition, these adolescents use relatively simple cognitive constructions, responding to situations and questions with few options (either/or, "black and white" thinking). If they remain at these stages over two or more years, they represent *arrested* ego development.[5]

A second group of adolescents are intensely involved with acceptance by friends and compliance with prevailing social rules. Their awareness of individual differences and complex views is at best limited. They hold and rarely question socially prized categories and slogans. In terms of ego development, these adolescents are at the conformist stages, frequently found during adolescent years. If they do not advance to higher stages, we classify them as *steady conformists*.

A third trajectory includes adolescents who express higher, postconformist ego stages. They show adherence to norms based on inner standards, increased distance or autonomy from parental views, abiding interest in mutuality with others, and a strong interest in complexity of experience, in paradox or contradiction. If they remain at these high levels, they represent *accelerated* ego development and contrast most strikingly with ego development arrests.

A fourth trajectory is *progressive* ego development, where the adolescent shifts upward from earliest preconformist stages to conformist, or from conformist to postconformist, over a two- to three-year period. There is also the *regressive ego development* trajectory, where the adolescent shifts downward from one set

---

[5]It should be noted that the trajectories are deliberately defined in terms of *levels* (rather than stages). Thus to be classified as "arrest", a subject must remain within one of *3 stages* that are conceptually linked (as preconformist). Similarly, progression must be from one of a set of linked stages (e.g. conformist) to another set (e.g. postconformist). Such an empirical definition minimizes exploitation of error variance by focusing on theoretically meaningful change, rather than slippage from 1 adjacent stage to the next.

EGO DEVELOPMENT TRAJECTORIES

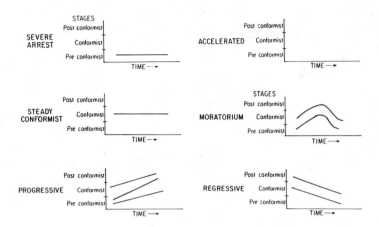

of stages (e.g., from conformist to preconformist) over the years. Finally there is a trajectory that we term (after Erikson, 1959) *psychosocial moratorium*, where the individual at first decreases and then increases levels of ego development. In the identity literature, such oscillations are discussed as representing "experimentation" by an adolescent as he or she tries out new roles and/or enacts conflicting yet significant ideals and wishes (Erikson, 1963; Marcia, 1980).

A major contributor to our understanding of coping styles is Norma Haan, who over the past 26 years has generated as Hold (1978) wrote: ". . .an original scheme for measuring the processes with which people cope with problems and defend against threats" (p. 139). Building on her clinical experience and work with longitudinal data sets at the Institute of Human Development at Berkeley, Haan (1977, 1983) focused on theoretical and empirical aspects of coping. Haan emphasized diversity in this area of functioning, conceptualizing twenty "ego processes" representing nuances of each individual's ways of dealing both with acute stress and continuing strains in every day life. From Haan's perspective, ego processes are the mechanisms used by adolescents and adults to deal with varied conflicts, affects, and external stresses. These processes include the use of intellectual resources (intellectuality), tolerance of ambiguity, empathy, denial, regression, and displacement.

Hann distinguished two types of ego processes: (a) coping processes, reflecting adaptive responses to stress; and (b) defending processes, ego processes representing maladaptive responses. More specifically, in her scheme, *coping* includes intellectuality, sublimation, and empathy in contrast to *defending*, represented by such processes as denial, displacement, and rationalization. Coping processes refer to those considerations and choices of actions that can be characterized as "more apt, differentiated, and sensitive" (Haan, 1977). On the other hand, defensive processes refer to considerations and actions that are more constricted, rigid, distorted, diffused, and obtuse. There are ten generic dimensions that can be expressed through either coping or defending modes. For instance, Haan (1965) included under the generic dimension "sensitivity," the processes empathy and projection:

> Projection involves a process of apprehending another's feelings, as does empathy, its counterpart. But projection is rigid, compelled, distorting, and undifferentiated, whereas empathy is flexible, purposive, reality oriented, and differentiated. (p. 374)

These processes can be further classified in terms of general functions: cognitive, self-reflexive (whereby people interact with their own feelings and thoughts), attention focusing, and emotion regulating. Table 9.1 lists and illustrates this taxonomy of ego processes.

A New View of Haan's Ego Processes

What is the connection between these *ego processes* and *ego development*? It is important first to be clear about distinctions between ego processes and ego development trajectories. An individual's *coping style* can be characterized by the profile of his or her most frequently used ego processes. Some individuals use primarily defending processes, whereas others show a predominance of coping, and still others will use a mixture of the two. Considering coping from this perspective is most germane to clarifying how coping may be related to adolescent development, because it leads to a more detailed identification of processes that are theoretically tied to ego development. Discovering links between these strategies and variations in current level or paths of ego development can illuminate how particular coping styles may be shaped by adolescent ego development.

We incorporate Haan's empirical assessment of coping into our studies, but only *after* converting her dichotomous categories into a two-tiered hierarchy with variations within each tier. At one pole of this theoretical continuum are those ways that an adolescent narrows his or her affective and cognitive responses to conflict and rigidly detaches from confronting difficulties at hand. At the other pole are differentiated and flexibly engaged ways that an adolescent may handle specific problems, involving such matters as developmental conflicts (bodily changes) or more situational difficulties (family conflicts over independence). In contrast to Haan, we make no assumptions about the outcome of applying these processes.

When using processes at the differentiated/engaged pole, the adolescent is more attuned to immediate options within situations and to future ramifications. Haan, Aertis, & Cooper (1985) wrote: "Thinking is differentiated; feeling is understood rather than blindly experienced. Negative feelings are understood rather than blindly experienced. Negative feeling are endured and positive feelings

TABLE 9.1
Taxonomy of Ego Processes[a]

Generic Processes	Differentiated/Engaging — Coping	Constricted/Detaching — Defending
	Cognitive Processes	
Discrimination:	Objectivity: person sees different sides of situations, even those contrary to his/her own.	Isolation: person misses connections and sees things as black or white.
Detachment:	Intellectuality: person is aware of the subtleties and nuances in situations and can reason abstractly.	Intellectualization: person uses broad terms devoid of detail, masking their feelings in abstract language.
Means-end Symbolization:	Logical Analysis: person recounts clear sequences of events and understands their consequences.	Rationalization: person reconstructs implausible chains of events in a self-serving manner, often attributing causes to outside sources.
	Reflexive-intraceptive Processes	
Delayed Response:	Tolerance of Ambiguity: person tolerates and considers complex situations which cannot be easily or immediately resolved.	Doubt: person shows difficulty making decisions and following through with them once they have already been made.
Sensitivity:	Empathy: person takes others' perspectives into account and responds sensitively.	Projection: person sees his/her own feelings and ideas reflected in others' behavior or expression.
Time Reversion:	Regression in service of the ego: person plays with ideas and feelings and enjoys sudden insights.	Regression: person does not take responsibility for him/herself and expects to be cared for by others in stressful or difficult situations.
	Attention-focusing Processes	
Selective Awareness:	Concentration: person focuses on tasks at hand and on the most relevant aspects of situations.	Denial: person selectively recounts the positive aspects of situations, leaving out the difficult ones.
	Emotion Regulating Processes	
Diversion:	Sublimation: person expresses both positive and negative emotions toward in relevant and socially acceptable ways.	Displacement: person displaces emotions from the instigating situation onto another person or thing in a safer context.
Transformation:	Substitution: person thoroughly and comfortably transforms uncivil feelings into more socialized forms.	Reaction formation: person reacts in overly socialized ways such that their actions seem strained, excessive, and brittle.
Restraint:	Suppression: person restrains emotions when appropriate to do so, but is nevertheless aware of those feelings.	Repression: person unintentionally curtails cognitive knowledge; his or her emotions, however, are left free-floating.

[a]Adapted from N. Haan, *Coping and Defending.* New York: Academic Press, 1977.

are enjoyed" (p. 130). An example of coping can be seen in the ego processes of intellectuality and regression in the service of the ego used by an adolescent to deal with her homesickness while abroad:

Interviewer: When you were feeling homesick, was there any way you tried to handle it or make it change in some way?

Adolescent: Well, I had this really strange thing. That was that; I have this infatuation with sky and clouds and rainbows, and when I draw, I love to draw things like that. So I would kind of look at the sky and think, well, that might have been over my house a day ago.

These ego processes reflect this adolescent's ability to use abstract ideas to solve problems and her ability to enjoy surprising aspects of even difficult situations.

In contrast, the adolescent relying on constricted/detaching processes experiences a narrowing of choices, a restriction of options, and overvaluation of past expectancies or solutions. These strategies are illustrated by another adolescent responding to his frustration when events do not transpire as he wishes:

Interviewer: Do you have any idea it is why you have this temper? Where it's coming from?

Adolescent: Builds up. See, my mother don't come to a family meeting; I get mad about that. I can't, I can't get . . . feel mad about that. I have a bad day in school; I get mad about that. Don't say nothin to anybody, and then somethin' will just trigger it, and I'll start— I'll start yellin at somebody or somethin'.

This adolescent uses regression and displacement, both considered by Haan to be defending processes. However, at the same time he also uses the coping process of objectivity. The displacement is clear as the adolescent is not directing his frustration at its source, whereas regression is apparent in his inability to be in charge of his own behavior and response. However, even as this adolescent is defending, he demonstrates the ability to be objective. In subsequent exchanges, he conveys his view that he is behaving inappropriately.

In summary, the coping processes and generic dimensions distinguished by Haan are clearly relevant to ego development, a relevance that we expand upon in the next section. On the other hand, her use of the contracting terms defensiveness and coping to distinguish these contrasting sets of processes is not as congenial. A major difficulty in Haan's work is the confounding of coping processes and coping outcomes (Holt, 1978). By defining which ways of coping are optimal or healthy, and which are "problematic" or "unhealthy," one loses the opportunity to tackle the significant question of how particular coping patterns may contribute to varied adaptive and maladaptive outcomes. In our view, the entire array of processes described by Haan have a potential for coping because all represent the adolescent's characteristic ways of dealing with problems. Along these lines, Haan et al. (1985) wrote that these characteristic ways "are determined by both situations and personal preference" (p. 131). Consequently in order to preserve Haan's important differentiation of coping processes and avoid confusion of process with outcome (defenses representing "maladaptive" processes), as well as a somewhat idiosyncratic use of the terms defense and defensiveness, we convert Haan's categories[6] into a continuum ranging from differentiated/engaging to constricted/detaching processes. Furthermore, to clearly distinguish this conceptual approach from the transactional/situational one represented by Lazarus and Folkman (1984), we conceptualize Haan's ego processes as "coping strategies." Table 9.1 includes this reconceptualization of the coping styles delineated by Haan.

Ego Development and Adolescent Coping Strategies

Through this theoretical transformation of Haan's dichotomy into a hierarchy, we position ourselves to analyze the relation of these strategies to stages and paths of ego development. Guiding our analysis is a two stage argument: (a) Adolescents at different ego levels and expressing different developmental paths (trajectories) will systematically differ in their coping strategies, and (b) these varied coping strategies will be reflected in different adaptive outcomes, with the more differentiated/engaged styles being linked with more favorable adjustment.

As summarized earlier, the construct of ego development refers to the individual's integrative processes and overall frame of reference. Major roots of this construct are drawn from cognitive-developmental theory (Piaget, 1932) and theories of self-system development (Sullivan, 1953). The linear series of stages posited in this scheme of development differ from one another along the lines of impulse control, conscious concerns, and interpersonal and cognitive styles. In brief, individuals at the earliest stages are impulsive, fearful, and have stereotyped cognitive styles and dependent or exploitative interpersonal styles. The three stages that share these more "primitive" characteristics are referred to as "preconformist" ones. In contrast, individuals who have reached later stages of ego development cope with inner conflict through high degrees of self-awareness, show much cognitive complexity, and have interpersonal styles that emphasize mutuality and respect for individual differences. These later stages are "postconformist" and less commonly found in any given population.

Loevinger's model of ego development does not assume or predict any relation between ego development and coping strategies. Nonetheless, her descriptions

---

[6]Haan also used a third distinction, fragmenting, referring to psychotic processes. We do not incorporate this third category in our current conversion.

of the personality (or character) styles unique for each stage imply that one should be able to find such coping correlates of these patterns. Consider, for example, Loevinger's and Wessler's (1970) descriptions of preconformist and postconformist individuals:

> The I–2 [impulsive] tends to dichotomize the world into good or bad, mean or nice, and clean or dirty; stereotype is the most conspicuous sign of this level . . . the I–2 subject seems unaware of mutuality or reciprocity between people . . . people are seen as sources of supply . . . affects are seen as bodily states or impulses rather than as differentiated inner feelings (pp. 56–58)

> The I–5 [autonomous] woman construes conflicting alternatives as aspects of many-sided life situations, as how things really are. She has a high tolerance for ambiguity . . . compares or collates three or more possibilities or aspects of a situation, such as appearances, actions, and feelings, again departing from an either-or view one often sees at I–4 [conscientious] (pp. 98)

The coping strategies delineated by Haan focus on how individuals regulate their responses to and management of stressful situations. Although a variety of psychological processes (cognitive, perceptual, behavioral) are included in these ways of regulating, there is an explicit hierarchy, stretching from the undifferentiated/detached to the differentiated/engaged, along which they can be arrayed. It is this hierarchy that closely aligns with the sequence of ego development stages— from impulsive (low cognitive complexity, exploitative interpersonal style, "sees people as sources of supply"), to autonomous (construes conflicting alternatives and cherishes mutuality). This alignment is, therefore, between a series of specific styles with more molar, holistic, stages. The stages of ego development frame the individual's understandings and behavioral options in given situations. The ways available for responding, framed by the stage of the individual's development, are his or her coping strategies. Our view represents a unidirectional model: The stages define the range and nature of the available coping strategies. It is an empirical question as to whether such a model is tenable or whether changes in coping strategies, occurring because of specific experiences, can in turn lead to ego development progressions or regressions. Examples of more specific predictions flowing from this more general statement are: Individuals at the lowest levels of ego development, where impulses are not experienced as one's own, are more likely to use strategies like regression or projection (Frank & Quinlan, 1976). At the highest stages, where mutuality and appreciation of individual differences are prized, increased use of empathy is to be expected, a prediction supported by findings of Carlozzi, Gaa, & Liberman (1983).

A second prediction from this integrative ego development/coping strategies model is that because at the higher stages more options will be available to the individual and he or she is aware of more complexity he or she has a greater range of choices and ways of connecting with others to utilize. In our schema this manifests itself in that a larger repertoire of coping strategies can be deployed. In other words, at the later stages, a higher number of strategies will be found in addition to more differentiated/engaged strategies.

THE ADOLESCENT AND FAMILY DEVELOPMENT RESEARCH PROGRAM

Before going into what we have learned about ego development and coping through our studies of adolescents, we first provide an overview of how we studied them. Without burdening the reader with technical detail about our methods (which can be found in Hauser et al., 1984), this section describes the groups we studied, how we observed them, and how we explored various aspects of individual development and coping.

In order to study a wide range of developmental patterns, we followed two groups: psychiatrically hospitalized adolescents likely to be at risk for later problems in their psychological development and high school freshmen with no foreseeable problems in their development. Our clinical experience suggested that many of the hospitalized adolescents would show early developmental arrests, functioning at low levels at ego development and probably not progressing to higher levels over the four years of the study. Although the hospitalized adolescents were not psychotic, there were strong reasons to expect that most of them would be developmentally impaired with respect to their perceptions of others, interpersonal styles, understanding of their surroundings, and impulse control.[7] In contrast, we expected that our group of high school freshmen with no apparent psychiatric problems would include many teenagers with progressive or accelerated ego development. Analyses of ego development in the first year of study (Hauser, et al., 1984) revealed results consistent with this original expectation.

The psychiatric patients consisted of successive adolescents admitted to the Children's Unit at McLean Hospital between autumn 1978 and winter 1980 who agreed to participate in the study. Most of these patients carried diagnoses of conduct disorder or depression. The average age was 13.9 for the patient group and 14.0 for the high school group. Members of both adolescent groups were predominantly from upper-middle-class and middle-class families.[8] Despite the demands of our procedures, all the adolescents and their families completed

---

[7]cf. Blos, P., *On adolescence*. New York: Free Press, 1962; Erikson, E. The Problem of Ego Identity. *Journal of American Psychoanalytical Association*, 1956, *4*, 56–121; Freud, A. On Adolescence. *Psychoanalytical Study of the Child*, 1958, *13*, 225–278; Weiner, I., *Psychological Disturbance in Adolescence*. New York: Wiley, 1970; Stierlin, H. *Separating Parents and Adolescents*. New York: Quadrangle, 1974

[8]Hollingshead (1957).

the various tests, interviews, and family discussion tasks. The total number of adolescents and families that entered the first year of the study was 146. One-hundred thirty-seven (high school adolescents = 75; patient adolescents = 62) subjects are included in analyses reported in this chapter. The nine missing subjects were omitted because of unavailable ego development protocols, missing interviews, or mechanical failures in recording of the interviews.

Shortly after agreeing to participate, each of the adolescents responded to the Washington University Sentence Completion Test of ego development (Loevinger & Wessler, 1970). On a second visit, within one month of the first, each adolescent met with one of our clinical interviewers for his or her first annual interview, which was audiotaped. The interview was an exploratory, semistructured one in which several topics were always covered in whatever order seemed most natural. These topics included school experience, peer relationships, family history, illness experience, and wishes/fantasies about the future. The interview was then transcribed and subsequently scored using Haan's Q–sort procedure (Haan, 1977; Haan et al., 1985), operationalizing the twenty coping strategies listed in Table 9.1. Trained raters (bachelor and graduate level psychology students, and a child psychiatrist) had an average interater reliability of .68. Reliabilities for the ego development ratings from each year were favorable (Hauser et al., 1984). As recommended by Loevinger and Wessler (1970), responses from each subject were removed from their original protocol and pooled for each stem. Following scoring, they were reassembled, and each protocol received a stage score (based on ogive distribution rules) and item sum score (a continuous interval score). (Cf. Hauser, 1976, for further discussion of these two scoring approaches). The ego development scoring was performed by a different group of raters than those rating the interviews. All correlational and regression analyses are based on adolescent item sum scores, whereas the trajectory classifications are based on adolescent stage scores.[9]

CONTRIBUTIONS OF ADOLESCENT EGO DEVELOPMENT TO ADOLESCENT COPING

Ego Development Stages and Coping Strategies: Cross-sectional Studies

Analyses of ego development and coping strategies from the first year of observations revealed numerous theoretically expected and substantial correlations between year one adolescent ego development stages and all but one of the coping strategies expressed by these adolescents. Table 9.2 presents these results.

---

[9]Besides helping us gauge each individual's ego development stage, the individual sets of sentence completions provide the equivalent of a rich written interview, offering many insights into adolescent and parental experiences of relationships with one another as well as their views of themselves, others, and their surroundings.

TABLE 9.2
Adolescent Coping Strategies and Ego Development Stages

Coping Strategy	High School	Psychiatric	All Adolescents
Tolerance of ambiguity	.115	−.114	.219***
Concentration	.463****	.302**	.639****
Logical analysis	.354***	.334***	.547****
Objectivity	.429****	.495****	.607****
Empathy	.287**	.296**	.418****
Intellectuality	.364***	.513****	.636****
Regression in the service of the ego	.297**	.423***	.573****
Sublimation	.046	.090	.436***
Substitution	.273*	.235*	.498****
Suppression	.178	.267*	.451****
Total differentiated/ engaging score	.473****	.454***	.683****
Denial	−.296**	−.414***	−.555****
Displacement	−.312	−.296	−.519***
Doubt/Indecision	−.319***	−.249	−.564***
Intellectualization	−.218ᵗ	−.101	−.172*
Isolation	−.396***	−.505****	−.622****
Projection	−.166	−.344***	−.453****
Rationalization	−.383***	−.268*	−.546***
Reaction formation	.273*	.211ᵗ	.071
Regression	−.359***	.190	−.536***
Repression	−.242*	−.427***	−.554***

$^t p<.10$ $*p<.05$ $**p<.01$ $***p<.009$ $****p<.0002$

In light of the possible impacts of psychiatric status on both ego development and coping, and the additional potential influences of social class (upper-middle, middle, lower-middle), age, and gender, we next examined the effects of adolescent ego development on adolescent coping strategies while statistically controlling for the effects these other variables. Hierarchical multiple regressions were carried out, with psychiatric status, age, gender, and social class entered first, followed by adolescent ego development. In addition, contributions by unique relations between adolescent gender and ego development were traced by including this interaction term as a final one in the multiple regression equations. Using this more stringent method, results again revealed significant predictive relations between adolescent ego development and coping strategies, with the exception of sublimation and tolerance of ambiguity. The proportion of variance explained ranged from 3% (suppression) to 15.4% (objectivity). It is also of interest that two significant gender-ego development interactions were found both for the constricting/detaching strategies. Girls with lower levels of ego development expressed higher levels of intellectualization, in contrast to the opposite pattern for boys with lower levels of ego development. Furthermore, boys at lower levels of ego development expressed more regression than did lower ego development girls.

Ego Development Trajectories and Coping: Longitudinal Studies

To what extent does an adolescent's coping expressed in his initial interviews anticipate the path of his or her subsequent ego development paths?

Based on two to three years of ego development scores, all of the adolescents were classified into the trajectories described and empirically defined earlier (separating early progression from advanced progression, and combining regression and moratorium subjects). Then, the year one coping strategy scores were analyzed through two multivariate analyses of covariance (MANCOVAs). One analysis was applied to the ten differentiated/engaging strategies, whereas the second analysis examined ten constricted/detaching strategies. Both sets of coping strategies were based on the year one clinical interviews. Covariates included psychiatric status, social class, and age of adolescent. These analyses revealed significant main effects for adolescent ego development trajectories. Follow-up univariate analyses of covariance (ANCOVAs) revealed that eleven coping processes distinguished the ego development trajectories that were to unfold over the next years (cf. Table 9.3). In addition, the total score for the differentiated/ engaged processes was significantly different among the trajectories. The general difference was that the *arrests* and *early progressive development* adolescents had significantly lower scores on the differentiated/engaging processes (e.g., concentration, intellectuality), and consistently higher scores on the disengaged/ constricted processes (e.g., displacement and denial).

In other words, when we search for "early coping signs" of ego development trajectories, we find that those adolescents who were to remain at very low levels of ego development or show paths of early progression (from preconformist to conformist) could already be discriminated in the first year interview. In contrast, with rare exception (substitution, doubt), adolescents showing the other trajectories could not be discerned by their early coping patterns.

CONCLUSIONS

Theoretical and empirical considerations point to ties between adolescent ego development and coping. Using a specific approach to coping strategies, one based on ego process conceptualizations, we predicted that specific types of coping strategies (e.g., constricted/detaching and differentiated/engaging) would be related to adolescent ego development. Analyses of adolescents drawn from high school and psychiatric populations were consistent with our predictions of how ego development influences adolescents' coping strategies. For instance,

TABLE 9.3
Coping Strategies and Adolescent Ego Trajectories

Coping Strategy	Trajectory					
	Arrest [a]	Early Progression	Conformist	Accel.	Adv. Prog.	Regression
Concentration	3.79[b]	4.53	6.17	6.24	5.77	6.11****
Intellectuality	4.14	4.69	6.49	7.10	6.25	2.93*
Objectivity	4.17	4.63	5.60	5.54	5.55	2.73*
Substitution	3.68	4.44	5.52	5.02	5.49	2.80
Regression in service of ego	5.24	5.21	6.96	7.35	6.73	2.54*
Total diff./ engaging score	4.39	4.91	5.99	6.03	5.84	4.00**
Denial	5.43	5.12	4.24	4.01	3.94	3.15*
Displacement	6.34	5.84	5.04	4.83	4.52	4.82***
Doubt & Indecsn.	5.38	4.51	2.93	3.43	3.78	2.54*
Rationalization	5.68	4.66	3.75	3.50	3.74	5.36****
Regression	6.18	5.25	3.57	3.76	4.58	4.23***
Isolation	5.81	5.25	3.52	3.18	3.48	2.33[t]

[a]All entries are mean scores. Where values differ significantly from others, they are underlined.
[b]Entries with same underlining differ significantly from all others on row.
[t]$p<.10$ *$p<.05$ **$p<.01$ ***$p<.005$ ****$p<.0006$

intellectuality and empathy were, as expected, strongly related to ego development. At higher levels of ego development, adolescents express more empathy and intellectuality. On the other hand, projection diminishes with higher ego development levels. These results provide still additional evidence for the construct validity of Loevinger's ego development test. Moreover, they underscore the value of applying an ego development perspective when studying coping variations in adolescence.

In addition to discovering ties between ego stages and coping strategies, we identified ways in which adolescents following varying ego development paths (based on longitudinal observations) differ in how they cope. The striking result of these ego development path analyses is that those adolescents who begin at the earliest stages and those that remain at these stages differ most in their coping patterns in the first year of observation—showing a preponderance of constricting and detaching strategies. We do not know if those adolescents whose development changes—such as progression or moratorium—will also show corresponding or parallel changes in their coping strategies. At this point, what these results indicate is that those adolescents whose baseline is low ego development also show coping strategies that are distinguished by a predominance of constricting and detaching ego processes.

Remaining to be explored is the question of how individual coping patterns themselves may change during adolescence and how such change is linked with ego development paths. Do all or certain coping strategies remain fixed for the adolescents who have arrested in their development? Do adolescents who are accelerated in their development also show strong changes across their coping strategies? Or are certain strategies more *resistant* to change, even alongside of striking developmental change? Will gender differences, until now not apparent in these analyses, become evident in time-based studies of adolescent coping patterns, especially when developmental paths are simultaneously assessed?

Our primary theme in this chapter is the critical importance of maintaining a developmental perspective when studying adolescent coping. Our argument is that an approach tracing how ego development influences coping promises to advance our understanding of adolescent coping, because such an approach goes beyond analyzing impacts of situational or demographic determinants and integrates concepts of development and adaptation, drawing relevant theoretical distinctions and current empirical instruments. Although situational and demographic forces are still important forces to be clarified, our perspective emphasizes the importance of *individual differences* among adolescents in terms of developmental status and paths of development.

REFERENCES

Block, J. (1971). *Lives through time*. Berkeley, CA: Bancroft.

Blos, P. (1962). *On adolescence: A psychoanalytic interpretation*. New York: Free Press.

Blos, P. (1979). *The Adolescent passage: Developmental issues*. New York: International Universities Press.

Brooks-Gunn, J., Petersen, A. C., & Eichorn, D. (Eds.). (1985). Time of maturation and psychosocial functioning in adolescence. [Special Issue]. *Journal of Youth and Adolescence, 14*, 149–264.

Browning, D. L. (1987). Ego development, authoritarianism, and social status: An investigation of the incremental validity of Loevinger's Sentence Completion Test (short form). *Journal of Personality and Social Psychology, 53*, 113–118.

Candee, D. (1974). Ego developmental aspects of new left ideology. *Journal of Personality and Social Psychology, 30*, 620–630.

Carlozzi, A. F., Gaa, J. P., & Liberman, D. B. (1983). Empathy and ego development. *Journal of Counseling Psychology, 30*(1), 113–116.

Erikson, E. H. (1956). The Problem of Ego Identity. *Journal of American Psychoanalytic Association, 4*, 56–121.

Erikson, E. H. (1959). Identity and the life cycle. *Psychological Issues, 1*, 1–171.

Erikson, E. H. (1963). *Childhood and society*. New York: Norton.

Freud, A. (1958). On adolescence. *Psychoanalytical Study of the Child, 13*, 225–278.

Frank, S., & Quinlan, D. (1976). Ego development and female delinquency: A cognitive-developmental approach. *Journal of Abnormal Psychology, 85*, 505–510.

Haan, N. (1965). Coping and defense mechanisms related to personality inventories. *Journal of Consulting and Clinical Psychology, 29*, 373–378.

Haan, N. (1977). *Coping and defending: Processes of self–environment organization*. New York: Academic Press.

Haan, N. (1983). The interactional morality of everyday life. In N. Haan, R. Bellah, P. Rabinow, & W. Sullivan (Eds.), *Social science as moral inquiry*. New York: Columbia University Press.

Haan, N., Aerts, E., & Cooper, B. A. B. (1985). *On moral grounds: The search for practical morality.* New York: New York University Press.

Hauser, S. T. (1976). Loevinger's model and measure of ego development: A critical review. *Psychological Bulletin, 83,* 928–955.

Hauser, S. T. (1978). Ego development and interpersonal style in adolescence. *Journal of Youth and Adolescence, 7*(4), 333–352.

Hauser, S. T., Houlihan, J., Powers, S. I., Jacobson, A. M., Noam, G. G., Weiss-Perry, B., Follansbee, D., & Book, B. K. (in press). Adolescent ego development within the family: Family styles and family sequences. *International Journal of Behavioral Development.*

Hauser, S. T., Pollets, D., Turner, B., Jacobson, A., Powers, S., & Noam, G. (1979). Ego development and self-esteem in adolescence. *Diabetes Care, 2*(6), 465–471.

Hauser, S. T., Powers, S., Noam, G., Jacobson, A., Weiss, B., & Follansbee, D. (1984). Familial contexts of adolescent ego development. *Child Development, 55,* 195–213.

Hauser, S. T., Powers, S. I., Noam, G., & Bowlds, M. K. (1987). Family interiors of adolescent ego development trajectories. *Family Perspective, 21*(4), 263–282.

Hauser, S. T., Jacobson, A. M., Milley, J., Wertlieb, D., Hershowitz, R., Wolfsdorf, J., & Lavori, P. (in preparation). Ego trajectories and adjustment to diabetes: Longitudinal studies of diabetic and acutely ill patients. In E. Susman, L. Feagens, & W. Ray (Eds.) *Emotion and cognition in child and adolescent health and development.* Hillsdale, NJ: Lawrence Erlbaum Associates.

Helson, R., & Wink, P. (1987). Two conceptions of maturity examined in the findings of a longitudinal study. *Journal of Personality and Social Psychology, 53*(3), 531–541.

Hill, J. P. (1987). Research on adolescents and their families: Past and prospect. *New Directions for Child Development: Adolescent Social Behavior and Health, 37,* 13–31.

Hollingshead, A. B. (1957). *Two factor index of social position* (mimeographed). Yale University, New Haven, CT.

Holt, R. R. (1978). Theory, no; method, yes. *Contemporary Psychology, 23,* 139–141.

Isberg, I. S., Hauser, S. T., Jacobson, A. M., Powers, S. I., Noam, G., Weiss-Perry, B., & Follansbee, D. (1989). Parental contexts of adolescent self-esteem: A developmental perspective. *Journal of Youth and Adolescence, 18*(1) 1–23.

Jacobson, A. M., Hauser, S. T., Powers, S., & Noam, G. (1985). The influence of chronic illness and ego development on self-esteem in diabetic and psychiatric adolescent patients. *Journal of Youth and Adolescence, 13,* 489–507.

Kirshner, L. A. (1988). Implications of Loevinger's theory of ego development for time-limited psychotherapy. *Psychotherapy, 25*(2), 220–227.

Lazarus, R. S., & Folkman, S. (Eds.). (1984). *Stress, appraisal, and coping.* New York: Springer.

Loevinger, J. (1976). *Ego development: Conceptions and theories.* San Francisco: Jossey-Bass.

Loevinger, J. (1979). Construct validity of the sentence completion test. *Applied Psychological Measures, 3,* 281–311.

Loevinger, J. (1985). Revision of the Sentence Completion Test for Ego Development. *Journal of Personality and Social Psychology, 48,* 420–427.

Loevinger, J., & Wessler, R. (1970). *Measuring ego development* (Vol. 1). San Francisco: Jossey-Bass.

Marcia, J. E. (1980). Identity in adolescence. In J. Adelson (Ed.), *Handbook of adolescent psychology.* New York: Wiley.

Noam, G., Hauser, S. T., Santostefano, S., Garrison, W., Jacobson, A., Powers, S., & Mead, M. (1984). Ego development and psychopathology: A study of hospitalized adolescents. *Child Development, 55,* 184–194.

Offer, D. (1969). *The psychological world of the teenager: A study of normal adolescent boys.* New York: Basic.

Petersen, A. C. (1988). Adolescent development. *Annual Review of Psychology, 39,* 583–607.

Petersen, A. C., & Spiga, R. (1982). Adolescence and stress. In L. Goldberger & S. Breznitz (Eds.), *Handbook of stress: Theoretical and clinical aspects* (pp. 515–528). New York: Free Press.

Piaget, J. (1932). *The moral judgment of the child.* London: Kegan, Paul.

Rosznafsky, J. (1981). The relationship of level of ego development to Q–sort personality ratings. *Journal of Personality and Social Psychology, 41,* 99–120.

Steinberg, L. (1981). Transformations in family relations at puberty. *Developmental Psychology, 17,* 833–840.

Steinberg, L., & Hill, J. (1978). Patterns of family interaction as a function of age, the onset of puberty, and formal thought. *Developmental Psychology, 14,* 683–684.

Stierlin, H. (1974). *Separating Parents and Adolescents.* New York: Quadrangle.

Sullivan, H. S. (1953). The interpersonal theory of psychiatry. In H. S. Perry & M. L. Gawel (Eds.), *The collected works of Harry Stack Sullivan: Volume I* (pp. 3–393). New York: Norton.

Vaillant, G. E. (1977). *Adaptation to life.* Boston: Little Brown.

Weiner, I. (1970). *Psychological disturbance in adolescence.* New York: Wiley.

10

Variation in Stress Reactivity During Adolescence

A. L. Greene
West Virginia University

Reed W. Larson
University of Illinois at Urbana-Champaign

PERSPECTIVES ON ADOLESCENT STRESS

At the end of a recent midterm exam, one struggling undergraduate wrote, "Adolescence is the last plight before adulthood." Although a bit muddled, this statement does reflect a traditional view of adolescence as an intrinsically stressful period of the life span (Blos, 1967; A. Freud, 1958; S. Freud, 1925; Hamburg, 1974). Within that perspective, the advent of exogenous stressors, such as parental divorce or school transition are thought to only exacerbate negative outcomes in a uniquely vulnerable period (Hetherington & Anderson, 1988; Simmons & Blyth, 1987; Wallerstein & Kelly, 1980). Consequently, adolescents are frequently described as moody, rebellious, and driven by libidinal urges that find expression in precisely the activities most feared by parents and teachers.

Although a host of studies clearly disconfirm this perception (Block, 1971; Douvan & Adelson, 1966; Greene & Boxer, 1986; Lerner & Knapp, 1975; Offer, 1969), it nonetheless remains a tacit assumption in much of the research on adolescent stress. Three factors have apparently contributed to its persistence in this literature: (a) an overreliance on adult informants and adult-based paradigms; (b) the perception of adolescence as an undifferentiated transition to adulthood; and (c) insufficient consideration of the developmental transitions that both characterize and differentiate adolescence.

Differentiating Adolescents

Considerable attention has been given to defining the relationship between adolescent stress and later adult pathology (Garmezy, 1981, 1983; Rutter, 1980, 1983). The logic for this emphasis has clear intuitive appeal: Early identification of those stressors likely to result in pathologic sequelae will facilitate earlier and more effective intervention (Danish, Smyer, & Nowak, 1980; Felner, Primavera, & Cauce, 1981). The unanimity of focus in the events typically examined (e.g., divorce, chronic illness, death of a parent) is not a solution to the problems involved in understanding adolescent stress. Rather it represents the almost undifferentiated application of adult stress paradigms to the study of children and adolescents (Greene, 1988). Rutter's (1983) following quotation illustrates this point:

> There are no comparable studies of children [or adolescents] in which the effects of different types of stress are contrasted systematically. However, we may utilize the adult findings as a guide in considering which might be the crucial aspects of life events that make them liable to provoke psychiatric disorder in children [and adolescents]. (p. 10; italics added)

The utility of such "adult stress" paradigms, however, is limited in three important respects. First, the sequence and timing of normative life event stressors (e.g., school transition, marriage) is different for adolescents than it is for adults (Hultsch & Plemons, 1979; Petersen & Spiga, 1982; Reese & Smyer, 1983). Understanding adolescent stress, therefore, requires some appreciation for the transitions that actually characterize the period rather than an unconsidered reliance on tallies of generic events. Second, adolescents and adults do not perceive the same events to be stressful nor do they attribute the same degree of salience or impact to the same, investigator-defined events (Greene, 1988; Yamamoto, 1979; Yamamoto & Felsenthal, 1982). Finally adolescents demonstrate unique patterns of responsivity to stress that distinguish their probable outcomes from those of adults (Swearingen & Cohen, 1985; Thoits, 1983).

Differentiating Adolescence

A second and related difficulty in the literature on adolescent stress is the lack of distinction between adolescent subperiods. Typically adolescence is viewed as an undifferentiated and often unpredictable period between childhood and adulthood. Yet a host of biological, psychological, and social transitions punctuate the period (Greene & Boxer, in press; Petersen & Taylor, 1980). The timing and (co)occurrence of these transitions demarcate early, middle, and late adolescent subperiods, with different developmental trajectories for males and females (Greene & Boxer, in press; Hamburg, 1974; Thornburg, 1983; Tobin-Richards, Boxer, & Peterson, 1982). Further, recent findings indicate that adolescents do not respond homogeneously to the same stressors (Felner, et al., 1981) and that different patterns of stress responsivity, as measured by self-reported dysphoria, for example, are associated with different subperiods (Moran & Eckenroade, 1988).

Developmental Mediators of Adolescent Stress

A final difficulty lies in the absent consideration of the developmental transitions (in affect, cognition, and levels of schooling) that distinguish adolescent subperiods and distinguish adolescents from children and adults (Compas, 1987a, 1987b; Maccoby, 1983). With a few notable exceptions (e.g., Petersen & Spiga, 1982; Tobin-Richards et al., 1982; Simmons & Blyth, 1987), researchers have largely overlooked the potentially mediating role of developmental transitions in the adolescent's perception of and responsivity to stress. The importance of such factors is perhaps best illustrated by considering the mediating role that may be played by the transitions in cognition and social context that characterize this period of the life span.

Cognitive Maturity

Significant changes in cognition emerge during adolescence (Flavell, 1982; Greene, in press; Inhelder & Piaget, 1958; Neimark, 1982). Over time, adolescents show greater capacity for abstraction and introspection in reasoning about self and others than do children (Flavell, 1982; Harris, Olthof, & Terwogt, 1981). To the extent that individual appraisal differentiates both stress perception and subsequent coping strategies (e.g., Lazarus & Folkman, 1984), the role of developing cognition in mediating adolescent stress vulnerability merits consideration.

Gains in cognitive maturity, for example, may facilitate the adolescent's decentration from immediate emotional experience (e.g., Labouvie-Vief, 1984). Thus, cognitively mature adolescents might be expected to show greater affective stability than those less cognitively mature. Conversely, however, the greater insight afforded by gains in cognitive maturity may heighten adolescents' awareness of internal experience and the complexity of external events (Greene, in press; Larson & Asmussen, 1988; Piaget, 1976). In such fashion, gains in cognitive maturity may actually heighten instability of affect and, thereby, increase stress vulnerability.

Social Contexts of Adolescence

Consideration also must be given to the time that adolescents spend in different social contexts. Over the course of the day, adolescents traverse different social contexts (e.g., school, peers, and family) that function as different opportunity systems (Csikszentmihalyi & Larson, 1984; Larson, 1983). Although time spent in the peer context is associated with excitement, self-extension, and vulnerability

(Douvan & Adelson, 1966; Larson, 1983), time spent alone (i.e., solitude) is often associated with lower affect, greater self-possession, and renewal (Larson & Csikszentmihalyi, 1980). Moreover, the frequency of changes that adolescents experience in those contexts (that is, between school, peers, and family, for example) is considerably higher than the frequency of comparable transitions experienced by adults.

Csikszentmihalyi and Larson (1984), for example, have suggested that the frequency of contextual transitions that adolescents experience (e.g., between school, family, and peers) may partially account for the greater affective variability observed among high school students as compared to adults. In such fashion, social context transitions may differentiate adolescent stress vulnerability. Of particular relevance to the present discussion is the likelihood that such context effects may vary for different adolescent subgroups (e.g., Simmons & Blyth, 1987).

Towards An Age-Appropriate Account of Adolescent Stress

As illustrated by the preceding discussion, the central issue in the study of adolescent stress is one of model appropriateness (Reese & Rodehaver, 1985). That is, putative accounts of age-related phenomena, such as adolescent stress, must incorporate consideration of the organismic features that emerge during and thereby distinguish the period of interest. Adult paradigms, with their attendant assumptions of continuity (see Costa et al., chapter 14 in this volume, for a related discussion), are of limited applicability to a period characterized chiefly by rapid change (Petersen & Taylor, 1980).

What seems needed, therefore, is a more finely differentiated account of adolescent stress, one that incorporates the developmental transitions that characterize different adolescent subperiods (e.g., cognition, pubertal onset, schooling) as well as the manner in which such transitions may differentially contribute to and/or mediate stress vulnerability and resilience (Compas, 1987a, 1987b; Maccoby, 1983).

As a first step towards that end, we began by examining developmental and contextual mediators of adolescents' daily affect over a seven-day period. As suggested previously, patterns of affectivity, such as low or negative affect or affective instability, are plausible markers of stress vulnerability. Further, such patterns (e.g., dysphoria, distress) are widely used indices of stress responsivity and outcome (e.g., Compas, 1987a; Compas, Slavin, Wagner, & Vannatta, 1986; Moran & Eckenroade, 1988; Rutter, 1983; Thoits, 1983). Despite that widespread usage, however, comparatively little is known about developmental differences in daily patterns of affectivity (see Csikszentmihalyi & Larson, 1984, for a notable exception) or the manner in which coterminous developmental transitions may differentiate the patterns observed.

EXAMINING DEVELOPMENTAL MEDIATORS
OF ADOLESCENT AFFECTIVITY

In the following sections of this chapter, we presented the findings of a recently completed investigation of adolescent daily experience. Following the considerations raised previously, two objectives guided that examination. The first was to examine patterns of adolescent affectivity as they related to gender, age, and cognitive maturity. The second purpose was to examine variation in affectivity across the contexts of adolescents' daily lives. Of particular interest to us in this regard were the interactions (i.e., between social context, gender, and cognitive maturity) that might differentiate patterns of affectivity among adolescent subgroups (i.e., elementary vs. junior high vs. high school students).

Sample

Four hundred eighty-three fifth- through ninth-grade students (9–15 years) participated in this study. The sample was stratified to achieve equal representation of SES (i.e., working class vs. white collar), sex, and grade. Seventy percent of the students originally contacted completed participation. Population surveys in two schools indicated that nonparticipation was unrelated to SES or self-esteem but was related to parental marital status. Students whose parents had remarried were more likely to decline participation than students whose parents were married or whose parents were separated, divorced, or widowed (Larson, 1989).

Procedure

Following the Experience Sampling Method (ESM) (Csikszentmihalyi & Larson, 1987), adolescents carried electronic pagers and a booklet of self-report forms for seven days. Students were paged seven times daily and completed a self-report form after each signal. Self-report forms requested information about adolescents' activities, social context, thoughts, moods, and feelings. On the whole, students were very cooperative and responded to 84% of the pager signals. A total of 18,022 self-reports were obtained, for an average of 37.3 assessments per student over a seven day period. At the conclusion of ESM sampling, interviews were conducted with each student to obtain additional data, including assessments of cognitive maturity and family background.

Measures

Internal Experience

Three measures of adolescents' internal experience were obtained through ESM sampling: average daily affect, affect variability, and the incidence of positive and negative feeling states.

Affect.   In response to each pager signal, students rated affect, using three bipolar semantic differential items, scaled from 1 to 7, where 7 represented the positive end of the scale (i.e., happy–unhappy, cheerful–irritable, and friendly–angry). Ratings for these items were aggregated across self-reports for each student to form a composite average daily affect score. Cronbach's alpha for this measure was .76.

Affect Variability.   Standard deviation scores in average daily affect were used to assess affect variability. Larger standard deviation scores indicated greater change in affect across self-ratings; smaller standard deviation scores indicated less change or greater stability of affect.

Feeling States.   During ESM sampling, students also completed thirteen 4-point unipolar items to describe how they were feeling (e.g., proud, calm, worried). Scores for each feeling state reflect the percentage of time that students endorsed each item.

Correlational analyses of these ratings yielded three positive (i.e., exuberance, tranquility, and acceptance) and three negative (i.e., distress, regret, and alienation) dimensions of feeling state. Table 10.1 presents the correlations obtained between the measures of internal experience.

Cognitive Maturity

Cognitive maturity was measured using an eight-item, self-administered volume conservation task (Linn & Pulos, 1983). Each problem was accompanied by a drawing of a beaker of water and two objects of differing weight, and required that students predict which object would displace the greater amount of water. Response choices to each item reflected the student's use of one of four hierarchically organized problem-solving strategies: *weight-only, weight-except-when-equal, volume-except-when-equal,* and *volume-only.*

Problem-solving strategies reflect adolescents' ability to cognitively decenter from the stimulus array accompanying each problem. Adolescents who employed immature strategies (i.e., *weight-only, weight-except-when-equal*), for example, were seduced by the array's appearance and selected the wrong answer. In contrast, adolescents who employed mature strategies (i.e., *volume-except-when-equal, volume-only*) achieved sufficient distance from misleading foils to select the correct solution. Cognitive maturity was scored by level (I–IV), corresponding to the adolescent's consistent or modal strategy use across the items of the task.

Social Context

Finally students identified their immediate social contexts following each pager signal. Four social contexts, accounting for 98.8% of all self-reports, were examined: time spent with family, time spent with peers, time spent in class, and time spent alone (i.e., solitude).

TABLE 10.1
Correlations Between Measures of Affectivity[a]

Feeling State Dimensions	Item Inter- Correlations	Average Daily Affect	Affect Variability
Exuberance (Proud, Great)	.73***	.49***	.10*
Regret (Guilty, Sorry, Embarrassed)	.62***	−.11*	.21***
Tranquility (Calm, In Control)	.62***	.32***	.04
Distress (Worried, Frustrated, Disappointed)	.55***	−.12**	.40***
Acceptance (Kindly, Warm, Accepted)	.68***	.49***	.12**
Alienation (Ignored, Lonely)	.64***	−.03	.26***

[a]Composite items for the feeling state dimensions presented parenthetically.
*$p<.05$
**$p<.01$
***$p<.001$

Developmental Variation in Internal Experience

As no significant differences were obtained between fifth and sixth graders and between seventh and eighth graders in the variables of interest, age groups were collapsed and will be referred to as elementary (i.e., fifth and sixth grade), junior high school (i.e., seventh and eight grade) and high school (ninth grade) students respectively. Repeated Measures MANOVA analysis indicated significant gender, $F(1,451) = 6.59$, $p < .001$, grade, $F(2,451) = 3.21$, $p < .001$, and social context, $F(3,768) = 3.16$, $p < .05$, effects, as well as a trend toward significant cognition effects, $F(3,451) = 1.51$, $p < .054$ in affectivity. Table 10.2 presents the mean scores obtained in that analysis by group. Results for each factor are discussed separately.

Grade

Elementary students reported the most positive affect of the three groups examined. They also were more likely to feel *exuberant, tranquil,* and *accepted.* Contrary to prior formulations (Blos, 1967; A. Freud, 1958; S. Freud, 1925; Hamburg, 1974), elementary-aged adolescents were no more variable in affect

TABLE 10.2
**Mean Scores on the Measures of Affectivity by Gender, Grade,
Cognitive Maturity, and Social Context**

	Gender		
	Females	Males	F
Average affect	5.21	4.93	9.67**
Affect variability	1.04	0.96	6.48*
Exuberance	33.12	34.34	n.s.
Regret	5.66	6.06	n.s.
Tranquility	46.88	49.16	n.s.
Distress	14.04	11.99	5.73*
Acceptance	38.40	31.95	4.99*
Alienation	8.24	8.11	n.s.

	Grade			
	Elementary	Junior High	Senior High	F
Average affect	5.26	4.96	4.84	10.65***
Affect variability	0.96	1.05	1.04	n.s
Exuberance	40.05	31.16	22.76	9.15***
Regret	5.03	7.35	4.11	n.s.
Tranquility	54.37	44.39	39.76	7.52***
Distress	10.84	15.17	13.39	5.56**
Acceptance	39.64	33.77	26.65	4.54*
Alienation	7.89	9.11	6.40	n.s.

	Cognitive Maturity				
	Level I	Level II	Level III	Level IV	F
Average affect	5.12	5.25	5.00	4.90	3.07*
Affect variability	1.03	0.97	0.99	1.04	2.71*
Exuberance	36.90	39.93	31.53	25.72	4.29*
Regret	7.85	5.15	5.90	4.03	n.s.
Tranquility	51.74	50.84	47.94	40.67	3.92**
Distress	14.67	12.31	13.28	11.46	n.s.
Acceptance	37.69	40.51	33.98	28.15	n.s.
Alienation	9.66	7.91	8.20	6.58	n.s.

(Continued)

202

TABLE 10.2
(continued)

	Social Context				
	Alone	With Family	In Class	With Peers	F
Average affect	4.84	5.02	5.16	5.39	39.20***
Affect variability	0.96	0.91	0.85	0.89	n.s.
Exuberance	29.80	32.60	33.20	37.90	7.51***
Regret	5.80	5.10	4.90	4.40	n.s.
Tranquility	45.40	43.60	40.90	42.30	n.s.
Distress	12.40	10.70	12.10	11.10	n.s.
Acceptance	28.40	34.70	34.10	40.30	10.96***
Alienation	10.20	7.60	5.80	6.00	11.60***

$*p<.05$
$**p<.01$
$***p<.001$

than junior or senior high students. However, that junior high school students experienced a higher incidence of *distress* than either elementary or high school students is congruent with previous investigations (e.g., Petersen & Spiga, 1982; Simmons & Blyth, 1987).[1]

Gender

Congruent with previous observations, females, although happier, also experienced greater affect variability and a higher incidence of *distress* than males (Compas, Davis, & Forsythe, 1985; Compas, et al., 1980; Thoits, 1983). As many parents can attest, although females' "high" was higher, it also was more apt to change. Females also experienced a higher incidence of *acceptance* (i.e., feelings of warmth, belonging) as compared to males. However, as we shall discuss shortly, those feelings of acceptance may not come without some cost.

Cognitive Maturity

Cognitive maturity was inversely associated with positive affect, *exuberance* and *tranquility*. Curiously, however, affect variability was greatest among the least as well as the most cognitively mature adolescents. Here we suspect that similar patterns of affectivity may manifest for different reasons.

Previous research suggests a positive association between cognitive maturity and an expanded understanding of emotion (Greene, in press; Harris et al.,

---

[1]For a fuller discussion of age trends in items comprising the affect scale, see Larson & Lampan-Petratis (1989).

1981; Piaget, 1976). The present findings are, in part, congruent with those speculations. As illustrated in Table 10.2, gains in cognitive maturity may lead to a heightened awareness of internal experience, which in turn may give rise to greater affective lability. The greater incidence of distress observed among gifted as compared to nongifted, adolescents provides support for this interpretation (Karnes, Oehler, & Jones, 1985; Leaverton & Hertzog, 1979). Conversely cognitive immaturity may impede the adolescent's ability to decenter from affective experience. Absent the skills for insight and self-regulation (Labouvie-Vief, 1982; Piaget, 1976), such adolescents may be "flooded" by affect and, thereby, be more vulnerable to stress.

Social Context

Not too surprisingly, adolescents experienced more positive affect and were more likely to feel *exuberant* and *accepted* with their peers than in any other social context. In contrast, solitude was associated with the highest incidence of *alienation*. Contrary to expectation (e.g., Greene, 1988), school was not associated with lower affect, greater affect variability, or a higher incidence of negative feeling states. As these findings indicate, the baseline of adolescents' internal experience differs considerably from one social context to another. When we consider the significant interaction that emerged in the incidence of *distress,* we find that different social contexts are associated with different patterns of affectivity and, as we shall argue, different patterns of stress vulnerability among different adolescents.

Figure 10.1 shows the significant Gender × Grade × Context interaction that emerged in the incidence of *distress,* $F(3,993) = 4.82, p < .002$. As indicated there, junior and senior school females experienced a high incidence of *distress* during periods of solitude and in the peer context. The latter finding is not uncommon in studies of adolescent stress: Females typically report greater distress and more difficulty among peers than do males (Compas et al., 1986; Greene, 1988; Thoits, 1983). Indeed Compas et al. (1986) reported intriguing data on the questionable (and apparently costly) benefits of social support networks for adolescent females. Given females' earlier facility with intimate relationships (Fischer, 1981), these data suggest that differences in social context also may index gender differences in stress vulnerability. Put another way, the context in which one is most embedded (reflected here in females' greater feelings of *acceptance*), is also the context in which one may be most vulnerable.

Perhaps the most striking aspect of FIG. 10.1, however, is the incidence of distress experienced by high school females in the family context. These data parallel Daniel Keating's (personal communication, March 15, 1988) observation that ninth grade females show a higher incidence and greater magnitude of family-related stress than do males. Borrowing from Chodorow (1978) and Gilligan

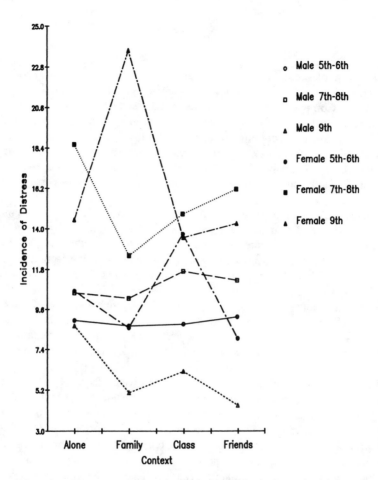

FIG. 10.1.   Three-way interaction between sex, grade, and social context in the incidence of distress.

(1982), it is arguable that greater relational identity, combined with earlier social expertise (Fischer, 1981), may well result in females' unique vulnerability to family perturbations during adolescence. Similarly Keating (personal communication, March 15, 1988) suggested that, among distressed families, adolescent females often assume a pseudoparenting role that entails affect management for the entire family. Thus, the normative socialization of females in the obligations of friendship and kinship (e.g., Chodorow, 1978; Gilligan, 1982; Hagestad, 1978; Troll & Bengtson, 1982) also may result in their greater vulnerability to the interactions that occur in those contexts.

CONCLUSIONS

Analysis of adolescents' internal experience yielded significant and theoretically consistent effects among the variables of interest. As in previous studies (Compas et al., 1985; Compas et al., 1986; Thoits, 1983) females, although happier, also experienced greater affect variability and a higher incidence of *distress*. Similarly the effects obtained for cognitive maturity (i.e., lower affect, lower incidence of positive feeling states, and higher incidence of distress) are consistent with prior accounts of the often paradoxical effects of developing insight and sophisticated reasoning capacity during adolescence (Greene, in press; Labouvie-Vief, 1982, 1984; Piaget, 1976).

Further, examination of social context differences in adolescents' internal experience revealed that different patterns of vulnerability and resilience may obtain in different social contexts based, in part, on the attributes and (developing) characteristics that adolescents bring to the setting. The interactions obtained between sex and social context (i.e., family and peers) in patterns of *distress* provide vivid illustration of this point.

Several questions remain to be examined in future investigations of adolescent stress. First, in the interests of simplicity, this chapter considered only two aspects of the developmental span that characterizes adolescence. For example, the concomitantly mediating influence of pubertal timing and onset, which has been well documented in other investigations (Petersen & Spiga, 1982; Petersen & Taylor, 1980; Simmons & Blyth, 1987; Tobin-Richards et al., 1982), is not considered here. Thus, future efforts will include consideration of pubertal status, timing, and other factors that differentiate adolescents and, thus, may differentially mediate stress vulnerability. Second, although we are in theoretical agreement with the subperiod approach discussed previously (e.g., Thornburg, 1983), only the early and midadolescent periods are represented in the present sample. Whether comparable (i.e., age-appropriate) patterns of internal experience also obtain among older adolescents is a question that remains to be examined. Finally we have yet to determine whether the patterns of internal experience or affectivity described here show good predictive validity to standardized measures of adolescent psychosocial adjustment, for example. As this question is a crucial test of the developmental differentiation hypothesis advocated here, our most immediate efforts will be structured to provide a more rigorous examination of the account developed thus far.

In summary, the present findings underscore the need for a more age-appropriate account (Reese & Rodehaver, 1985) of adolescent's vulnerability to stress, one that incorporates the developmental transitions (e.g., in cognition and social context) that configure and distinguish adolescent subperiods. As illustrated by the present investigation, such transitions may act to mediate patterns of stress vulnerability and resilience during adolescence. Thus, studies of adolescent stress are strengthened by considering the attributes and capabilities that adolescents bring to the contexts of daily life.

ACKNOWLEDGMENTS

The authors are grateful to Mary Chandler and Paul Bly for their assistance in the data analyses presented here.

The research reported in this chapter was supported by a grant awarded to Reed W. Larson (Principal Investigator), Anita L. Greene, and Maryse Richards (Coprincipal Investigators) by the National Institute of Mental Health (1 R01 MH38324, "Stress in Daily Life During Adolescence").

REFERENCES

Blook, J. (1971). *Lives through time*. Berkeley, CA: Bancroft.

Blos, P. (1967). The second individuation process of adolescence. *Psychoanalytic Study of the Child, 22,* 162–186.

Chodorow, N. (1978). *The reproduction of mothering*. Berkeley: University of California Press.

Compas, B. E. (1987a). Stress and life events during childhood and adolescence. *Clinical Psychology Review, 7,* 275–302.

Compas, B. E. (1987b). Coping with stress during childhood and adolescence. *Psychological Bulletin, 101,* 399–403.

Compas, B. E., Davis, G. E., & Forsythe, C. J. (1985). Characteristics of life events during adolescence. *American Journal of Community Psychology, 13,* 677–691.

Compas, B. E., Slavin, L. A., Wagner, B. M., & Vannatta, K. (1986). Relationship of life events and social support with psychological dysfunction among adolescents. *Journal of Youth and Adolescence, 15,* 205–221.

Csikszentmihalyi, M., & Larson, R. W. (1984). *Being adolescent: Conflict and growth in the teenage years*. New York: Basic.

Csikszentmihalyi, M., & Larson, R. W. (1987). The reliability and validity of the Experience Sampling Method. *Journal of Nervous and Mental Diseases, 175,* 526–536.

Danish, S. J., Smyer, M. A., & Nowak, C. A. (1980). Developmental intervention: Enhancing life-event processes. In P. B. Baltes & O. G. Brim (Eds.), *Life-span development and behavior* (pp. 339–363). New York: Academic Press.

Douvan, E., & Adelson, J. (1966). *The adolescent experience*. New York: Wiley.

Felner, R. D., Primavera, J., & Cauce, A. M. (1981). The impact of school transitions: A focus for preventive efforts. *American Journal of Community Psychology, 9,* 449–459.

Fischer, J. L. (1981). Transitions in relationship style from adolescence to young adulthood. *Journal of Youth and Adolescence, 10,* 11–14.

Flavell, J. H. (1982). On cognitive development. *Child Development, 53,* 1–10.

Freud, A. (1958) Adolescence. *Psychoanalytic Study of the Child, 13,* 255–278.

Freud, S. (1925). Three contributions to the sexual theory. *Nervous and Mental Disease Monograph Series* (No. 7). New York: Nervous and Mental Disease Publishing.

Garmezy, N. (1981). Children under stress: Perspectives on antecedents and correlates of vulnerability and resistance to psychopathology. In I. A. Rabin, J. Aronoff, A. M. Barclay, & R. A. Zucker (Eds.), *Further explorations in personality* (pp. 196–269). New York: Wiley.

Garmezy, N. (1983). Stressors of childhood. In N. Garmezy & M. Rutter (Eds.), *Stress, coping and development in children* (pp. 43–84). New York: McGraw Hill.

Gilligan, C. (1982). *In a different voice: Psychological theory and women's development.* Cambridge, MA: Harvard University Press.

Greene, A. L. (1988). Early adolescents' perceptions of stress. *Journal of Early Adolescence, 8,* 391–403.

Greene, A. L. (in press). Formal operations and other aspects of personality development during adolescence. *Adolescence.*

Greene, A. L., & Boxer, A. M. (1986). Daughters and sons as young adults: Restructuring the ties that bind. In N. Datan, A. L. Greene, & H. W. Reese (Eds.), *Life-span developmental psychology: Intergenerational relations,* (pp. 125–150). Hillsdale, NJ: Erlbaum Associates.

Greene, A. L., & Boxer, A. M. (in press). Transitions through adolescence: A view of the issues. In A. L. Greene & A. M. Boxer, *Transitions through adolescence: Research and theory in life-span perspective* (pp. xxx). Hillsdale, NJ: Lawrence Erlbaum Associates.

Hagestad, G. O. (1978). *Role change and socialization in adulthood: The transition to the empty nest.* Unpublished manuscript, Committee on Human Development, University of Chicago.

Hamburg, B. A. (1974). Early adolescence: A specific and stressful stage of the life cycle. In G. Coehlo, D. A. Hamburg, & J. E. Adams (Eds.), *Coping and adaptation.* New York: Basic.

Harris, P. L., Olthof, T., & Terwogt, M. M. (1981). Children's knowledge of emotion. *Journal of Child Psychology and Psychiatry, 22,* 247–261.

Hetherington, E. M., & Anderson, E. R. (1988). The effects of divorce and remarriage on early adolescents and their families. In M. D. Levine & E. R. McAnarney (Eds.), *Early adolescent transitions* (pp. 49–68). Lexington, MA: D. C. Heath.

Hultsch, D. F., & Plemons, J. K. (1979). Life events and life span development. In P. B. Baltes & O. G. Brim (Eds.), *Life-span development and behavior* (pp. 1–31). New York: Academic Press.

Inhelder, B., & Piaget, J. (1958). *The growth of logical thinking.* New York: Basic.

Karnes, F. A., Oehler, J. J., & Jones, G. E. (1985). The relationship between electromyogram level and the children's personality questionnaire as measures of tension in upper elementary gifted students. *Journal of Clinical Psychology, 41,* 169–172.

Labouvie-Vief, G. (1982). Dynamic development and mature autonomy: A theoretical prologue. *Human Development, 25,* 161–191.

Labouvie-Vief, G. (1984). Logic and self regulation from youth to maturity: A model. In M. L. Commons, F. A. Richards, & C. Armon (Eds.), *Beyond formal operations: Late adolescent and adult cognitive development* (pp. 158–179). New York: Praeger.

Larson, R. W. (1983). Adolescents' daily experience with family and friends: Contrasting opportunity systems. *Journal of Marriage and the Family, 45,* 739–750.

Larson, R. W. (1989). Beeping children and adolescents: A method for studying time use and daily experience. *Journal of Youth and Adolescence, 18,* 511–530.

Larson, R. W., & Asmussen, L. (1988, November). *Anger, worry and hurt: An enlarging world of negative emotion.* Paper presented at the Conference on Adolescent Stress, Social Relationships and Mental Health, University of Massachusetts-Boston, Boston, MA.

Larson, R. W., & Csikszentmihalyi, M. (1980). The significance of time alone in adolescent development. *Journal of Current Adolescent Medicine, 2,* 33–40.

Larson, R. W., & Lampan-Petraitis, C. (1989). Daily emotional states as reported by children and adolescents. *Child Development, 60,* 1250–1260.

Lazarus, R. S., & Folkman, S. (1984). *Stress, appraisal, and coping.* New York: Springer.

Leaverton, L., & Hertzog, S. (1979). Adjustment of the gifted. *Journal for the Education of the Gifted, 2,* 149–152.

Lerner, R. M., & Knapp, J. R. (1975). Actual and perceived intrafamilial attitudes of late adolescents and their parents. *Journal of Youth and Adolescence, 4,* 17–36.

Linn, M. C., & Pulos, S. (1983). Male–female differences in predicting displaced volume: Strategy usage, aptitude relationships, and experience influences. *Journal of Educational Psychology, 75,* 86–96.

Maccoby, E. E. (1983). Social-emotional development and response to stressors. In N. Garmezy & M. Rutter (Eds.), *Stress, coping and development in children* (pp. 217–234). New York: McGraw-Hill.

Moran, P., & Eckenroade, J. (1988, March). *Social stress and depression during adolescence: Gender and age differences.* Paper presented at the Biennial Meeting of the Society for Research on Adolescence, Alexandria, VA.

Neimark, E. D. (1982). Adolescent thought: Transition to formal operations. In B. B. Wolman (Ed.), *Handbook of developmental psychology* (pp. 486–502). Englewood Cliffs, NJ: Prentice-Hall.

Offer, D. (1969). *The psychological world of the teenager.* New York: Basic.

Petersen, A. C., & Spiga, R. (1982). Adolescence and stress. In L. Goldberger & S. Breznitz (Eds.), *Handbook of stress: Theoretical and clinical aspects* (pp. 515–528). New York: Free Press.

Petersen, A. C., & Taylor, B. (1980). The biological approach to adolescence: Biological change and psychological adaptation. In J. Adelson (Ed.), *Handbook of adolescent psychology* (pp. 117–168). New York: Wiley.

Piaget, J. (1976). *The grasp of consciousness.* Cambridge, MA: Harvard University Press.

Reese, H. W., & Rodehaver, D. (1985). Problem solving and complex decision-making. In J. E. Birren & K. W. Schaie (Eds.), *Handbook of the psychology of aging* (pp. 475–499). New York: Van Nostrand-Rheinhold.

Reese, H. W., & Smyer, M. A. (1983). The dimensionalization of life events. In K. A. McCluskey & E. Callahan (Eds.), *Life-span developmental psychology: Nonnormative life events* (pp. 1–33). New York: Academic Press.

Rutter, M. (1980). The long-term effects of early experience. *Developmental Medicine and Child Neurology, 22,* 800–915.

Rutter, M. (1983). Stress, coping, and development: Some issues and some questions. In N. Garmezy & M. Rutter (Eds.), *Stress, coping and development in children* (pp. 1–41). New York: McGraw-Hill.

Simmons, R. G., & Blyth, D. A. (1987). *Moving into adolescence: The impact of pubertal change and school context.* New York: Aldine De Gruyter.

Swearingen, E. M., & Cohen, L. H. (1985). Life events and psychological distress: A prospective study of young adolescents. *Developmental Psychology, 21,* 1045–1054.

Thoits, P. A. (1983). Dimensions of life events that influence psychological distress: An evaluation and synthesis of the literature. In H. B. Kaplan (Ed.), *Psychological stress: Trends in theory and research* (pp. 33–102). New York: Academic Press.

Thornburg, H. D. (1983). Is early adolescence really a stage of development? *Theory into Practice, 31,* 79–84.

Tobin-Richards, M., Boxer, A. M., & Petersen, A. C. (1982). The psychological significance of pubertal change: Sex differences in the perception of self during early adolescence. In J. Brooks-Gunn & A. C. Peterson (Eds.), *Girls at puberty: Psychosocial perspectives* (pp. 127–154). New York: Plenum.

Troll, L. E., & Bengtson, V. L. (1982). Intergenerational relations throughout the life span. In B. Wolman (Ed.), *Handbook of developmental psychology* (pp. 890–911). Englewood Cliffs, NJ: Prentice-Hall.

Wallerstein, J. S., & Kelly, J. B. (1980). *Surviving the break up: How children and parents cope with divorce.* New York: Basic.

Yamamoto, K. (1979). Children's ratings of the stressfulness of experiences. *Developmental Psychology, 15,* 581–582.

Yamamoto, K., & Felsenthal, H. M. (1982). Stressful experiences of children: Professional judgments. *Psychological Reports, 50,* 1087–1093.

V

ADULTHOOD

11

Social Supports and Physical Health: Symptoms, Health Behaviors, and Infectious Disease

Sheldon Cohen
Carnegie Mellon University

Since the mid 1970s, there has been a strong interest among behavioral and medical scientists alike in the possible roles that social networks and social supports play in influencing physical health. This interest received substantial impetus in 1979 from the publication of data from a nine-year prospective study of the residents of Alameda County, California (Berkman & Syme, 1979). The study found that a "social integration" index—including questions about marital status, having friends, associating with neighbors, and belonging to formal and informal groups—was related to mortality. Initially healthy persons who were more socially integrated (i.e., had more friends, family and neighbor interactions, belonged to groups, etc.) lived longer than their less integrated counterparts. Apparently something about the social environment had an important influence on health.

This ground-breaking study raised at least as many questions as it answered. First, it was unclear how the social environment would influence physical health. What psychological, behavioral, and biological mechanisms linked the social environment to physical morbidity and mortality? Second, the quality of measurement of the social environment in the Alameda County Study (as well as later epidemiologic studies reporting similar results, e.g., Blazer, 1982; House, Robbins, & Metzner, 1982; Schoenbach, Kaplan, Fredman, & Kleinbach, 1986) was not state-of-the-art, and the conceptual underpinning of the social integration index was virtually nonexistent. What did the index actually measure, and what other conceptualizations of the social environment would influence health?

Because many of these issues are primarily psychological in nature, the time was ripe for psychologists to get involved. Potential contributions included the provisions of: (a) theoretical underpinnings for various conceptualizations of

213

social networks and supports, (b) hypotheses about how social supports influence health, and (c) psychometrically valid instruments for the measurement of social networks and social supports.

My own interests in this area were kindled during the late 1970s, and I have been involved in research on the relation between social support and health ever since. This chapter provides an overview of nearly ten years of research that I and my colleagues have done in this area and presents a representative sampling of this work. The work I report is meant to exemplify approaches psychologists can take to this problem but *is not* intended to be a comprehensive coverage of areas where important contributions can be made. I begin by summarizing some of the basic theoretical assumptions made when we began this course of study and by briefly discussing the development of a social support scale. I then summarize a series of studies we conducted on the influences of social supports on psychological and physical symptoms. This work was essential in the process of instrument development and in clarifying a number of theoretical questions. Discussion of the symptom work is followed by summaries of our more recent work on the roles social supports play in determining two "harder" outcomes: health behaviors and biologically verified disease. Included are studies on perceived support as a buffer of the effects of stress on quitting smoking and ongoing work on the role of social supports in susceptibility to infectious disease.

STRESS-BUFFERING VERSUS MAIN EFFECT MODELS

There were few data on the influence of support systems on physical health when the Alameda County study was published. However, John Cassel (1976; also see Cobb, 1976), a social epidemiologist at the University of North Carolina, had proposed that social support positively influenced health and well-being, and he suggested a possible mechanism for this influence—stress-buffering. The idea of the stress-buffering hypothesis is that social support operates by protecting people against the pathogenic effects of stressors. That is, stressors put one at risk for disease, but stressor related risk is reduced or totally ameliorated when those confronted with stressors have strong social support networks. An important corollary of this hypothesis is that outside of facing stressful events, social support is not really important.

Figures 11.1B and 11.1C present two theoretical versions of the data predicted by the stress-buffering model. Figure 11.1C represents an extreme version, suggesting that support totally ameliorates the influence of stress on health outcomes. (Symptoms are used as an example in the figure). Figure 11.1B represents a more moderate version of the hypothesis, suggesting that support attenuates the influence of stress but does not provide total protection. Both versions of the stress-buffering hypothesis are supported by a statistical interaction of stress and social support.

The alternative hypothesis is that stress is not really an issue in social support's

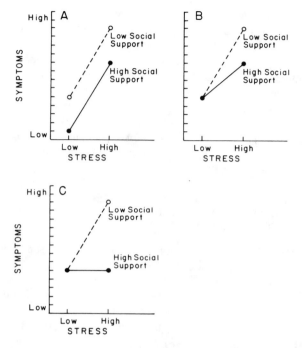

FIG. 11.1. Depiction of main effect of social support on symptomatology and two forms of the stress-buffering interaction. Reprinted from Cohen & Wills (1985).

influence on health. That is, having social support is beneficial to health overall, irrespective of stressor exposure. This is termed the main effect hypothesis, because it predicts a main effect of social support *without* a statistical interaction between stress and social support. Figure 11.1A represents this alternative.

The focus of most of the work discussed in this chapter is on establishing and understanding the stress-buffering hypothesis. However, many of the studies pit the main effect and stress-buffering hypotheses against one another. Moreover, near the end of the chapter, I return again to discussing the main effect model. At any rate, FIG. 11.1 provides a template to compare with results of the studies I report, providing an aid in interpreting which of the models is supported by each study.

Support Concepts and Support Mechanisms

Although there are still very few studies comparing the stress-buffering and main effect models in the prediction of physical disease, the literature on the relative efficacy of these models in the prediction of psychological symptomatology has grown enormously over the last ten years. In 1985, Tom Wills and I published an integrative review article of this work (Cohen & Wills, 1985). The published review included over 40 studies comparing the main-effect and stress-buffering hypotheses.

The Cohen and Wills (1985; also see Kessler & McLeod, 1985) review found support for both main effect and stress-buffering models. However, which model was supported in any specific study depended on the nature of the social support or network measure that was used. Stress-buffering effects were found with measures that assessed *perceived availability* of social support. Main-effects were found with measures that assessed *degree of integration* in a larger social network. This latter measure is the social integration type measure used in the Alameda County mortality study.

Psychologic Mediators of the Relation between Social Support and Health

What are the psychologic and behavior factors that link the social environment to health? In the following section, I selectively review some alternative mechanisms. (A detailed discussion of mechanisms linking support to health can be found in Cohen, 1988). The focus is on the influences of the social environment on the *onset and progression* of disease. Although many of the arguments also apply to disease recovery, a thorough treatment of recovery requires additional considerations such as the influence of support on disease symptoms, rehabilitative behaviors, availability and quantity of caretaking, and so forth. Finally the discussion and models (FIGS. 11.2 and 11.3) are limited to paths moving in one direction, from support to health or illness. Alternative paths are excluded for the sake of brevity. Their exclusion is not, however, intended to reflect any hypotheses about their existence.

Main-effect model.   Figure 11.2 represents the main-effect hypothesis—social support directly influences health and well-being irrespective (independent) of stress levels. Because our review suggested that main effects are driven by *social*

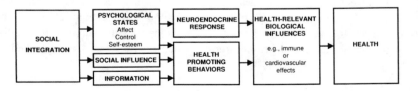

FIG. 11.2.   Main-effect model of the psychological and biological pathways linking social integration to the onset and progression of disease. All indicated paths move in one causal direction. The exclusion of alternative paths is not intended to reflect any hypotheses about their existence.

integration, the explanations I present are directed at this conceptualization of social networks. First, social integration may facilitate health-promoting behaviors. Persons with stronger networks may take better care of themselves (e.g., exercise, drink less, and smoke less). Better self-care could occur, because an integrated network makes persons feel better about themselves (e.g., elevated self-esteem and feelings of control), because networks provide accurate information in regard to a healthier life style, or because networks apply social pressures on members to engage in health promoting behaviors. (Of course, networks can also provide inaccurate information or apply social pressures to engage in behaviors detrimental to health, e.g., McKinlay, 1973; Sanders, 1982; Seeman, Seeman, & Sayles, 1985). Second, belonging to an integrated network may cause positive changes in psychological states (affect, control, self-esteem) that influence neuroendocrine response (cf. Bovard, 1959). Hormones released (or suppressed) as a response to these states are presumed to influence disease pathogenesis through their effects on biological systems more proximate to disease outcomes (e.g., the immune and cardiovascular systems) (cf. Ader, 1981; Glass, 1977). Third (not represented in FIG. 11.3), integrated social networks may prevent disease by providing material aid, for example, the provision of food, clothing, and housing could limit exposure to risk factors such as insufficient diet and exposure to cold. Finally social integration may influence health merely because it indirectly reflects exposure to stress (not represented in FIG. 11.3). For example, social networks may provide warnings and information that help persons avoid stressor confrontation. Alternatively weak social networks (isolation) may act as stressors and hence *not belonging* to an integrated network may put persons under disease risk.

Stress-buffering model.   Figure 11.3 represents the stress-buffering hypothesis. In this case, I focus on explanations for the role *perceived availability of social support* plays in this process. The theory in developing this model was that people

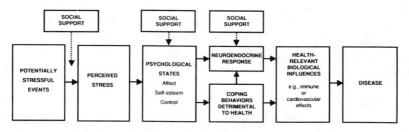

FIG. 11.3. Stress-buffering model of psychological and biological pathways linking perceived availability of support to health and well-being. All indicated paths move in one causal direction. The exclusion of alternative paths is not intended to reflect any hypotheses about their existence.

confront objective stressful events and appraise whether or not they can cope with those events (Lazarus, 1966; Lazarus & Folkman, 1984). If they find the event threatening or otherwise demanding, and at the same time find their coping resources inadequate, they experience stress. We will refer to this state as perceived or appraised stress. The appraisal of stress is presumed to result in negative psychological states that either trigger behaviors detrimental to health, or biological processes (e.g., elevated neuroendocrine response) that put persons under risk for various diseases.

Perceived support can enter into this model through its influence on the stress appraisal process; that is, a supportive network may help by providing information regarding how threatening an event actually is, suggesting effective coping responses and/or providing aid in coping (e.g., Cohen & McKay, 1984; Thoits, 1985). The perception of support may merely reflect these processes. However, because the appraisal process is cognitive in nature (i.e., it all goes on in your head), the mere belief that such resources are available may be enough to short-circuit stressor appraisal. This argument suggests that perceived support works not because it provides a reasonable approximation of available resources, but because the *belief* that support is available is what is critical in appraising whether events are stressful (e.g., Wethington & Kessler, 1986).

Perceived support may also operate after a situation is appraised as stressful, between stress appraisal and the illness outcome (cf. House, 1981). This could occur through reappraisal of a situation initially judged as stressful, through the facilitation of successful coping with stress-induced affect (Thoits, 1985), through the discouragement of unhealthy behavioral coping styles, or by directly short-circuiting a stress-triggered biological process (e.g., damping neuroendocrine response).

There is another theoretical prediction regarding stress-buffering effects that is important for the work I am going to discuss. We predicted that there must be a *match* between the needs elicited by a stressor and the available support resources in order to get a stress-buffering effect (Cohen & McKay, 1984; Cohen & Wills, 1985). For example, if you lose your job, having friends who will gladly give (or loan) you money may be appropriate support. On the other hand, if a spouse, parent, or friend dies, having friends who will give you money is not very helpful. So there is a need for a match between the kinds of resources that are available and the kinds of needs that are elicited by the stressful events that one confronts.

What is proposed earlier is a specific matching hypothesis (i.e., there needs to be a match between the specific needs elicited by a stressor and available social resources). Tom Wills and I also suggested a more global matching hypothesis; there are some globally useful resources that are helpful in confronting a wide range of stressors (Cohen & Wills, 1985). One of these resources is appraisal support—having people you can talk to about problems, who can help define problems, provide ways of coping with problems, and ways of coping with stress-triggered affect. The other one is self-esteem support—having people who make you feel better about yourself. We felt that appraisal would serve as a global resource because the appraisal of most stressors is subject to information provided by others. (For exceptions, see discussion of social comparison as a model for social support in Cohen & McKay, 1984). We felt that self-esteem would operate as a global resource, because many stressors are in fact threats to self-esteem (cf. Wills, 1985).

Measuring Perceived Social Support

Our early work focused on the stress-buffering hypothesis. Although the literature suggested that studies using perceived support measures (and appropriate methodologies) often found stress-buffering effects, there were almost as many measures as there were studies. Moreover, the measures available at that time were impure in terms of what concept they represented and lacked in terms of traditional psychometric validation.

For the reasons I just outlined and because I wanted a measurement instrument that assessed different types of social resources, the first step was to design a measure of perceived availability of social support. I wanted a scale score that reflected the total perceived availability of social support as well as subscale scores reflecting different types (or functions) of social resources. In developing the Interpersonal Support Evaluation List (ISEL), we focused on four functions that I had proposed as important in stress-buffering: appraisal support—having people to talk to about problems; self-esteem support—having people who make you feel better about yourself; belonging support—having others to do things with; and tangible support—having people who would provide material aid (Cohen & McKay, 1984). Separate forms of the ISEL were designed for both college students (Cohen & Hoberman, 1983) and for the general population (Cohen, Mermelstein, Kamarck, & Hoberman, 1985). Psychometrics on these scales have been reported in over 10 studies and are summarized in Cohen et al. (1985).

Subscale independence. There has been some controversy recently as to whether the ISEL subscales actually differentiate between different support functions (House & Kahn, 1985; Sarason, Shearin, Pierce, & Sarason, 1987). In response, let me refer you to the recent work of Jeff Brookings (Brookings & Bolton, 1988) that reports a confirmatory factor analysis of the student scale. Brookings found that the models that held up best were the ones that combined all of the subscales (entire ISEL score) *and* the one that proposed the four separate subscales. In our own work with more standard factor analysis, we have consistently (across samples) found independent factors for appraisal and tangible support. We often find that self-esteem support is also relatively independent, but it occasionally (especially in adult samples) clusters with appraisal. In most cases, however, belonging is so highly correlated with appraisal that we are unable to separate them empirically. As will be apparent from the studies we discuss later, even with some overlap between scales, discriminating between support functions has proved to be empirically useful.

THE SYMPTOM STUDIES

The first study using the ISEL examined the possibility that perceived support buffered the effects of negative life events on symptomatology. The subjects were 70 undergraduates at the University of Oregon (Cohen & Hoberman, 1983). Figure 11.4 presents the data when the entire ISEL is considered. As apparent from the figure, when depressive symptoms were the outcome, we found the stress-buffering interaction that was predicted (similar to FIG. 11.1B).[1] We find a similar effect with physical symptoms, although there is an unpredicted cross-over with those under low stress having somewhat higher symptomatology related with higher levels of support. Figure 11.5 presents similar data from a study of 112 Oregon undergraduates conducted one year later. In this case, we found a stress-buffering effect with both depressive and physical symptoms without a cross-over in the physical symptoms data.

Also of importance are the subscale data. Subscale data from the Cohen and Hoberman study indicate stress-buffering effects for appraisal, belonging, and self-esteem support. Neither a main nor buffering effect was found in the case of tangible support. Unfortunately subscale data from the second Oregon student study are not available.

The next study is not from our lab, but because it used the ISEL in testing the stress-buffering hypothesis, it provides relevant information for our discussion. These data are from a sample of 92 University of Delaware students collected by Larry Cohen (L. Cohen, McGowan, Fooskas, & Rose, 1984). The study was longitudinal—stress and symptoms were measured at the onset of the study and stress, social support, and symptoms measured two months later. Cohen analyzed the data cross-sectionally at time 2 and prospectively, predicting time 2 symptomatology from time 1 stress and time 2 support while controlling for time 1 symptoms. Both the cross-sectional and prospective analyses indicated support for a stress-buffering effect of the overall ISEL. Figure 11.6 shows the effect for the cross-section at

---

[1]No statistical analyses are reported in this chapter. Most of the individual studies have been published elsewhere with detailed statistical descriptions of the analyses reported in the original publications. When an effect of stress-buffering is indicated, a significant ($p < .05$) stress × support interaction was found. The interaction is tested after the main effects of stress and main effects of social support have already been entered into the equation (see Cohen & Wills, 1985; Reis, 1984). In order to avoid Type I error, subscale analyses of the ISEL have been done only when the overall stress × ISEL effect is significant. They are considered exploratory. Data reported in the cold study are all based on correlations with $p < .05$ or better.

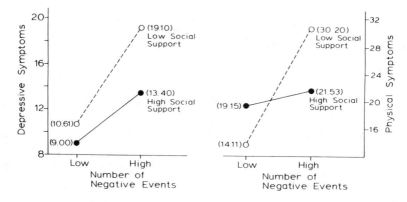

FIG. 11.4. Depiction of the interaction between number of negative life events and perceived availability of social support in the prediction of physical and depressive symptoms from a sample of 70 University of Oregon undergraduates. Reprinted from Cohen and Hoberman (1983) with permission of V. H. Winston and Sons, Inc.

time 2. Subscale contributions varied somewhat across analyses. Time 2 analyses predicting scores on the Beck Depression Inventory (BDI) indicated appraisal, self-esteem, and belonging were operative, while the prospective analysis of BDI scores indicated that only the self-esteem scale was operative.

Figure 11.7 presents data from a longitudinal study of 64 people participating in a clinic-based smoking cessation program (Cohen et al., 1985; Mermelstein,

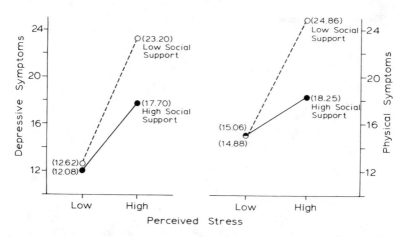

FIG. 11.5. Depiction of the interaction between perceived stress and perceived availability of social support in the prediction of physical and depressive symptoms from a sample of 112 University of Oregon undergraduates.

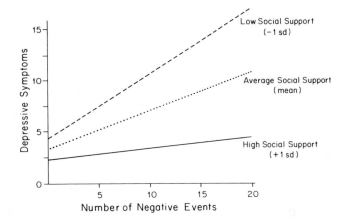

FIG. 11.6.   Depiction of the interaction between number of negative life events and social support from a sample of 92 University of Delaware undergraduates. Adopted from FIG. 2 in Cohen et al. (1984).

Cohen, Lichtenstein, Kamarck, & Baer, 1986). It is a six-week prospective study, with perceived stress, social support, and physical symptoms measured at time 1, and physical symptoms measured again at time 2. The analysis predicted symptoms at time 2 from time 1 stress and support, controlling for time 1 symptoms (cf. Monroe, 1983). As apparent from the left side of the figure, there is a stress-buffering effect for the overall ISEL scale. If you examine the role of the separate subscales, the effect is almost entirely attributable to the appraisal scale. The effect of appraisal is depicted on the right side of the figure.

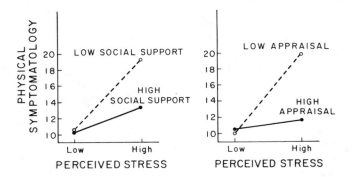

FIG. 11.7.   Depiction of the interaction between perceived stress and perceived availability of social support in the prediction of physical symptomatology from a sample of 64 persons enrolled in a clinic smoking cessation program. The figure on the left is based on the scores from the entire ISEL. The figure on the right is based solely on the ISEL Appraisal subscale.

Threshold or continuous effect? Figure 11.8 is reversed in orientation to attract your attention, because it is slightly different in content. These are data from a study of 609 incoming freshman at Carnegie Mellon University [CMU] (Cohen, Sherrod, & Clark, 1986). One of the questions we addressed in this study was whether stress-buffering effects occurred at a particular threshold of perceived support, or whether the apparent protective influence of perceived support increased in a continuous linear fashion. In short, does some minimum amount of social support protect persons, with additional social support not making any difference? The first thing to notice about the figure is that we again found a stress-buffering effect of the ISEL. Second, as social support increases, the difference in symptomatology between low and high stress decreases. In other words, the more social support available to persons under high stress, the better off they are (i.e., the closer they are to being like the low-stress group). Hence, we found a linear effect, not a threshold effect. Finally the stress-buffering effect of the ISEL in this study was attributable to the appraisal, self-esteem, and belonging subscales. All three demonstrated stress-buffering effects, but there was no buffering effect of tangible support.

Are stress-buffering effects an artifact of personality? My concern with this question arose out of an issue raised by Ken Heller (1979; Heller & Swindle, 1983). Specifically Heller suggested that stress-buffering effects of social support may be due to differences in social competence. In short, the argument was that socially competent people are both more able to attract social support and more able to cope with stressful events.

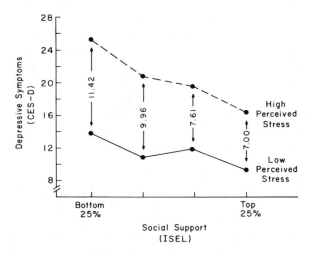

FIG. 11.8.   Depiction of the interaction between perceived stress and social support from a sample of 609 freshman undergraduates at Carnegie Mellon University.

We examined the issue of whether social skills could account for the stress-buffering effects in the study of CMU freshman discussed earlier. As you recall from FIG. 11.8, perceived support operates as a stress buffer in this study. In an additional analysis, we investigated the possible role of three social skills: social confidence, self-disclosure, and social anxiety. In a regression analysis, we forced the three main effects of these scales in first, then life events and social support, then the interactions between stressful life events and the social skills scales, and finally the interaction between life events and social support. In short, we tested for the possibility that the stress-buffering effect of social support occurred above and beyond (independent of) any similar effects of the social skills measures. The results indicated that the support effect held up, even after controlling for the possible influence of these three social skills (Cohen, Sherrod, & Clark, 1986).

These are not, of course, the only personality measures that may account for the stress-buffering effects. However, to make a strong argument that perceived support is acting as a proxy for any personality variable, one would need to show that the variable under consideration operates as a stress buffer. In order to determine which factors may provide an alternative explanation for support effects, we critically reviewed the published studies on personality factors as stress buffers (Cohen & Edwards, 1989). Studies of the following personality factors were included in our review: anomie, arousal, and sensation seeking; coping flexibility; coping styles; hardiness; locus of control; private self-consciousness; self-esteem; social interests; social skills; and Type A behavior. We concluded that locus of control is the only personality factor whose stress-buffering capabilities receive any substantial support. When defined as a generalized concept applying only to control of things outside oneself, the data are fairly consistent with the operation of internal control as a stress buffer. I do not want to deny that any of these other factors act as stress buffers but to suggest that there is no convincing evidence at this time that this is true.

In sum, there is considerable evidence that perceived support operates as a stress buffer but little that plausible proxy variables do. There are no published studies directly addressing the possibility that locus of control, the one variable that appears to operate as a stress buffer, underlies the perceived support effect. However, studies demonstrating that persons with *internal* control and high levels of social support are less impacted by stress than persons with *external* control and high levels of social support indicate that control operates as a moderator of stress by support interaction, not as a proxy for support (Lefcourt, Martin, & Saleh, 1984; Sandler & Lakey, 1982). Hence, up until this point, proxy explanations of perceived support effects seem unfounded.

Are perceptions of available social support valid?   An issue related to the discussion of personality proxies is whether measures of perceived social support reflect the actual availability of support or merely a grossly distorted representation of the availability of social resources. It is conceivable that persons have biased cognitive representations of their social environments. Moreover, these biases could be driven by stable individual differences in personality. Several investigators have addressed the issue of whether perceived availability of social support really is a reflection of people's social support systems. Carolyn Cutrona (1986), Amiram Vinokur and his colleagues (Vinokur, Schul & Caplan, 1987), and Harry Reis (personal communication) have all done independent work where they measured the perceived availability of social support in people and subsequently had them track their interpersonal interactions over some period of time. All three studies found that perceived availability of social support corresponded with people's reports of the support available to them in their environment. Particularly interesting in this context is Harry Reis' work. Using the ISEL, Reis found that people who are high on the appraisal scale (who said that they had people they could talk to about problems, who could help them cope with problems) subsequently reported having more interactions in which they talked to friends about problems than people who were lower on that scale.

Summary.   Our work on perceived availability of support as a buffer of cumulative stress effects on symptomatology clearly and consistently indicates stress-buffering effects of the overall ISEL scale. These effects were found in both cross-sectional and prospective studies, and typically suggest a partial (see FIG. 11.1b) ameliorative effect. The effect also appears to be linear in nature, that is, it increases with increasing perceptions of support. In most studies, appraisal and/or self-esteem support were at least partly responsible for stress-buffering effects. However, belonging was often similarly operative. Only tangible support was consistently ineffective. We used cumulative stress measures as opposed to looking at specific stressors (e.g., exams, bereavement, or unemployment), therefore, the reviewed work does not provide a good test of the hypothesis that support is effective only when it matches the needs elicited by stressful events. The general effectiveness of appraisal and self-esteem support are, however, consistent with our argument that these two types of support operate as global resource.

The studies examining possible alternative explanations for the perceived social support effect suggest little evidence for such alternatives. Stress-buffering effects of perceived support survive analyses where social-skill effects are partialled out, and perceived support seems to reflect the actual availability of social resources.

PERCEIVED SOCIAL SUPPORT AND SMOKING CESSATION AND MAINTENANCE

As mentioned earlier, a primary path through which social support could influence health is by influencing health relevant behaviors. Smoking is the behavior most strongly linked with physical health outcomes, thus, studying the role of support in smoking behavior seemed like the appropriate place to start. Hence, Ed

Lichtenstein and I began a program of research on the role of social supports in quitting smoking and maintaining abstinence. We began by considering how social networks could influence people's attempts to quit smoking. We looked at a number of different possibilities (see Cohen, Lichtenstein, Mermelstein, Kingsolver, Baer, & Kamarck, 1988, for a detailed discussion). However, for the purpose of this chapter, I would like to stick with the stress-buffering issue. Our thinking in this area was that stress makes it harder to quit smoking and maintain abstinence, and that support should help protect quitters from the deleterious effects of stress on the quitting process (see Shiffman et al., 1986; Wills & Shiffman, 1985). Moreover, although environmental and social stressors were important considerations in this context, we felt that it was even more important to consider the stress created by the act of quitting. If perceived social support operated as a stress buffer, persons with higher scores on the ISEL would be more likely to succeed at this stressful task. We assume all quitters are under relatively high levels of stress and, hence, are concerned here with a main effect of perceived availability of support rather than an interaction between stress and support.

Our analysis got a little more complicated in that we broke up the sequence of quitting into different stages: the decision to quit, quitting itself, early maintenance (defined as the first three months after quitting), and late maintenance (three to twelve months after quitting) (see discussion of stages by Prochaska & DiClemente, 1983; and by Brownell, Marlatt, Lichtenstein, & Wilson, 1986; our theoretical discussion of support and stages in Cohen et al., 1988). We hypothesized that stress would be particularly important for cessation and early maintenance but relatively unimportant for late maintenance. This hypothesis partly derived from existing evidence that we and others had collected suggesting that stress was important during the early stages of quitting (Cohen, 1986; Cohen, Kamarck, & Mermelstein 1983; Shiffman, 1982) and partly from our gut feelings that the early stages were the most likely points for stress to interrupt the quitting process. The studies I will discuss do not address the decision to quit stage but only the last three stages. We predicted that perceived availability of social support would predict who quits smoking and success at early but not late maintenance.

We have, in the last eight years, conducted four one-year prospective studies. In these studies, people are given the perceived social support measure (the ISEL) upon entering the study—before starting to quit smoking. The first three studies each involved between 50 and 70 persons enrolled in formal smoking cessation programs run at a university clinic (Baer, 1987; Cohen et al., 1988; Mermelstein et al., 1986). The fourth study included 465 people in the Pittsburgh community who were quitting smoking by themselves, 70 of whom were administered the ISEL. As noted previously, in all four studies, we assessed perceived support before participants began the quitting process and then followed them for one year after their expected quit date.

The results of these studies are summarized in Table 11.1. As apparent from the table, in one clinic study, the total ISEL score predicted *cessation,* and the appraisal and self-esteem subscales were responsible for the effect. However, the consistent finding is clearly for *early maintenance.* Across three of the four studies, we found that those who quit (for at least 24 hours) were more likely to still be abstinent at three months, if they had high scores on the ISEL.[2] In the first two of those studies, the effects were due primarily to the appraisal scale. In the self-quitting study, none of the subscales were independently related to outcome. The one piece of datum that is inconsistent with our *stage* prediction occurs in the third study. Unexpectedly the ISEL also predicted long-term maintenance. That is, persons with higher ISEL scores who were abstinent at three months were more likely to be abstinent at twelve months than their counterparts with lower scores.

In short, the data roughly fit our model. Overall, there is strong evidence for the positive influence of high levels of perceived social support and suggestive evidence for the argument that stress and, therefore, the perceived availability of support are most important during quitting and early maintenance.

THE COMMON COLD STUDY

Although there has been a great deal of research on the influence of social supports on symptomatology, there are few data linking any conceptualization of support to the onset of a biologically verified disease. This section provides a description of our ongoing work on the effects of social integration and social support on susceptibility to infectious disease. The foci of this work include establishing relations between support and biologically verified disease, and identifying behavioral, psychological and biological mediators of support-disease links.

This study is being conducted in collaboration with David Tyrrell and Andy Smith of the Common Cold Unit (CCU), which is part of the Medical Research Council in Britain. The CCU runs clinical trials to assess the effects of various cold viruses. Over the 30 or so years that the Common Cold Unit has been running trials, they have found that there is tremendous variability in who among those exposed to viruses develop colds. Up until now, attempts to explain this variability have primarily been immunologic in nature. (For exceptions, see Broadbent, Broadbent, Phillpotts, & Wallace, 1984; Totman, Kiff, Reed, & Craig, 1980).

---

[2]Given a directional hypothesis and the replicative purpose of studies 2 through 4, the use of a two-tailed test in evaluating the relation between support and three-month continuous abstinence is quite conservative. One-tail probabilities for studies 2 and 3 would be .03 and .05 respectively. It is also possible to calculate the joint probability corrected for chance differences of finding these three-month results across the four studies. The nonsignificant probability for study 2 is not readily available, therefore, I will make the conservative assumption that it is 1. Hence, the joint probability corrected for chance is $1 \times .05 \times .06 \times .10/ .5^4 = .005$.

TABLE 11.1
Stages at Which Pretreatment ISEL (and ISEL Subscales) Predicted Smoking Cessation and Maintenance in Four Prospective Studies[1]

| | Stage of Cessation[2] | | |
	Cessation (End of Treatment)	Early Maint. (3 Mo. Post)	Late Maint. (12 Mo. Post)
Clinic Study I		ISEL Total (Appraisal)	
Clinic Study II	ISEL Total (Appraisal & Self-Esteem)		
Clinic Study III		ISEL Total* (Appraisal)	ISEL Total (Appraisal)
Self-quit Study IV		ISEL Total**	

[1]There were no significant effects in cells where the scale and subscale are not indicated. In all cases where effects occurred, persons with higher social support scores were more likely to quit or remain abstinent.

[2]The cessation state represents the predictions of quitting smoking for at least 24 hours. The early maintenance stage represents prediction of smoking status at 3 months for 24-hour quitters. The late maintenance stage represents prediction of smoking status at 12 months for persons who were abstinent at 3 months.

   $p < .05$, if no asterisk
   *$p < .06$
   **$p < .10$

Overall, however, the previral challenge antibody levels standardly used by the CCU have not been extremely successful in predicting outcome. It is clear that persons with specific neutralizing antibody to a virus (those who have been previously exposed to the virus) are at least partially protected from reinfection. However, beyond that, there has not been much variance accounted for.

In my collaboration with the CCU, we are examining whether we can predict response to viral challenge from a psychological profile taken prior to challenge. In particular, the emphasis is on assessing the possible roles of social integration and perceived social support in suspectibility to infection and in specifying the psychologic, behavioral, and immunological pathways that link support to susceptibility. When completed, the study will include over 1,000 volunteers, allowing adequate power for testing hypotheses that require multiple controls and an opportunity for split-sample replication.

Main effect and stress-buffering models.   We are testing both the main effect and buffering models discussed earlier (FIGS. 11.2 & 11.3). In the case of main effects, we are specifically testing the proposal that social integration has a main effect on susceptibility to infection, with more integrated persons showing less infection and less symptomatology. Psychological mediators of a social integration–infection link that we are considering include increased personal control, self-esteem, and positive affect, and decreased negative affect. Health behavior mediation under consideration includes decreased smoking and drinking, increased exercise, improved diet, and quality of sleep. Finally immune mediation is being assessed by a number of measures of both humoral and cellular immunity.

In the case of stress-buffering effects, we are testing the proposal that stress increases susceptibility to infection and that high levels of perceived support protect (or buffer) against this increased risk. We hope to determine the point at which perceived support short circuits the stress–disease process by assessing objective stressful events, stress perceptions, and negative affective responses. (Recall that we proposed earlier that support may intervene between the objective event and perception of that event and/or after an event has been appraised as stressful—see FIG. 11.3.) We are also interested in identifying psychological, behavioral, and biological pathways that link stress to infection. Hypothesized psychological pathways we are testing include lowered personal control, self-esteem, and positive affect, and elevated negative affect. The five measures of health behavior discussed earlier will be used to assess whether stress influences on susceptibility are mediated by health behaviors. Here the assumption is that stress may result in coping behaviors deleterious to health (e.g., increases in smoking and drinking, decreases in exercise and sleep, and a poorer diet), and as a consequence place persons under greater risk for infection. If perceived support operates as a stress buffer in this case, no relation between stress and health behaviors would be expected for those with high levels of support.

Trial description.   Healthy volunteers are recruited to participate in a nine-day, live-in isolation trial at the CCU. Before arriving at the unit, demographics and medical histories are obtained through the mail. Prior to viral exposure, each volunteer is given a thorough physical examination, has blood drawn, and nasal secretion samples are taken. Psychological measures and health behaviors are also assessed during this three-day, prechallenge period. Late on the third day or early on the fourth, the volunteers are exposed (in nasal drops) to a cold virus or to a placebo. Over the remainder of the trial, their biologic and symptomatologic responses are carefully tracked. Nasal secretion samples are collected daily to detect viral shedding (cellular reproduction of the virus). Handkerchiefs (tissues) used by volunteers are placed in plastic bags and sealed—they are later counted and weighed to assess the amount of nasal secretion, and daily symptom interviews are conducted by a physician blind to psychologic and immune status and to their experimental condition. On the ninth day of the trial, ratings of volunteer satisfaction with their flatmates, physician clinical ratings, and volunteer clinical ratings of their cold are all obtained. Three weeks after the beginning of the trial, a final blood sample is collected (by volunteer's own physician or local hospital) to look at serum antibody levels that take that long to change.

At the end of the trial, volunteers are classified into three outcome categories: clinical cold, subclinical cold, and not infected. To be assigned to the clinical cold classification, a volunteer must show both biologic (a four-fold increase in the production of specific antibodies to the virus and/or virus shedding—cellular reproduction of the virus) and symptomatologic responses (e.g., headache, runny nose, fever, handkerchief use, etc.). Those in the subclinical cold category demonstrate biologic infection but *do not* have cold symptoms. Finally those in the not-infected category show neither biologic nor symptomatologic indications of being exposed to the virus. On the average, roughly one-third of the volunteers fall in each category.

Some preliminary results.   The evidence discussed in the following section is preliminary, based on approximately 300 volunteers. These data are cross-sectional in nature. That is, they involve correlations between the psychosocial factors, health behaviors, and immune function at entering the trial. We need very large numbers to provide a fair test of the stress-buffering hypothesis (cf. Reis, 1984), therefore, I will limit the discussion to the main effect (social integration) model.

As discussed earlier, social integration may influence disease susceptibility through a number of psychological states and/or through health behaviors. In this study, we conceptualized social integration as the number of important roles persons hold (Thoits, 1983). A scale—the Social Network Index (SNI)—was developed that assessed both the number of roles (e.g., spouse, parent, child, employee, student) and the number of relationships across these roles. The associations reported here are found for both measures but are generally stronger for the number of important relationships measure. First, let us ask, if social integration is associated with psychological states. The preliminary data indicate positive correlations between social integration and positive affect, self-esteem, and personal control. There is *no* association of social integration and negative affect. Moreover, social integration is also associated with all five health behavior measures. The greater the level of social integration, the less smoking and drinking, the better diet and sleep, and the more exercise. Finally social integration is correlated with a number of the cellular immune measures in the study. However, whether these relations are indicative of relatively higher levels of immunocompetence in regard to the virus challenge must await analyses of infection susceptibility. In sum, preliminary data suggest the plausibility of many of the pathways between social integration and disease discussed earlier (see FIG. 11.2). The lack of a relation between social integration and negative affect suggests, however, that stress triggered by isolation may not be the underlying cause of SI effects on health. However, this sample is less likely to include the truly isolated individuals who are present in the general population samples and, hence, may not provide an adequate test of the isolation hypothesis.

CONCLUSIONS

The epidemiological data on the role of social integration in morbidity and mortality have clearly established that the social environment plays an important role in health and well-being (see review in Cohen, 1988). Our own work suggests that pathways through which such effects occur depend on the particular conceptualization of the social environment one chooses to study. Social integration appears to promote health irrespective of stress levels, whereas perceived availability of social support operates as a stress buffer.

The particular focus of this chapter has been stress-buffering effects. We have discovered that when a perceived availability of social support measure is used, these effects reliably occur in the prediction of psychological and physical symptoms.[3] Moreover, perceived support is also related to success in quitting smoking and maintaining abstinence, especially in the first three months after quitting. In both the symptom and smoking behavior data, the effects are primarily attributable to appraisal and self-esteem support—two types of support that are presumed to be effective in the face of a wide range of stressors.

Work on possible artifactual explanations for these effects suggest that they are robust in the face of controls for such artifacts. They are not explicable in terms of social skills or other obvious personality variables. Moreover, perceived support is not a grossly biased estimate of available support but rather provides at least a rough representation of the support available in the social environment.

The role of social integration in producing main effects on health has been discussed only in the context of the study of susceptibility to cold viruses. Preliminary data from this study provide evidence for a number of pathways through which social integration might influence disease susceptibility. Social integration is positively associated with a number of beneficial psychological states and with engaging in health-promoting behaviors. Moreover, social integration is also associated with cellular immune modulation that might provide a more direct (than health behaviors) biologic explanation for the link between social integration and disease susceptibility.

ACKNOWLEDGMENTS

This chapter is based on an invited address delivered to the American Psychological Association, August, 1987, and adapted for the Eleventh Biennial West Virginia University Conference on Life-Span Developmental Psychology. Preparation of this chapter was supported by an NIMH Research Scientist Development Award (K02 MH00721). Research reported in the chapter was supported by

---

[3]This assumes appropriate sample, adequate sample size, an influence of stress on the health outcome, and reliable instruments (Cohen & Wills, 1985).

grants from the National Science Foundation (BNS 77–08576), the National Heart Lung and Blood Institute (HL29547), the National Cancer Institute (CA38243), the National Institute of Allergies and Infectious Diseases (AI23072), and the Office of Naval Research (N00014–88–K–0063).

REFERENCES

Ader, R. (1981). *Psychoneuroimmunology*. New York: Academic Press.

Baer, J. (1987). *Perceived social support, smoking in the social network and smoking relapse: A followup report*. Unpublished manuscript, Department of Psychology, University of Washington, Seattle.

Berkman, L. F., & Syme, S. L. (1979). Social networks, host resistance, and mortality: A nine-year follow-up study of Alameda County residents. *American Journal of Epidemiology, 109,* 186–204.

Blazer, D. G. (1982). Social support and mortality in an elderly community population. *American Journal of Epidemiology, 115,* 684–694.

Bovard, E. (1959). The effects of social stimuli on the response to stress. *Psychological Review, 66,* 267–277.

Broadbent, D. E., Broadbent, M. H. P., Phillpotts, R. J., & Wallace, J. (1984). Some further studies on the prediction of experimental colds in volunteers by psychological factors. *Journal of Psychosomatic Research, 28,* 511–523.

Brookings, J. B., & Bolton, B. (1988). Confirmatory factor analysis of the Interpersonal Support Evaluation List. *American Journal of Community Psychology, 16,* 137–147.

Brownell, K. D., Marlatt, G. A., Lichtenstein, E., & Wilson, G. T. (1986). Understanding and preventing relapse. *American Psychologist, 41,* 765–782.

Cassel, J. C. (1976). The contribution of the social environment to host resistance. *American Journal of Epidemiology, 104,* 107–123.

Cobb, S. (1976). Social support as a moderator of life stress. *Psychosomatic Medicine, 38,* 300–314.

Cohen, L. H., McGowan, J., Fooskas, S., & Rose, S. (1984). Positive life events and social support and the relationship between life stress and psychological disorder. *American Journal of Community Psychology, 12,* 567–587.

Cohen, S. (1986). Contrasting the hassle scale and the perceived stress scale. *American Psychologist, 41,* 716–719.

Cohen, S. (1988). Psychosocial models of the role of social support in the etiology of physical disease. *Health Psychology, 7,* 269–297.

Cohen, S., & Edwards, J. R. (1989). Personality characteristics as moderators of the relationship between stress and disorder. In R. W. J. Neufeld (Ed.), *Advances in the investigation of psychological stress* (pp. 235–283). New York: Wiley.

Cohen, S., & Hoberman, H. (1983). Positive events and social supports as buffers of life change stress. *Journal of Applied Social Psychology, 13,* 99–125.

Cohen, S., Kamarck, T., & Mermelstein, R. (1983). A global measure of perceived stress. *Journal of Health and Social Behavior, 24,* 385–396.

Cohen, S., Lichtenstein, E., Mermelstein, R., Kingsolver, K., Baer, J., & Kamarck, T. (1988). Social support interventions for smoking cessation. In B. H. Gottlieb (Ed.), *Creating support groups: Formats, processes and effects.* New York: Sage.

Cohen, S., & McKay, G. (1984). Social support, stress and the buffering hypothesis: A theoretical analysis. In A. Baum, J. E. Singer, & S. E. Taylor (Eds.), *Handbook of psychology and health.* (Vol. 4, pp. 253–268). Hillsdale, NJ: Lawrence Erlbaum Associates.

Cohen, S., Mermelstein, R., Kamarck, T., & Hoberman, H. (1985). Measuring the functional components of social support. In I. G. Sarason & B. Sarason (Eds.), *Social support: Theory, research and applications* (pp. 73–94). The Hague: Martinus Nijhoff.

Cohen, S., Sherrod, D. R., & Clark, M. S. (1986). Social skills and the stress-protective role of social support. *Journal of Personality and Social Psychology, 50,* 963–973.

Cohen, S., & Wills, T. A. (1985). Social support, stress and the buffering hypothesis. *Psychological Bulletin, 98,* 310–357.

Cutrona, C. E. (1986). Behavioral manifestations of social support: A microanalytic investigation. *Journal of Personality and Social Psychology, 51,* 201–208.

Glass, D. C. (1977). *Behavior patterns, stress, and coronary disease.* Hillsdale, NJ: Lawrence Erlbaum Associates.

Heller, K. (1979). The effects of social support: Prevention and treatment implications. In A. P. Goldstein & F. H. Kanfer (Eds.), *Maximizing treatment gains: Transfer enhancement in psychotherapy.* (pp. 353–382). New York: Academic Press.

Heller, K., & Swindle, R. W. (1983). Social networks, perceived social support and coping with stress. In R. D. Felner, L. A. Jason, J. Moritsugu, & S. S. Farber (Eds.), *Preventive psychology; research and practice in community intervention* (pp. 87–103). New York: Pergamon.

House, J. S. (1981). *Work stress and social support.* Reading, MA: Addison-Wesley.

House, J. S., & Kahn, R. L. (1985). Measures and concepts of social support. In S. Cohen & S. L. Syme (Eds.), *Social support and health* (pp. 83–108). New York: Academic Press.

House, J. S., Robbins, C., & Metzner, H. L. (1982). The association of social relationships and activities with mortality: Prospective evidence from the Tecumseh Community Health Study. *American Journal of Epidemiology, 116,* 123–140.

Kessler, R. C., & McLeod, J. D. (1985). Social support and mental health in community samples. In S. Cohen & S. L. Syme (Eds.), *Social support and health* (pp. 219–240). New York: Academic Press.

Lazarus, R. S. (1966). *Psychological stress and the coping process.* New York: McGraw-Hill.

Lazarus, R. S., & Folkman, S. (1984). *Stress, appraisal and coping.* New York: Springer.

Lefcourt, H. M., Martin, R. A., & Saleh, W. E. (1984). Locus of control and social support: Interactive moderators of stress. *Journal of Personality and Social Psychology, 47,* 378–389.

McKinlay, J. B. (1973). Social networks, lay consultation and help-seeking behavior. *Social Forces, 51,* 275–292.

Mermelstein, R., Cohen, S., Lichtenstein, E., Kamarck, T., & Baer, J. (1986). Social support and smoking cessation maintenance. *Journal of Consulting and Clinical Psychology. 54,* 447–453.

Monroe, S. M. (1983). Social support and disorder: Toward an untangling of cause and affect. *American Journal of Community Psychology, 11,* 81–96.

Prochaska, J. O., & DiClemente, C. C. (1983). Stages and processes of self-change of smoking. Toward an integrative model of change. *Journal of Consulting and Clinical Psychology, 51,* 390–395.

Reis, H. T. (1984). Social interaction and well-being. In S. Duck (Ed.), *Personal relationships, Vol. 5; Repairing personal relationships* (pp. 21–45). London: Academic Press.

Sanders, G. S. (1982). Social comparison and perceptions of health and illness. In G. S. Sanders & J. Suls (Eds.), *The social psychology of health and illness* (pp. 129–157). Hillsdale, NJ: Lawrence Erlbaum Associates.

Sandler, I. N., & Lakay, B. (1982). Locus of control as a stress moderator: The role of control perceptions and social support. *American Journal of Community Psychology, 10,* 65–80.

Sarason, B. R., Shearin, E. N., Pierce, G. R., & Sarason, I. G. (1987). Interrelations of social support measures: Theoretical and practical implications. *Journal of Personality and Social Psychology, 52,* 813–832.

Shoenbach, V. J., Kaplan, B. H., Fredman, L., & Kleinbach, D. G. (1986). Social ties and mortality in Evans County, Georgia. *American Journal of Epidemiology, 123,* 577–591.

Seeman, M., Seeman, T. E., & Sayles, M. (1985). Social networks and health status: A longitudinal analysis. *Social Psychology Quarterly, 48,* 237–248.

Shiffman, S. (1982). Relapse following smoking cessation: A situational analysis. *Journal of Consulting and Clinical Psychology, 50,* 71–86.

Shiffman, S., Shumaker, S., Abrams, D., Cohen, S., Garvey, A., Grunberg, N., & Swann, G. (1986). Models of smoking relapse. *Health Psychology, 5,* 13–27.

Thoits, P. A. (1983). Multiple identities and psychological well-being: A reformulation and test of the social isolation hypothesis. *American Sociological Review, 48,* 174–187.

Thoits, P. A. (1985). Social support processes and psychological well-being: Theoretical possibilities. In I. G. Sarason & B. Sarason (Eds.), *Social support theory: Research and applications* (pp. 51–72). The Hague: Martinus Nijhoff.

Totman, R., Kiff, J., Reed, S. E., & Craig, J. W. (1980). Predicting experimental colds in volunteers from different measures of recent life stress. *Journal of Psychosomatic Research, 24,* 155–163.

Vinokur, A., Schul, Y., & Caplan, R. D. (1987). Determinants of perceived social support: Interpersonal transactions, personal outlook, and transient affective states. *Journal of Personality and Social Psychology, 53,* 1137–1145.

Wethington, E., & Kessler, R. C. (1986). Perceived support, received support, and adjustment to stressful life events. *Journal of Health and Social Behavior, 27,* 78–89.

Wills, T. A. (1985). Supportive functions of interpersonal relationships. In S. Cohen & S. L. Syme (Eds.), *Social support and health* (pp. 61–82). New York: Academic Press.

Wills, T. A., & Shiffman, S. (1985). Coping and substance use: A conceptual framework. In S. Shiffman & T. A. Wills (Eds.), *Coping and substance use* (pp. 3–24). Orlando, FL: Academic Press.

Patterns in Coping With Controllable and Uncontrollable Events

Peggy A. Thoits
Vanderbilt University

Recently considerable interest has focused on the consequences of uncontrollable stress and the ways in which individuals cope with it. Whether uncontrollable stressors elicit giving-up behavior (Abramson, Seligman, & Teasdale, 1978) or renewed efforts to master problems (Silver & Wortman, 1980; Wortman & Brehm, 1975) has been an ongoing debate within social psychology. Much of the research on this issue has been experimental in design; the evidence to date yields inconsistent findings (Wortman & Silver, 1987). However, both the learned helplessness model and Wortman and Brehm's "integrative reactance model" predict that when individuals perceive aversive events as controllable, they will engage in problem-solving efforts; when individuals perceive events as uncontrollable, they will (fairly quickly, according to Abramson et al. and eventually according to Wortman and Brehm) reduce their problem-solving attempts.

Uncontrollable events and perceptions of uncontrollability also have been a concern of stress researchers, both psychologists and sociologists alike. Using surveys and case-control comparisons, stress researchers have shown that uncontrollable negative life events are causally implicated in depression (see review in Thoits, 1983) and that external control orientations increase the likelihood of individuals succumbing to stress (Pearlin, Lieberman, Menaghan, & Mullan, 1981; Thoits, 1987a; Turner & Noh, 1983; Wheaton, 1980). Stress researchers have assumed that a generalized belief that one lacks personal control will decrease the probability of the individual engaging in problem-solving behavior, even when such attempts might be appropriate.

Thus, there is a broad consensus among social psychologists and stress researchers that perceived control should influence coping. Folkman (1984) specified these predictions further. Folkman proposed that when stressors are appraised

235

as uncontrollable, individuals will engage in proportionately more emotion-focused coping and fewer problem-focused attempts. When stressors are appraised as controllable, individuals will use proportionately more problem-focused strategies than emotion-focused ones. She further posited that when appraisals of stressors are accurate (e.g., when objectively uncontrollable stressors are correctly perceived as uncontrollable), using the appropriate type of coping for the situation will be a more effective stress buffer, reducing physical illness or psychological distress.

These are reasonable predictions, and recent research supports the relationship between control perceptions and problem-focused versus emotion-focused coping (Billings, Cronkite, & Moos, 1983; Folkman, 1984; Folkman & Lazarus, 1985; Folkman, Lazarus, Dunkel-Schetter, DeLongis, & Gruen, 1986; Stone & Neale, 1984). However, there are ambiguities in the term "perceived control." For example, perceived control has been used to refer to predictable versus unpredictable stress (Thompson, 1981), to causal responsibility for a stressful event (self-blame) (Bulman & Wortman, 1977), and to noncontingent outcomes of problem-solving efforts when control over outcomes was initially assumed (Abramson et al., 1978). Additionally there are other meanings that control might have. For example, to have control could mean a perceived ability to prevent a stressful event, an ability to change the circumstances that created stress (Folkman, 1984), or an assumption of responsibility for solving or resolving a stressful event (Brickman et al., 1982). These varieties of meaning may have different implications for coping findings, especially if the interpretation of control is left open to a respondent who is questioned about his/her appraisals of and ways of coping with a stressor.

These considerations suggest that it would be instructive to examine the relationships among coping, event outcomes, and perceived controllability when different potential meanings of controllability are assessed. This is the primary purpose of this chapter. Other than expecting to find a positive relationship between perceived control (as indicated by the perceived ability to *change* a stressful situation—the most common meaning of the term) and the use of problem-focused strategies, and a relationship between problem-solving and positive outcomes, no other hypotheses will be developed here a priori. Various meanings of control should influence coping responses and event outcomes, but in what ways they do so will be left open to exploration. Throughout the remainder of this chapter, the term "control" will refer to a perception that one can change a situation for the better, with other potential meanings of control described in terms of anticipation, preventability, and so on.

The model of coping that undergirds this exploration borrows from previous work by Lazarus and his colleagues (e.g., Lazarus & Folkman, 1984) and Pearlin and Schooler (1978) but is elaborated further by my own work on the nature of emotion (Thoits, 1984, 1985). Following Lazarus, the model assumes that individuals must cope with two sources of difficulty when facing an environmental demand—somehow solving or adjusting to the demand itself (problem-focused coping) and regulating the emotional distress engendered by the demand (emotion-focused coping) (Lazarus & Folkman, 1984). Following Lazarus and Folkman (1984) and Pearlin and Schooler (1978), I further assume that there are two basic modes of changing the problem or the emotional reaction: behavioral and cognitive. Behavioral responses consist of actions taken to confront or avoid a stressful situation or to directly alter an undesired emotional state. Cognitive responses consist of efforts to change the *meaning* of the situation or of the emotional reaction. Thus, a four-fold table of coping responses is implied: Situations can be altered behaviorally or cognitively, and emotional reactions can be altered behaviorally or cognitively.

However, the literature on emotion indicates that emotions themselves are complex, consisting of a number of associated components. These include, in addition to their situational antecedents, physiological changes, expressive gestures, and the cultural labels that identify the feeling (Thoits, 1984). Each of these latter components can be manipulated both behaviorally and cognitively for the purpose of changing feelings; therefore, a more elaborate model of coping responses is implied (see FIG. 12.1).

I argue that there are 7 distinguishable types of coping response (7 because it

FIG. 12.1.   More Complex Model of Coping

	MODE:	
TARGET:	*BEHAVIORAL*	*COGNITIVE*
SITUATION-FOCUSED STRATEGIES	Act, confront Seek info, advice, practical aid Withdraw, leave	Reinterpret situation Distraction Thought-stopping Accept the situation Fantasize solution, or escape
EMOTION-FOCUSED STRATEGIES		
(A) PHYSIOLOGY	Hard exercise Use drugs/alcohol Relaxation techniques	Biofeedback Meditation Progressive Desen-sitization Hypnosis
(B) EXPRESSIVE GESTURES	Catharsis Hide Feelings	Fantasy release Prayer
(C) EMOTIONAL LABEL	(N.A.)	Reinterpret feelings

is not possible to behaviorally alter an emotional label)—behavioral or cognitive manipulations of the problematic situation and behavioral or cognitive manipulations of *aspects* of the problematic emotional reaction. Specific examples of techniques that might be used in each category are indicated in FIG. 12.1 and are examined in the analyses that follow.

This model includes virtually all of the coping techniques that have been identified by previous researchers. For example, Pearlin and Schooler (1978) identified three broad strategies: changing the situation, managing the emotional distress, and reinterpreting the meaning of the situation. Stone and Neale (1984) identified eight modes of coping—direct action, seeking social support, situation reinterpretation, distraction, acceptance, tension–release, catharsis, and prayer. Factor analyses of the Ways of Coping Checklist developed by Lazarus and his colleagues (Aldwin, Folkman, Schaefer, Coyne, & Lazarus, 1980; Vitaliano, Russo, Carr, Maiuro, & Becker, 1985) revealed a number of coping factors, depending on the analytic strategy that is employed. These include confrontive coping, planful problem-solving, support-seeking, positive reappraisal, distancing, accepting responsibility, self-control, and escape–avoidance. Thus, the exploratory coping model (see FIG. 12.1) is compatible with previous inductive and empirical work on coping responses.

METHODS

Procedures

Two hundred undergraduates at a midwestern university were asked to write detailed descriptions of two recent emotional experiences that were important to them, one negative emotional experience and one positive. (The protocols were counterbalanced; half asked for the positive experience first, half for the negative experience first.) Within each situation, respondents were asked to describe how they handled the situation, how they handled their feelings, and how the situation turned out. These descriptions were coded independently for content by two research assistants and myself (reliability estimates are reported following). The protocol included a number of closed-ended questions about those experiences as well, including probes for perceived expectedness, preventability, controllability, responsibility for causing, and responsibility for solving the situation. Respondents' sociodemographic characteristics were the final items assessed in the protocol. For the purposes of this chapter, only the content of the negative-experience descriptions are analyzed.

The Sample

Out of 200 protocols, only one, containing obviously facetious responses, was unusable, resulting in a sample N of 199. The sample consisted of 106 women (53.3%) and 93 men (46.7%). The mean age was 19; freshmen or sophomores comprised 91% of the sample. Ninety-two percent were white. Only 1.5% were married, and 1.5% were divorced; 97% had never been married. Protestants were in the majority (48%); Catholics composed 29.6% of the sample, Jews 8.7%, other religions 3.6%, and 10.2% claimed no religious affiliation. Respondents' fathers had completed college, on average; their mothers had some years of college education, on average. In short, this was a predominantly white, Protestant, middle-class sample of unmarried college students.

Coding Procedures

A preliminary content-coding scheme was devised based on recurrent themes in the first 50 protocols, then existing codes were refined or new codes were added as other categories emerged during the coding process. Protocols were coded independently by two out of three raters in batches of 10; disagreements between coders were then discussed and resolved prior to the next round of coding. Prior to resolutions, interrater agreements were at or above 79.9% on all variables, with the exception of "how the situation turned out," which had an interrater agreement of 67%.

Negative Events

Respondents' situational descriptions were first coded into three categories: The situation described a discrete event, an ongoing strain, or both. A situation was categorized as a discrete event, if it represented the onset of a major change in the individual's life circumstances (e.g. parents announce that they will seek a divorce; a sibling is diagnosed as having cancer; a love relationship is ended). A situation was categorized as an ongoing strain, if no change onset was described, and if the difficulty had persisted for longer than one week (e.g., continuous conflicts with a parent, continuous conflicts with a roommate, continued illness of a loved one). If a situation included both a discrete event and an ongoing strain (e.g., the respondent had repeated fights with his/her lover and eventually decided to end the relationship), then it was coded as strain plus event. The majority of descriptions (72.9%) referred to a discrete event; 22.6% included both an event and a strain, whereas 4.5% described only an ongoing strain. The analyses following exclude respondents who described only an ongoing strain.

Situations then were coded for the specific events that were described, using 50 event categories. Up to 4 events were coded for each description, because many focal events had antecedents or consequences. For example, discovering a lover's infidelity frequently was followed by a major quarrel, which in turn resulted in the relationship being ended. The mean number of coded events per description was 1.6.

The number of lines written to describe each emotional experience also was counted as a rough indicator of the expressivity (or motivation) of each respondent. Respondents wrote a mean of 26 lines to describe their negative experience (range from 3 to 99). As expected, the order in which these descriptions were requested affected the number of lines written; respondents wrote a mean of 29 lines, if they described their negative experience first and a mean of 22 lines if second (p=.001). Respondents worked steadily on the protocol for an hour to an hour and a half; therefore, these order effects likely reflect fatigue.

Women wrote significantly more lines than men for each requested experience. For the negative experience, females wrote a mean of 30.3 lines, whereas males wrote a mean of 20.7 (p<.001). This gender difference held regardless of the order in which the negative and positive emotional experiences were requested. This raises the possibility that gender differences in expressivity (or motivation) may have affected our coding of respondents' negative event experiences. However, there were no significant gender differences in the mean numbers of events or strains that were coded. Gender differences in expressivity (or motivation) also might affect the number of coping strategies that were spontaneously mentioned by respondents. Previous analyses revealed significant sex differences in the number of coping strategies reported (Thoits, in press); thus, gender and number of lines written were controlled in all analyses reported following.

Respondents were asked "how long ago" the negative situation they described had happened. Described situations occurred an average of 1.7 years ago. There were no significant gender differences in time since the situation had occurred, nor did the number of lines written vary by time since occurrence.

Given the sample, the negative emotional experiences described by these respondents were restricted in range. Financial difficulties were rare in the protocols, as of course were descriptions of marital, parenting, or occupational difficulties. On the other hand, unexpectedly, academic difficulties did not predominate in the protocols (only 5 respondents described reactions to academic failure). Rather respondents described what Kessler and McLeod (1984) called "network events"—i.e., reactions to difficulties experienced by loved ones (family and friends)—and they described "respondent events" (i.e., reactions to their own difficulties, the bulk of which involved interpersonal problems with family members, friends, and lovers as well as the deaths of loved ones). There were no significant gender differences in the frequency of these broad types of events, although women more frequently described a death than men. Although the stressful experiences described by these respondents are not representative of all possible stressors, for the purpose of exploring the theoretical relationship between perceived controllability and coping, these data are still useful.

Described events ranged in severity. Some were highly traumatic—such as witnessing a close friend's fatal accident, finding the body of a parent who had committed suicide, and having been raped. Others were major events—such as the death of a close relative, family member seriously ill, or parents' divorce. Others were moderately stressful events—such as being arrested or caught in the act of wrongdoing, having a love relationship end, and being expelled from a team or fraternity house. Still others were relatively minor and common events—

such as leaving home to come to college, experiencing a temporary separation from a lover, having an argument with a family member or friend, being the subject of gossip, losing a game to an opposing team, and moving residence. All respondents were asked to write about a negative experience that was important to them; therefore, the perceived stressfulness of that experience was not directly assessed in the protocol. Event severity might have affected the number and types of coping strategies that respondents reported (presuming that more severe events require more, and more varied, coping efforts). Therefore, some analyses following control for each event that was coded in order to examine this potential bias.

Perceptions of Events

Closed-ended items probed for respondents' perceptions of the situations they had described. Possible responses to each of these questions were "no," "to some extent," and "yes." Anticipation was assessed with the following question: "At the time, did you *anticipate or expect* that the situation would happen?" (emphasis in the original). Preventability was assessed, if the respondent answered "to some extent" or "yes" to the anticipation question: "Did you believe that you could have *prevented* the situation from happening?" Controllability was assessed with this phrasing: "At the time, did the situation seem like one that you could *control*—that is, did you think you could change the situation for the better?" Causal responsibility was indicated with: "Did you believe that you were *responsible* for the event happening?" Finally to indicate responsibility for problem-solving, the question was: "Did you believe that you were responsible for *solving* the situation?"

Coping Strategies

Respondents were asked how they handled the situation that they had described and, in a second question, how they handled their feelings. Their open-ended responses to both questions were content-coded first into 37 distinguishable coping strategies. Up to 7 strategies were coded for each respondent (4 respondents described 8). These then were collapsed into 18 subtypes of coping, based on the coping model outlined in the introduction (see FIG. 12.1 and Appendix 12.1). To these were added three miscellaneous strategies; these types of coping emerged from the content coding and could not be reliably classified as to their target and mode (see Appendix 12.1).

The reader might wonder why the 37 initial coded strategies were not grouped into the broader categories shown in Appendix 12.1 on the basis of a factor analysis of the items. Exploratory work indicated that a coping typology could not be derived from factor analysis for several reasons. First, coping strategies were complexly interrelated. Some strategies were used in conjunction with others, some were used to the exclusion of others, and some regularly followed others in chronological sequence. Consequently no clear typology emerged, even from an oblique rotation that allowed for correlations among coping factors.

Second, several strategies within a theoretical category did not "hang together," because individuals selected only one of those strategies to achieve the same implicit function. For example, talking to family, to friends, or to authority figures are alternative ways of seeking social support, theoretically. Yet these strategies did not correlate highly, because individuals tended to use one support source in preference to others.

Third, a single strategy could serve several latent functions simultaneously or could serve different latent functions for different people. For example, in these data, going for a drive correlated with spending time alone, thinking through a situation, leaving a situation permanently (i.e., a decision was apparently made during the drive), trying not to think about the situation, engaging in strenuous exercise, and using drugs or alcohol. In other words, going for a drive could help a person make decisions, could distract the person from the problem, or could exhaust or deaden feelings. For some, driving might serve all of these functions; for others, driving might serve one function and not others.

For these several reasons, no further attempt was made to construct coping factors empirically. Instead, strategies were grouped on theoretical grounds, and these groupings were modified only slightly on the basis of an inspection of their intercorrelations. No attempt was made to classify strategies on the basis of the underlying functions they served (e.g., problem solving, escape/avoidance), because this could not be done without explicit probes to verify the perceived functions of each strategy (see Stone & Neale, 1984). Instead strategies were grouped only on the basis of their mode of action (behavioral or cognitive) and the apparent target of those actions (the situation, aspects of feelings).

Outcomes

Respondents were asked in the protocols to report how the negative situation that they described had turned out. Two dimensions emerged from the content coding of their replies: The valence of the outcome was positive, negative, or had mixed positive and negative aspects, and the effects of the situation had ended or were continuing. Outcome valence was coded ordinally: 1 if negative, 2 if mixed positive and negative, and 3 if positive. Whether the effects of the event had ended or were continuing was indicated by a dummy variable, 1 if ended, 0 if continuing.

RESULTS

The majority of respondents perceived their described situation as unanticipated (61.6%), not preventable (79.6%), and uncontrollable (66.8%). Slightly over half regarded the situation as one for which they were not causally responsible (56.3%) and as one they were not responsible for solving (54.5%). Table 12.1

TABLE 12.1
Intercorrelations Among Event Perceptions

Perceptions	1.	2.	3.	4.	5.
1. Anticipation	—				
2. Preventability	.44***	—			
3. Controllability	.15*	.27***	—		
4. Causal Responsibility	−.01	.23***	.31***	—	
5. Respon. for Solving	.13[+]	.20**	.09	.23**	—

[+]p < .10   *p < .05   **p < .01   ***p < .001

reports the intercorrelations among these responses. Although several of these perceptions are significantly related to one another, the low correlations indicate that they capture different aspects of perceived "control." (The correlation of .44 between anticipation and preventability reflects a skip pattern: Preventability was asked only if the respondent had anticipated the event at least to some extent; otherwise the event was assumed to be nonpreventable.)

Determinants of Perceptions

Two classes of variables might influence event perceptions—respondents' social characteristics and the types of events that they chose to describe. To assess these factors, each perception variable (coded ordinally 0 = no; 1 = to some extent; 2 = yes) was first regressed on the social characteristics of the individual (gender, age, race, marital status, father's education, mother's education, and religion), while controlling for the number of lines in the event description and the order in which the negative event description was requested in the protocol (first or second). Only gender, age, and number of lines significantly influenced perceptions (data not shown), so these variables were retained as controls in the next analysis.

Next, each event perception was regressed on a set of seven dummy variables that indicated the type of event experienced (i.e., family network event, friend network event, death of a loved one, problem with family member, problem with friend, problem with lover, and other problem). Gender and age were controlled in each equation. The number of lines written was controlled only in the causal responsibility equation, since it influenced only this perception.

The results of these regressions are shown in Table 12.2. Females are more likely to have anticipated the situation, viewed it as preventable, and perceived it as controllable (i.e., changeable).[1] Older respondents were more likely to see

---

[1]However, when the effects of specific events were controlled in an analysis of covariance model, gender differences in viewing events as preventable and controllable disappeared. Women still perceived events as more expected or anticipated after the effects of specific events were controlled.

the situation as preventable and controllable, and believed themselves to be causally responsible for it. Significantly more lines were written to describe the situation when respondents believed themselves causally responsible (perhaps reflecting a need to justify or explain the problems that they had caused).

Respondents believed themselves not responsible for causing and not responsible for solving family network events—events that had happened to family members, not themselves. They believed that they were not responsible for solving problems that had happened to their friends as well. Deaths were perceived as unanticipated and not preventable; respondents also saw themselves as not responsible for causing a death, appropriately enough. Note that although there is a tendency to view deaths as uncontrollable ($b = -.07$), this was not a significant effect. (Of 29 respondents who described a death, 76% perceived it as uncontrollable.) In other words, deaths were viewed as just as uncontrollable as other types of events.

Respondents believed themselves responsible for solving their interpersonal problems with family members and not responsible for causing interpersonal problems with their friends. Problems with lovers were unrelated to any perceptions. Finally, miscellaneous other problems were perceived as unanticipated and uncontrollable.

The results in Table 12.2 raise the question of whether event perceptions depend more on individual factors or on the events themselves. To examine this,

TABLE 12.2
Perceptions Regressed on Gender, Age, and Types of Events

	Anticip	Prevent	Control	Respon Cause	Respon Solve
Variables					
Female (0,1)	$.13^+$	$.14^*$	$.12^+$	$-.04$	$.003$
Age	$.03$	$.20^{**}$	$.13^+$	$.16^*$	$.07$
# Lines Written	—	—	—	$.20^{**}$	—
Family Network Event	$-.12$	$-.11$	$-.02$	$-.19^*$	$-.18^*$
Friend Network Event	$-.11$	$.03$	$-.11$	$.01$	$-.15^+$
Death	$-.16^+$	$-.18^*$	$-.07$	$-.15^+$	$-.12$
Problem with Family	$.04$	$-.09$	$.08$	$.06$	$.17^*$
Problem with Friend	$.04$	$-.05$	$-.05$	$-.19^*$	$.08$
Problem with Lover	$-.06$	$.10$	$.14$	$.09$	$.02$
Other Problem	$-.21^*$	$-.12$	$-.17^+$	$-.02$	$.09$
N	189	187	185	190	168
R^2	$.07$	$.12$	$.11$	$.17$	$.12$

$^+p < .10$ $^* < .05$ $^{**}p < .01$ $^{***}p < .001$
Note: Ns vary due to missing values on some variables. Standardized coefficients are presented.

each of the respondent's event perceptions was regressed on the specific event experienced, using an analysis of covariance model. Specifically, mean perception scores were calculated for each of the 50 coded events, using in the calculation of means only the subgroups of individuals who had experienced each particular event. Many respondents actually described more than one discrete event within their situational description; therefore, mean perceptions for the main, or focal, event only were calculated to avoid interdependence among event effects in the analyses. Each respondent then received a mean score (on anticipation, preventability, controllability, etc.) for the particular event he or she had experienced. These mean event perception scores were used in a subsequent regression analysis. (Regressing respondents' actual perceptions on a set of dummy variables for each of the 50 events would have accomplished the same purpose.) The results (not shown) indicate that 32% of the variance in anticipation, 32% of the variance in preventability, 26% in controllability, 37% in perceptions of causal responsibility, and 41% in responsibility for solving the situation were attributable to the event itself. Thus, although events importantly influence event perceptions, considerable variation remains in perceptions to be accounted for by other factors.

Perceptions and Coping Responses

The next issue, central to this chapter, is whether these various event perceptions actually influenced individuals' choices of coping responses. Table 12.3 reports the frequency with which respondents mentioned each type of coping.

The five most frequently used coping strategies were expressing feelings (catharsis), direct action, hiding feelings, reinterpreting the situation, and seeking support. In other words, behavioral manipulations of the situation, behavioral manipulations of expressive gestures, and cognitive reinterpretations of the situation were the most frequently mentioned techniques. On average, respondents reported using 3.7 specific strategies for handling their situation.

Each coping response that had been used by 5% or more of the sample (see Table 12.3) next was regressed on respondents' sociodemographic characteristics, the number of lines written, and the order in which the negative event description was requested in the protocol. Preliminary results (not shown) indicate that gender, age, religion, number of lines, and order significantly affected the likelihood of using specific coping strategies. Then each coping strategy was regressed on the five perception variables, while gender, age, religion, number of lines, and order were controlled. The results of these analyses are shown in Table 12.4.[2]

Differences in coping responses by gender and religious affiliation are apparent. Women used significantly more coping strategies than men overall and were

---

[2]Although probit analysis would be the more appropriate technique to use for dichotomous dependent variables, regression results are reported here, because most readers are more familiar with this method. Probit analyses replicated the findings reported in Table 12.4.

TABLE 12.3
Strategies Used to Cope with Negative Events (Percent of Sample Mentioning Strategy)

Strategy	Total Sample (N = 188)
Catharsis	64.4
Direct action	39.9
Hide feelings	38.8
See it differently	38.3
Seek support	34.0
Leave the situation	20.7
Think it through	15.4
Thought-stopping	13.8
Distraction	7.5
Accept it	7.5
Exercise	5.9
Prayer	5.9
Use drugs/alcohol	4.8
Fantasy expression	4.3
Fantasy solution	4.3
Wait	4.3
Write about it	4.3
Other physiological	3.2
Desensitization	1.1
Music	1.1
Redefine feelings	0.0
Mean strategies used	3.7

Note: Percentages are based on dummy variables indicating whether each type of coping was used by the respondent or not. Means are based on the number of strategies actually coded for each respondent.

more likely to seek support, see the situation differently, and express their feelings freely (catharsis). Men were significantly more likely to accept the situation and engage in strenuous physical exercise as coping strategies. Compared to Protestants (the omitted comparison group), Catholics used significantly fewer coping strategies, were less likely to seek social support or think through the situation, and were more likely to accept the situation and use drugs or alcohol. Individuals with no religious affiliation were more likely to leave the situation and use drugs or alcohol. These gender and religious differences generally remained significant when a control for the event itself was added to the equations in an analysis of covariance model (results not shown).[3] These patterns suggest that

---

[3]The mean probability of using each coping strategy for each of the 50 coded events was calculated for those subgroups of individuals who had experienced the same event. Each respondent then received a mean score (for number of coping responses, taking direct action, seeking support, and so on) for

there are subcultural differences in coping, independent of the nature of events, that may be a result of socialization.

Table 12.4 shows that, compared to other perceptions, perceived control was related to using more types of coping. When respondents perceived control, they used more strategies overall and were likely to take direct action, to try not to think about it, to distract themselves, to express their feelings freely, and not to pray. (Conversely, if events were perceived as uncontrollable, respondents were *less* likely to take action, to stop thinking about it, to distract themselves, to express their feelings freely, and were more likely to pray.) These findings support the widespread assumption in the coping literature that perceived controllability and problem-solving (taking action) are positively related. Unexpectedly they also suggest that more efforts at emotional regulation are necessary when events are perceived as controllable (and not when events are uncontrollable). Apparently respondents attempted to regulate the distress that might interfere with their problem-solving efforts.

Other perceptions were related to coping responses. If a negative event was anticipated, individuals were more likely to accept it and hide their feelings. If an event was perceived as not preventable, respondents were more likely to reinterpret its meaning (try to see the situation differently). If individuals believed that they were causally responsible for the occurrence of a negative event, they were more likely to try to see the situation differently and less likely to engage in hard physical exercise. Finally, perceived responsibility for solving a situation positively influenced the likelihood of taking direct action. These patterns suggest that potentially different meanings of "perceived control" in fact have different consequences for coping.

Outcomes

An important question is whether the outcomes of respondents' events were influenced by their initial perceptions and/or by the number and types of coping strategies that they used.

Twenty-four percent of respondents reported a negative outcome, 36% reported mixed positive and negative outcomes, and 40% reported positive consequences. The sample was evenly split between those whose situations had ended or were continuing in their effects. These two dimensions were correlated .28 (p< .001), indicating that positive outcomes were associated with situations that had ended.

To determine whether event perceptions had direct influences on reported

---

the particular event he or she had experienced. The appropriate mean score was controlled in each equation shown in Table 12.4. Again, this procedure is equivalent to adding 50 dummy variables to each equation—dummies that indicate the respondent's experience or nonexperience of a particular event.

TABLE 12.4
The Effects of Event Perceptions on the Use of Coping Strategies,
Controlling for Respondents' Social Characteristics[a]

	No. of Strats.	Direct Action	Seek Support	Leave	Think Through
Variables					
Female (0,1)	.23**	−.13	.23**	.04	−.11
Age	−.01	.07	−.05	−.07	−.10
Catholic (0,1)	−.16*	.08	−.14+	−.11	−.15+
Jewish (0,1)	−.08	.03	−.07	−.02	−.08
No religion (0,1)	.05	−.01	−.12	.17*	.12
Anticipated	−.07	.04	−.14	−.13	−.06
Preventable	.01	.07	.04	−.02	.07
Controllable	.14+	.15+	.08	.13	−.14
Causal responsib.	−.05	.06	.01	−.08	.09
Respon. for solving	.13+	.22**	.09	−.05	.03
N	160	160	160	160	160
R^2	.22	.18	.11	.07	.11

	See Sit Differ	Accept	Thought Stop	Distract
Female (0,1)	.25*	−.19*	−.04	.05
Age	.03	.02	−.02	−.01
Catholic (0,1)	−.10	.20*	.09	−.01
Jewish (0,1)	−.02	.09	−.12	.12
No religion (0,1)	.06	.04	.03	.03
Anticipated	.05	.18*	.01	−.15
Preventable	−.21*	.01	−.07	.10
Controllable	−.07	−.14	.24**	.20*
Causal responsibility	.16+	−.09	−.07	−.14
Respon. for solving	.03	−.11	.13	.02
N	160	160	160	160
R^2	.10	.14	.10	.08

	Cathars	Hide Feelings	Exercise	Alcoh/Drugs	Pray
Female (0,1)	.21**	.04	−.20*	−.03	.10
Age	.02	.01	−.11	.05	−.01
Catholic (0,1)	−.06	.02	−.09	.16+	−.12
Jewish (0,1)	.04	−.03	−.04	−.04	−.12
No religion (0,1)	−.12	−.04	−.00	.23**	−.13
Anticipated	−.01	.19*	−.05	−.10	.05
Preventable	−.02	−.13	.12	.12	−.02
Controllable	.16+	−.02	.02	−.11	−.16+
Causal responsibility	−.13	−.02	−.18+	−.03	.04
Respon. for solving	.12	−.05	.07	.08	−.07
N	160	160	160	160	160
R^2	.15	.05	.09	.11	.06

+$p < .10$ *$p < .05$ **$p < .01$ ***$p < .001$

[a]Note: Standardized coefficients are presented. Ns are lower in this analysis due to missing values on the event-perception variables. All equations include controls for number of lines written and the order in which the negative experience description was requested in the protocol (coefficients not shown, for simpler presentation). Number of lines written significantly increased the number of strategies used and positively influenced use of particular strategies; order (first, second) significantly decreased the number and use of particular strategies.

outcomes, each outcome variable was regressed on the five perception indicators, with sociodemographic characteristics, number of lines written, and order of description controlled. Perceptions were unrelated to the valence or to the persistence of event outcomes (results not shown). Even within subgroups of respondents whose situational effects had ended versus those whose situational effects persisted, perceptions were unrelated to the valence of event outcomes (results not shown). Thus, initial event perceptions do not directly affect the outcomes of those events. Instead perceptions affect outcomes indirectly by influencing coping responses (Table 12.4).

Next, separately by whether situational effects had ended or not, the valence of the outcome was regressed on the set of 13 coping strategies, with respondents' social characteristics, number of lines written, and the order of description controlled. Coping strategies significantly influenced reported outcomes only for situations that had continuing persistent effects; thus, only these results are shown in Table 12.5.

Trying to see the situation differently, freely expressing feelings, engaging in strenuous exercise, and praying produced a more positive outcome in situations

TABLE 12.5
The Effects of Coping Strategies on Reported Outcomes,
for Situations with Continuing Effects Only[a]

Strategy	Outcome
Direct action	.11
Seek support	−.05
Leave the situation	−.16
Think situation through	−.05
See situation differently	.30*
Accept the situation	.16
Thought-stopping	−.02
Distraction	−.03
Express feelings freely	.31*
Hide feelings	−.05
Hard exercise	.22[+]
Use alcohol/drugs	.08
Pray	.23*
N	88
R^2 (adjusted)	.12

[+]$p < .10$ *$p < .05$
[a]Note: Standardized coefficients are reported. Outcome is coded 3 = positive, 2 = mixed positive and negative aspects, 1 = negative. Controlled in the equation, but not shown here, are gender, age, religion, father's education, mother's education, number of lines written, and order of event description. Only the coefficient for Catholic was significant (b = .24, p = .05).

that had continuing effects. In Lazarus's terms, only emotion-focused coping strategies were significantly associated with more positive outcomes. Interestingly, none of the strategies that might be described as problem-solving efforts (taking action, seeking support, leaving the situation, and thinking through the situation) were significantly related to outcome valence.

Perhaps the effects of problem-solving efforts are not evident in Table 12.5, because they depend on perceived situational control. Folkman (1984) argued that responding to controllable situations with problem-solving efforts and to uncontrollable situations with emotion-focused efforts should produce better outcomes than vice versa. More specifically, Folkman argued that when events are *accurately* perceived as controllable or uncontrollable then the use of problem-focused or emotion-focused responses respectively are more likely to produce positive outcomes. Unfortunately, no indicators of the accuracy of respondents' perceptions are available in this study. However, it is still possible to examine outcomes of various coping strategies under differing conditions of perceived control.

The sample was stratified into two groups: those who perceived their situation as uncontrollable (i.e., unchangeable), and those who viewed it as controllable, or controllable to some extent. Separately by whether the effects of the situation had ended or were continuing and by perceived controllability, the valence of the respondent's outcome was regressed on the 13 strategy variables, with social characteristics, number of lines written, and order of event description controlled. The results are shown in Table 12.6.

Coping strategies produced positive outcomes (that persisted) only when individuals perceived uncontrollability. Surprisingly, taking action significantly *increased* the likelihood of a positive continuing outcome only when an event was viewed as uncontrollable. Trying to see the situation differently, accepting the situation, expressing feelings freely, and engaging in strenuous exercise also produced more positive (continuing) outcomes. In short, problem-focused *and* emotion-focused coping were efficacious responses to an uncontrollable event (at least as outcomes were reported by respondents).

How are we to understand these results? Why were problem-solving attempts unrelated to outcomes when individuals perceived that they had situational control? Returning to respondents' qualitative accounts, it appeared that this was because problem-solving efforts were not always successful, despite respondents' best efforts. Conversely, why were problem-solving attempts related to persistent, more positive outcomes when individuals perceived a lack of situational control? It appeared that problem-solving attempts actually could dampen the negative consequences of an uncontrollable event, or in some cases, increase respondents' self-respect for having tried. Two examples drawn from the protocols can illustrate these points.

The first example shows that problem-solving behavior can go awry in a situation perceived as controllable. An 18-year-old female wrote:

TABLE 12.6
The Effects of Coping Strategies on Reported Outcomes, by
Perceived Controllability and Persistence of Situational Effects[a]

| | No Perceived Control | | Perceived Control | |
| | Contin. | Ended | Contin. | Ended |
Strategy	Outcome	Outcome	Outcome	Outcome
Direct action	.37*	.06	.19	.20
Seek support	.09	−.11	−.27	−.64
Leave the situation	.001	−.52**	.07	.65
Think situation through	−.25	.13	.30	.02
See situation differently	.46**	.03	.68	.57
Accept the situation	.27+	−.30	—	—
Thought-stopping	−.12	−.09	−.46	−.25
Distraction	.13	—	.49	.15
Express feelings	.47**	.18	.03	−.38
Hide feelings	.02	.27	−.47	−.57
Hard exercise	.24+	−.13	.49	−.05
Use alcohol/drugs	.08	−.01	.50	—
Pray	.17	.12	1.05*	.63
N	57	51	30	25
R^2 (adjusted)	.34	.03	.00	.00

$^+p < .10$ $*p < .05$ $**p < .01$
[a]Note: Standardized coefficients are reported. Outcome is coded 3 = positive, 2 = mixed positive and negative aspects, 1 = negative. Controlled in the equations, but not shown here, are gender, age, religion, father's education, mother's education, number of lines written, and order of event description.

About the middle of the summer, a really good friend of mine told me she was pregnant and wanted to have an abortion. She asked if I'd help her. After we had talked it over, and she was sure this was what she wanted, I agreed to help her. We live in a *really* small town, and she wanted to keep it quiet. I knew a girl I worked with would be able to [get] the info I needed for me, so I asked her, just saying it wasn't for me. Apparently she didn't believe me, because she started telling people I was pregnant and wanted an abortion. What was worse was everybody else still believes her, no matter what is said. . . . At least she did get me the info, and my friend did get an abortion, but now she's sorry she did it and told me over Thanksgiving that I should have stopped her. I don't even care if I see anybody at home again. Of course, not everybody believes it, but that's kind of hard to remember.

This young woman rated her situation as unanticipated but controllable, adding, "At first, I just thought I was helping out a friend. I didn't think it would be any big deal." She did not see herself as responsible for the event happening and did not respond to the solution–responsibility question. In answer to how she handled the situation and her feelings, she replied, "I have tried talking to people, but it doesn't seem to be helping. I have tried talking to both the girl who had the abortion and the girl spreading the rumor. The girl spreading the rumor just says she doesn't know what I'm talking about and walks away. The girl who had the abortion says she doesn't want to talk to me anymore." In answer to "How did the situation turn out?" she replied, "I'm hoping the rumor will blow over by Christmas. I'm also hoping the girl who had the abortion will be speaking to me again, because I really wish I could help her. I'm tired of her trying to make me feel as if it's my fault." This young woman's efforts at direct problem-solving have been unsuccessful thus far, and the negative effects of the situation persist.

The positive consequences of taking action when faced with an uncontrollable situation can be illustrated with the following example. A male, 19-years-old, wrote:

> I was having a terrible weekend. I went home for my best friend's marriage. He is still in high school, but we were very close. Anyway, he was quitting school to get married, and I went back to say goodbye and offer what support I could. Anyway, in the meantime, I stopped by my father's to get a box of my stuff to bring back [to school], and while doing this I left a key on the kitchen table (a key that they leave hidden outside). They (he and my stepmother) called me after the wedding and said I should come over. I stopped, and they gave a lecture on how immature and irresponsible I was (20 minutes). I replied that I was leaving for the reception. My stepmom said, "Just forget *everything*" ([meaning] money for school), if I left. I did. When I got back to school, I realized that I had 2 tests the next day. I stopped by work to get a hug for good luck from Karen, my boss, my friend, the love in my life right now. I had just totally severed the last cord with my hometown. Instead of a hug, Karen made some smartass comment. I stomped out, left a note in her car, and went and failed my tests. I felt so hurt, confused, and betrayed. My friend (Karen) came by and was crying and apologizing. She moved in last week, but I lost something with that experience, some "trust" that we had. I just hope I can get it back.

On the probe questions, this young man rated his negative experience as not anticipated, not preventable, and uncontrollable and indicated that he did not feel causally responsible but did believe that he was responsible "to some extent" for solving the situation. In reply to, "What, if anything, did you do about the situation?" he responded, "Left a note, talked, forced the make-up situation." In response to, "How did you handle your emotion(s)?" he wrote, "I left the bad situation and went off by myself. I expressed myself in a note and tried to work the problem out. The thought of giving up only briefly flashed across my mind." In reply to, "How did the situation turn out?" he wrote, "Still working on it (improving)." Here problem-solving efforts helped ameliorate the consequences of what were perceived to be uncontrollable circumstances.

These examples suggest that when a situation is perceived as controllable, problem-solving efforts still may have negligible or negative consequences. And when a situation is perceived as uncontrollable, acting on it (in conjunction with emotion-focused strategies) still can prevent or reduce continuing negative consequences.

DISCUSSION AND CONCLUSIONS

The purpose of this chapter is to reexamine the relationship between perceived control and coping responses, with attention to different aspects or meanings of control. Most often in the literature, controllability refers to the person's ability to alter a stressful situation. As expected, the perceived *changeability* of a situation increased individuals' use of problem-focused coping strategies as well as the total number of strategies they used overall. However, other aspects of control affected coping responses as well. Most notably, anticipating a negative situation increased emotion-focused coping responses (accepting the situation, hiding one's feelings). Viewing a negative situation as not preventable or oneself as causally responsible increased what might be called perception-focused coping (reinterpreting the meaning of the situation) (Pearlin & Schooler, 1978), and accepting personal responsibility for solving a situation predicted the use of problem-focused coping strategies. These previously understudied control perceptions are important, because they elicit specific coping strategies that are associated with more positive continuing event outcomes. Attention to these additional aspects of perceived control seems warranted in future research. In particular, it may be useful to explore whether coping responses are better predicted by specific *combinations* of these perceptions; for example, problem-solving efforts may more often follow uncontrollable events for which an individual also assumes responsibility for causing or solving.

In the course of the analysis, several additional intriguing findings emerged that call for further study. Controllable (i.e., changeable) events elicited not only problem-focused efforts but numerous emotion-focused efforts as well (thought-stopping, distraction, catharsis). If one assumes that two sources of stress (solving the problem and managing feelings) accompany controllable events (Lazarus & Folkman, 1984), then these findings are not surprising. However, many researchers implicitly assume that uncontrollable situations require more or more varied coping efforts—especially more emotion-focused efforts—than controllable ones do (e.g., Silver & Wortman, 1980; Wortman & Silver, 1987). The findings here suggest that this is not the case, but more rigorous testing clearly is required.

Especially unexpected was the finding that problem-solving efforts in response to *un*controllable events can result in somewhat better continuing outcomes. This suggests some indirect support for aspects of Wortman's and Brehm's (1975) "integrative reactance model" but also a possible qualifier to it. Wortman and Brehm argued that when individuals initially expect to be able to influence an important outcome, exposure to loss of control will at first increase their motivation to obtain the desired outcome. The greater the initial expectation of control, the more problem-solving a person will attempt prior to giving up, and the more depressed he or she will become after giving up.

Unfortunately, no measure of initial expectations for control over *outcomes* was obtained in this study. However, it was clear that individuals did engage in problem-solving even when they perceived their situations as unchangeable, consistent with Wortman and Brehm. However, in contrast to Wortman and Brehm's predictions, and Folkman's as well (1984), the reported outcomes of those efforts were not especially negative. It appears that some aspects of an uncontrollable situation still can be changed for the better. Moreover, attempting to exercise control against seemingly stacked odds may help protect individuals' self-esteem and morale in the face of adversity. Clearly more research is needed on these issues, because if these speculations are valid, they suggest a potentially fruitful way to intervene in the situations of individuals facing uncontrollable stressors.

To end on a sociological note, the findings in this chapter also suggest that there are subcultural differences in coping responses that cannot be attributed to the nature of the events that individuals experience. Variations were found in the use of specific coping techniques by gender and religious affiliation. Research with samples less homogeneous in socioeconomic characteristics might discern coping patterns by race/ethnicity and social class as well. The specific coping strategies used preferentially by these different groups have implications for the persistence and positivity of event outcomes (see also Pearlin & Schooler, 1978); therefore, these subcultural differences deserve further study. Systematic variations in the use of effective and ineffective coping techniques eventually may help explain the higher rates of psychological distress and disorder in lower status groups.

APPENDIX 12.1. COPING STRATEGIES

Behavioral Strategies. Situation as Target

Direct Action: Acted on situation to try to change it; confronted or discussed the problem with person involved; gathered information for solving the problem; read books about the situation.

Substituted new situation for the old (e.g., found another lover, another job).

Seek Social Support: Talked to family member(s) for advice/help.

Talked to friend(s) for advice/help.

Consulted therapist/minister/other authority figure.

Leave the Situation: Left the situation permanently.

Left or avoided the situation temporarily.

Went off by self for long walks or drives.

Withdrew from contact with others.

Cognitive Strategies. Situation as Target

Think It Through: Analyzed the situation; thought through the situation; analyzed the alternatives; made a plan of action; made a decision.

See It Differently: Saw the situation in a new way; reinterpreted the meaning of the situation; tried to see the positive side; had a realization or told self something about the situation.

Compared self to others who were worse off.

Accept it: Accepted the situation; became resigned.

Thought-Stopping: Tried not to think about it; refused to think about it.

Distraction: Kept busy doing useful things to distract self; distracted self by watching TV/socializing/reading novels.

Fantasy Solution: Fantasized a magical solution to the situation; wished for a magical resolution or reversal of circumstances.

Behavioral Strategies. Physiology as Target.

Use Drugs/Alcohol: Took pills (legal or illegal); smoked marijuana; drank alcohol.

Exercise: Engaged in hard physical exercise.

Other Physiological: Used muscle-relaxation techniques; broke things to exhaust self, ate, slept.

Cognitive Strategies. Physiology as Target

Desensitization: Used progressive desensitization techniques, hypnosis.

Behavioral Strategies. Expressive Gestures as Target

Catharsis: Expressed emotion freely when alone; expressed emotion with/to others who were involved in the situation; expressed emotion freely with/to others who were not involved in the situation; expressed emotion freely (context unknown).

Hide Feelings: Controlled expressive behaviors (tried not to cry, hid feelings from others, went on as usual, acted as if nothing had happened); suppressed the emotion (method unspecified).

Cognitive Strategies. Expressive Gestures as Target

Fantasy Expression: Fantasized expressing true feelings; wanted to or visualized aggression against someone.

Prayer: Prayed, spoke to God.

Cognitive strategies. Emotion Label as Target

Redefine: Reinterpreted existing feelings as different ones; told self I wasn't feeling what I was.

Miscellaneous Strategies

Write: Wrote in journal; wrote a letter that was never sent; wrote a poem about it.

Music: Listened to music; played an instrument.

Wait: Waited for situation or feelings to pass; let time pass; endured it.

ACKNOWLEDGMENTS

This chapter was prepared for presentation at the Conference on Life-Span Development, Morgantown, West Virginia, March 24–27, 1988. I am grateful to Kris Baughman and Lori Sudderth for their careful and conscientious research assistance on this project and to Larry Griffin for his helpful comments and suggestions regarding analysis.

REFERENCES

Abramson, L. Y., Seligman, M. E. P., & Teasdale, J. D. (1978). Learned helplessness in humans: Critique and reformulation. *Journal of Abnormal Psychology, 87,* 49–74.

Aldwin, C., Folkman, S., Schaefer, C., Coyne, J. C., & Lazarus, R. S. (1980). *Ways of coping: A process measure.* Paper presented at the Annual Convention of the American Psychological Association, Los Angeles.

Billings, A. G., Cronkite, R. C., & Moos, R. H. (1983). Social-environmental factors in unipolar depression: Comparisons of depressed patients and nondepressed controls. *Journal of Abnormal Psychology, 92,* 119–133.

Brickman, P., Rabinowitz, V. C., Karuza, J., Jr., Coates, D., Cohen, E., & Kidder, L. (1982). Models of helping and coping. *American Psychologist, 37,* 368–384.

Bulman, R. J., & Wortman, C. B. (1977). Attributions of blame and coping in the "real world": Severe accident victims react to their lot. *Journal of Personality and Social Psychology, 35,* 351–363.

Folkman, S. (1984). Personal control and stress and coping processes: A theoretical analysis. *Journal of Personality and Social Psychology, 46,* 839–852.

Folkman, S., & Lazarus, R. S. (1985). If it changes it must be a process: Study of emotion and coping during three stages of a college examination. *Journal of Personality and Social Psychology, 48,* 150–170.

Folkman, S., Lazarus, R. S., Dunkel-Schetter, C., DeLongis, A., & Gruen, R. (1986). The dynamics of a stressful encounter: Cognitive appraisal, coping, and encounter outcomes. *Journal of Personality and Social Psychology, 50,* 992–1003.

Kessler, R. C., & McLeod, J. (1984). Sex differences in vulnerability to undesirable life events. *American Sociological Review, 49,* 620–631.

Lazarus, R. S., & Folkman, S. (1984). *Stress, appraisal, and coping.* New York: Springer.

Pearlin, L. I., Lieberman, M. A., Menaghan, E. G., & Mullan, J. T. (1981). The stress process. *Journal of Health and Social Behavior, 22,* 337–356.

Pearlin, L. I., & Schooler, C. (1978). The structure of coping. *Journal of Health and Social Behavior, 19,* 2–21.

Silver, R. L., & Wortman, C. B. (1980). Coping with undesirable life events. In J. Garber & M. E. P. Seligman (Eds.), *Human helplessness: Theory and applications* (pp. 279–340). New York: Academic Press.

Stone, A. A., & Neale, J. M. (1984). New measure of daily coping: Development and preliminary results. *Journal of Personality and Social Psychology, 46,* 892–906.

Thoits, P. A. (1983). Dimensions of life events that influence psychological distress: An evaluation and synthesis of the literature. In H. B. Kaplan (Ed.), *Psychosocial stress: Trends in theory and research* (pp. 33–103). New York: Academic Press.

Thoits, P. A. (1984). Coping, social support, and psychological outcomes: The central role of emotion. In P. Shaver (Ed.), *Review of personality and social psychology* (vol. 5, pp. 219–238). Beverly Hills, CA: Sage.

Thoits, P. A. (1985). Self-labeling processes in mental illness: The role of emotional deviance. *American Journal of Sociology, 92,* 221–249.

Thoits, P. A. (1987). Gender and marital status differences in control and distress: Common stress versus unique stress explanations. *Journal of Health and Social Behavior, 28,* 7–22.

Thoits, P. A. (in press). Gender differences in coping with emotional distress. In J. Eckenrode (Ed.), *The social context of coping.* New York: Plenum.

Thompson, S. C. (1981). Will it hurt less if I can control it? A complex answer to a simple question. *Psychological Bulletin, 90,* 89–101.

Turner, R. J., & Noh, S. (1983). Class and psychological vulnerability among women: The significance of social support and personal control. *Journal of Health and Social Behavior, 24,* 2–15.

Vitaliano, P. P., Russo, J., Carr, J. E., Maiuro, R. D., & Becker, J. (1985). The Ways of Coping Checklist: Revision and psychometric properties. *Multivariate Behavioral Research, 20,* 3–26.

Wheaton, B. (1980). The sociogenesis of psychological disorder: An attributional theory. *Journal of Health and Social Behavior, 24,* 208–229.

Wortman, C. B., & Brehm, J. W. (1975). Responses to uncontrollable outcomes: An integration of reactance theory and the learned helplessness model. In L. Berkowitz (Ed.), *Advances in experimental social psychology* (vol. 8, pp. 277–336). New York: Academic Press.

Wortman, C. B., & Silver, R. C. (1987). Coping with irrevocable loss. In G. R. VandenBos & B. K. Bryant (Eds.), *Cataclysms, crises, and catastrophes: Psychology in action* (pp. 189–235). Washington, DC: American Psychological Association.

VI

OLDER ADULTHOOD

13

Attachment, Social Support, and Coping With Negative Life Events in Mature Adulthood

Toni C. Antonucci
The University of Michigan

The goal of this chapter is both theoretical and empirical. Theoretically it is proposed that attachment and social support can be viewed under the broader rubric of social relations. The convoy model of social relations (Antonucci, 1985; Kahn & Antonucci, 1980; Plath, 1980) is presented within this context as a theoretical framework within which to view social relations, including attachment and social support, over the life course. The second portion of the chapter is designed to empirically examine social relations within the convoy model, using the individual's ability to cope with negative life events as an illustrative case.

CONVOYS OF SOCIAL RELATIONS: ATTACHMENT AND SOCIAL SUPPORT

The convoy model suggests that as people develop and mature, they move through life both protected and sometimes made vulnerable by their social relationships. This view is based on both the attachment and social support literatures. The model emphasizes the importance of viewing social relations within a life-span context, of considering social relations as often, but not always, having stable and enduring qualities, and as having an important and cumulative influence on the individual. Although the voluminous research in the areas of helping, loving, caregiving, social support, friendships, close relationships, attachments, and affiliative behaviors are clearly related, they have unfortunately rarely been integrated or even benefitted from relevant empirical findings (cf. Antonucci, 1990; Berscheid & Peplau, 1983; Brehm, 1984; Cairns, 1977). In addition, these research endeavors have largely been focused empirically and theoretically within limited age groups (e.g., college students, old people, parent–infant pairs) and have generally been considered either positively or negatively (e.g., helpful friendships, dysfunctional families). The convoy model argues that all types of social relations need to be organized and understood within a single rubric and within a life-span, developmental, dynamic framework. In this chapter, an effort is made to emphasize and explicate how the theoretical and empirical research on attachment and social support can inform our general knowledge of social relations. This section begins with a brief review of both the traditional and more recent life-span views of attachment. It is followed by a consideration of the theoretical and empirical evidence available in the field of social support. The section ends with an integration of the two with the Convoy Model of Social Relations.

Attachment—Theory and Research

Traditionally attachment researchers have focused on mother–infant dyads. Ainsworth's (1964) early work stressed that the mother–child relationship is important, because the mother provides the infant with a secure base from which to explore the world. Ainsworth proposed that mothers and other significant caregivers, through responsiveness and contingent interaction, help these infants come to view the world as orderly, predictable, and interesting. Indeed the most advanced stage of attachment, as originally outlined by Bowbly (1969), is the goal-corrected partnership. At this stage, which occurs towards the end of the first year of life, the infant begins to infer the mother's feelings and motives; the dyad develops set goals and specifically plans to influence each other's behavior. This allows the development of a truly contingent and interactive partnership wherein each member of the dyad influences and is influenced by what the other does or might do. These dyadic relationships are often the vehicle through which many basic needs are provided and through which the infant comes to view the world as nonthreatening and stimulating. With the increased abilities of the child, the relationship develops from one in which the mother primarily responds to the infant to one that is mutually responsive.

The research with children has been dominated by child psychologists whose perspective has focused for many years almost exclusively on infant development. The field was advanced considerably by Mary Ainsworth's research (see Ainsworth, Blehar, Waters, & Wall, 1978, for a summary) and most specifically by her development of the attachment measurement technique known as the Strange Situation (Ainsworth et al., 1978). This technique was designed for use with one-year-olds and is only appropriate with young children; therefore, most research by child psychologists has been restricted to the period from twelve to thirty-six months. In what has turned out to be a fortuitous turn of events, many child developmental psychologists began longitudinal studies with these infants and have, thus, become increasingly interested in the long-term influence of the mother–child relationship on both other social relationships and other aspects of development (Arend, Gove, & Sroufe, 1979; Cassidy, 1988; Egeland & Farber, 1984; Ford & Thompson, 1985; Hartup, 1989; Main & Cassidy, 1988). Ainsworth and others (cf. Ainsworth et al., 1978) convincingly demonstrated that securely attached infants are provided with a secure base from which to explore their surroundings; therefore, it seemed both logical and reasonable that these early attachment relationships would have far-reaching effects. Recent work by many of these same investigators has been quite successful in demonstrating these relationships (see Bretherton & Waters, 1985; Main, Kaplan & Cassidy, 1985; Parkes & Stevenson-Hinde, 1982, for examples of this work).

In recent years, child developmental psychologists who have previously been concerned with the mother–infant attachment relationship have suggested that attachment should be viewed as life-span concept. As Bretherton and Waters (1985) noted, in many ways this recent development is a rediscovery of the original work of Bowlby (1969) as well as a notion specifically explored by others over a decade ago (cf. Antonucci, 1976; Kahn & Antonucci, 1980; Lerner & Ryff, 1978; Troll & Smith, 1976). Clinical evidence has also supported such an approach. Although not specifically using the attachment paradigm, mental health researchers have documented a relationship between depressed adults and their early parental relationships (e.g., Brown & Harris, 1978) as well as childhood links to later social problems (Robins, 1966). More directly, several researchers recently highlighted the clinical implications of attachment both in later childhood and adulthood (Belsky & Nezworski, 1988; Erickson, Egeland, & Sroufe, 1985; Lewis, Feiring, McGuffog, & Jaskir, 1984; Skolnick, 1986). Similarly, the child abuse literature has documented the relationship between being abused as a child and being a child abuser as an adult, another indirect indication of the life-span influence of early attachment relationships (Parke & Collmer, 1975). This work emphasizes the long-term effects of social relations by noting that children who have insecure attachments or poor early social relations are significantly more likely to manifest troublesome behaviors or mental health problems in later childhood or adulthood. In addition, there is research that suggests that attachment relations may be cumulative; that is, infants securely attached to their mothers at a young age remain so at a later age (Main et al., 1985) and that infants securely attached to their mothers are more likely to develop secure attachments with other people (Lewis, 1984). Hence, there is accumulating evidence of the long-term and cumulative effects of attachment relationships.

An interesting additional point should be made with respect to how attachment is seen to affect the individual. At the broad theoretical level, it is assumed that secure attachment enables the individual to view the world as an interesting and nonthreatening place to explore. It can be said that attachment is thought to have a direct or main effect on the individual's well-being. On the other hand, Ainsworth's Strange Situation is actually a measure of the indirect or buffering effect of social relations. The strange situation is a series of eight increasingly stressful separation and reunion episodes wherein infant responses are observed. It essentially examines the degree to which secure relationships buffer or enable the infant to withstand stress. Directly parallel research can be said to exist in the social support and social networks literatures.

Social Support—Theory and Research

"Modern" interest in social support is usually traced to Cassel (1976) and Cobb (1976), who noted the importance of supportive others in promoting "host resistance," that is, the ability of an individual to resist infection or illness. A significant link between social support and mortality has been demonstrated (Berkman & Syme, 1979; Blazer, 1982; House, Robbins, & Metzner, 1982) making social support the focus of much recent research. Social relations have long been known to affect mental health, most notably depression (Schaefer, Coyne, & Lazarus, 1981) and negative affect (Rook, 1984), but also the ability to cope with stressful life events (Kasl & Cooper, 1987) and physical illness (Brubaker, 1987; Ell, Mantell, Hamovitch, & Nishimoto 1989). Research in the area of depression is particularly illustrative, because it has been demonstrated that depressed individuals have generally smaller networks, often have experienced important losses in childhood, and have problematic or negative interactions with their network members (Brown & Bifulco, 1985; Coyne, Wortman & Lehman, 1988; Dean, Kolody & Wood, 1990; Fondacaro & Moos, 1987; Hammer 1981). However, as more extensive studies of social support and health become available, it becomes increasingly clear that very little is known about the processes and mechanisms through which this effect is accomplished (Antonucci & Jackson, 1987; Berkman, 1988; Cohen, 1988; Heller, Swindle, & Dusenbury, 1986; Pearlin & Turner, 1987; Wallston, Alagna, DeVellis, & DeVellis, 1983). The research examining the effect of social support on the general health and well-being of the individual has been labeled main or direct effect research; whereas the research exploring how social relations help an individual resist the negative effects of stress is generally known as the buffering- or indirect-effect of social support. These labels, although not often used in the attachment literature, clearly parallel the two views of attachment outlined previously.

Convoy Model of Social Relations

The convoy model argues that social relations can be characterized as hierarchical, developmental, and causally related to specific antecedents and consequences. This model was originally developed by Kahn and Antonucci (see Antonucci, 1985; Kahn, 1979; Kahn & Antonucci, 1980) and is only summarized briefly here. Special effort will be made to explicate the link between attachment and social support theory and research.

Social relations of both the attachment and social support type can readily be seen to be hierarchical. This simply affirms that some relations are more close and important than others. The attachment research with its primary emphasis on mother–child relationships, followed only much more recently by research on father, grandparents, and other caregiver attachments, has clearly recognized this hierarchy. The research on social support and social networks also assumes that some relationships are more significant than others. These are the relationships that are most often measured or examined. They include relations with spouse, parents, and children. Secondary level relations might be those with other relatives, friends, or coworkers. The convoy model assumes that the closeness of social relations vary. There are some people with whom an individual might be considered intimately connected, whereas there are others who are decreasingly important members of their social networks.

The developmental nature of social relations has also been recognized by both literatures. It is recognized that as infants grow and mature, they become increasing able to be active and interactive partners in the attachment relationship. Similar observations have been made of the mother, who may not be growing and maturing in the same physical sense as the infant but who often is growing and maturing in her capabilities and sensitivity as a mother. The social support literature has thus far mostly recognized that relationships develop over time as a result of shared experiences, expectations, and events (Levitt, in press). Family system and organizational theorists have recognized this at a still broader level, noting that as individual members of a system grow and develop so does the nature of the relationship among individual members of that organization (Kreppner & Lerner, 1989). Ainsworth et al., (1978) and others showed that even as the actual capabilities of the infants change and develop, there is underlying stability in the attachment relationship itself. This continuity or stability of relationship has been demonstrated over the first year of life and up through the early and middle stages of childhood (e.g., Antonucci & Levitt, 1984; Egeland & Farber, 1984; Main & Cassidy, 1988; Skolnick, 1986). We assume a direct parallel in adult relationships (i.e., that social relationships tend to be stable and continuous over time). Similarly, much of the attachment research has noted that infant relationships vary in quality. Hence, the discussion of relationships as secure, anxious, or avoidant. We assume that adult social relationships are exactly parallel, that some social interactions are consistently characterized as warm, nurturant, supportive (i.e., as continuing to provide the individual with a secure base from which to explore and interact with the world) as well as a cushion or buffer that helps an individual cope with the stresses or strains of life. Furthermore, as Main, Kaplan, and Cassidy (1985) suggested, relationships can be similarly anxious or avoidant.

Finally, the convoy model assumes that there are antecedent and consequent conditions that influence social relations. As Ainsworth and other attachment researchers have empirically demonstrated, the mother influences the developing relationship with her child. However, also important is a greater understanding of what influences the mother; that is, what are the antecedent conditions that influence how the mother interacts with her child either generally or in any specific situation. The social support research has similarly demonstrated that social relations are influenced by the properties of the individual such as age, gender, ethnic group membership, marital status, or by situational characteristics (e.g., organizational membership, roles occupied, employment status).

Empirical Investigations

In an effort to understand how social relations influence the individual, investigators have sought to explore both qualitative and quantitative aspects of attachment and social support. The intensive study of the first year of life by Mary Ainsworth and her colleagues (1978) examined both aspects of the mother–infant interactive sequences. Although the quantitative data are interesting, the most useful and predictive data have been the qualitative judgments of attachment security (Ainsworth et al., 1978; Antonucci & Levitt, 1984; Main & Cassidy, 1988). Research concerning the characteristics of social support and social networks has offered similar insights concerning social relations. Of particular interest to the theoretical basis of social relations is the finding that although both quantitative and qualitative characteristics of relations influence the health and well-being of the individual, it is the qualitative characteristics of the relationships that are the most predictive (e.g., Antonucci & Akiyama, 1987a). These findings are interpreted as providing evidence of a psychological basis for understanding how and why social relations are important and effective. The social support and social networks' empirical evidence essentially indicates that although the size, gender, and age of a social network may provide useful information, more critical (and predictive) is how individuals evaluate their social relationships. In the present chapter, data are presented that offer related empirical evidence concerning the hierarchical, developmental, and causal effects of social relations among adults. Data are presented from a study of social relations among mature adults. Although childhood and young adult data are not available, it is believed that these findings are useful, because they provide representative data that substantiate a life-course continuity of attachment and social support that can be viewed under the general rubric of convoys of social relations. Paralleling the infant data, adult data assessing the hierarchical and stable nature of social relations suggests both a clear hierarchical organization of relationships and a considerable amount of stability. The qualitative versus quantitative aspects of social relationships are investigated through an examination of the relative impact of size (quantity) versus satisfaction (quality) with social relationships in helping the individual cope with negative life events.

The Sample

The data presented in this chapter are based on the first national study of social support among mature adults. The original sample consisted of 718 adults fifty years of age and older living in the coterminous United States. They were first interviewed in 1980. In 1984, all available respondents were recontacted for a telephone interview. Approximately 404 men and women were reinterviewed. Details of both samples are available from the final reports of those projects (Antonucci, Kahn, Harrison, & Payne, 1986; Kahn & Antonucci, 1984) and from recent publications (Antonucci & Akiyama, 1987a, 1987b; Antonucci, Kahn, & Akiyama, 1989).

The integration of the attachment and social support literatures into one comprehensive theory of social relationships would argue for both continuity and stability in social relationships, except under unusual circumstances. However, most adult researchers have assumed that with age there is a dramatic reduction in the number of people with whom one has social relationships. Our data suggest that this is not so.

Hierarchical Relationships

The convoy model proposes that people hierarchically organize their social relations, that is to say relations with some are closer and more intimate than relations with others. Using the concentric circles diagram described by Antonucci (1986), we asked people to name those people who were so close and important to them that it was hard to imagine life without them (inner circle); people who were not quite *that* close but still important (middle circle), and people not already mentioned but who are close enough and important enough in your life that they should be in your network (outer circle). Men and women in this national sample were readily able to distribute their social relations over these three levels of intimacy. Ninety-seven percent of the spouses were in the inner circle; ninety-eight percent of the children and eighty-six percent of siblings were included in the inner or middle circle, whereas thirty-seven percent of friends were listed as members of the outer circle. Clearly people are able to hierarchically organize their social relations. For example, although not all spouses were members of the inner network, the majority of spouses were considered relations that were "so close and important that it is hard to imagine life without them."

Stability of Social Relations

The availability of two waves of data regarding social relations among a representative sample of mature adults makes it possible to examine the stability of these relationships. A unique strength of these data is that they are longitudinal, but an important limiting aspect of wave 1 and 2 is that information for the first wave of data concerning social relations was collected during a face-to-face interview using the concentric circles diagram (Antonucci, 1986) as a focal point for gathering detailed information about social relations. Data for the second wave were collected by telephone. It was, therefore, not possible to use the concentric circles diagram, and a reliance on summary measures of the detailed assessment of certain social relations characteristics was necessary.

Nevertheless, parallel support variables from wave 1 and wave 2 are consistently and significantly correlated. Network size, presence of spouse in network, number of family members, and frequency of contact are all related from wave 1 to wave 2. Reports of what others do for you are also consistently correlated. Of the six supports assessed in both waves, wave 1 reports are significantly correlated with wave 2 reports of having others reassure you, care for you when you are ill, talk with you when you are upset, talk with you about your health, people you confide in and people who respect you (only marginally significant for the latter two). Adequacy of social relations, measured using an index of two variables (Would you want more people in your network? Would you want more people you could depend on?), was also significantly correlated between the two waves. These data, collected four years apart for a national representative sample of mature adults, offer considerable weight to the proposition that there is stability over time in social relations.

Age Differences in Social Relations

The data suggest that there are fewer age differences in social relations than often hypothesized. There were no significant age differences in the number of people in the support networks of older people as compared with younger people (see Antonucci & Akiyama, 1987b for details). Although close examination of the actual numbers suggests that with advanced age there does tend to be some reduction in the number of people nominated as close and important, this reduction is not statistically significant. Similarly, size of network at wave 1 is significantly correlated with size of network at wave 2 despite the differences in interview technique and question format.

There were also no significant differences by gender in network composition; both men and women of all ages have more women in their network. There are no age differences in the number of people from whom respondents received support. Several other variables, however, did show significant differences by age. Older people are more likely to have network members who are older and are likely to have known their network members longer. Older people are less likely to live within an hour's drive of their network members than younger people, and older people have less contact with their network members. These latter findings are influenced by the increased probability that younger people are married and hence, living in "close proximity" to an additional member of their support network. Whereas there were no age differences in the number of people our respondents received support from, older respondents indicated that they provided less support to others than did younger respondents. Although complete data are not available from the two waves, analyses indicate that, despite differences in methodology, the report of support received from others is significantly correlated from 1980 to 1984.

Social Relations and Coping with Life Events

The attachment and the social support literatures suggest that social relations provide a positive base for people that help them function both under normal situations and under stress. In this section, longitudinal data from our sample of mature men and women are used to examine whether or not social relations have a positive effect even in the presence of negative life events. Two questions are addressed in the following analyses: (a) Do social relations as reported four years earlier affect an individual's life satisfaction even when they experience negative life events four years later and, if so, (b) which characteristics of social relations, quantity or quality, are most influential? The measures and assessment tools are described first.

Support measures used in these analyses were collected at the time of the first wave of data collection in 1980. The negative life events were assessed in 1984. Quantity of social support was assessed as size of network, that is, the number of people respondents nominated as individuals who were close and important to them. Quality of social support was assessed as the average of the responses to two questions concerning satisfaction with network. Respondents were asked how satisfied they were with their family life, and separately how satisfied they were with their friendships. Responses ranged from one to seven (1 = completely dissatisfied to 7 = completely satisfied). A series of questions, adapted from the Holmes and Rahe Scale (1967), were asked regarding negative life events. For the present analyses, most frequent events were considered: death of spouse, death of another close family or friend, serious illness or injury to a close family member or friend, and a summary score of all eleven negative life events assessed.

In order to examine the relative influence of the quantitative and qualitative characteristics of social relations on life satisfaction, the following analytic strategy was adopted. Ordinary least squares regression analyses were utilized. Analyses were conducted for each network characteristic, that is, size of and satisfaction with network, separately for each of the three negative life events as well as the total negative life events score. The results are summarized in Table 13.1 and, consistent with the infant attachment literature, suggest that qualitative measures of social support are more predictive of life satisfaction than quantitative measures.

Table 13.1 presents the regression analyses utilizing life satisfaction as the dependent variable and each type of support variable. Age and sex are also entered into each regression equation. The Fs and R^2s are provided in the bottom portion of the table. Most clear from Table 13.1 is that the regression analyses using network size as the social support variable do not account for a very high proportion of the variance. In fact, none of the first four regression analyses summarized in Table 13.1 are significant. The asterisks next to each predictor variable indicates that the variable was significantly related to the criterion variable. As examination of the first four columns indicates, although the negative

TABLE 13.1
Predicting Life Satisfaction from Age, Gender, Social Support,
and Negative Life Events

	Beta Coefficients							
Age	.01	.07	.07	.04	.04	.03	.03	.01
Gender	.15	.08	.08	.08	.08	.09$^+$	.08	.08
Network Size	−.04	−.04	−.03	−.03				
Network Satisfaction					.21**	.20**	.20**	.20**
Spouse Died	−.10*				−.11*			
Others Died		.02				.00		
Family Ill			−.09$^+$				.09$^+$	
Total Negative Life Events				−.13*			−.13*	
F	2.20	1.20	2.00	2.69	6.49**	5.20**	6.00**	6.89**
R^2 Adjusted	.02	.01	.02	.03	.06	.05	.06	.07

$^+p < .10$
$*p < .05$
$**p < .01$

life events of having a spouse die and total negative life events score are both negatively related to life satisfaction, neither the size of network nor the overall regressions are significant.

The last four columns in Table 13.1 summarize the results of the same analyses, substituting network satisfaction for size of network. Examination of the Fs and R^2s indicates that the proportion of variance accounted for in these analyses are larger and reach statistical significance. Two negative life events are significantly and negatively related to life satisfaction: spouse died and total negative life events. In all four regression equations, network satisfaction is positively related to life satisfaction.

Before summarizing these findings and discussing their theoretical implications, consider a note about a methodological issue. Both the life satisfaction and the network satisfaction variables use the same question phrasing and response choices; therefore, the issue of artificial inflation of the relationship between the two variables is raised. To address this question, a parallel set of analyses were conducted using a three-level happiness variable as the dependent variable. Results from this second set of analyses are not presented but are quite similar to those presented here, adding to our confidence in the pattern of findings reported previously.

The analyses summarized in Table 13.1 support the case for the differential effectiveness of qualitative over quantitative support. Regression analyses using network size as the support variable were not significantly related to life satisfaction whereas analyses using network satisfaction were. These analyses thus provide supporting evidence of the direct or main effects of support and suggest that this effect is carried by qualitative rather than quantitative support.

In summarizing these findings, we note that these data do not permit the examination of the indirect or buffering effects of social support. Cohen and Wills (1985) recently reviewed this literature and noted that evidence concerning the buffering effect is equivocal. Their extensive review of the literature led them to the conclusion that the buffering effect is present only when the support provided is specific to the stressful event experienced. No such measures were available in the present data set; thus, a buffering effect as suggested by Cohen and Wills, that is, with support measures specific to the crises, could not be assessed. Nevertheless, we did attempt a buffering analyses using the generalized measures that were available and paralleling the regression analyses reported previously. We were unable to document a buffering effect in any of these analyses.

The regression analyses reported above support the proposition that social support has a main or direct effect on general well-being. Our findings further permit a distinction between quantitative and qualitative measures of support. Parallel analyses using both wave 2 support and negative life events data are also significant, in fact, accounting for two to four times the amount of variance. The analyses reported in this chapter in many ways represent a conservative test of the influence of supportive relations, because the support measures used in these analyses were assessed four years earlier at time 1 whereas the negative life events were assessed at time 2. This type of analyses has been highly unusual in the literature, mainly because of the lack of availability of longitudinal, detailed data concerning social relations. The findings lend support to the long-term or life-span view of social relations that has been proposed in this chapter by indicating that early support has a positive influence on well-being, even in the presence of negative life events.

It is unfortunate that the data concerning the role of social support being provided specific to the negative life event were not available. Such data would have permitted the examination of both the direct and indirect effect of social relations. Ramifications of these findings are discussed below as they relate to the life-span theoretical model of convoys of social relations proposed in the first half of this chapter.

SUMMARY AND CONCLUSIONS

In this chapter, it is proposed that attachment and social support research be integrated under the broader rubric of social relations. The convoy model of social relations is suggested as representing the necessary theoretical framework. A review and reconsideration of past work, as well as the presentation from a short-term longitudinal study of adulthood, lends support for this integrative approach. The lack of age differences in the support networks of adults fifty years of age and over indicate significant stability. Analyses reported in this chapter indicate that satisfaction with network, but not necessarily size of network, is significantly related to well-being both for those who are experiencing negative life events and those who are not.

These analyses highlight the psychological as well as the long-term effects of social relationships. That people's social networks differed so little over a cross-sectional span of almost fifty years (the oldest respondent in the wave 1 data collection was 98) suggests a significant similarity in network characteristics. Although one must be careful not to confuse cross-sectional with longitudinal data, in this case a lack of age differences in the cross-sectional analyses and the presence of significant correlations in the longitudinal data, both lead to the same conclusion. Structural characteristics of social relations are relatively stable over time. In addition, the regression analyses that did capitalize on the use of longitudinal data was also consistent with earlier views in indicating that early social relations affect later well-being both when individuals experience life events and when they do not. This longitudinal view suggests that the recent work of attachment researchers on extending the concept across the life-span (cf. Belsky & Nezworski, 1988; Bretherton & Waters, 1985) and of early child developmental psychologists who are integrating the work on social networks of mothers with the relationships and development of their children (Cochran & Brassard, 1979; Colletta, 1981; Crnic, Greenberg, Ragozin, Robinson, & Basham, 1983; Crockenberg, 1981; Levitt, Weber, & Clark, 1986; Zarling, Hirsch & Landry, 1988) should be expanded and applauded. The present chapter is meant to be another step in this exciting new direction that represents an integration of the work of attachment theorists, life-span developmental psychologists, and adult development researchers.

ACKNOWLEDGMENTS

Preparation of this manuscript was supported in part by a Research Career Development Award (#AG))271) and a Research Grant (#RO1 AG06146) to the author from the National Institutes on Aging.

The data computation on which this paper is based employed the OSIRIS IV computer software package, which was developed by the Institute for Social Research of The University of Michigan, using funds from the Survey Research Center, the Inter-University Consortium for Political Research, National Science Foundation, and other sources. I would like to thank Mary Levitt for comments on an earlier version of this manuscript and Halimah Hassan for help with the data analyses.

REFERENCES

Ainsworth, M. D. (1964). Patterns of attachment behavior shown by the infant in interaction with his mother. *Merrill-Palmer Quarterly, 10,* 51–58.

Ainsworth, M. D. S., Blehar, M. C., Waters, E., & Wall, S. (1978) *Patterns of Attachment.* Hillsdale, NJ: Lawrence Erlbaum Associates.

Antonucci, T. C. (1976). Attachment: A life span concept. *Human Development, 19,* 135–42.

Antonucci, T. C. (1985). Personal characteristics, social support, and social behavior. In E. Shanas & R. H. Binstock (Eds.), *Handbook of aging and the social sciences,* (pp. 94–129). New York: Van Nostrand Reinhold.

Antonucci, T. C. (1986, Summer). Measuring social support networks: Hierarchical mapping technique. *Generations,* 10–12.

Antonucci, T. C. (1990) Social supports and social relationships in R. H. Binstock & L. K. George (Eds.), *The handbook of aging and the social sciences, 3rd Edition* (pp. 205–226. San Diego, CA: Academic Press.

Antonucci, T. C., & Akiyama, H. (1987a). An examination of sex differences in social support among older men and women. *Sex roles, 17,* 737–749.

Antonucci, T. C., & Akiyama, H. (1987b). Social networks in adult life and a preliminary examination of the convoy model. *Journal of Gerontology, 42,* 519–527.

Antonucci, T. C., & Jackson, J. S. (1987). Social support, interpersonal efficacy and health. In L. L. Carstensen & B. A. Edelstein (Eds.), *Handbook of clinical gerontology* (pp. 291–311). New York: Pergamon.

Antonucci, T. C., Kahn, R. L., & Akiyama, H. (1989). Psychosocial factors and the response to cancer symptoms. In R. Yancik & J. Yates (Eds.), *Cancer in the elderly: Approaches to early detection and treatment* (pp. 40–52). New York: Springer.

Antonucci, T. C., Kahn, R. L., Harrison, R., Payne, B. C. (1986). *Cancer symptoms in the elderly: Support and responses.* Final report to the National Cancer Institute, #R01 CA36580.

Antonucci, T. C., & Levitt, M. J. (1984). Early prediction of attachment security: A multivariate approach. *Infant Behavior and Development, 7,* 1–18.

Arend, K., Gove, F. I., & Sroufe, L. A. (1979). Continuity of individual adaptation from infancy to kindergarten: A predictive study of ego-resiliency and curiosity in preschoolers. *Child Development, 58,* 958–959.

Belsky, J. & Nezworski, T. (1988). *Clinical implications of attachment,* Hillsdale, NJ: Lawrence Erlbaum Associates.

Berkman, L. F. (1988). The changing and heterogenous nature of aging and longevity: A social and biomedical perspective. *Annual Review of Gerontology and Geriatrics, 8,* 37–88.

Berkman, L. S., & Syme, S. L. (1979). Social networks, host resistance, and mortality: A nine year follow-up study of Alameda County residents. *American Journal of Epidemiology, 109,* 186–204.

Berscheid, E., & Peplau, L. A. (1983). The emerging science of relationships. In H. H. Kelley, E. Berscheid, A. Christensen, J. H. Harvey, T. L. Huston, G. Levinger, E. McClintock, L. A. Peplau, & D. R. Peterson (Eds.), *Close relationships* (pp. 1–19). New York: Freeman.

Blazer, D. G. (1982). Social support and mortality in an elderly population. *American Journal of Epidemiology, 115,* 684–694.

Bowlby, J. (1969). *Attachment and loss: Volume 1. Attachment.* New York: Basic.

Brehm, S. S. (1984). Social support processes. In J. C. Masters & K. Yarkin-Levin (Eds.), *Boundary areas in social and developmental psychology* (pp. 107–130). New York: Academic Press.

Bretherton, I., & Waters, E. (Eds.), (1985). In Growing points of attachment theory and research. *Monographs of the Society for Research in Child Development, 50,* (1–2, Serial No. 209).

Brown, G. W., & Bifulco, A. (1985). Social support, life events and depression. In I. Sarason & B. R. Sarason (Eds.), *Social support: Theory, research, and applications* (pp. 349–370). The Hague: Nijhoff.

Brown G. W., & Harris, T. (1978). *Social origins of depression.* New York: Free Press.

Brubaker, T. (1987). *Aging, health and family, long term care.* Newbury Park, CA: Sage.

Cairns, R. B. (1977) Beyond social attachment: The dynamics of interactional development. In T. Alloway, P. Pliner, & L. Krames (Eds.), *Attachment behavior* (pp. 1–24). New York: Plenum.

Cassel, J. (1976). The contribution of the social environment to host resistance. *American Journal of Epidemiology, 104,* (3), 253–286. New York: Academic Press.

Cassidy, J. (1988). Child–mother attachment and the self in six-year-olds. *Child Development, 59,* 121–134.

Cobb, S. (1976). Social support as a moderator of life stress. *Psychosomatic Medicine, 38,* 300–314.

Cochran, M. M., & Brassard, J. A. (1979). Child development and personal social networks. *Child Development, 50,* 601–616.

Cohen, S. (1988). Psychosocial models of the role of social support in the etiology of physical disease. *Health Psychology, 7,* 269–297.

Cohen S., & Wills, T. A. (1985). Stress, social support, and the buffering hypothesis. *Psychology Bulletin, 98,* 310–357.

Colletta, N. D. (1981). Social support and the risk of maternal rejection by adolescent mothers. *Journal of Psychology, 109,* 191–197.

Coyne, J. C., Wortman, C. B., & Lehman, D. R. (1988). The other side of support: Emotional over involvement and miscarried helping. In B. Gottlieb (Ed.), *Marshaling social support: Formats, processes, and effects.* New York: Sage.

Crnic, K. A., Greenberg, M. T., Ragozin, A. S., Robinson, N. M., & Basham, R. B. (1983). Effects of stress and social support on mothers and premature and full-term infants. *Child Development, 54,* 209–217.

Crockenberg, S. B. (1981). Infant irritability, mother responsiveness, and social support influences on the security of infant–mother attachment. *Child Development, 52,* 857–865.

Dean, A., Kolody, B., & Wood, P. (1990). The effects of various sources of social support on depression in elderly persons. *Journal of Health and Social Behavior, 31,* 148–161.

Egeland, B., & Farber, E. A. (1984). Infant–mother attachment. Factors related to its development and changes over time. *Child Development, 55,* 753–771.

Ell, K. O., Mantell, J. E., Hamovitch, M. B., & Nishimoto, R. H. (1989). Social support, sense of control and coping among patients with breast, lung, or colorectal cancer. *Journal of Psychosocial Oncology, 7,* 63–89.

Erickson, M., Egeland, B., & Sroufe, L. A. (1985). The relationship between quality of attachment and behavior problems in preschool in high risk sample. In I. Bretherton & E. Waters (Eds.), *Growing points in attachment theory and research* (pp. 147–186). *Monographs of the Society for Research in Child Development, 50* (1–2, Serial No. 209).

Fondacaro, M. R., & Moos, R. H. (1987). Social support and coping: A longitudinal analysis. *American Journal of Community Psychology, 15,* 653–673.

Ford, M. E., & Thompson, R. (1985). Perceptions of personal agency and infant attachment: Toward a life-span perspective. *International Journal of Behavioral Development, 8,* 377–405.

Hammer, M. (1981). Social supports, social networks, and schizophrenia. *Schizophrenia Bulletin, 7,* 45–57.

Hartup, W. W. (1989). Social relationships and their development significance. *American Psychologist, 44,* 120–126.

Heller, K., Swindle, R. W., & Dusenbury, L. (1986). Component social support processes: Comments and integration. *Journal of Consulting and Clinical Psychology, 54,* 466–470.

Holmes, T. H., & Rahe, R. H. (1967). The Social Readjustment Rating Scale. *Journal of Psychosomatic Medicine, 11,* 213–218.

House, J. S., Robbins, C., & Metzner, H. C. (1982). The association of social relationships and activities with mortality: Perspective evidence from the Tecumseh community health study. *American Journal of Epidemiology, 116,* 123–140.

Kahn, R. L. (1979). Aging and social support, In M. W. Riley (Ed.), *Aging from birth to death: Interdisciplinary perspectives.* Boulder, CO: Westview.

Kahn, R. L., & Antonucci, T. C. (1980). Convoys over the life course: Attachment, roles, and social support. In P. B. Baltes & O. G. Brim (Eds.), *Life span development and behavior* (Vol. 3, pp. 253–286). New York: Academic Press.

Kahn, R. L., & Antonucci, T. C. (1984). *Social supports of the elderly: Family/friends/professionals.* Final report to the National Institute on Aging, #AGO1632.

Kasl, S., & Cooper, C. L. (Eds.). (1987). *Stress and health issues in research methodology* (pp. 143–165). Chichester: Wiley.

Kreppner, K., & Lerner, R. M. (1989). *Family systems and life-span development.* Hillsdale, NJ: Lawrence Erlbaum Associates.

Levitt, M. J., (in press). Attachment and close relationships: A life span perspective. In J. L. Gewirtz & W. F. Kurtines (Eds.), *Intersections with attachment.* Hillsdale, NJ: Lawrence Erlbaum Associates.

Levitt, M. J., Weber, R. A., & Clark, M. C. (1986). Social network relations as sources of maternal support and well-being. *Developmental Psychology, 22,* 310–316.

Lerner, R., & Ryff, G. (1978). Implementation of the life-span view of human development: The sample case of attachment. In P. B. Baltes (Ed.), *Life-span development and behavior* (vol. 1, pp. 1–44). New York: Plenum.

Lewis, M., (Ed.). (1984). *Beyond the dyad.* New York: Plenum.

Lewis, M., Feiring, C., McGuffog, C., & Jaskir, J. (1984). Predicting psychopathology in six-year-olds from early social relations. *Child Development, 55,* 123–137.

Main, M. (1985, April). *An adult attachment classification system.* Paper presented at the biennial meeting of the Society for Research in Child Development, Toronto.

Main, M., & Cassidy, J. (1988). Categories of response to reunion with the parent at age 6: Predictable from infant attachment classifications and stable over a 1-month period. *Developmental Psychology, 24,* 415–426.

Main, M., Kaplan, N., & Cassidy, J. (1985). Security in infancy, childhood, and adulthood: A move to the level of representation. In I. Bretherton & E. Waters (Eds.), *Growing points of attachment theory and research. Monograph of the Society for Research in Child Development, 50* (1–2), Serial No. 209.

Parke, R. D., & Collmer, C. W. (1975). Child abuse: An interdisciplinary analysis. In E. M. Hetherington (Ed.), *Review of child development research* (pp. 509–590). Chicago: University of Chicago Press.

Parkes, C. M., & Stevenson-Hinde, J. (1982). *The place of attachment in human behavior.* New York: Busic.

Pearlin, L. I., & Turner, H. A. (1987). The family as a context of the stress process. In S. Kasl & C. L. Cooper (Eds.), *Stress and health issues in research methodology* (pp. 143–165). Chichester, England: Wiley.

Plath, D. (1980). *Long engagements.* Stanford, CA: Stanford University Press.

Robins, L. N. (1966). *Deviant children grown up.* Baltimore: Williams & Wilkins.

Rook, K. S. (1984). The negative side of social interaction: Impact on psychologic well-being. *Journal of Personality and Social Psychology, 46,* 1097–1108.

Shaefer, C., Coyne, J. C., & Lazarus, R. S. (1981). The health-related functions of social support. *Journal of Behavioral Medicine, 4,* 381–406.

Skolnick, A. (1986). Early attachment and personal relationships across the life course. In P. B. Baltes, D. L. Featherman, & R. M. Lerner (Eds.), In *Life-span Development and Behavior* (vol. 7, 173–206). Hillsdale, NJ: Lawrence Erlbaum Associates.

Troll, L. E., & Smith, J. (1976). Attachment through the life-span: Some questions about dyadic bonds among adults. *Human Development, 19,* 156–170.

Wallston, B. S., Alagna, S. W., DeVellis, B. M., & DeVellis, R. F. (1983). Social support and physical health. *Health Psychology, 2,* 367–393.

Zarling, C. L., Hirsch, B. J., Landry, S. (1988). Maternal social networks and mother-infant interactions in full-term and very low birth weight, preterm infants. *Child Development, 59*(1), 178–185.

Personality, Defense, Coping, and Adaptation in Older Adulthood

Paul T. Costa, Jr.
Alan B. Zonderman,
Robert R. McCrae
Gerontology Research Center
National Institute on Aging, National Institutes of Health
Baltimore, Maryland

Dividing the life span into discrete segments is always more or less arbitrary, and this seems to be particularly true with regard to coping processes. Older people—provided that they are cognitively intact, as most are—are fundamentally adults, and in most respects, they cope with stress as do adults of other ages. There are, it appears, some age-related changes in the nature of the stressors typically encountered, with concommitant changes in the coping strategies adopted; once situational effects are taken into consideration, however, there appear to be few age differences in the use of any of a wide range of coping processes. Coping, however, is sometimes contrasted with defense, and researchers who identify themselves with this latter tradition have been particularly concerned with issues of development. In this chapter, we briefly summarize theory and research on the development of defense mechanisms in adults and present new cross-sectional data on some putative measures of defenses. We will then turn to research on ways of coping and their relation to age. Finally we will discuss the general process of adaptation to aging and its stresses.

AGE AND DEFENSE MECHANISMS

Long before stress and coping became a topic worthy of such a volume as this, psychologists and psychiatrists were concerned with processes of defense. In the work of Haan (1965, 1977) and Vaillant (1977), models of defense were closely linked to longitudinal studies. Thus, it seems appropriate to begin our discussion with an examination of theory and research on the use of defense mechanisms in adulthood.

Stress and coping researchers often take a dim view of the concept of defense. They tend to believe it is relevant, if at all, only to cases of psychopathology and that it presents insuperable obstacles to scientific measurement. Those who retain an interest in defense mechanisms (e.g., Horowitz, 1988; Vaillant & Drake, 1985) view them as the foundation of psychological health: Without the relatively automatic operation of basic defenses, the rational decisions needed for effective coping would be impossible. Furthermore, although the assessment of defenses is not easy, they believe it is worth attempting. Recent assessments of coping research (Aldwin & Revenson, 1987) demonstrate that newer approaches to coping do not have all the answers; it may well be time to reconsider the role of defenses in psychological adaptation. We will begin with an examination of three instruments designed to assess defenses, both as an illustration of different approaches to their measurement and as an introduction to some new data on age and the use of defenses.

Conceptualizing and Measuring Defenses

The concept of defense is central to psychoanalysis and to many psychodynamic systems that have evolved from it (A. Freud, 1936; S. Freud, 1894/1955; Horney, 1945). In brief, defense mechanisms are thought to be ways of distorting reality in order to manage distressing feelings. The distortion may range from innocent rationalization to the development of chronic neurotic symptoms; the variety of ways in which people can deceive themselves is at least as great as the number of ways in which people can cope with problems they consciously face.

Although the existence of defenses is axiomatic for most clinical and personality psychologists, the data in support of this assumption is remarkably weak (Kline, 1981). Much has been made of studies of perceptual defense that demonstrate that individuals require a few milliseconds longer to recognize an emotionally laden word than a neutral word, but it is a great inferential leap from such data to the elaborate defensive structures hypothesized by classical psychoanalysis (cf. Klein, 1970). In large part, the limited evidence in favor of defensive processes is due to the difficulty of assessing them reliably and validly, a difficulty that is inherent in the concept itself.

We call behavior *defensive* if it is in some sense inconsistent with objective reality, when reality might be too painful to face directly. It is usually possible to assess the behavior, but it is much more difficult to define reality. Older individuals, despite the proximity of death, generally do not show evidence of a heightened fear of death (Kastenbaum & Costa, 1977). To claim this as an instance of denial, we would have to assert that death really is a threat—especially a threat to older people—and we simply have no basis for such an assertion.

Some people view it as a release or as a passage to a new and better life. Are they merely rationalizing? Who can say?

Stereotypes of old age have portrayed it as a dismal portion of the life span, and evidence that older men and women are generally as happy and satisfied with life as are younger individuals (Costa & McCrae, 1984; McCrae & Costa, 1988) is taken by many as evidence of defensive distortion. However, the appearance of happiness among older people is so common that we would have to assume that older people in general were prone to the use of fairly primitive defenses, and this assumption is inconsistent with the fact that most cope relatively well and realistically with events such as retirement, death of spouse, and personal illness.

Psychologists who are committed to the notion of widespread defensive processes tend to take a dim view of self-reports about any important issue and claim (with some logic) that self-reports of defensive behavior are meaningless. Many have, therefore, relied on projective techniques to assess defenses (e.g., Bellak, 1973). As Kahana (1978) noted, projective tests remain enormously popular despite incessant criticism of their reliability and validity and their generally meager empirical basis. Although they may be of value in the interaction of client and therapist, these techniques have provided little data that could contribute to a scientific understanding of defenses in old age.

Consequently, researchers who believe in the importance of defenses but who also wish to do rigorous research have had to devise new techniques and make certain assumptions about the data provided by subjects. Gleser and Ihilevich (1969; Ihilevich & Gleser, 1986) designed the Defense Mechanisms Inventory (DMI) to measure five broad defenses: Turning Against Object, Projection, Principalization, Turning Against Self, and Reversal. Ten vignettes are presented, and the subject is asked to select which from a set of five responses he or she would be most and least likely to make in the situation; the five responses are intended to represent the five defenses. Because the situation is hypothetical, the subject is thought to have sufficient distance to respond accurately; and because the subject is forced to choose among defenses, the possibilities for socially desirable responding are minimized. Although the five mechanisms were intended to measure a wide range of defenses, factor analyses clearly show that there are only two independent factors in the DMI: Turning Against Object and Projection are contrasted with Principalization and Reversal in the first; Turning Against Self is the second. The first factor seems to represent the degree of socialization in defensive responses and has been shown to be correlated with ratings of the personality dimension of Agreeableness vs. Antagonism (Costa, McCrae, & Dembroski, 1989.)

Haan (1965, 1977) relied on a classification of 10 defense mechanisms derived from the work of Kroeber (1963), and her subjects were rated on their use of each by interviewers and other clinical psychologists who reviewed extensive information on life history, present status, and social interactions. These ratings were then used to select MMPI items that differentiated the high from the low users on each mechanism. It was possible to develop reliable scales for seven mechanisms: Regression, Repression, Denial, Displacement, Intellectualizing, Projection, and Doubt. Because an empirical criterion-group item selection strategy was used, there was no need to assume that the subjects responded accurately to the MMPI items: Regardless of subjects' motivations in answering questions, certain items distinguished individuals who used a defense, and those items made up a scale. Subsequent research with these scales has provided some evidence of their validity (Morrissey, 1977).

Bond, Gardner, Christian, and Sigal (1983) acknowledged that individuals could not be expected to report defensive behavior accurately but thought that respondents could provide information from which defenses could be inferred: "A statement like, 'People tell me that I often take anger out on someone other than the one at whom I'm really angry,' might tap displacement even if the subject is unaware of his defensive behavior at the time it is happening" (p. 334). They constructed an inventory of items intended to measure such "conscious derivatives" of 25 defense mechanisms and described four broad defensive styles on the basis of a factor analysis of these items: Maladaptive Action Pattern, Image-Distorting, Self-Sacrificing, and Adaptive defenses. Because these scales are based on covarying clusters of conscious self-descriptions, they resemble more conventional, rational scales of personality measurement. A rational interpretation of item content supports the labels for Maladaptive Action Pattern, Self-Sacrificing, and Adaptive defenses. The Image-Distorting defenses consist of items intended to measure splitting, primitive idealization, and omnipotence with devaluation, but an examination of the items provides a somewhat more prosaic interpretation: The scale seems to tap a sense of superiority to others and a judgmental, intolerant style that suggests that arrogance and narrow-mindedness of antagonistic people (Costa et al., 1989). An alternative label might be *superiority*.

Building on the conceptual work of Haan and her predecessors, Vaillant (1976, 1977) identified 15 defense mechanisms that he classified as immature (projection, schizoid fantasy, hypochondriasis, passive aggression, acting out, and dissociation), neurotic (reaction formation, isolation, displacement, and repression), or mature (humor, altruism, sublimation, suppression, and anticipation). As we will see, "maturity" for Vaillant implies both better mental health and further psychological development. Using the archives of longitudinal studies, Vaillant inferred the use of defense mechanisms from life history data by noting the ways in which individuals described the way they handled crises. Most of the individual mechanisms showed adequate interrater reliability (Vaillant, 1977), and global maturity of defense (the degree to which mature mechanisms are preferred over immature mechanisms) has been shown to be related to psychological health and adult adjustment, seen in such criteria as stable marital relationships, career success, and the absence of psychiatric hospitalization (Vaillant & Drake, 1985).

Defenses and Aging

There is relatively little data on age differences or changes in the use of defenses, and almost none that includes assessments in old age. Haan (1977) attempted to assess changes between childhood and two points in adulthood, using ratings of coping and defense based on life-history data and interviews. The ipsative nature of the Q–sorts used to assess defenses posed methodological problems in comparing data from one period with those from others, so no firm conclusions could be drawn about changes in the average use of coping or defense mechanisms, particularly between the two adult assessments.

Vaillant resolved some of these problems in his analyses of defenses in the Grant Study of Adult Development (Vaillant, 1976). He rated 1,782 vignettes from 95 men for ages less than 20, 20 to 35, and over 35. There were clear increases between adolescence and adulthood in the use of mature mechanisms, and corresponding decreases in the use of immature mechanisms. Change continued in the same direction between early and middle adulthood but was much reduced in magnitude. Most personality research suggests that stability in personality is not reached until age 30 (Costa & McCrae, 1980), and it is possible that changes in maturity of defenses follow the same pattern. We could find no longitudinal studies of defenses that traced subjects over age 65.

Our own data can provide some information based on cross-sectional studies. Participants in the Baltimore Longitudinal Study of Aging (BLSA; Shock et al., 1984) and their spouses have been enrolled in a program of research on personality, stress, and coping since 1979. In 1980, 182 of them completed the Defense Mechanisms Inventory (DMI; Ihilevich & Gleser, 1986). Between 1981 and 1988, 477 of them took a computer-administered version of the MMPI, from which Haan's (1965) Defense Scales were calculated. In 1987, 293 completed the Defense Style Questionnaire (DSQ; Bond et al., 1983). The men in these samples ranged in age from 23 to 92; the women ranged from 20 to 85.

A first question concerns the validity of these instruments as measures of defense in the present sample. Although better evidence would come from a comparison with observer ratings, intercorrelation of the three sets of self-reported defense mechanisms provides one basis for evaluating construct validity. Some predictable correlations are found: DMI Turning Against Self is related to DSQ Self-Sacrificing defenses ($r = .26$, $N = 88$, $p < .05$); DMI Principalization is related to DSQ Adaptive defenses ($r = .25$); and DMI Reversal is related to MMPI Denial ($r = .49$, $N = 77$, $p < .001$). There are also some clear failures: DMI Projection is unrelated to MMPI Projection ($r = .10$, $n.s.$), and DMI Turning Against Object is unrelated to MMPI Displacement ($r = .09$, $n.s.$). The strongest and most numerous correlations are with the MMPI Denial and Doubt scales, which show an opposite pattern of correlates—not surprisingly, given the correlation between these two scales of $-.59$. Individuals who score high on MMPI Denial and low on MMPI Doubt also score high on Principalization,

Reversal, and Adaptive defenses, and score low on Turning Against Object, Projection, and Maladaptive Action Pattern defenses. These individuals present themselves as using relatively more mature, socialized, and desirable defenses. It is impossible to tell from these data whether this self-presentation is based on denial, as the MMPI scale suggests, or is an accurate report of adaptive defenses, as the DSQ scale suggests.

The first column of Table 14.1 gives the correlations of age (at the time of testing) with the five DMI defenses, the seven MMPI scales and the 4 factors from the DSQ. Age is positively correlated with DMI Principalization and Reversal, MMPI Repression, Denial, and Intellectualizing, and DSQ Self-Sacrificing defenses; it is negatively correlated with DMI Turning Against Object and Projection, and DSQ Maladaptive Action Pattern defenses. Note that the four significant correlations with DMI scales are highly redundant, because these four scales are strongly intercorrelated. Age is unrelated to Turning Against Self, Regression, Displacement, Projection, Doubt, Image-Distorting defenses (Superiority), and Adaptive defenses. (The same general pattern is seen when analyses are done separately for men and women.) Most of the correlations are relatively small in magnitude, especially given the wide age range involved; however, the stronger of the correlations appear to present a consistent picture of older individuals as being more forgiving and willing to meet adversity cheerfully, and less prone to take offense or to vent frustrations on others. When the individual items of the DSQ were correlated with age, the only notable correlate ($r = .40$) was the item: "We should never get angry at people we don't like."

As we will see, these data are consistent with earlier studies of coping mechanisms that showed lower use of hostile reactions among middle-aged and older men and women (McCrae, 1982). However, it must be recalled that both that study and the present one are cross-sectional, and it is plausible to argue that these effects represent generational differences. Younger cohorts have grown up in what is in many respects an increasingly violent world, and they may have a greater acceptance of aggression as an effective and healthy way to respond to frustration and conflict. Longitudinal studies are clearly needed here.

In the case of the DMI, which shows the strongest pattern of correlations with age, another explanation is possible. The DMI presents a series of hypothetical situations and asks the respondent how he or she would react. Many of the situations are most relevant to young people (e.g., concern dating or starting a first job), and it may be difficult for older subjects to identify with the protagonist. In these cases, older subject may endorse an abstract, socially desirable response that does not accurately describe their own typical response to frustration. These data may tell us more about how older people believe they should cope than how they actually do. Interestingly the DSQ item most strongly related to age ("We should never get angry at people we don't like") also concerns an attitude rather than a description of behavior.

It is possible that age differences in coping may not be linear. In particular,

TABLE 14.1
Correlations of Age and Personality with Defense Mechanism Scales

Variable	Age	Self-Reported NEO–PI Factors				
		N	E	O	A	C
Defense Mechanisms Inventory (DMI)						
Turning Against Object	-37***	24**	-13	23**	-14	-20*[b]
Projection	-27***	12	-22*	07	-04	-11
Principalization	21**	-23**	26**	10	-01	27**[b]
Turning Against Self	08	05	-11	-16	23**	01
Reversal	40***	-23**	21*	-24**	03	11
Haan MMPI Scales						
Regression	-01	32***[b]	05	-19**[a]	-10	-21***[a,b]
Repression	21***	05	-06	-11	19**	24***[b]
Denial	12**	-44***	29***[a,b]	-13*	06	29***[b]
Displacement	03	46***[a,b]	-05	-11	-09	02
Intellectualizing	10*	-25***[a]	-13*[a,b]	15*	-30***	10
Projection	07	24***	-10	-12	-12*	06
Doubt	-03	57***[a,b]	-36***	-01	02	-15*
Defense Style Questionnaire (DSQ)						
Maladaptive Action Pattern	-12*	47***[a]	-15*[b]	-10	-09	-29***[b]
Image-Distorting (Superiority)	-05	03	11	-05	-42***[a,b]	-09
Self-Sacrificing	27***	-03	06	-01	24***[a,b]	06
Adaptive	11	-31***[a]	19**	33***[a,b]	08	08

Note: For age, N = 182 for DMI, 477 for MMPI, 292 for DSQ; for NEO–PI, N = 127 for DMI, 274 for MMPI, 261 for DSQ. Decimal points are omitted. NEO–PI = NEO Personality Inventory.

[a]Replicated (p < .05, one-tailed) in NEO–PI factors from spouse ratings, N = 60 for MMPI, 100 for DSQ, spouse ratings not available for DMI.

[b]Replicated (p < .05, one-tailed) in NEO–PI factors from mean peer ratings, N = 88 for DMI, 112 for MMPI, 157 for DSQ.

*p < .05
**p < .01
***p < .001

there may be an increase in maturity of defenses among young adults and a regression to less mature defenses among older adults. To examine these possibilities, curvilinear regressions were conducted, predicting each of the defense scales from age and age squared. Only two of the 16 regressions showed significant curvilinearity: Turning Against Others increased until about age 40, and decreased thereafter; Self-Sacrificing defenses decreased to about age 48 and increased after that. These effects, however, were small, accounting for less than 3% of the variance in defense scale scores. It is not clear that either of these patterns is consistent with the hypothesis of growth and subsequent regression.

In general, although there are some differences in which older and younger individuals respond to these scales, it would be hard to characterize defensive patterns of older people as either better or worse, more or less mature or adaptive. On the DSQ scales, older individuals are significantly less likely to use Maladaptive Action Pattern defenses, but the association is quite small in magnitude. At a minimum, however, it appears reasonable to conclude that defenses do not become maladaptive with age.

Defense and Personality

Within the psychoanalytic tradition, it has been assumed that defenses are a more or less stable part of the individual's personality or character—indeed, Haan (1977) defined personality in terms of coping and defense as "the fundamental and persistent organizational strategies that people use to interregulate various aspects of themselves" (p. 1). Most maturational theories assume some sort of continuity, and theories of adult development that revolve around styles of defense (e.g., Vaillant, 1977) presuppose some stability of defense. These views lead to two straightforward questions: Are defensive styles themselves stable, and are they systematically related to stable personality traits?

Longitudinal data are required to answer the first question, but few longitudinal studies have been reported. Haan's studies of men and women at two ages (30 and 40 in one sample, 37 and 47 in another) give information on the ten-year stability of rated defense styles. Significant positive correlations were found in at least one of the four subsamples for 18 of the 20 coping and defense styles; the median stability coefficient for the 10 defenses was $r = .21$. This very modest evidence of stability in defenses must be viewed both in terms of the validity of the Haan constructs and the fact that independent raters were employed at the two time periods. Interrater unreliability doubtless attenuated the correlations considerably.

A somewhat different approach was used by Vaillant, Bond, and Vaillant (1986). Clinical ratings of defenses based on life-history data gathered at age 47 were correlated with self-reports on the DSQ obtained six to ten years later. Global ratings of maturity of defense from these two assessments showed a correlation of .35 ($p < .001$). These data provide somewhat stronger evidence for the stability of defenses, as well as for the clinical validity of the DSQ. Like traits, defenses show evidence of stability in adulthood.

Any examination of the relations between defenses and personality traits immediately encountered difficulties in assessment. Personality is usually measured by self-report instruments, but believers in defenses typically distrust self-reports. The interpretation of correlations is, therefore, problematic. For example, Haan (1965) correlated her MMPI defense scales with MMPI clinical scales and found that Denial was negatively associated with scales measuring psychopathology. Both Haan (1977) and Morrissey (1977) interpreted this as evidence that subjects high in Denial distort their MMPI responses to present socially desirable portraits of themselves. Alternative explanations include the possibilities that denial is a more effective and mature mechanism than previously expected, or that the Haan scale is a poor measure of denial, or—perhaps most likely—that the Haan scale does not differentiate between genuine denial of undesirable traits and truthful avowal of desirable traits.

It is impossible to resolve these ambiguities within the realm of self-reports, but external observers can provide another, less biased perspective (McCrae & Costa, 1983). We, therefore, include peer (McCrae & Costa, 1987) and spouse (Costa & McCrae, 1988) ratings from subsamples as well as self-reports in our examination of these defenses.

The instrument used for the measurement of personality is the NEO Personality Inventory (NEO–PI; Costa & McCrae, 1985), which assesses aspects of all five of the major dimensions of normal personality identified in a number of different lines of research (Amelang & Borkenau, 1982; Digman & Inouye, 1986; Goldberg, 1981). Factor scores are used to provide optimal measure of each of the five factors of Neuroticism, Extraversion, Openness to Experience, Agreeableness, and Conscientiousness (McCrae & Costa, 1989). The NEO–PI has parallel forms for self-reports and ratings, and factors can be scored from either form.

Table 14.1 gives correlations between self-reported NEO–PI factors and the DMI, MMPI, and DSQ scales. Footnotes to the table indicate replications of the findings using either spouse or mean peer ratings of personality. Despite the smaller sample sizes for ratings, half of the significant correlations in Table 14.1 are replicated when observer ratings replace self-reports in the measurement of personality. For example, people who score high on MMPI denial describe themselves as low in Neuroticism and high in Extraversion and Conscientiousness, and at least two of these three claims are supported by external observers (correlations with Neuroticism were negative but nonsignificant in both spouse and peer raters). Although it might be argued that observers are taken in by the individual's defenses, that view is implausible. Surely spouses and friends of many years will have as good or better a basis for assessing true personality as clinical raters reviewing a few hours of life-history interview will have of assessing defenses. The most likely explanation is that these defense scales are in fact related to personality.

Perhaps the most interesting findings presented in Table 14.1 have to do with the associations of personality traits with Bond et al.'s four defense styles. The dimension of Agreeableness is related to two of the DSQ styles: Agreeable individuals use Self-Sacrificing defenses, whereas antagonistic individuals use Image-Distorting defenses (Superiority). In dealing with conflict, agreeable people defer to others, whereas disagreeable people assert their superiority.

Adaptive defense mechanisms were associated with the personality traits of low Neuroticism and high Extraversion and Openness; Maladaptive action defenses were associated with Neuroticism and low Extraversion and Conscientiousness. Bond's scales are also known to be related to Vaillant's assessments of defensive maturity (Vaillant et al., 1986), which in turn are related to success in life (Vaillant, 1977). It would seem pausible to speculate that low Neuroticism and high Extraversion, Openness, and Conscientiousness may lead to a better adjustment in life, and it is possible that characteristic ways of coping or defending provide part of the mechanism that explains the link between personality and life success.

Summary: Defenses and Aging

The concept of defense has played a much larger role in the history of psychology than the parallel concept of coping, but progress in assessing defenses has been slow. When scales from three of the better validated instruments are correlated with age across the range from 20 to 92, most show little or no relation to age. There is some evidence that older people are more prone to report the use of defenses that suggest strong socialization, but it is not yet clear whether this is a generational or a maturational effect. Longitudinal studies provide some support for the stability of defense within the adult years, and there is cross-observer evidence that defenses are related to personality traits. Because personality traits are known to be highly stable well into old age, it seems likely that defensive styles may also persist throughout adulthood.

Vaillant's (1977) view of adult development emphasizes the increasing maturation of defenses, and he has presented evidence of this process between adolescence and middle age. Although there is as yet no comparable longitudinal data for the later years of adulthood, cross-sectional data offer little basis for believing that adult development continues in this regard. For adults over age 30, it appears that maturity of defenses reflects psychological adjustment rather than continuing adult development.

AGE DIFFERENCES IN THE USE
OF COPING MECHANISMS

Although the concept of defense dates back at least to Freud, and stress has been intensively studied since the 1950s, coping has emerged as a major focus of attention only in the past decade (Costa & McCrae, 1989). The new paradigm, based largely on the work of Lazarus (1966; Lazarus, Averill, & Opton, 1974;

Lazarus & Folkman, 1984) is characterized by a number of distinctive features. Coping is seen as an effort to deal with a perceived threat, loss, or challenge; it may serve to resolve the problem or to reduce distress (or both); it is a dynamic process in which a variety of different strategies may be adopted simultaneously or successively. Coping responses are seen as conscious (if not necessarily fully rational) behaviors that can be studied directly through self-reports. Finally coping is considered to be the specific response of a given individual to a particular stressor rather than an enduring and cross-situationally invariant style. Consequently most recent research has requested that subjects describe their responses to a specified event or circumstance. Whether individuals have characteristic coping styles, perhaps related to enduring personality dispositions, remains an empirical question.

Although many researchers have adopted this general paradigm, and many have used the Ways of Coping checklist (Folkman & Lazarus, 1980) or some modification of it as their coping instrument, there has been virtually no consensus on the specific number or nature of coping mechanisms. Different combinations of items are used to measure anywhere from 2 to 28 different coping mechanisms, and, although some mechanisms (like direct action and seeking social support) are common to most studies, there is no clear agreement on labels, making comparisons difficult.

Several recent studies using this general paradigm have addressed the question of age differences in coping. In one of the first of these, McCrae (1982) examined age differences in the use of coping mechanisms in a study of adults aged 21 to 91. A preliminary examination of a life-events checklist had shown that there were clear age differences not only in the specific events experienced (birth of child for the younger adults; death of spouse for the older) but also in the general categories of threat, loss, and challenge. Young adults reported more family- and job-related challenges; older adults reported more threatening health problems for themselves or their spouses. These differences are illustrated in FIG. 14.1, which gives the mean number of life events from a standard list classified as either challenges, threats, or losses (see McCrae, 1982, for specifics).

Controlling for type of stressor was clearly indicated, and two methods were used in two separate subsamples. In the first, subjects were asked to describe their coping efforts in response to a significant life event chosen and categorized by the investigator as a threat, loss, or challenge; type of stressor was controlled statistically in this study. In the second, each individual was asked to select three separate events—one a threat, one a loss, and one a challenge—and then complete a shortened coping questionnaire about each.

After controlling for type of stressor, only two of 28 finely differentiated coping mechanisms showed replicated age differences: Younger adults (under age 50) more frequently reported hostile reaction and the use of escapist fantasy than did middle-aged or older adults. There were no significant age differences in either study for the use of rational action, seeking help, perseverence, isolation of affect, expression of feelings, distraction, intellectual denial, self-blame, taking

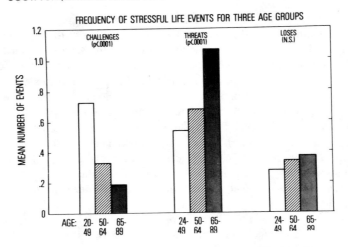

FIG. 14.1. Distribution of challenges, threats, and losses in three age groups.

one step at a time, social comparison, substitution, drawing strength from adversity, avoidance, withdrawal, active forgetting, or passivity. Lazarus and DeLongis (1983) reported a similar absence of age differences in their community-based study.

Studies that have found age differences have generally not been consistent. In a study of coping with interpersonal conflicts, Quayhagen and Quayhagen (1982) found that older adults used less help seeking and problem solving, but more affectivity (emotional ventilation). The increased use of emotional ventilation is at variance with the decreased use of hostile reactions reported by McCrae (1982). Quayhagen and Quayhagen found no differences in existential growth, fantasy, or minimization of threat. Folkman, Lazarus, Pimley, and Novacek (1987) found that, across a range of stressful situations, older respondents used less confrontive coping (e.g., "stood my ground and fought") and were less likely to seek social support; they were more likely to use distancing and positive reappraisal. Irion and Blanchard-Fields (1987), using a smaller sample but similar coping scales, also found that older individuals used less confrontive coping in dealing with threat (but not challenge). They did not replicate any of the other findings of Folkman et al. (1987). Felton and Revenson (1987) examined age differences in coping with chronic illness in middle-aged and older adults; by restricting the stress to illness, they reduced the confounding of age with type of stress. They reported lower use of emotional expression, self-blame, and information-seeking in their older subjects but no age differences in the use of cognitive restructuring, threat minimization, or wish-fulfilling fantasy (recall that McCrae found decreased use of escapist fantasy in older adults).

Although comparison between studies is made difficult by the different concepts and labels used for different coping mechanisms, it appears clear that there is no consistent pattern of age differences across these studies. Where they occur, age differences appear to be small in magnitude and specific to the particular sample and stress examined. Pending the results of longitudinal studies, the findings on age and coping begin to resemble those for age and personality traits, where stability in adulthood, rather than growth or decline, is the rule (Costa & McCrae, 1988).

Coping and Personality

No one claims that personality should be seen as a collection of ways of coping, and Folkman and Lazarus (1980) argued that patterns of coping do not show the cross-situational consistency that might be expected of personality traits. This does not mean, however, that personality traits may not be related to preferred ways of coping, and in fact several studies show systematic relations. When we examined correlations between Neuroticism, Extraversion, and Openness and use of 27 discrete coping mechanisms, we found a meaningful pattern of replicated results. Extraversion was associated with increased use of rational action, positive thinking, substitution, and restraint; Openness was positively associated with the use of humor and negatively associated with the use of faith; Neuroticism was associated with a wide range of maladaptive coping mechanisms, including hostile reaction, escapist fantasy, self-blame, sedation, withdrawal, wishful thinking, passivity, and indecisiveness (McCrae & Costa, 1986). Most of these correlations with Neuroticism were replicated in a study of victims of the Three Mile Island nuclear accident (Costa & McCrae, 1989); in addition, there was a suggestion that Neuroticism interfered with the use of adaptive coping mechanisms (such as self-adaptation and faith) as well as promoting the use of ineffective coping mechanisms in that sample.

Vickers, Kolar, and Hervig (1989) used a different scoring for the Ways of Coping to assess eight coping mechanisms: problem solving, caution, negotiation, seeking support, self-blame, positive reappraisal, escape, and minimization. Correlations with the domain scales of the NEO–PI replicated some previous findings—for example, Neuroticism was related to self-blame and escape, and Extraversion was related to problem solving and positive reappraisal—and suggested some new ones. Most striking were correlations with Conscientiousness, which was strongly related to problem solving ($r = .44$, $p < .001$), as well as to seeking support and positive reappraisal. These associations suggest that individuals high in Conscientiousness use a variety of strategies for actively dealing with their problems. Clearly the role of personality in coping is a topic that requires and deserves continued research.

THE PROCESS OF ADAPTATION

We are still learning about the specific ways of coping individuals use to deal with stress, but we have long known that there must be some general processes of adaptation that allow individuals to return to normal functioning after major changes have disrupted their lives: The healing effects of time are proverbial. Maintaining or reestablishing equilibrium seems to be a basic characteristic of organisms at many levels, and adaptation has been extensively studied in perceptual processes (Helson, 1964) as well as in more global areas like psychological well-being (Brickman & Campbell, 1971). The simple passage of time and repeated exposure to the situation gradually brings about an adjustment that may or may not be associated with specific coping or defense mechanisms.

A 30-year-old adult who awoke one morning to find the face of an 80-year-old in the mirror would probably be severely traumatized. An 80-year-old sees the same face with equanimity: Fifty years of slow change have allowed a gradual and generally painless adaptation. Similar processes change expectations with regard to health, vigor, and life left to live; along with these lowered expectations may come a keener appreciation for the small pleasures in life or a broader investment in the welfare of humanity as a whole. Many of the negative stereotypes of aging seem to stem from the inability of younger individuals to appreciate the changes that time will make in their values and expectations. Seen through the eyes of the old, the life of the old is not depressing or threatening.

Adaptation also occurs when changes are abrupt, although the adjustment may be more painful and require more active effort. Of all the threats of old age, none is more stressful for most individuals than the loss of a spouse. For a small minority, grief or the disruption of life routines even seems to hasten death (Stroebe & Stroebe, 1987) within the first year or two after bereavement. In the long run, however—and widows especially are likely to survive their spouses by many years—most individuals adapt to the loss of a loved one and to the accompanying chronic losses of income and social and emotion support. In a ten-year follow-up of a national probability sample, widowed men and women showed little or no difference from married individuals on measures of self-rated health, activities of daily living, social network size, extraversion, openness to experience, psychological well-being, or depression (McCrae & Costa, 1988). These findings do not mean that the loved one has been forgotten or that the sense of loss does not remain. However, individuals learn to accept their loss, and widowhood ultimately ceases to have much effect on day-to-day mood and functioning.

We interpreted these findings as evidence of psychological resilience: an ability to adapt to even the most stressful circumstances over time. Further, we saw no evidence that resilience was diminished by age itself, because the findings were clearly demonstrated in widows over age 65 and as old as 85. The view that older people are rigid and unable to adapt to life changes finds no support in this study.

This study, however, examined only the long-term consequences of widowhood, not the process of grieving or of rebuilding a new life. In the long run, individuals will probably return to their own characteristic level of functioning. In the short run, however, many would benefit from help—whether professional or informal—to relieve their distress and deal with the new demands of daily life. It is here that research on coping and defense should find an important application. Studies to date indicate that what works for younger adults will also work for older adults, and that older men and women are not rigid in their coping nor destined to use primitive and ineffective methods of defense. These findings should bring encouragement to researchers seeking ways to help older people cope.

ACKNOWLEDGMENTS

Thanks are due to Michael Bond for providing the Defense Style Questionnaire.

REFERENCES

Aldwin, C. M., & Revenson, T. A. (1987). Does coping help? A reexamination of the relation between coping and mental health. *Journal of Personality and Social Psychology, 53,* 337–348.

Amelang, M., & Borkenau, P. (1982). Über die faktorielle Struktur und externe Validität einiger Fragebogen-Skalen zur Erfassung von Dimensionen der Extraversion und emotionalen Labilität [On the factor structure and external validity of some questionnaire scales measuring dimensions of extraversion and neuroticism]. *Zeitschrift für Differentielle und Diagnostische Psychologie, 3,* 119–146.

Bellak, H. G. (1973). *Ego functions in schizophrenics, neurotics, and normals.* New York: Wiley.

Bond, M., Gardner, S. T., Christian, J., & Sigal, J. J. (1983). Empirical study of self-rated defense styles. *Archives of General Psychiatry, 40,* 333–338.

Brickman, P., & Campbell, D. T. (1971). Hedonic relativism and planning the good society. In M. H. Appley (Ed.), *Adaptation level theory: A symposium* (pp. 287–302). New York: Academic Press.

Costa, P. T., Jr., & McCrae, R. R. (1980). Still stable after all these years: Personality as a key to some issues in adulthood and old age. In P. B. Baltes & O. G. Brim, Jr. (Eds.), *Life span development and behavior* (Vol. 3, pp. 65–102). New York: Academic Press.

Costa, P. T., Jr., & McCrae, R. R. (1984). Personality as a lifelong determinant of well-being. In C. Malatesta & C. Izard (Eds.), *Affective processes in adult development and aging* (pp. 141–157). Beverly Hills, CA: Sage.

Costa, P. T., Jr., & McCrae, R. R. (1985). *The NEO Personality Inventory manual.* Odessa, FL: Psychological Assessment Resources.

Costa, P. T., Jr., & McCrae, R. R. (1988). Personality in adulthood: A six-year longitudinal study of self-reports and spouse ratings on the NEO Personality Inventory. *Journal of Personality and Social Psychology, 54,* 417–434.

Costa, P. T., Jr., & McCrae, R. R. (1989). Personality, stress, and coping: Some lessons from a decade of research. In K. S. Markides & C. L. Cooper (Eds.), *Aging, stress, social support and health* (pp. 267–283). New York: Wiley.

Costa, P. T., Jr., McCrae, R. R., & Dembroski, T. M. (1989). Agreeableness vs. antagonism: Explication of a potential risk factor for CHD. In A. Siegman & T. M. Dembroski (Eds.), *In search of coronary-prone behavior: Beyond Type A* (pp. 41–63). Hillsdale, NJ: Lawrence Erlbaum Associates.

Digman, J. M., & Inouye, J. (1986). Further specification of the five robust factors of personality. *Journal of Personality and Social Psychology, 50,* 116–123.

Felton, B. J., & Revenson, T. A. (1987). Age differences in coping with chronic illness. *Psychology and Aging, 2,* 164–170.

Folkman, S. & Lazarus, R. S. (1980). An analysis of coping in a middle-aged community sample. *Journal of Health and Social Behavior, 21,* 219–239.

Folkman, S., Lazarus, R. S., Pimley, S., & Novacek, J. (1987). Age differences in stress and coping processes. *Psychology and Aging, 2,* 171–184.

Freud, A. (1936). *The ego and the mechanisms of defense.* New York: International Universities Press.

Freud, S. (1955). The neuro-psychoses of defense. In J. Strachey (Ed. and Trans.), *The standard edition of the complete psychological works of Sigmund Freud* (Vol. 3, pp. 45–61). London: Hogarth. (Original work published 1894)

Gleser, G., & Ihilevich, D. (1969). An objective instrument for measuring defense mechanisms. *Journal of Consulting and Clinical Psychology, 33,* 51–60.

Goldberg, L. R. (1981). Language and individual differences: The search for universals in personality lexicons. In L. Wheeler (Ed.), *Review of personality and social psychology* (Vol. 2, pp. 141–165). Beverly Hills, CA: Sage.

Haan, N. (1965). Coping and defense mechanisms related to personality inventories. *Journal of Consulting Psychology, 29,* 373–378.

Haan, N. (1977). *Coping and defending.* New York: Academic Press.

Helson, H. (1964). *Adaptation-level theory.* New York: Harper & Row.

Horney, K. (1945). *Our inner conflicts.* New York: Norton.

Horowitz, M. J. (1988). *Introduction to psychodynamics: A new synthesis.* New York: Basic.

Ihilevich, D., & Gleser, G. C. (1986). *Defense mechanisms: Their classification, correlates, and measurement with the Defense Mechanism Inventory.* Owosso, MI: DMI Associates.

Irion, J. C., & Blanchard-Fields, F. (1987). A cross-sectional comparison of adaptive coping in adulthood. *Journal of Gerontology, 42,* 502–504.

Kahana, B. (1978). The use of projective techniques in personality assessment of the aged. In I. C. Siegler, M. Storandt, & M. F. Elias (Eds.), *The clinical psychology of aging* (pp. 145–180). New York: Plenum.

Kastenbaum, R., & Costa, P. T., Jr. (1977). Psychological perspectives on death. In M. R. Rosenzweig & L. W. Porter (Eds.), *Annual Review of Psychology, 28,* 225–249.

Klein, G. S. (1970). *Perception, motives, and personality.* New York: Knopf.

Kline, P. (1981). *Fact and fantasy in Freudian theory* (2nd. ed.). London: Methuen.

Kroeber, T. C. (1963). The coping functions of the ego mechanisms. In R. W. White (Ed.), *The study of lives* (pp. 178–198). New York: Atherton.

Lazarus, R. S. (1966). *Psychological stress and the coping process.* New York: McGraw-Hill.

Lazarus, R. S., Averill, J. R., & Opton, E. M., Jr. (1974). The psychology of coping: Issues of research and assessment. In G. V. Coelho, D. A. Hamburg, & J. F. Adams (Eds.), *Coping and adaption* (pp. 249–315). New York: Basic.

Lazarus, R. S., & DeLongis, A. (1983). Psychological stress and coping in aging. *American Psychologist, 38,* 245–254.

Lazarus, R. S., & Folkman, S. (1984). *Stress, appraisal, and coping.* New York: Springer.

McCrae, R. R. (1982). Age differences in the use of coping mechanisms. *Journal of Gerontology, 37,* 454–460.

McCrae, R. R., & Costa, P. T., Jr. (1983). Social desirability scales: More substance than style. *Journal of Consulting and Clinical Psychology, 51,* 882–888.

McCrae, R. R., & Costa, P. T., Jr. (1986). Personality, coping, and coping effectiveness in an adult sample. *Journal of Personality, 54,* 385–405.

McCrae, R. R., & Costa, P. T., Jr. (1987). Validation of the five-factor model of personality across instruments and observers. *Journal of Personality and Social Psychology, 52,* 81–90.

McCrae, R. R., & Costa, P. T., Jr. (1988). Psychological resilience among widowed men and women: A 10-year followup of a national survey. *Journal of Social Issues, 44,* 129–142.

McCrae, R. R., & Costa, P. T., Jr. (1989). Rotation to maximize the construct validity of factors in the NEO Personality Inventory. *Multivariate Behavioral Research, 24,* 107–124.

Morrissey, R. F. (1977). The Haan model of ego functioning: An assessment of empirical research. In N. Haan, *Coping and defending* (pp. 250–279). New York: Academic Press.

Quayhagen, M. P., & Quayhagen, M. (1982). Coping with conflict: Measurement of age-related patterns. *Research on Aging, 4,* 364–377.

Shock, N. W., Greulich, R. C., Andres, R., Arenberg, D., Costa, P. T., Jr., Lakatta, E. G., & Tobin, J. D. (1984). *Normal human aging: The Baltimore Longitudinal Study of Aging* (NIH Publication No. 84–2450). Bethesda, MD: National Institutes of Health.

Stroebe, W., & Stroebe, M. S. (1987). *Bereavement and health.* New York: Cambridge University Press.

Vaillant, G. E. (1976). Natural history of male psychological health: V. The relation of choice of ego mechanisms of defense to adult adjustment. *Archives of General Psychiatry, 33,* 535–545.

Vaillant, G. E. (1977). *Adaptation to life.* Boston: Little Brown.

Vaillant, G. E., Bond, M., & Vaillant, C. O. (1986). An empirically validated hierarchy of defense mechanisms. *Archives of General Psychiatry, 43,* 786–794.

Vaillant, G. E., & Drake, R. E. (1985). Maturity of ego defenses in relation to *DSM–III* Axis II personality disorder. *Archives of General Psychiatry, 42,* 597–601.

Vickers, R. R., Jr., Kolar, D. W., & Hervig, L. K. (1989). *Personality correlates of coping with military basic training* (Report No. 89–3). San Diego, CA: Naval Health Research Center.

VII

EPILOGUE

Life-Course Perspectives on the Study of Adversity, Stress, and Coping: Discussion of Papers From the West Virginia Conference

Bertram J. Cohler
The University of Chicago

If there is one summary comment that can be made, it is that psychological processes cannot be studied except in the context of both variations in social surround and change over time. Evidence presented here shows quite clearly that means used for coping with role strains and both expected or normative, and unexpected, generally adverse circumstances vary with changes in social context including the course of life itself. Indeed viewed from the perspective of life-course social science, failure to consider these issues of context and timing compromises the significance of findings.

THE SOCIAL ORGANIZATION OF LIVES

These chapters represent turning points in our study of lives over time. The disciplines reflected in the study of human development have moved beyond consideration of childhood as a discrete point in time to a consideration of childhood within the context of the course of life. This view is implicit in the definition provided by Baltes, Reese, and Lipsitt (1980), in their definition of life-span developmental psychology as "concerned with the description, explanation, and modification (optimization) of developmental processes in the human life-course from birth to death" (P. 66). The concept of life course, as contrasted with the more traditional concept of life span, emphasizes the significance of such issues as cohort and social timing as dimensions of critical importance for the study of lives, including consideration of stress and adversity, and coping and resilience. This is consistent with Hagestad's and Neugarten's (1985) following observation:

A life span orientation in psychology and a life course perspective differ in their key intellectual concerns. Whereas the former focuses a good deal of attention on intrapsychic phenomena, the later emphasizes turning points when the "social persona" undergoes change. In particular, a life course approach concentrates on age-related transitions that are socially created, socially recognized, and socially shared. (p. 35)

Findings reported in this volume may be best studied in the context of life-course social science. In order to realize this goal, it is first necessary to consider the concepts underlying these presentations and then to integrate these findings into a larger context.

Cohort and Life Course

The formulation of the concept of cohort, powerfully elaborated at the second Life-Span Conference (Nesselroade & Reese, 1973), marked a fundamental shift in the study of lives over time. Although introduced principally in terms of significance of the cross-sequential research design for method for study of change over time, once the power of this construct is recognized, it becomes impossible to study lives from an individual differences perspective. It is as a consequence of a particular social context that persons define self and others, understand so called "inner" or "motivational" states, and understand personal changes over time. Little else is constant except the interplay of social factors and particular life experiences.

Cohort and Life-Course Study

The power of the concept of cohort is that it provides a means for studying the impact of sociohistorical forces upon individual lives and also provides the means for specifying the extent of change over time (Cain, 1967; Riley, 1973; Riley & Fener, 1968; Ryder, 1965). This has been most clearly demonstrated in the Seattle project (Schaie, 1984; Schaie, Labouvie, & Buech, 1973), and in Glen Elder's pioneering study point in the course of life at the time of the Great Depression upon future adjustment (Elder, 1974, 1979, 1986; Elder & Rockwell, 1978, 1979). Life course differs from life span precisely in terms of this emphasis upon personal attributes as derived from shared understanding of self and others, and of the passage of time itself.

The Social Organization of Development

There is a second concept of equal significance, first introduced by Gergen (1977) in his critically important paper celebrating Klaus Riegel's career: Chance is an important factor determining change in lives over time and requires much more systematic study. Much of continuity experienced over the course of life may be a result of a continuing effort at management of meanings in order to realize narrative coherence. For example, such early life adversity as the death or illness of parents, or of other disruptions in family life, becomes a focus of personal struggle leading to enhanced resilience. The physician, inspired in career choice by the effort to find a cure for an illness afflicting a family member, parents particularly concerned with provision of emotional security for offspring as a reaction to disruptions that they had encountered as children, or unusually success-ful persons deliberately seeking to overcome childhood poverty, all provide examples of this effort at managing meanings in order to resolve past adversity and realize enhanced experience of continuity through subsequent life experiences.

This sense-making activity is largely shaped by normative context, such as changes expectable at particular points in the course of life. Parent loss is an expectable life change for a middle-aged adult, but an eruptive, unexpected change for a seven-year-old. Clinical study suggests that young children are unable to understand the finality of death or to engage in mourning (Garber, 1981; Wolfenstein, 1979). Further, the child lacks a convoy of consociates experiencing this life change, able both to provide support, and also able to provide anticipatory socialization or preparation in dealing with this loss from continuing experiences of others suffering similar adversity. The "off-time" nature of the loss may be a major factor in the finding, reported both in clinical–observational and systematic counted-data studies that the death of a parent has a major and continuing adverse impact upon adjustment later in life (Altschul & Pollock, 1988).

The socially structured or organized manner in which chance, or aleatoric accounts, is experienced by persons, together with life circumstances of particular persons, forms the basis of a life story or developmental narrative. For example, in our society, events are believed to relate to each other in a causal manner; developmental psychology was founded on the study of the extent to which earlier events might "determine" later events. Although the impact is often believed to be indirect, or different as different points in the course of life (the concept of the so-called "sleeper effect") (Clarke & Clarke, 1981; Kagan & Moss, 1963; Livson & Peskin, 1980; Peskin & Livson, 1981), it is assumed that events occurring earlier in the course of life must in some manner influence those occurring later. Learning theory and psychoanalysis are among accounts of devel-opment most strongly reflecting this socially constructed understanding of the relationship between past, present, and future (Geertz, 1973; Ricoeur, 1984). At least to some extent, findings regarding continuity and change over time reflect this understanding of past and present that is shared alike by respondent and investigator.

Neugarten (1969) has noted that change rather than continuity may be the most important factor in the study of development, while Gergen suggested that the most important factor to study is the manner in which we construct narratives of development and changes over time. These narratives provide a presently understandable account of the course of life to date. This developmental narrative optimally includes a followable account that makes sense of adversity and change, both positive such as a job promotion, and adverse such as unexpected personal losses or family discord. Failure to maintain an account that is coherent, or coherence attained at the cost of possible changes in the life story, leads to personal distress, ultimately experienced as a sense of impending fragmentation, as portrayed by Kohut and his associates studying psychopathology of the self (Kohut, 1971, 1974, 1975, 1977, 1978, 1984; Kohut & Wolf 1978; Strozier, 1975).

Gergen's pioneering discussion of the aleatoric perspective has received additional support as a result of the introduction into social science study of the concept of chaos theory, pioneered in the physical sciences. We make order, construct patterns, and see continuity over time in phenomena that intrinsically may not enjoy such order. As Gleick (1987) argued in his recent review of chaos theory, physical scientists long believed that if one could do an experiment or write down an equation, order could be created out of seeming disorder. Only more recently has it been recognized that this is a fiction reflecting our need to order nature, portrayed by Levi-Strauss (1966) in his essays on *The Savage Mind*, rather than nature itself.

Disorder is inherent in both in nature and in the study of lives over time. What is important to observe is the manner in which we organize this disorder into a coherent framework called developmental social science. Viewed from another perspective, discontinuity over time, has critical implications for social science study. Indeed one of the reasons why psychoanalysis has been such an advocate of continuity theory may be that psychopathology has a unique capacity to organize lives over time. Psychopathology reflects a particularly rigidly maintained story of the course of life in which particular factors earlier in time have determined later outcomes. For example, an adult's insistence that present distress is a result of early parental loss through death or desertion, or continuing parental discord, reflects reliance on this shared linear narrative, often based on random or chance events, organized into a coherent life story tenaciously maintained across subsequent life experiences.

Finally it should be noted not only that persons continually reorder understandings of the past in order to render a life marked by accidents of fate and chance into a coherent, linearly ordered story (Gergen, 1977; Cohler, 1982), but that the very nature of the life constructed or the story told changes over time within particular cohorts and as a function of place in the course of life (it is clearly important to separate the effects, for example, of being middle-aged from being in the generation in the middle in terms of presently existing age-grades).

Life-course perspectives become particularly important in the study of what is viewed as role strain and adversity (Thoits, 1983), and in the use of particular coping techniques significant in managing such adversity (Pearlin 1980, 1983). For example, studies of subjectively and objectively evaluated health show that the respondent's own understanding of present health status may be more relevant than that of health professionals as a correlate of feelings of well-being (Shanas, Townsend, Wedderburn, Friis, Milhoj, & Stehower, 1968). Multiple afflictions may be unusual in a middle-aged adult but quite common along older persons. As one respondent observed, "I may have things wrong with me, but you ought to see my next door neighbor!" Indeed as long as physical mobility is retained, persons are not greatly troubled by other health problems. This point is dramatically underscored in Antonnucci's discussion of soul support and aging (chapter 13 in the present volume).

The *understanding* or narrative fashioned regarding available support systems also varies according to point the course of life. Younger persons appear to find the physical presence of others necessary to function as a source of support, being in the proximity of others who may be of help to them, whereas older persons seem to derive comfort from the memory or reminiscence of such support provided in the past, using memory of support as a means of relieving present distress. [Reliance upon particular coping techniques also varies both with point in the life course and cohort (Costa, Zonderman, & McCrae, chap. 14 in this volume; Felton & Revenson, 1987; McCrae, 1982; McCrae & Costa, 1988; Quayhagen & Quayhagen, 1982), have shown some modest age differences in the means adults use for coping with personal distress; Older adults appear to cope with problems in a more "matter of fact" manner than younger adults, but also rely on more conventional approaches.] Their review of findings by other investigators studying aging and changes in means of dealing with distress supports the view that, although age differences are relatively modest, there does seem to be increased reliance upon personal psychological rather than social resources across the second half of life (Neugarten, 1979; Neugarten & Datan, 1974).

These older adults are members of a cohort characterized by lower levels of education and psychological mindedness than more recent cohorts, as Costa and his colleagues observed; therefore, age and cohort membership interact in leading to these findings. Indeed there may be little generalization that may be made about modes used for coping with adversity without considering age, place in the course of life of persons being studied, and cohort membership. Quayhagen and Quayhagen (1982), Lieberman and Tobin (1983), Lazarus and DeLongis (1983), Hoffine, Folkman, and Lazarus (1989) and Folkman (1984; chap. 2, this volume) all reported on increased reliance upon psychological rather than social coping resources among older as contrasted with younger adults (Greenblatt, Becerra, & Serofetinides, 1982), and shift towards a more intraceptive perspective portrayed by Neugarten (1973, 1979) as "interiority." Further, as both Lieberman and Tobin (1983) and Gutmann (1987) suggested, some means of dealing with life-changes, such as externalization or "projection," that might be regarded as maladaptive at younger ages are highly adaptive among older adults. For example, projection and expression of hostility outward is highly related to surviving relocation from independent living to residential care, and to increased longevity while in residential care.

Social Timetables, Adult Roles, and Stressful Life Events

A final concept significant in life course study of stress and coping concerns the issue of the time table for events (Roth, 1963). Assumption and enactment of particular social roles is understood in a temporal manner, with such assumption characterized as on time, in terms of the expectable course of life in our society, or as "early" or "late" comparing assumption of a particular role by a person related to others. Indeed, chronological age has little relevance for a social understanding of lives over time except as socially organized. Age, just as time, is socially constructed. As Neugarten, Moore, and Lowe (1965) showed, there is consensus regarding not only the very duration of life itself but also regarding the ages at which particular role transitions or life-events may be anticipated.[1] Children learn this time table for the course of life during the preschool years (Farnham-Diggory, 1966) and are well socialized into such expectations by adolescence. It is precisely this social definition of the course of life that transforms study of the life span or life cycle into study of the life course (Hagested & Neugarten, 1985).

Although there may be consensus among persons regarding the expectable course of life in the same manner as in the quite different means used for evaluating prestige and style of life reflected in social status (Warner & Lunt, 1941; Warner, Meeker, & Ells, 1949; Blau & Duncan, 1967/1978), this timetable shifts across cohorts, reflecting sociohistorical change (Kohli & Meyer, 1986; Neugarten, 1979). However, within particular cohorts there is general agreement on the timetable for specific role transitions such as leaving school, marriage, birth of first child, grandparenthood, death of own parents, retirement, widowhood, and so forth. As Roth (1963) noted:

> Each individual uses the timetable norms of the group as a yardstick to measure his own progress. From a comparison of his own rate of progress with the norm, he can determine whether he is behind, on, or ahead of schedule. In order to know what norms to apply as a yardstick, the individual must have a model group with which he identifies—a group with which he believes he closely shares relevant career characteristics and experiences, and from whose members he may obtain information about future expectations in his timetable. (p. 116)

Life changes taking place too early or late in terms of those that may be expected have important implications for the experience of psychological well-

---

[1]Consensus regarding the expectable course of life provides the basis of age stratification in society (Linton, 1942; Riley, 1971, 1976; Elder, 1975; Ragan & Wales, 1980). Age functions to differentially allocate scarce resources and rewards, including prestige, honor, and remuneration based on occupational attainment. This "ageism" must be differentiated from age categorization, understood as consensual understanding of regularized and expectable actions that endure over time and that are characteristic of particular ages within particular cohorts of persons.

being or morale. In general, those life events taking place early off-time have greater negative impact than those taking place late off-time. Adolescent parenthood and unexpected death of a spouse over the early to middle adult years are example of such adverse, early off-time, stressful life events (Russell, 1980; Bankoff, 1983; Antonucci, 1976, 1985, chapter 13 in this volume). Not only are early off-time events unexpected, providing little opportunity for preparation, but in addition there is a lack of consociates (Plath, 1980), role colleagues (Hagestad, 1974), or a social convoy (Antonucci & Akiyama, 1987; Kahn, 1979; Kahn & Antonucci, 1980; Rowe & Kahn, 1987) to serve as a source of assistance and support in dealing with these events (Lowenthal & Robinson, 1976).

Timing and Sequence of Role Transitions

Although much of the discussion of role transitions and morale across the course of life has concerned issues of timing and accessibility to consociates available to assist in reduction of attendant strain and in anticipatory socialization, concern with issues of timing of role entrances (and exits) is intertwined with the issue of the sequence in which these expectable roles are negotiated. As both Hogan (1978, 1980, 1981) and Runyan (1980) showed, there is an expectable order as well as an expectable time for assumption of the adult role portfolio. When entrance into a role such as parenthood occurs prior to entrance into expectable roles, the orderly process of adult role acquisition is disrupted, enhancing the sense of disordered timing (Seltzer, 1976) characteristic of such off-time role transitions as early widowhood and early parenthood. Although, as Furstenberg (1987) showed, there may later be some "catch-up" in terms of expectable adult outcomes, off-time/off-sequence role transitions interfere with such later outcomes as advancement at work (Hogan, 1981) or realization of such family goals as effective socialization of offspring and provision of personal and economic support for family members among single, adolescent-mother headed households.

Timing of role entrances, transitions, exits, and losses, understood both in terms of expectable point in the course of life and in terms of the orderly nature of careers in the larger sense of expectable life plan, were first portrayed by the social philosopher Schutz (Schutz & Luckmann, 1973) and is closely related to concepts of stress, adversity, and resilience. Indeed the concept of stress, applied to unexpected, usually adverse events of the sort first scaled by Holmes and Rahe (1967), is best understood as a problem in the generally early off-time role transitions, exits, and losses noted here.

Stress, Role Strain, and Coping

Although there are some late off-time role transitions such as among women having fertility problems, it is principally those early off-time events that are so unexpected, that are adverse principally because of their unexpected occurrence at a particular point in the expectable course of life. Early retirement due to disability is another example of these adverse stressful events. Such unexpected, adverse events should be differentiated from another so-called stressor, role-related strain and overload. From the perspective first outlined at the West Virginia Life-Span Conference by Pearlin (1975), strain refers to the adverse consequences engendered in realization of expectable adult roles. Strain may result from role conflicts arising from simultaneous demands of two or more equally salient role identities, such as the parent of a school-aged child called to a meeting at the time of a scheduled outing or school activity, or role overload, such as among parents with one or more preschool aged children, or over-scheduled professionals. One consequence of continuing role strain is the experience of hassles, as portrayed by Lazarus, Folkman, and their colleagues, varying over time, and measured through self-report checklists (Lazarus, Folkman, 1984; Folkman, chap. 1 in this volume). Pearlin (1975, 1983) argued that strains may be best studied with regard to specific roles, although findings suggest that domains of strains across multiple adult roles have structural similarity.

Little is known about role strains as contrasted with adverse, unexpected life-changes among children and adolescents. Indeed much of study to date has focused on issues of strain and coping across the adult years when, with expectable full role portfolios of work, marriage, parenthood, and participation within the family of adulthood, men and women are confronted with the task of juggling often incompatible, conflicting role expectations (Cohler & Boxer, 1984). One way of understanding findings reported by Anita Greene and Reed Larson (chap. 10 in this volume), and Bruce Compas and his associates (chap. 6 in this volume) is that many of these findings refer to role strain, in the terms initially employed by Pearlin and his colleagues, rather than stress, in the sense of unexpected, adverse life changes. Indeed Compas referred to the distinction between hassles and strain. Wagner, Compas, and Howell (1988) also suggested that it is possible to study the relationship of role strain or daily hassles in relation to adversity. Compas and his colleagues showed that much of the variance in the relation of stress (strain and adversity) is accounted for by strain rather than major, adverse life changes. Indeed the pathway that they suggest is that adversity leads to enhanced strain which, in turn, leads to formation of psychological symptoms.

Compas noted another problem posed by the study of stress and strain across the years of middle childhood and adolescence: The fact that family stress accounts for 40% of variance in child outcome shows that children serve as "pass-through" agents for their parents. Parental experience of both role strain and adversity is passed across generations, appearing as behavior problems in offspring. These findings argue for a family conception of stress. Both Cohler (1983) and Pruchno, Blow, and Smyer (1984) argued for a conception of the family consistent with Burgess' (1926) original formulation as the "unity of interacting personalities." Adversity affects not just a single family member or even a dyad but rather a complex, intertwined family system. When a parent becomes ill, grandparents, aunts and uncles, and often relatives at even a greater genealogical distance are drawn into the situation, providing alternate caretaking for offspring, social services, and even financial support (Cohler, Gallant, Grunebaum & Kaufman, 1983).

It is also possible that the function of children as pass-through agents varies with age: Offspring expression of adversity and role strain affecting parents may be more evident in younger children than in adolescents. Again Compas' findings suggest that, among adolescents, parental adversity is less likely to be directly reflected in offspring behavioral problems but that this outcome is a function of the meanings that parents attribute to adversity. Reflecting both Thomas' (1928) discussion of the definition of the situation and Blumer's (1962) discussion of meanings embedded in roles, adolescents appear much more able than younger children to understand and respond to parental experience of adversity. Again it is important to understand the foundations of apparent individual differences in adolescent ability to cope with adversity. Some offspring deal with parental adversity through means such as parentification, taking over the parental role, or through distancing oneself from the family, becoming more involved in own projects and activities. Parental role strain and unexpected adversity may also lead to quite different child and adolescent behavioral outcomes. As Compas noted, it is essential that we carry out longitudinal research focused on the experience both of role strain and adversity as it impacts upon boys and girls over time.

Findings reported by Greene and Larson support Compas' call for longitudinal study separately for boys and girls, noting the importance both of considering the ecology or normative context in which particular role strains are likely to appear. For example, in a cross-sectional study, fifth grade is a time of relatively positive sense of well-being, whereas ninth grade appears to be a particular time of distress, especially when teenagers are alone. Adolescent boys find both time alone and time spent with peers less inherently a source of strain than time spent with family. Adolescent girls find both peers and family to be a source of conflict. Ninth-grade girls are particularly likely to report relations with family to be a source of strain. Girls are more likely than boys to become enmeshed in family conflict and to identify with parental discord. This is consistent with observations reported by Komarovsky (1950, 1956, 1962), Chodorow (1974, 1978, 1989), and Cohler and Grunebaum (1981), that women are socialized into interdependence and kin-keeping to a far greater extent than men. Confronted with family discord, boys are able to escape into athletics, computers, and other activities whereas girls are more likely to remain enmeshed in family conflict.

Coping With Role Strain and Adverse Life Changes

Coping, therefore, refers to the means used in dealing with both adversity, including that engendered by off-time role transitions and role strain and overload. There are at least three different conceptions of coping in the contemporary literature and well exemplified by the present volume: the ego-psychological or individual differences approach, first exemplified in Kroeber's (1963) report and later extended by Haan (1977) and by Hauser and his colleagues (Hauser et al., 1984, 1987; chapter 9 in this volume); studying stress and coping in the families of adolescents, a social psychological approach pioneered by Lazarus, Averill, and Opton (1974), Lazarus and Folkman (1984), and by Billings and Moos (1981) and Moos and Billings (1982); and the sociological approach pioneered by Pearlin (1980, 1983) and Pearlin and Schooler (1978) and extended by Pearlin and his associates (Pearlin, Lieberman, Menaghan, & Mullen, 1981).

This contemporary approach to study of coping and mastery is markedly at variance with that emerging from the drive psychology of traditional psychoanalytic formulations, including those of ego-psychology. Rather than focusing on means used by individuals in order to protect against emergence of unacceptable wishes, from the perspective of contemporary social science perspectives, coping responses represent strategies used by persons in an effort to deal with problems posed by life context that permit avoidance of feeling of distress and continued positive self-esteem (Menaghan, 1983). Lazarus and Folkman (1984) defined coping as "constantly changing cognitive and behavioral efforts to manage specific external and/or internal demands that are appraised as taxing or exceeding the resources of the person (p. 141).

Efforts to distinguish between the concepts of defense and coping, as in the ego-psychological tradition represented by Lois Murphy (1960a, 1960b, 1962, 1970, 1974), Kroeber (1963), Haan (1977), and others are as irrelevant as the distinction between intrapsychic conflict and that stemming from person–environment interactions (Lazarus & Folkman, 1984). Study of the process of appraisal and response to specific threatening events is of particular significance for those working within this tradition (Antonovsky, 1979, 1987; Billings & Moos, 1981; Costa & McCrae, 1989; Costa, Zonderman, & McCrae, chap. 14 in this volume; Lazarus, 1966; Lazarus & Folkman, 1984; Mechanic, 1962, 1974, 1977; Menaghan, 1983; Moos & Billings, 1982; Pearlin & Schooler, 1978).

Investigators working within the social psychological tradition of coping research assume a continuing process in which the meaning of transactions with the real world are evaluated in terms of both possible disruptions of present adjustment and also potential for ever increased sense of efficacy or competence (Janis & Mann, 1977; Lazarus & Folkman, 1984; Mechanic, 1974, 1977). These investigators portray a feedback system similar to the TOTE system portrayed by Miller, Galanter, & Pribram (1960), in which continuing, or primary, appraisal of the stream of experience is able to provide first warning of possible disruptions of present adjustment, including both immediate threats characterized as eruptive events, anticipated life-changes, and opportunities for increased realization of personal satisfaction such as are presented by accepting new responsibilities at work. Secondary appraisal provides further evaluation of means for dealing with the threat or reality of disruption of adjustment as well as for taking advantage of challenges or opportunity. Reappraisal of the success of these actions, planned or enacted, leads to further modification in actions designed either to deal with adversity or to take advantage of opportunity.

Lazarus and Folkman (1984) suggest that coping serves two major functions, managing or changing the problem (problem-focused coping) and regulating own response to the problem (emotion-focused coping). Although such emotion-focused techniques as "psyching" oneself to meet a challenge may be useful in some specific contexts, the problem with this approach is that it may also lead to distortion of reality, making solution of the problem even more difficult. In contrast, problem-focused coping requires cognitive reappraisal of the event posing challenge to adjustment and then acting on the basis the problem defined. Focusing on the experience of students taking doctoral examinations, Mechanic (1974) proposed a three-step process of dealing with situational demands, creating the motivational state necessary to meet those demands, and maintenance of the capacity required to deal with the event.

Menaghan (1983) and Lazarus and Folkman (1984) emphasized the significance of appreciating available resources, enduring styles of response to challenging events, and efforts directed at meeting those challenges in understanding the coping process. Csikszentmihalyi (1975) proposed that challenge or "flow" is characterized by the experience of a balance between circumstances and skills and talents. Increased anxiety is experienced when persons feel available skills lacking in order to deal with circumstances, whereas boredom results from skills and talents much greater than required in order to deal with circumstances.

Antonovsky (1979, 1987), Kobasa (1979, 1982) and Kobasa, Maddi, and Kahn (1982), and Lazarus and Folkman (1984), all stressed the significance of health and vitality in meeting these challenges, whereas Bandura (1977, 1982), Block and Block (1980), Gurin and Brim (1984), and Lazarus and Folkman (1984) also emphasized the importance of maintaining sense of self-efficacy or control, as well as having social skills and being able to use available social supports. However, Pearlin and Schooler (1978) and Menaghan (1983) questioned the significance of generalized coping styles, including trait conceptions of coping, noting that, at least in study of response to role strain and overload, there is little consistency of techniques used across roles.

Although generally accepting the concept of coping as a process of appraisal, action, and reappraisal, most clearly discussed in work by Pearlin and his associates and by the Lazarus research group, Billings and Moos (1981) and Moos and Billings (1982) further extended study of coping processes by focusing explicitly upon factors affecting choice of coping method. Distinguishing between cognitive or psychological, and action or behavioral strategies, these investigators have delineated three particular methods or strategies, including active coping or focusing upon personal appraisal of challenging events and most effective response, active behavioral coping, involving particular actions to overcome the challenge, and avoidance coping, the goal of which is to avoid confrontation with challenging events.

Moos and Billings (1982) suggested that this tripartite distinction of method of coping, together with the locus of coping as either problem- or emotion-focused, will provide the most complete possible understanding of response to challenge. The problem with this approach is that it also makes assumptions about coping styles invariant across situations that have not been supported either in the investigators' own research or that of Pearlin and Schooler (1978).

Pearlin and Schooler (1978) provided a first approach to the study of coping from a third, or sociological, approach, focusing on the actions and thoughts that persons engage in when confronted by strains encountered in particular roles. From this perspective, coping responses represent particular actions salient to particular roles. Coping functions to change the situation out of which the strainful experience arose, response controlling the meaning of these experiences of strain, and accompanying feelings of role overload and conflict. The important factor here is the meaning of the definition of particular roles. Implicit in both the ego-psychological or individual difference formulation and the social-psychological formulation is a similar concern with meaning. Consistent with the perspective first explored by Pearlin and Schooler, and stated more clearly by Blumer (1962, 1969/1976) in his discussion of the symbolic interactionist perspective, our concern is with understandings or meanings that persons attach to performing particular roles in a presently defined manner. Although personality and context shape the selection of one from among many coping responses in hierarchy of such responses, the focus in the sociological perspective is the role-determined set of such responses (Thoits, 1983). Pearlin and his colleagues suggested that, although there may be some common factors underlying coping with strains attendant upon particular roles, coping is much more generally role-specific. Particular role strains are differentially saturated with underlying dimensions on which all coping techniques are presumably based.

Folkman and Lazarus have been particularly articulate in their critique of this sociological approach (Folkman, 1984, chap. 1 in this volume; Folkman & Lazarus, 1980; Lazarus & Folkman, 1984). They claim that so-called coping techniques are actually more general than Pearlin and Schooler are willing to acknowledge. Folkman and Lazarus further have suggested that this approach makes it difficult to determine the processes underlying coping techniques. Finally Folkman and Lazarus have believed that personality dimensions are implicitly embedded in the coping techniques reported in Pearlin and Schooler's initial work and, by extension, Pearlin's more recent work as well. As Folkman (chap. 1 in this volume) has stated, coping efforts are made in response to an effort to appraise and respond to stress. The source of the disagreement between social psychological and sociological approaches may lie in the use made of the term stress. This term may be distinguished in terms both of unexpected, adverse life-changes as contrasted with socially defined, expectable role transitions. One approach would be to limit discussions of coping to response to unexpected circumstances, such as in Kai Erikson's (1976) vivid portrayal of community response to disaster, and that so-called coping in response to role strain and overload, as well as that related to expectable transitions in terms of personal response to management of strains emerging from the management of expectable roles, including role transitions.

Normative Perspectives and Developmental Study of Coping and Mastery

Normative transitions, adverse events, and role strains appear to have particular associated coping responses not generalizable across events or roles. Particular coping responses are always a function of complex interactions between person and event in the manner suggested by Stern (1970), Stern, Stein, and Bloom (1956), and French, Rogers, and Cobb (1974). All adversity is not alike, just as particular role strains have particular meaning for persons at particular points in the life course. Issues of resilience and mastery must be phrased in more specific terms than in research to the present, taking into account distinctions between the three major sources of challenge to adjustment, role strain, normative transitions, and adverse eruptive life changes as well as factors entering into appraisal of the meaning of these events (Brim & Ryff, 1980).

With the exception of studies by Fiske (Lowenthal) and her colleagues (Fiske, 1980a, 1980b; Lowenthal & Chiriboga, 1973; Lowenthal, Thurnher, & Chiriboga, 1975) and by Pearlin, Lieberman, and their colleagues (Menaghan, 1983; Pearlin et al., 1981), there has been little continuing study of the impact of life changes over time and across cohorts. Little is known about continuity over time in coping styles when confronted with particular life changes. [Selection of particular strategies for solving problems is a consequence not only of life changes, but also of place in the course of life.]

For example, among younger persons, increased suspiciousness and preoccupation with the motives of others is not a very effective means for dealing with adversity. However, among very old persons, this so-called paranoid stance predicts to increased longevity after transition from independent living to residential care (Lierberman & Tobin, 1983). Some persons are able to overcome particular adversity or deal with particular role strains at particular points in the course of life; they may be unable to cope with stress and strains at either earlier or later points. Findings from studies of onset and recovery from schizophrenia suggest that older patients with episodic forms of this disturbance appear more resilient when confronted with personally salient adversity than at earlier ages (Cohler & Ferrono, 1986). Once again, it becomes clear that the most interesting questions in the study of resilience and coping, as in the study of vulnerability, concern changes in the significance of particular strategies of solving problems associated with particular points in the course of life.

Further, particular means used in coping with the impact of role strains, normative events, and unexpected adversity characteristic of persons within one cohort experiencing particular sociohistorical events in common may not be characteristic of other cohorts. Other than in Elder's continuing study of the Depression cohort (Elder, 1979, 1986; Elder, Liker & Cross, 1984; Elder, Nguyen, & Caspi, 1985; Elder & Rockwell, 1979), there has been little concern with determining the intertwined effects of aging, phase of life course, and cohort as factors associated with selection of particular coping styles when confronted with changes resulting from normative transition, unexpected adversity, and role strains.

Consideration of continuity and change over time must also include study of issues of coherence and sense of self in responding to challenges posed by adversity and change. Appraisal and response to life changes is closely related to present conception of self, including perceived self-efficacy and control (Bandura, 1977, 1982) and presently experienced coherence or narrative of the life history as a whole (Antonovsky, 1979; Cohler, 1982; Epstein, 1981; Kris, 1956). This personal narrative, reflecting the coherence of a presently remembered past, experienced present, and anticipated future, and defined by factors as diverse as enduring temperamental influences, place in the course of life, and effects of sociohistorical events affecting a particular cohort, govern the manner in which particular coping strategies are defined as relevant.

Finally it should be noted that the capacity to use effective strategies in dealing with adversity and challenge is a function not just of life changes but also of place in the course of life. Some persons are able to overcome particular adversity or deal with particular role strains at particular points in the course of life; they may be unable to cope with stress and strains at either earlier or later points. Findings from studies of onset and recovery from schizophrenia suggest that older patients with episodic forms of this disturbance appear more resilient when confronted with personally salient adversity than at earlier ages (Cohler & Ferrono, 1986).

Rather than viewing development as linear or epigenetic, with past experience directly determining present adjustment, findings such as those reviewed by Emde (1981) and Emde and Harmon (1984), and reports of the adult outcome of a woman fistula fed as an infant (Engel, 1967; Engel & Reichsman, 1956; Reichsman, 1977; Viderman, 1979) suggest that the course of development may be more flexible than suggested by both psychoanalytic and cognitive epistemology. Across the course of childhood, as in adult, personality development remains open to a variety of influences, including social context and unexpected life changes. To date, we may have been more successful in understanding the impact of expectable changes across the course of development than in understanding the impact of unexpected adversity upon the subsequent course of adjustment. At least to some extent, the impact of adversity may be more reversible than has been recognized (Clarke & Clarke, 1976; Kagan, Klein, Finley, Rogoff, & Nolan, 1979). Increased focus on the meaning of life changes for persons is critically important in understanding the manner in which life changes shape both intention and action (Neugarten, 1969).

As Felsman and Vaillant (1987) suggested, the nature of misfortune may be less important than its duration. Temporary disruptions of maternal care may be less adverse than continuing instability of the caretaker–child bond (Rutter, 1972/1981, 1979). Emphasis upon issues of continuity, focusing, emphasizing, enduring, early-formed, stable coping styles may lead to disregard of such other factors as family milieu, development, and even unpredictable life circumstances, which also influence both nature and change of coping styles over time (Garmezy, 1983; Rutter, 1981/1983, 1984; White & Associates, 1978; White, Kaban, & Attanucci, 1979; White & Watts, 1973).[2]

Process study of coping across the adult years, focusing on the complex interplay of person and situation, has suggested there are relatively few, consistent individual differences over time in preferred manner of resolving problems (Pearlin & Schooler, 1978; Menaghan, 1983; Lazarus & Folkman, 1984). To date, other than in pioneering studies of Rutter 1981), and Garmezy and his associates (Garmezy, 1981, 1983; Garmezy & Tellegen, 1984), there has been little effort to use this social psychological approach in the study of coping across the childhood years.

There has been little study of developmental factors related to selection of coping strategies (Sroufe & Rutter, 1984; Earls, Beardslee & Garrison, 1987; Felsman & Vaillant, 1987; Fisher, Kokes, Cole, Perkins & Wynne, 1987). Changes noted through middle childhood and adolescence in preferred coping strategies are a function both of the extent to which social context affects the choice of coping strategy (Earls, Beardslee, & Garrison, 1987; Pearlin, Lieberman, Menaghan, & Mullen, 1981; Rutter, 1984), as well as a shift from maturational factors to those based on social context, as the most significant factor in personality development and change, such as selection of coping strategies (Cohler & Boxer, 1984; Rutter, 1981/1983; Werner & Smith, 1982).

Particularly during the early childhood years, limitations upon particular coping strategies are a function of such maturational factors as difficulty in conceiving of the future, which limits the child's capacity to engage in grief and mourning

---

[2]There has been much interest in the significance of the caretaker–child relationship in the origins of the capacity for resilience. On the one hand, findings from B. White's longitudinal study of the origins of competence suggests that early social exchange between child and caretaker has relatively little lasting impact on the development of competence; much of the contact between mother and child centered on teaching the child to speak. On the other hand, as Bowlby (1977), Sroufe (1979; Sroufe, Fox, & Pancake, 1983), Werner and Smith (1982), and Musick, Stott, Spencer, Goldman, and Cohler (1987) all have noted, the quality of the child's attachment bonds to the caretaker appears related both to increased sense of self-reliance during childhood and also to later resilience when confronted by adversity.

(Garber, 1981). Differences in the means by which children and adults evaluate and respond to adversity and opportunity are still not clearly understood. Rutter (1981/1983) suggested that, as temperamental characteristics are modified by experience, there may be increased variability in the manner in which children are able to respond to problems created by life circumstances, leading to increased variability and differentiation in perceiving and responding to these problems.

Social Time, Role Strain, and Coping Across the Course of Life

In the definition provided by Baltes, Reese, and Lipsitt (1980), the concept of life-span developmental psychology was proposed to cover the course of human life. However, the concept of life course itself was not further elaborated in the definition. It is clear that this course is a socially defined one, with both ages and transitions in and out of major roles, and the expectable course of human life as the major factors determining this definition. So-called life stress is but another manner of understanding generally early off-time, adverse, eruptive life-events. Issues of social timing are critical in determining response to such transitions from early childhood through oldest age. Depending on the nature of such personal resources as temperament, particular life experiences, and shared outlook upon self and others shaped by individual and collective life-historical events, as well as experience of available personal resources and social supports, persons react or cope with transitions in quite different ways. Research on stress, coping, and support must not only take into consideration issues of social timing and nature of life change (expectable role transition vs. eruptive/off-time event) but also cohort, including socially determined interactions with other such events, point in the course of life at which the study is to take place, and whether coping techniques are to be studied in conjunction with role strains, role transitions, or eruptive events.

Chapters in the present volume represent an important effort to understand stress and coping in terms of developmental and social factors. These studies consider several interrelated themes. A first set of studies pertains to issues of adversity, risk, and resilience, particularly across the years of early childhood. Tiffany Field (chap. 3 in this volume) surveys sources of risk and adversity, and means of intervention among premature infants. Although dealing with a different domain of behavior, E. Mark Cummings' and his associate's demonstration of the impact of parental anger on the child's organization of experience is based on a similar set of assumptions (E. M. Cummings & J. Cummings, 1988; J. Cummings, Pellegrini, Notarius, & M. Cummings, 1989; Cummings & El-Sheikh, chap. 7 in this volume). If a question may be raised regarding the assumptions underlying Fields' investigation, it concerns whether differences reported in prenatal and perinatal adjustment continues to make a difference over time and, if so, how this experience is transformed over time. For example, in her report of the ultrasound project, if children are born with better neurological organization and lessened distress, to what extent does this more resilient status establish an anlage for a later, good, child–caretaker tie? Is this difference significant for all babies, or only those in which parents are particularly anxious about providing such care.

The question posed in different ways in studies of both Fields and Cummings is when a difference begins to have impact upon later development. Cummings' findings show that children become distressed when their parents argue and fight. Parental marital discord has an obvious and immediate impact upon the organization of the child's behavior. Again this supports Compas' observation that, particularly among younger children, parental discord has direct impact upon the child's report of behavioral problems. J. Cummings has shown that children from homes showing more anger are more likely to try and break up other childrens' fights (J. Cummings et al., 1989). Further, boys and girls respond to anger in different ways, with boys becoming more angry and girls more distressed. Even young children can differentiate types of parental discord (silent and smoldering versus overt anger) (E. M. Cummings, Vogel, J. S. Cummings, & El-Sheikh, in press). Again the ecology in which anger is observed by children is important: Young children experiencing anger at home are more apt to get involved in the discord, whereas observing such anger in a laboratory setting, children turn to other adults for help.

Studies of the offspring of psychiatrically ill and well parents show similar short-term results. Particularly among offspring of parents showing depressive mood, but present to some extent among parents with a bipolar disorder as well, but not among the children of chronic schizophrenic mothers, lowered parental mood and expression of anger has a similarly disorganizing short-term impact upon the child's state (Cohler, 1987). These findings are consistent with those of Tronick and his associates (Cohn, Tronick, 1989; Gianino & Tronick, 1988; Tronick, 1989; Tronick, Cohn, & Shea, 1986), Emde and his colleagues (Emde, 1984; Emde & Source, 1983), and D. Stern's studies of parental expression of personal distress and offspring development (Stern, Hofer, Haft, & Dore, 1984; Cramer & Stern, 1988), all of which show that parental failure to remain attuned to the child's affective state, reflecting in turn parental emotional unavailability and lack of empathy, adversely affect the child's play, synchronicity observed in the mother–child interaction, and the child's own affective response (Stern, 1985). These findings are consistent with recent psychoanalytic perspectives regarding development of the self, reflected in the recent work of Kohut and his associates (Kohut, 1977, 1984; Wolf, 1988). Cummings' work is of particular importance for study of the impact of parental affective disorder upon the child's adjustment. The question remains of the longer-term impact of maternal unavailability and lack of maternal referencing for the child's personality development across the child years and into adulthood.

This issue of resilience and "protective" factors, and of vulnerability, is well represented in the longitudinal studies reported both by Egeland (chap. 4 in this volume) and by Compas (chap. 6 in this volume). Each of these studies is concerned with problems of vulnerability and resilience in a group of school children. Issues of continuity and change are important for each study. Again the question is whether findings such as those reported by Egeland and his colleagues regarding changes from first to third grade reflects fundamental developmental processes or fluctuations in the stability of measures across groups studied. What is needed is a larger-scale collaborative study of childhood mental health similar to that of the group working on adult affective disorders. Collaborative studies permit sharing of instruments across groups, decreasing both type I and type II errors. Typological classification, such as that attempted by Compas and his associates, using cross-classification of stress and behavior problems provides a useful guide to future research in this area. Findings reported by Egeland (Farber & Egeland, 1987) and by Compass show that adversity as such is less important than the nature of the child's response and that of the family. Finally both of these studies show the importance of considering issues of resilience and protective factors in response to adversity among groups of children differing over time in kind of adversity experienced.

A second set of problems concerns means used to cope with adversity. In a somewhat different manner, chapters in the present volume by Folkman, Thoits, Karraker, Costa and his associates and Hauser and his associates all deal with these issues of coping. For Costa and Hauser, although in somewhat different ways, coping is understood primarily in individual difference terms, whereas Karraker raises issues regarding the origins of these individual differences and provides a clear and helpful taxonomy for dealing with these issues. Folkman and Thoits deal with coping from the social psychological perspective, concerned with the meaning of adversity for persons and normative dimensions that underlie coping. Cummings takes advantage of this approach in his study of the means by which children cope with discord in the home and in the laboratory. He reports that there is a significant transformation in the manner in which children deal with observation of anger in the home. Although very young children respond to the display of anger by calling for parental attention, beginning at about age five, children begin to rely on problem-focused coping, attempting to intervene and dispel conflict at home.

A third set of problems concerns issues of social surround and social support as factors intervening in the process of managing adversity in order to enhance feelings of personal comfort. As each researcher has noted, we still do not understand the means by which social support intervenes in order to reduce the impact of adversity. Antonucci suggests that the meaning of support differs across the adult years, whereas Sheldon Cohen focuses on the psychobiological foundations of social support. Beginning with her collaborative work with Robert Kahn and continuing on in reports from survey studies, Antonucci and her colleagues have demonstrated the significance of the social convoy of support for adults. Among adults, this support is more reciprocal than among children, and there is good agreement regarding the extent of reciprocity reflected in a particular role relationship. She also has focused on the developmental context of such support; carrying through on the theme of a life-course approach to the study of stress and coping, Antonucci here suggests that expectations regarding social support differ over time: For example, older adults expect to receive more support than they give, justifying this inequity in terms of a life time in which they have given more than they received. Persons implicitly balance their accounts of equity.

Cohen follows a tradition established by Schachter's experimental social psychological study of stress. Ultimately we will attain greater understanding of the complex interplay between being with others as a source of support and central nervous system changes. It should be noted that this issue of brain chemistry and social support is relevant for both persons and need, and caregivers or caretakers. For example, in studies now under way, Kiecolt-Glaser and Glaser (1989) have been studying the impact upon family caregivers of patients with Alzheimer's disease in order to determine the nature of adverse changes in the neuroimmunological system resulting from the process of rendering care.

Too often in studies of social support and adjustment, there is much attention to demonstration of the positive impact of social support upon those experiencing particular adversity and insufficient attention to the impact of caregiving upon the caregiver. As Cohen has noted, there is a different impact of social support upon those giving and receiving care. Although the recipient experiences relief, the provider of care may experience enhanced role strain and overload as a consequence of making this care available. Caregiving, just as other social relationships, is a reciprocal process. This is well illustrated not just in the problem of offspring caring for older parents with dementia or other infirmities but also parents caring for offspring with afflictions ranging from such life-threatening illnesses as cancer to serious psychiatric disability in either childhood or adulthood (Cook & Cohler, 1986; Cohler, Pickett, & Cook, 1990).

Finally there is the issue of the changing significance of social support across the course of life. It is clear that younger persons enjoy support and participating in a groups as a source of support. This is clear from continuing findings from a study being conducted by Anita Greene and Reed Larson, that adolescents show the most positive social mood while with friends. It is less clear that social participation is of equal significance for older persons. Indeed it is possible that reminiscence may be more significant as a source of social support than face-to-face interaction. In our own study of aging and personality change, an older woman, assumed to be depressed by nursing home staff, sat alone for hours at a bridge table. Discussion with this woman revealed that she had recently lost the last of four bridge partners participating in a game across the course of her adult years. She now found solace in remembering games they had played together and other games with her now deceased husband and other couples. These had been among the most pleasant moments of this woman's life, and she was able to find solace in later life through remembering these pleasant times. One of the factors associated with increased depression in the early phases of Alzheimer's disease is the problem that is posed by no longer being able to remember the past and, as a result, no longer being able to find such solace in memories.

CONCLUSIONS

Over the past decade, there has been markedly greater sophistication regarding the significance of ecology and experience in understanding changes in lives over time. In his study on *The nature of prejudice*, Allport (1954) provided a lens model for the study of social phenomena. Focusing the lens at ever greater power leads to increasing understanding of the origins of individual differences in such phenomena as determinants of feelings of well-being and psychological symptoms. It is important to begin with the recognition of a socially constructed course of life. Within any society, persons share common expectations regarding transitions in social life; children appear to learn this social time table within the first years of life, and whereas older adults appear to grant greater flexibility and variability in this social time table than younger adults, there is continuing appraisal of own attainments in terms of those that are expectable. Ultimately, particularly across the second half of life, shared understandings regarding the expectable duration or finitude play an increasingly important role in this evaluation of social timing (Neugarten & Datan, 1974).

Life changes and response to these changes must be understood within the context of this socially constructed time table. Life changes such as widowhood, which are expectable role transitions, appear to have a much less malignant input for adjustment in later life than in young to middle adulthood. Bankoff's (1983) findings, reported by McCrae and Costa (1988), suggest that the duration of most intense grief is in the first six months following widowhood. At the end of this time, the sense of well-being is approximately as it had been prior to the loss. Death of a spouse for a thirty-year-old man or woman means both lack of socialization into this role and lack of a convoy of consociates who have also experienced this loss from whom to seek support. Indeed there are important gender differences as well: Widowhood has markedly greater adverse impact upon older men losing a wife than upon older wives losing a husband, as shown by differential rates of institutionalization of older widows and widowers (Troll, Miller & Atchley, 1979).

Although the greatest concern has been focused on those major life changes, such as widowhood, that occur in an early, off-time, adverse manner, the greatest impact upon the lives of most persons may not be from these major changes but from strain accompanying day-to-day role performance, referred to by Lazarus and Folkman as "hassles." Although, as Compas and his colleagues have noted, role strain may be the outcome of adversity in performance of these major adult roles, strain and overload may be experienced as a consequence of the effort to manage the role portfolio characteristic of adult lives in postindustrial society. Further, experience of strain and attendant impact upon mental health may not just be a consequence of social timing but also of context and gender. Boys and girls respond both in quite different ways to expectable strains in family relations and in quite different ways across the years of childhood and adolescence. Indeed as Cummings' findings suggest, observation of family discord has quite different impact for children at home and in the laboratory setting.

Next steps in research in this area must recognize more completely these complex issues of setting, age, and present role portfolio in understanding mental health outcomes. Cross-sequential studies of the response to role strain and adversity are critically needed. Coping responses when confronted by strain and adversity vary over time, with education and age, and as a function of setting in which they are observed. Coping appears to be jointly constructed on the basis of age, social context, and meanings attributed by persons to experiences across the course of life. The repertoire of coping increases with age, particularly between early and middle childhood, just as with the setting. Problem-centered coping may be more valuable for some settings and for some problems than for other settings and problems. Particular forms of coping appear to related both to type of problem and to setting. A life-course perspective, permitting integration of person and social context, offers promise of increasing our understanding of stress and coping.

REFERENCES

Allport. G. (1954). *The nature of prejudice.* Cambridge, MA: Addison-Wesley

Altschul, S., & Pollock, G. (Eds.). (1988). *Childhood bereavement and its aftermath.* New York: International Universities Press.

Antonovsky, A. (1979). *Health, stress, and coping.* San Francisco: Jossey-Bass.

Antonovsky, A. (1987). *Unraveling the mystery of health: How people manage stress and stay well.* San Francisco: Jossey-Bass.

Antonucci, T. (1976). Attachment: A life-span concept. *Human Development, 19,,* 135–142.

Antonucci, T. (1985). Personal characteristics, social support. and social behavior. In R. Binstock & E. Shanas (Eds.), *Handbook of aging and the social sciences* (2nd Ed., 94–128). New York: Van Nostrand & Reinhold.

Antonucci, T., & Akiyama, H. (1987). Social networks in adult life and a preliminary examination of the convoy model. *Journal of Gerontology, 42,* 519–527.

Baltes, P., Reese, H., & Lipsitt, L. (1980). Life-span developmental psychology. *Annual Review of Psychology, 31* 65–110.

Bandura, A. (1977). Self-efficacy: Toward a unifying theory of behavioral change. *Psychological Review, 84* 191–215.

Bandura, A. (1982). Self-efficacy mechanism in human agency. *American Psychologist, 37,* 122–147.

Bankoff, L. (1983). Social support and adaptation to widowhood. *Journal of Marriage and the Family, 45,* 827–839.

Billings, A., & Moos, R. (1981). The role of coping responses and social resources in attenuating the stress of life events. *Journal of Behavioral Medicine, 4,* 139–157.

Blau, P., Duncan, O. D. (1978). *The American occupational structure.* New York: Free Press. (Original work published 1967)

Block, J., & Block, J. (1980). The role of ego-control and ego-resiliency in the organization of behavior. In W. A. Collins (Ed.), *Development of cognition, affect, and social relations: The Minnesota Symposia on Child Psychology, Volume 13* (39–102). Minneapolis, MN: University of Minnesota Press.

Blumer, H. (1962). Society as symbolic interaction. In A. Rose (Ed.), *Human behavior and social processes* (pp. 179–192). Boston: Houghton-Mifflin.

Brim, O. G., Jr. & Ryff, C. (1980). On the properties of life-events. In. P. B. Bates & O. G. Brim, Jr. (Eds.), *Life-span development and behavior* (vol. 3; pp. 368–388). New York: Academic Press.

Bowlby, J. (1973). Self-reliance and some conditions that promote it. In R. Gosling (Ed.), *Support, innovation and autonomy* (pp. 23–48). London: Tavistock.

Bowlby, J. (1977). The making and breaking of affectional bonds. In Aetiology and Psychopathology in the height of attachment theory, *British Journal of Psychiatry, 30,* 201–210.

Burgess, E. (1926). The family as a unity of interacting personalities. *Family, 7,* 3–9.

Cain, L. (1967). Age status and generational phenomena: The new old people in contemporary America. *The Gerontologist, 7,* 83–92.

Chodorow, N. (1974). Family structure and feminine personality. In. L. Lamphere & M. Rosaldo (Eds.), *Women, culture, and society* (pp. 43–66). Stanford, CA: Stanford University Press.

Chodorow, N. (1978) *The reproduction of mothering: Psychoanalysis and the sociology of gender.* Berkeley: University of California Press.

Chodorow, N. (1989). *Feminism and psychoanalytic theory.* New Haven: Yale University Press.

Clarke, S. D. B., & Clarke, A. M. (Eds.). (1976) *Early experience: Myth and evidence.* New York: Free Press.

Clarke, S. D. B., & Clarke, A. M. (1981). "Sleeper effects" in development. Fact or artifact? *Developmental Review, 1,* 344–360.

Cohler, B. (1982). Personal narrative and life course. In. P. B. Baltes & O. G. Brim, Jr. (Eds.), *Life-span development behavior* (pp. 206–243). New York: Academic Press.

Cohler, B. (1983). Autonomy and interdependence in the family of adulthood: A psychological perspective. *The Gerontologist, 23* 33–39.

Cohler, B. (1986). Reflections on the study of offspring of parents with major psychopathology. In National Mental Health Association, *The prevention of mental-emotional disabilities* (pp. 89–95). Arlington, VA: National Mental Health Association.

Cohler, B. (1987). Adversity, resilience and the study of lives. In E. J. Anthony & B. Cohler (Eds.), *The invulnerable child,* New York: Guilford.

Cohler, B., & Boxer, A. (1984). Middle adulthood: Settling into the world-Person, time and context. In D. Offer & M. Sabshin (Ed.), *Normality and the life course: A critical integration* (pp. 145–203). New York: Basic.

Cohler, B., & Ferrono, C. (1986). Schizophrenia and the life course. In N. Miller & G. Cohen (Eds.), *Schizophrenia and aging* (pp. 189–200). New York: Guilford Press.

Cohler, B., Gallant, D., Grunebaum, H., & Kaufman, C. (1983). Social adjustment among schizophrenic, depressed and well mothers and their school aged children. In H. Morrison (Ed.), *Children of depressed parents: Risk, identification, and intervention* (pp. 65–98). New York: Grune & Stratton.

Cohler, B., & Grunebaum, H. (1981). *Mothers, grandmothers, and daughters.* New York: Wiley.

Cohler, B., Pickett, S., & Cook, J. (1990). The psychiatric patient grows older: Issues in family care. In B. Lebowitz & E. Light (Eds.), *Aging and caregiving* (pp. xxx–xxx). New York: Springer.

Cohn, J., & Tronick, E. (1989). Specificity of infant's response to mother's affective behavior. *Journal of the American Academy of Child Psychiatry, 28*, 242–248.

Cook, J., & Cohler, B. (1986). Reciprocal socialization and the care of offspring with cancer and with schizophrenia. In N. Datan, A. Greene, & H. Reese (Eds.), *Life-span developmental psychology: Intergenerational relations* (pp. 223–244). Hillsdale, NJ: Lawrence Erlbaum Associates.

Costa, P., & McCrae, R. (1989). Personality, stress, and coping: Some lessons from a decade of research. In K. S. Markides & C. L. Cooper (Eds.), *Aging, stress, social support and health.* New York: Wiley.

Cramer, B., & Stern, D. (1988). Evaluation of changes in mother–infant brief psychotherapy: A single case study. *Infant Mental Health Journal, 9*, 20–45.

Csikszentmihalyi, M. (1975). *Beyond boredom and anxiety.* San Francisco: Jossey-Bass.

Cummings, E. M., & Cummings, J. (1988). A process oriented approach to childrens' coping with adults' angry behavior. *Developmental Review, 8*, 296–321.

Cummings, J., Pellegrini, D., Notarius, D., & Cummings, M. (1989). Children's responses to angry adult behavior as a function of marital distress and history of interparent hostility. *Child Development, 60*, 1035–1043.

Cummings, E. M., Vogel, D., Cummings, J. S., & El-Sheikh, M. (1978). Childrens' responses to different forms of expression of anger between adults, *Child Development, 25*, 490–498.

Earls, F., Beardslee, W., & Garrison, W. (1987). Correlates and predictors of competence in young children. In E. J. Anthony & B. J. Cohler (Eds.), *The invulnerable child* (pp. 84–105).

Elder, G. (1986). Military times and turning points in men's lives, *Developmental Psychology, 22*, 233–245.

Elder, G., Caspi, A., & Nguyen, T. V. (1985). Resourceful and vulnerable children: Family influences in hard times. In R. K. Silbereisen & K. Eyferth (Eds.), *Development in context: Integrative perspectives on youth development.* New York Springer (In Press)

Elder, G., Liker, J., & Cross, C. (1984). Parent–child behavior in the Great Depression. In P. B. Baltes & O. G. Brim, Jr. (Eds.), *Life-span development and behavior: Volume 6* (pp. 111–159). New York: Academic Press.

Elder, G., Nguyen, T. V., & Caspi, A. (1985). Linking family hardship to childrens' lives, *Child Development, 56*, 361–375.

Elder, G., Rockwell, R. (1978). Economic depression and post-war opportunity: A study of life-patterns and health. In R. Simmons (Ed.), *Research in community and mental health* (pp. 249–304). Greenwich, CT: JAI Press.

Elder, G., Rockwell, R. (1979). The life-course and human development: An ecological perspective. *International Journal of Behavioral Development, 2*, 1–21.

Elder, G. H., Jr. (1974). *Children of the great depression.* Chicago: University of Chicago Press.

Elder, G. H., Jr. (1979). Historical change in life patterns and personality. In P. B. Baltes & O. G. Brim, Jr. (Eds.), *Life-span development and behavior: Volume 2* (pp. 118–161). New York: Academic Press.

Emde, R. (1981). Changing models of infancy and the nature of early development: Remodeling the foundation. *Journal of the American Psychoanalytic Association, 29*, 179–219.

Emde, R. (1984). The affective self: Continuities and transformations from infancy. In J. Call, E. Galenson, & R. Tyson (Eds.), *Frontiers in infant psychiatry. I* (pp. 38–54). New York: Basic.

Emde, R., & Source, J. (1983). The rewards of infancy: Emotional availability and maternal referencing. In J. Call, E. Galenson, & R. Tyson (Eds.), *Frontiers of infant psychiatry: Volume I* (pp. 17–30). New York: Basic.

Emde, R., & Harmon, R. (1984). Entering a new era in the search for developmental continuities. In R. Emde & R. Harmon (Eds.), *Continuities and discontinuities in development* (pp. 1–11). New York: Plenum.

Engel, G. (1962). *Psychological development in health and disease.* Philadelphia: Saunders.

Engel, G. (1967). Ego development following severe trauma in infancy. *Bulletin of the Association of Psychoanalytic Medicine, 6*, 57–61.

Engel, G., & Reichsman, F. (1956). Spontaneous and experimentally induced depressions in an infant with a gastric fistula. *Journal of the American Psychoanalytic Association, 4*, 428–452.

Epstein, S. (1981). The unity principle versus the reality and pleasure principles, *or* the tale of the scorpion and the frog. In M. Lynch, Norem-Hebeisen, & K. Gergen (Eds.), *Self-concept: Advances in theory and research* (pp. 27–37). Cambridge, MA: Ballinger-Harper & Row.

Erikson, K. (1976) *Everything in its path: Destruction of community in the Buffalo Creek flood.* New York: Simon & Schuster.

Farber, E., & Egeland, B. (1987). Invulnerability among abused and neglected children. In E. J. Anthony & B. Cohler (Eds.), *The invulnerable child* (pp. 253–288). New York: Guilford Press.

Farnham-Diggory, S. (1966). Self, future, and time: A developmental study of the concepts of psychotic, brain-damaged, and normal children. *Monographs of the Society for Research in Child Development, 31* (Whole No. 1).

Felsman, J. K., & Vaillant, G. (1987). Resilient children as adults: A forty year study. In E. J. Anthony & B. Cohler (Eds.), *The invulnerable child* (pp. 289–315). New York: Guilford Press.

Felton, B., & Revenson, T. (1987). Age differences in coping with chronic illness. *Psychology and Aging, 2*, 164–170.

Fisher, L. Kokes, R., Cole, R., Perkins, P., & Wynne, L. (1987). Competent children at risk: A study of well functioning offspring of disturbed parents. In E. J. Anthony & B. Cohler (Eds.), *The invulnerable child* (pp. 211–228). New York: Guilford Press.

Fiske, M. (1980a). Changing hierarchies of commitment in adulthood. In E. Erikson N. Smelser (Eds.), *Themes of work and love in adulthood* (pp. 238–264). Cambridge, MA: Harvard University Press.

Fiske, M. (1980b). Tasks and crises of the second half of life: The interrelationship of commitment, coping and adaptation. In J. Birren & R. B. Sloan (Eds.), *Handbook of mental health and aging* (pp. 337–373). Englewood Cliffs, NJ: Prentice-Hall.

Folkman, S. (1984). Personal control and stress and coping processes: A theoretical analysis. *Journal of Personality and Social Psychology, 46*, 839–852.

Folkman, S., & Lazarus, R. (1980). An analysis of coping in a middle-aged community sample. *Journal of Health and Social Behavior, 21*, 219–239.

French, J. R. P., Jr., Rodgers, W., & Cobb, S. (1974). Adjustment as a person–environment fit. In G. C. Coelho, D. Hamburg, & J. Adams (Eds.), *Coping and adaptation* (pp. 316–333). New York: Basic.

Furstenberg, F. (1987). *Adolescent mothers in later life.* New York: Cambridge University Press.

Garber, B. (1981). Mourning in children: Toward a theoretical synthesis. *Annual For Psychoanalysis, 9*, 9–19.

Garmezy, N. (1981). Children under stress: Perspectives on antecedents and correlates of vulnerability and resistance to psychopathology. In A. I. Rabin, J. Aronoff, A. M. Barclay, & R. Zucker (Eds.), *Further explorations in personality* (pp. 196–269). New York: Wiley-Interscience.

Garmezy, N. (1983). Stressors of childhood. In N. Garmezy & M. Rutter (Eds.), *Stress, coping and development in children* (pp. 43–84). New York: McGraw-Hill.

Garmezy, N., & Tellegen, A. (1984). Studies of stress-resistant children: Methods, variables, and preliminary findings. In F. L. Morrison, C. Lord, D. P. Keating (Eds.), *Applied developmental psychology. Volume I* (pp. 231–287). York: Academic Press.

Geertz, C. (1973). Person, time, and conduct in Bali. In C. Geertz, *The interpretation of cultures* (pp. 360–411). New York: Basic.

Gergen, K. (1977). Stability, change, and chance in understanding human development. In N. Datan & H. Reese (Eds.), *Life-span developmental psychology: Dialectical perspectives on experimental research* (pp. 135–158). New York: Academic Press.

Gergen, K. (1982). *Toward transformation in social knowledge.* New York: Springer-Verlag.

Gianino, A., & Tronick, E. (1988). The mutual regulation model: The infant's self and interactive regulation of coping and defense. In T. Field, P. McCabe, & N. Schneiderman (Eds.), *Stress and coping* (pp. 47–68). Hillsdale, NJ: Lawrence Erlbaum Associates.

Gleick, J. (1987). *Chaos: Making a new science.* New York: Viking.

Greenblatt, M., Becerra, R., & Serafetinides, E. (1982). Social networks and mental health: An overview. *The American Journal of Psychiatry, 139,* 977–984.

Gurin, P., & Brim, O. G., Jr. (1984). Change in self in adulthood: The example of sense of control. In P. B. Baltes & O. G. Brim, Jr. (Eds.), *Life-span development and behavior. Volume 6* (pp. 281–334). New York: Academic Press.

Gutmann, D. (1987). *Reclaimed powers: Toward a psychology of men and women in later life.* New York: Basic.

Haan, N. (1977). *Coping and defending: Processes of self–environment organization.* New York: Academic Press.

Hagestad, G. (1974). *Middle aged women and their children: Exploring changes in a role relationship.* Unpublished doctoral dissertation, University of Minnesota.

Hagestad, G., & Neugarten, B. (1985). Age and the life-course. In R. Binstock & E. Shanas (Eds.), *Handbook of aging and society* (2nd Ed., pp. 35–61). New York: Van Nostrand-Reinhold.

Hauser, S., Book, B., Houlihan, J., Powers, S., Weiss-Perry, B., Follansbee, D., Jacobson, A., & Noam, G. (1987). Sex differences within the family: Studies of adolescent and parent family interactions. *Journal of Youth and Adolescence, 16,* 199–220.

Hauser, S., Powers, S., Noam, G., Jacobson, A., Weiss, B., & Follansbee, D. (1984). Familial contexts of adolescent ego development. *Child Development, 55,* 195–213.

Hogan, D. (1978). The variable order of events in the life-course. *American Sociological Review, 43,* 573–586.

Hogan, D. (1980). The transition to adulthood as a career contingency. *American Sociological Review, 45,* 261–276.

Hogan, D. (1981). *Transitions and social change: The early lives of American men.* New York: Academic Press.

Holmes, T., Rahe, R.R. (1967). The social readjustment rating scale. *Journal of Psychosomatic Research, 11,* 213–218.

Huffine, C., Folkman, S., & Lazarus, R. (1989). Psychoactive drugs, alcohol, and stress and coping process in older adults. *American Journal of Drug and Alcohol Abuse, 15,* 101–113.

Janis, I. L., & Mann, L. (1977). *Decision making.* New York: Free Press/Macmillan.

Kagan, J. (1979). The form of early development: Continuity and discontinuity in emergent competencies. *Archives of General Psychiatry, 36,* 1047–1054.

Kagan, J., Klein, R., Finley, G., Rogoff, B., & Nolan, E. (1979). A cross-cultural study of cognitive development. *Monographs of the Society for Research in Child Development, 44,* (Serial No. 180).

Kagan, J., & Moss, H. (1963). *From birth to maturity.* New York: Wiley.

Kahn, R. (1979). Aging and social support. In M. Riley (Ed.), *Aging from birth to death* (pp. 77–91). Boulder, CO: Westview Press.

Kahn, R., & Antonucci, T. (1980). Convoys over the life course: Attachment, roles, and social support. In P. B. Baltes & O. G. Brim, Jr. (Eds.), *Life-span development and behavior. Volume 3* (pp. 254–286). New York: Academic Press.

Kahn, R., & Antonucci, T. (1981). Convoys of social support: A life-course approach. In S. Kiesler, J. Morgan, & V. Oppenheimer (Eds.), *Aging: Social change* (pp. 383–405). New York: Academic Press.

Kaufman, C., Grunebaum, H., Cohler, B., & Cramer, E. (1979). Superkids: Competent children of schizophrenic mothers. *American Journal of Psychiatry, 136,* 1398–1402.

Kiecolt-Glaser, J., Glaser, R. (1989). Caregiving, mental health and immune function. In E. Light & B. Lebowitz (Eds.), *Alzheimer's disease treatment and family stress: Direction for research,* Washington, DC, U.S. Government Printing Office, 245–266.

Kobasa, S. (1979). Stressful life events, personality, and health: An inquiry into hardiness. *Journal of Personality and Social Psychology, 37,* 1–11.

Kobasa, S. (1982). The hardy personality: Toward a social psychology of stress and health. In G. S. Sanders & J. Suls (Eds.), *Social psychology of health and illness* (pp. 3–32). Hillsdale, NJ: Lawrence Erlbaum Associates.

Kobasa, S., Maddi, S., & Kahn, S. (1982). Hardiness and health: A prospective study. *Journal of Personality and Social Psychology, 42,* 168–177.

Kohli, M., & Meyer, J. (1986). Social structure and social construction of life stages. *Human Development, 29,* 145–180.

Kohut, H. (1971). *The analysis of the self.* New York: International Universities Press (Monographs of the Psychoanalytic Study of the Child, No. 1).

Kohut, H. (1977). *The restoration of the self.* New York: International Universities Press.

Kohut, H. (1974/1978). Remarks about the formation of the self-letter to a student regarding some principles of psychoanalytic research. In P. Ornstein (Ed.), *The search for the self: Selected writings of Heinz Kohut, 1950–1978* (vol. 2, pp. 737–770). New York: International Universities Press.

Kohut, H. (1975/1978). The psychoanalyst in the community of scholars. In P. Ornstein (Ed.), *The search for the self: Selected writings of Heinz Kohut 1950–1978* (Vol. 2, pp. 685–724). New York: International Universities Press.

Kohut, H. (1984). *How does psychoanalysis cure.* Chicago: University of Chicago Press.

Kohut, H. (1985). Self psychology and the sciences of man. In C. Strozier (Ed.), *Self psychology and the humanities: Reflections on a new psychoanalytic approach by Heinz Kohut* (pp. 73–94). New York: Norton.

Kohut, H., & Wolf, E. (1978). The disorders of the self and their treatment: An outline. *International Journal of Psychoanalysis, 59,* 413–425.

Komarovsky, M. (1950). Functional analysis of sex roles. *American Sociological Review, 15,* 508–516.

Komarovsky, M. (1956). Continuities in family research: A case study. *American Journal of Sociology, 62,* 466–469.

Komarovsky, M. (1962). *Blue-collar marriage.* New York: Random House.

Komarovsky, M. (1973). Presidential address; Some problems in role analysis. *American Sociological Review, 38,* 649–662.

Kris, E. (1956). The personal myth: A problem in psychoanalytic technique. *Journal of the American Psychoanalytic Association, 4,* 653–681.

Kroeber, T. (1963). The coping functions of the ego mechanisms. In R. W. White (Ed.), *The study of lives* (pp. 178–197). New York: Aldine/Atherton.

Lazarus, R. (1966). *Psychological stress and the coping process.* New York: McGraw-Hill.

Lazarus, R. (1980/1981). The costs and benefits of denial. In B. P. Dohrenwend & B. S. Dohrenwend (Eds.), *Stressful life events and their contexts* (pp. 131–156). New York: Neale Watson/Prodist.

Lazarus, R., Averill, J., & Opton, E. M., Jr. (1974). The psychology of coping: Issues of research and assessment. In G. Coelho, D. Hamburg, & J. Adams (Eds.), *Coping and adaptation* (pp. 248–315). New York: Basic.

Lazarus, R., & DeLongis, A. (1983). Psychological stress and coping in aging. *American Psychologist, 38,* 245–254.

Lazarus, R., & Folkman, S. (1984). *Stress, appraisal and coping.* New York: Springer.

Levi-Strauss, C. (1962/1966). *La pensee sauvage* (The savage mind). Chicago: University of Chicago Press.

Lieberman, M., & Tobin, S. (1983). *The experience of old age: stress, coping and survival.* New York: Basic.

Linton, R. (1942). Age and sex categories. *American Sociological Review, 7,* 589–603.

Livson, N., & Peskin, H. (1980). Perspectives on adolescence from longitudinal research. In J. Adelson (Ed.), *Handbook on adolescence* (pp. 47–98). New York: Wiley.

Lowenthal, M. F., & Chiriboga, D. (1973). Social stress and adaptation: Toward a life-course orientation, In C. Eisdorfer & M. P. Lawton (Eds.), *The psychology of adult development and aging* (pp. 281–310). Washington, DC: American Psychological Association.

Lowenthal, M., & Robinson, B. (1976). Social networks and isolation. In R. Binstock & E. Shanas (Eds.), *Handbook of aging and the social sciences* (pp. 432–456). New York: Van Nostrand-Reinhold.

Lowenthal, M. F., Thurnher, M., Chiriboga, D. & Associates. (1975). *Four states of life: A comparative study of men and women facing transitions.* San Francisco, Jossey-Bass.

McCrae, R. (1982). Age differences in the use of coping mechanisms. *Journal of Gerontology, 37,* 454–460.

McCrae, R. & Costa, P. (1986). Personality, coping, and coping effectiveness in an adult sample. *Journal of Gerontology, 54,* 385–405.

McCrae, R., & Costa, P. (1988). Psychological resilience among widowed men and women: A 10-year follow-up of a national survey. *Journal of Social Issues, 44,* 129–142.

Mechanic, D. (1962). *Students under stress: A study in the social psychology of adaptation.* New York: Free Press/Macmillan.

Mechanic, D. (1974). Social structure and personal adaptation: Some neglected dimensions. In G. Coelho, D. Hamburg, & J. Adams, *Coping and adaptation* (pp. 32–46). New York: Basic.

Mechanic, D. (1977). Illness, behavior, social adaptation, and the management of illness: A comparison of educational and medical models. *Journal of Nervous and Mental Disease, 165,* 79–87.

Menaghan, E. (1983). Individual coping efforts: Moderators of the relationship between life stress and mental health outcomes. In H. Kaplan (Ed.), *Psychosocial stress: Trends in theory and research* (pp. 157–191). New York: Academic Press.

Miller, G., Galanter, E., & Pribram, K. (1960). *Plans and the structure of behavior.* New York: Holt-Dryden.

Moos, R., & Billings, A. (1982). Conceptualizing and measuring coping resources and processes. In L. Goldberger & S. Breznitz (Eds.), *Handbook of stress* (pp. 212–230). New York: Free Press/Macmillan.

Murphy, L. (1960a). The child's way of coping: A longitudinal study of normal children. *Bulletin of the Menninger Clinic, 24,* 136–143.

Murphy, L. (1960b). Coping devices and defense mechanisms in relation to autonomous ego functions. *Bulletin of the Menninger Clinic, 24,* 144–153.

Murphy, L. (1962). *The widening world of childhood.* New York: Basic.

Murphy, L. (1970). The problem of defense and the concept of coping. In E. J. Anthony & C. Koupernik (Eds.), *The child in his family: Volume II* (pp. 65–86). New York: Wiley.

Murphy, L. (1974). Coping, vulnerability, and resilience in childhood. In G. V. Coelho, D. Hamburg, & J. Adams (Eds.), *Coping and adaptation* (pp. 69–100). New York: Basic.

Musick, J., Stott, F., Spencer, K. K., Goldman, J., & Cohler, B. (1987). Maternal factors related to vulnerability and resiliency in young children at risk. In. E. J. Anthony & B. Cohler (Eds.), *The invulnerable child* (pp. 229–252). New York: Guilford Press.

Nesselroade, J., & Reese, H. (1973). *Life-span developmental psychology: Methodological issues.* (Proceedings of the Second West Virginia Life-Span Conference). New York: Academic Press.

Neugarten, B. (1969). Continuities and discontinuities of psychological issues into adult life. *Human Development, 12,* 121–130.

Neugarten, B. (1973). Personality change in late life: A developmental perspective. In C. Eisdorfer & M. P. Lawton (Eds.), *The psychology of adult development and aging* (pp. 311–335). Washington, DC: American Psychological Association.

Neugarten, B. (1979). Time, age and the life-cycle. *American Journal of Psychiatry, 136,* 887–894.

Neugarten, B., & Datan, N. (1974). Sociological perspectives on the life cycle. In P. Baltes & K. W. Schaie (Eds.), *Life-span developmental psychology: Personality and socialization* (pp. 53–69). New York: Academic Press.

Neugarten, B., Moore, J., & Lowe, J. (1965). Age norms, age constraints, and adult socialization. *American Journal of Sociology, 70,* 710–717.

Pearlin, L. (1975). Sex roles and depression. In N. Datan & L. Ginsberg (Eds.), *Life-span developmental psychology: Normative life crises* (pp. 191–207). New York: Academic Press.

Pearlin, L. (1980) The life-cycle and life strains. In H. Blalock, Jr. (Ed.), *Sociological theory and research* (pp. 349–360). New York: Free Press/Macmillan.

Pearlin, L. (1982). The social contexts of stress. In L. Goldberger & S. Breznitz (Eds.), *Handbook of stress* (pp. 367–379). New York: Free Press/Macmillan.

Pearlin, L. (1983). Role strains and personal stress. In H.B. Kaplan (Ed.), *Psychosocial stress: Trends in theory and research* (pp. 3–32). New York: Academic Press.

Pearlin, L., Lieberman, M., Menaghan, E., & Mullen, J. (1981). The stress process. *Journal of Health and Social Behavior, 22,* 237–256.

Pearlin, L., & Schooler, C. (1978). The structure of coping. *Journal of Health and Social Behavior, 19,* 2–21.

Peskin, H., & Livson, N. (1981). Uses of the past in adult psychological health. In D. Eichorn, J. Clausen, N. Haan, M. Honzik, & P. Mussen (Eds.), *Present and past in middle life* (pp. 154–183). New York: Academic Press.

Plath, D. (1980). Contours of consociation: Lessons from a Japanese narrative. In P.B. Baltes & O.G. Brim, Jr. (Eds.), *Life-span development and behavior. Volume 3* (pp. 287–305). New York: Academic Press.

Pruchno, R., Blow, F., & Smyer, M. (1984). Life events and interdependent lives: Implications for research and intervention. *Human Development, 27,* 31–41.

Quayhagen, M., & Quayhagen, M. (1982). Coping with conflict: Measurement of age-related patterns, *Research on Aging, 4,* 364–377.

Ragan, P., & Wales, J. (1980). Age stratification and the life course. In J. Birren & R. B. Sloane (Eds.), *Handbook of mental health and aging* (pp. 591–615). Englewood Cliffs, NJ: Prentice-Hall.

Reichsmann, F. (1977). An example of psychophysiologic research. In R. Simons & H. Parades (Eds.), *Understanding human behavior in health and disease* (pp. 447–460). Baltimore: Williams & Wilkins.

Ricoeur, P. (1984). *Time and narrative: Volume 1.* (K. McLaughlin & D. Pellauer, trans.). Chicago: University of Chicago Press.

Riley, M. (1971). Social gerontology and the age stratification of society. *The Gerontologist, 11,* 79–87.

Riley, M. (1973). Aging and cohort succession: Interpretations and misinterpretations. *The Public Opinion Quarterly, 37,* 35–49.

Riley, M. (1976). Age strata in social systems. In R. Binstock & E. Shanas (Eds.), *Handbook of aging and the social sciences* (pp. 189–217). New York: Van Nostrand-Reinhold.

Riley, M., & Foner, A. (1968). (Eds.), *Aging and society. Volume I: An inventory of research findings.* New York: Russell-Sage.

Roth, J. (1963). *Timetables: Structuring the passage of time in hospital treatment and other careers.* Indianapolis, IN: Bobbs-Merrill.

Rowe, J., & Kahn, R. (1987, July 10). Human aging: Usual and successful. *Science, 237,* 143–149.

Runyan, M. (1980). A stage-state analysis of the life course. *Journal of Personality and Social Psychology, 38,* 951–962.

Russell, C. (1980). Unscheduled parenthood: Transition to "parent" for the teenager. *The Journal of Social Issues, 36,* 45–63.

Rutter, M. (1981). *Maternal deprivation reassessed* (2nd ed.). London: Penguin. (Original work published 1972).

Rutter, M. (1979). Maternal deprivation, 1972–1978: New findings, new concepts, new approaches. *Child Development, 50,* 283–305.

Rutter, M. (1981/1983). Stress, coping and development: Some issues and some questions. In N. Garmezy, & M. Rutter (Eds.), *Stress, coping and development* (pp. 1–41). New York: McGraw-Hill.

Rutter, M. (1984). Continuities and discontinuities in socioemotional development: Empirical and conceptual perspectives. In R. Emde & R. Harmon (Eds.), *Continuities and discontinuities in development* (pp. 41–68). New York: Plenum.

Ryder, R. (1965). The cohort as a concept in the study of social change. *American Sociological Review, 30,* 843–861.

Schaie, K. W. (1984). The Seattle longitudinal study: A 2-year exploration of the psychometric intelligence of adulthood. In K. W. Schaie (Ed.), *Longitudinal studies of personality* (pp. 64–135). New York: Guilford Press.

Schaie, K.W., Labouvie, G., & Buech, B. (1973). Generational and cohort-specific differences in adult cognitive behavior: A fourteen-year study of independent samples. *Developmental Psychology, 9,* 151–166.

Schutz, A., & Luckmann, T. (1973). *The structures of the life-world.* Evanston, IL: Northwestern University Press.

Seltzer, M. (1976). Suggestions for the examination of time disordered relationships. In J. Gubrium (Ed.), *Time, roles, and the self in old age* (pp. 111–125). New York: Human Sciences Press.

Shanas, E., Townsend, P., Wedderburn, D., Friis, H., Milhoj, P., & Stenhower, J. (1968). *Old people in three industrial societies.* New York: Atherton.

Sroufe, L. A. (1979). The coherence of individual development. *American Psychologist, 34,* 834–841.

Sroufe, L. A., Fox, N., & Pancake, V. (1983). Attachment and dependency in developmental perspective. *Child Development, 54,* 1615–1627.

Sroufe, L., & Rutter, M. (1984). The domain of developmental psychopathology. *Child Development, 55,* 17–29.

Stern, D. (1985). *The interpersonal world of the infant: A view from psychoanalysis and development psychology.* New York: Basic.

Stern, D., Hofer, L., Haft, W., & Dore, J. (1984). Affect attunement: The sharing of feelings between mother and infant by way of inter-modal fluency. In T. Field & N. Fox (Eds.), *Social perception in infants* (pp. 249–268). Norwood, NJ: Ablex.

Stern, G. (1970). *People in context: measuring person–environment congruence in education and industry.* New York: Wiley.

Stern, G., Stein, M., & Bloom, B. (1956). *Methods in personality assessment.* New York: Free Press-Macmillan.

Strozier, C. (1985). (Ed.). *Self-psychology and the humanities: Reflections on a new psychoanalytic approach.* New York: Norton.

Thoits, P. (1983). Dimensions of life events that influence psychological distress: An evaluation and synthesis of the literature. In H. B. Kaplan (Ed.), *Psychosocial stress: Trends in theory and research* (pp. 33–103). New York: Academic Press.

Thomas, W. I. (1928). *The unadjusted girl.* Boston: Little Brown.

Thomas, W. I., & Thomas, D. S. (1928). *The child in America: Behavior problems and programs.* New York: Knopf.

Troll, L., Miller, S., & Atchley, R. (1979). *Families in later life.* Belmont, CA: Wadsworth.

Tronick, E. (1989). Emotions and emotional communication in infancy. *American Psychologist, 44* 112–119.

Tronick, E., Cohn, J., & Shea E. (1986). The transfer of affect between mothers and infants. *In* T. Brazelton & M. Yogman (Eds.), *Affective development in infancy* (pp. 11–25). Norwood, NJ: Ablex.

Viederman, M. (1979). Monica: A 25-year longitudinal study of the consequences of trauma in infancy. *Journal of the American Psychoanalytic Association, 27,* 107–126.

Wagner, B., Compas, B., & Howell, D. (1988). Daily and major life-events: A test of an integrative model of psychosocial stress. *American Journal of Community Psychology, 16,* 189–205.

Warner, W. L., Lunt, P. (1941). *The social life of a modern community.* New Haven, CT: Yale University Press.

Warner, W. L., Meeker, M., & Ells, K. (1949). *Social class in America.* New York: Harper & Row/Science Research Associates.

Werner, E., & Smith, R. (1977) *Kauai's children come to age.* Honolulu: University Press of Hawaii.

Werner, E., & Smith, R. (1982). *Vulnerable but invincible: A study of resilient children.* New York: McGraw-Hill.

White, B. L., & Associates. (1978). *Experience and environment: Volume 2.* Englewood Cliffs, NJ: Prentice-Hall.

White, B. L., & Watts, J. C. (1973). *Experience and environment: Volume 1*. Englewood Cliffs, NJ: Prentice-Hall.

White, B. L., Kaban, B., & Attanucci, J. (1979). *The origins of human competence: The final report of the Harvard Preschool Project*. Lexington, MA: Lexington Books/D.C. Heath.

Wolf, E. (1988). *Treating the self: Elements of clinical self-psychology*. New York: Guilford Press.

Wolfenstein, M. (1979). How is mourning possible? *The Psychoanalytic Study of the Child, 21,* 93–123.

Author Index

Subject Index